Viva

Spelling Dictionary

BUD WILEMAN
ROBIN WILEMAN

Viva Books
New Delhi | Mumbai | Chennai | Kolkata | Bengaluru | Hyderabad | Kochi | Guwahati

This edition first published
in 2010 by

Viva Books Private Limited
4737/23, Ansari Road, Daryaganj
New Delhi 110002
Tel: 011-4224 2200, Fax: 011- 422 2240
E-mail: vivadelhi@vivagroupindia.net
http://www.vivagroupindia.com

Reprinted 2011

ISBN: 978-81-309-1255-4

Printed in India by Anand Sons, Delhi.

In gratitude to all those children and adults who helped with the spelling in this dictionary.

ACKNOWLEDGEMENTS

The editors are grateful for the assistance rendered by consultants to the first edition.

BESSANA C. SEWELL, B.Ed., G.D.S.E., G.T.C., Ad.Dip.T., A.T.C.L., M.A.C.E.
Australian Remedial Education Association Consultant
ALISON J. GRIFFITHS, B.A., Dip.Ed., G.D.S.E.
Australian Remedial Education Association Consultant
JOHN J. CROUGH, B.A., A.Ed., M.Ed. Admin.

FOREWORD

This is a book that deals with an age old problem.

"Please, how do you spell 'inconceivable'?"
"Why don't you look it up in the dictionary?"
"I did, but it's not there!"

Of course it was there, but not in the form sought by the puzzled inquirer, who was trying to find "inconseavable".

In English, there is no simple relationship between speech sounds and their graphic representation: a single sound may be written in a number of different ways. However, far from being a haphazard arrangement, English spelling is based on a complex system of rules which govern the interrelationship of a word's visual appearance, sound and meaning. Sometimes, as in the K sound in s*k*ip (Scandinavian) and s*ch*izoid (Greek), the word's origin determines the spelling. On other occasions it is the grammatical function, as in "there" and "their", which both derive from Old English.

The visual patterns also impose limitations on meaning, and they may give readers significant clues. For example, the homonyms "to", "too", and "two" have differing syntactic and semantic functions; "night" and "knight" are both nouns, but mean different things.

For struggling readers and writers, the whole system can be bewildering, and the rules difficult to learn. What can be done to help? One possibility is to reform spelling so that it becomes phonetically regular. G.B. Shaw left a legacy to that end, and some beginning reading and writing schemes such as the Initial Teaching Alphabet have attempted the task. However, such alleged reforms would result in considerable problems for those who have already learnt to read and write, and would deprive all readers of the valuable clues to meaning inherent in the present system.

The alternatives are, firstly, to find more efficient ways of teaching spelling in context as a system of auditory and visual patterns that contribute to our understanding of the printed word and, secondly, to provide writers with a key to correct spellings of incidental words as they need them.

The *Spelling Dictionary* provides such a key. It consists of a lexicon of words commonly used, containing not only their correct spellings but also common misspellings, so that the reader can look up "inconseavable" or "inconceivable" and find the accepted form of the word. The incorrect spellings are easily identified both by indentation and a blue lettering.

While there are other spelling dictionaries on the market, this is the first one based on Australian usage. The list of words presented and their misspelled forms are the result of research by the editors.

The lexicon has been compiled after consulting distinctively dictionaries, and the misspellings drawn from a range of spelling tests, lists of commonly misspelt words, and the editors' own experience. An additional advantage is the provision of a set of simple guidelines to help inexperienced or erratic spellers to improve their mastery of written language.

The *Spelling Dictionary* is designed to help those people who, although their oral conversation is adequate, may not be able to spell all the words they know. It will be an invaluable reference for the many children and adults with problems in this area, as well as for the teachers who are endeavouring to help them.

Dr. Patricia Long,
Chairperson
Special Education Department,
Melbourne College of Advanced Education

INTRODUCTION

How to Find a Word.

If possible, write down what you think is the spelling of the word you wish to find. Decide what are the first two or three letters.
Find these in the dictionary by looking at the left hand column. If you have the correct spelling you will find the word printed in **black**.
If you have the incorrect spelling you will find the word printed in **blue**, in the second left hand column. You will then find the correct spelling in **black** in the right hand column.
If you do not find the word, check any directions that may be given e.g.

Look under **de-** if the word is not under **di**.

Then proceed as above. Check how close you were to the correct spelling and if necessary learn the correct spelling.

How to Learn the Correct Spelling.

Say the word and the letters.
Look at the word carefully.
Write the word three times.
Close your eyes and think of the word. **Write it down** with your eyes closed.
Check to see you are correct.
Write the word in a sentence so that you will remember its meaning as well as its spelling.
Consult a standard dictionary if you are unsure of the meaning.

About the Dictionary.

You will see that all the words, correct spellings and incorrect spellings are listed in alphabetical order.

Nouns
To form the plural of most nouns add **"s"** to the word.
e.g. rabbit, rabbits.
Where the plural may be difficult, you are given help.
e.g. injury, -ries (for 'injuries')
goose, geese
piano, pianos
You will find hints to help you with plurals on page ix.

Verbs

Verbs listed in the dictionary give the endings for the past tense, the past participle and the present participle. Most verbs have the same word for the past tense and the past participle.

e.g. reach, -ed, -ing for reach, **reached,** reaching.

Where difficulty could occur with the spelling, you are given further help.

e.g. collide, -lided, -liding for collide, collided, colliding.
erase, erased, erasing

Where the past tense and the past participle are different, the words are given in full.

e.g. sing, sang, sung, singing.

You will find hints to help you with verbs on page ix.

Adjectives

Where there may be difficulty in spelling the comparative and superlative forms, further help is given.

e.g. dizzy, dizzier, dizziest.

Adverbs

Where the ending **-ly** is given, it is added to the word.

e.g. mythical, -ly for **'mythically'**.

Where there is a change in spelling, further help is given.

e.g. haste, -tily for **'hastily'**.
palpable, -bly for **'palpably'**.

SOME SPELLING HINTS

1. For short sounding words (one syllable words) *that do not end in* **e**, double the last letter when adding -ed, -er or -ing, e.g. ban, banned; jog, jogger; fit, fitting.
2. In short words *that end in* **e** where the central vowel sound is said the same way as the letter name – e.g. make – drop the **e** when -ed, -er or -ing are added, e.g. cope, coped; make, maker; bite, biting.
   Short words keep the **e** when -ly is added, e.g. tame, tamely; time, timely.
3. Short words (one syllable) ending in **y**, preceded by a vowel, keep the **y** when -ed, -er or -ing are added, e.g. key, keyed; buy, buyer; toy, toying.
   If the **y** is preceded by a consonant, when -ed, or -er are added, the **y** is changed to **i**, e.g. try, tried; fly, flier.
   The **y** is kept when adding -ing, e.g. try, trying.
4. Longer words ending in **y**, change the **y** to **i** when adding other parts, e.g. berry, berries; marry, marriage; happy, happiness; hurry, hurried; funny, funnily; heavy, heavier and heaviest.
   However, when adding -ing, the **y** is kept, e.g. hurry, hurrying; bury, burying.
5. Vowels that can be doubled are **e** (been) and **o** (moon) and sometimes **u** (vacuum); **a** and **i** are not doubled in English words.
6. Letters that can be doubled in the middle of a word are **b**, **d**, **f**, **g**, **m**, **n**, **r**, **s**, **t**, and **z**.
7. In short words, **f**, **l**, **s** and **z** at the end of a word are doubled, e.g. cuff, doll, pass, buzz.
8. If **full** is added to the end of a word, one **l** is dropped, e.g. helpful, until.
9. When **all-** or **well-** are added to the front of a word, one **l** is dropped, e.g. already, welcome.
10. When **dis-** and **mis-**, meaning 'not', are placed in front of a word, the **s** is not doubled – e.g. disable, misbehave – unless the main word begins with **s**, e.g. disservice, misspell.

    Also when **un-** is placed in front of a word, the **n** is not doubled – e.g. unmade – unless the main word begins with **n**, e.g. unnecessary.

    Similarly, when **in-** is placed in front of a word, the **n** is not doubled – e.g. insane – unless the main word begins with **n**, e.g. innumerable.

PLURALS

1. Most words add **s** to form the plural – e.g. cat, cats, but words that end in a sibilant sound (-s, -sh, -ss, -tch, -x) add **es**, e.g. gases, wishes, masses, catches, foxes.

2. Most words ending in **f** change the **f** to **v** and add **es**, e.g. thief, thieves. There are some exceptions, so check the word.
3. Most words ending in **o** add **es**, e.g. potato, potatoes. Exceptions are foreign words, so check the word if you are unsure.
4. Words ending in **y**, *preceded by a consonant*, change the **y** to **i** and add **es** – e.g. ferry, ferries, but words ending in **y**, *preceded by a vowel*, add **s**, e.g. day, days; monkey, monkeys.
5. Words ending in **ful** usually put the **s** after the stem word, e.g. cupful, cupsful. However the placement of **s** at the end of the word is now becoming acceptable, e.g. cupful, cupfuls.
6. Some words add **en** or **ren** to the stem word, e.g. ox, oxen; child, children.
7. Some foreign words change the ending and add **a**, **ae**, **i**, e.g. compendium, compendia; formula, formulae, bacillus, bacilli.

POSITION OF LETTERS

1. In **'ee'** sound words, **c** is always followed by **ei**, e.g. receive, ceiling. Most others have **ie**, e.g. believe, priest. However, there are many exceptions so check the word if you are unsure.
2. **q** is always followed by **u** in English words.
3. No English words end in **j** or **v**.
4. If **g** and **h** come together, **g** is always before **h**, e.g. eight, enough.
5. **ck** never starts a word.

SOUND

1. If a long word (more than one syllable) ends in the sound **'shun'**, it could be spelt -tion, -sion, -cion.
2. **ti, si** and **ci** make the **'sh'** sound, but not at the beginning of a word.
3. A long word ending in the **'j'** sound could be -age, -ege, -ige, -dge. Check the word if you are not sure.
4. A long word ending in the **'ree'** sound could be -ary, -ery, -ory, -ury or -ry. Check the word if you are not sure.
5. Very short words (one syllable) ending in **y** make the **'i'** sound as in sly, pry, sky.
6. Words ending in the **'ul'** sound could be spelt -ble, -al, -el, -il, -ol, -le. Check the word if you are not sure.
7. Most words ending in the **'ize'** sound are usually spelt **-ise**, e.g. analyse, paralyse. Some exceptions are capsize, prize.

Aa

aback
abacus, abaci, abacuses
abait abate
abakus abacus
abalone
abalonie abalone
abandon, -ed, -ing
abandonment
abase, abased, abasing
abasement
abashed
abate, abated, abating
abatement
abators abattoirs
abattoirs
abatwaz abattoirs
abayance abeyance
abbess (nun)
abbess abyss (hole)
abbey, -beys
abbie abbey
abbot
abbreviate, -ated, -ating
abbreviation
abcence absence
abdacate abdicate
abdicate, -cated, -cating
abdication
abdomen
abduckshun abduction
abduct
abduction
abductor
abel able
aberation aberration
aberrant
aberration
abet, abetted, abetting
abeyance
abeyense abeyance
abhor, abhorred, abhorring
abhore abhor
abhorent abhorrent
abhorrent, -ly
abidance
abidanse abidance
abide, abode, abided, abiding
abilitee ability
abilitey ability
ability, -ties
abismal abysmal
abiss abyss
abject, -ly
abjective objective
abjekt abject
abjure, -jured, -juring
ablaze
able, abler, ablest
able-bodied
ablushun ablution
ablution
abnegashun abnegation
abnegate, -gated, -gating
abnegation
abnormal, -ly
abnormality, -ties
aboard
abode
abolish
abolishment
abolishun abolition
abolitionary
abolitionist
abollish abolish
A-bomb
abominabel abominable
abominable
abominably
abominate, -nated, -nating
abomination
abord aboard
aboriginal
Aborigine
aborshun abortion
abort, -ed, -ing

abortion
abortive, -ly
abound, -ed, -ing
about
above
aboveboard
abowt — about
abracadabra
abradant
abrade, abraded, abrading
abrasion
abrasive
abreast
abrest — abreast
abridge, abridged, abridging
abridgment
abrige — abridge
abroad
abrogate, -gated, -gating
abrupt, -ly
abruptness
absail — abseil
abscess
abscond, -ed, -ing
absconder
abseil, -ed, -ing
absence
absense — absence
absent, -ed, -ing
absentee
absenteeism
absent-minded
absess — abscess
absinth
absolushun — absolution
absolute, -ly
absolution
absolutism
absolutist
absolve, -solved, -solving
absorb, -ed, -ing
absorbency
absorbensy — absorbency
absorbent
absorbshun — absorption
absorption
absorptive
abstain, -ed, -ing
abstane — abstain
abstemious, -ly
abstemius — abstemious
abstenshun — abstention
abstention
abstinence
abstinense — abstinence
abstinent, -ly
abstract, -ed, -ing
abstraction
abstrakshun — abstraction
abstrakt — abstract
abstruse, -ly
absurd, -ly
absurdity
abundance
abundant, -ly
abundence — abundance
abundent — abundant
abusave — abusive
abuse, abused, abusing
abusive, -ly
abut, abutted, abutting
abuttal
abysmal, -ly
abyss (hole)
acacia
academic
academician
academishun — academician
academy, -mies
accacia — acacia
accademic — academic
accademy — academy
accede, -ceded, -ceding (agree)
accede — exceed (surpass)
accelerate, -rated, -rating
acceleration
accelerator
accent, -ed, -ing
accentual, -ly
accentuate, -ated, -ating
accept, -ed, -ing
acceptabel — acceptable
acceptability

acceptable, -bly
acceptance
  acceptense — acceptance
access
  accessable — accessible
accessary, -ries (crime)
  accessibel — accessible
accessibility
accessible, -bly
  accessibul — accessible
accession
accessory, -ries (extra)
accident
accidental, -ly
acclaim, -ed, -ing
acclamation
acclimatise, -tised, -tising
accolade
accommodate, -dated, -dating
accommodation
  accomodation — accommodation
accompaniment
accompanist
accompany, -nied, -nying
  accompanyment — accompaniment
accomplice
accomplish, -ed, -ing
accomplishment
  accompliss — accomplice
accord, -ed, -ing
accordance
  accordanse — accordance
accordant, -ly
accordingly
accordion
accordionist
accost, -ed, -ing
account, -ed, -ing
  accountabel — accountable
accountability
accountable
accountably
  accountabul — accountable
accountancy
accountant
  accoustic — acoustic
accredit, -ed, -ing
accreditation
  accreshun — accretion
accretion
  accrew — accrue
  accross — across
accrual
accrue, -crued, -cruing
  accult — occult
  accumen — acumen
accumulate, -lated, -lating
accumulation
accumulative
accumulator
accuracy
  accurasy — accuracy
accurate, -ly
accurateness
accursed
accusation
accuse, -cused, -cusing
accuser
accustom, -ed, -ing
  accute — acute
ace
  acelerate — accelerate
  acerage — acreage
  acerbait — acerbate
acerbate, -bated, -bating
acerbic
acerbity
  acerige — acreage
acetate
acetic (acid)
  acetic — ascetic (hermit)
  acetilene — acetylene
acetylene
ache, ached, aching
  acheivable — achievable
  acheive — achieve
  achievabel — achievable
achievable
  achievabul — achievable
achieve, achieved, achieving
achievement
achiever
acid
acidic

acidify, -fied, -fying
acidity
ackers
acknowledge, -edged, -edging
acknowledgment

> For other ack- words, look under ac- or acc- .

aclaim acclaim
aclamation acclamation
acme
acne
acolade accolade
acommodate accommodate
acommodation accommodation
acompanist accompanist
acompany accompany
acomplice accomplice
acomplish accomplish
acord accord
acordion accordion
acorn
acost accost
acount account
acoustic
acoustical, -ly
acoustics
acquaint, -ed, -ing
acquaintance
acquaintanse acquaintance
acquiesce, -esced, -escing
acquiescence
acquiescent, -ly
acquiess acquiesce
acquire, -quired, -quiring
acquisition
acquisitive, -ly
acquit, -quitted, -quitting
acquittal
acre
acreage
acredit accredit
acrid, -ly
acrimonious, -ly
acrimony, -nies
acrobat
acrobatic
acrobatically
acrobatics
acrofobia acrophobia
acrophobia
acropolis
across
acrylic
acryllic acrylic
act, -ed, -ing
acter actor
acting
action
actionabel actionable
actionable
actionabul actionable
activate, -vated, -vating
active
activism
activist
activity, -ties
actor
actress
actual, -ly
actuality, -ties
actually
actuarial, -ly
actuary, -ries
actuate, -ated, -ating
acuity
acumen
acupuncture
acupuncturist
acupunshur acupuncture
acute, -ly
acuteness
adage
adagio
adajio adagio
adamant
adament adamant
adapt, -ed, -ing
adaptabel adaptable
adaptability
adaptable
adaptabul adaptable
adaptation
adaption

Word	Correct spelling
adaptive, -ly	
adaptor	
adda	adder
addendum, -da	
adder	
addicshun	addiction
addict, -ed, -ing	
addiction	
addictive	
addishun	addition
addition (add)	
addition	edition (book)
additional, -ly	
additive	
addled	
address, -ed, -ing	
adduce, -duced, -ducing	
adducibel	adducible
adducible	

> For other add- words, look under **ad-**.

Word	Correct spelling
adenoid	
adept, -ly	
adeptness	
adequacy	
adequasy	adequacy
adequate, -ly	
adherant	adherent
adhere, -hered, -hering	
adherence	
adherense	adherence
adherent, -ly	
adheshun	adhesion
adhesion	
adhesive, -ly	
adjacent, -ly	
adjasent	adjacent
adjectival, -ly	
adjective	
adjetival	adjectival
adjetive	adjective
adjoin, -ed, -ing	
adjourn, -ed, -ing	
adjournment	
adjudicate, -cated, -eating	
adjudication	
adjudicative, -ly	
adjudicator	
adjunct	
adjure, -jured, -juring	
adjurn	adjourn
adjurnment	adjournment
adjust, -ed, -ing	
adjustabel	adjustable
adjustable, -bly	
adjustabul	adjustable
adjustment	
admeral	admiral
administer, -ed, -ing	
administrabel	administrable
administrable	
administrabul	administrable
administrate, -trated, -trating	
administrater	administrator
administration	
administrative, -ly	
administrator	
admirable, -bly	
admiral	
admiralty, -ties	
admiration	
admire, -mired, -miring	
admirer	
admishun	admission
admissable	admissible
admissibel	admissible
admissible, -ly	
admissibul	admissible
admission	
admit, -mitted, -mitting	
admittance	
admittanse	admittance
admittedly	
admonish, -ed, -ing	
admonishun	admonition
admonition	
ad nauseam	
ado	
adobe	
adolescence	
adolescent	
adolesense	adolescence
adolesent	adolescent

adopshun	adoption
adopt, -ed, -ing	
adoption	
adoptive, -ly	
adorabel	adorable
adorable	
adorably	
adorabul	adorable
adoration	
adore, adored, adoring	
adorn, -ed, -ing	
adornment	
adorrable	adorable
adorre	adore
adrenalin	
adress	address
adrift	
adroit, -ly	
adroyt	adroit
adulate, -lated, -lating	
adulation	
adulatory	
adult	
adulterate, -rated, -rating	
adulteration	
adulterer	
adulteress	
adulterous	
adultery, -teries	
adulthood	
adultry	adultery
advacate	advocate
advance, -vanced, -vancing	
advancement	
advanse	advance
advansement	advancement
advantage, -taged, -taging	
advantageous, -ly	
advantaje	advantage
advenscher	adventure
advenshur	adventure
advent	
adventure, -tured, -turing	
adventureous	adventurous
adventurer	
adventuresome	
adventurous, -ly	
adverb	
adverbial, -ly	
adversary, -saries	
adverse, -ly	
adversery	adversary
adversity, -ties	
advert, -ed, -ing	
advertise, -tised, -tising	
advertisement	
advertiser	
advertisment	advertisement
advice (opinion)	
advice	advise (give advice)
advisabel	advisable
advisability	
advisable, -bly	
advisabul	advisable
advise, -vised, -vising (give advice)	
advise	advice (opinion)
advised, -ly	
adviser	
advisery	advisory
advisory	
advocacy	
advocasy	advocacy
advocate, -cated, -cating	
advokate	advocate
adze	
aegis	
aeon	
aerate, -rated, -rating	
aerator	
aerial, -ly	
aerobatics	
aerobics	
aerodrome	
aerodynamics	
aeronautical, -ly	
aeronautics	
aeronortics	aeronautics
aeroplain	aeroplane
aeroplane	
aerosol	
aerospace	
aesthetic	

aetiologist
aetiology
afable affable
afadavit affadavit
afair affair
afar
afasia aphasia
afect affect (pretend)
afect effect (result)
afectation affectation
afected affected
afected effected
afection affection
afectionate affectionate
afective affective
afeild afield
affabel affable
affability
affable
affableness
affably
affabul affable
affadavit affidavit
affair
affare affair
affecshun affection
affect, -ed, -ing (pretend)
affectation
affection
affectionate, -ly
affective, -ly (emotion)
affective effective (actual)
affidavit
affiliate, -ated, -ating
affiliation
affilliation affiliation
affinity, -ties
affirm, -ed, -ing
affirmation
affirmative, -ly
affix, -ed, -ing
afflicshun affliction
afflict, -ed, -ing
affliction
afflictive, -ly
affluence
affluense affluence
affluent, -ly
afford, -ed, -ing
affordable
affordabul affordable
affraid afraid
affray
affresh afresh
affro afro
affront, -ed, -ing
afield
afinity affinity
afirm affirm
afirmative affirmative
afix affix
aflict afflict
afliction affliction
afloat
afluent affluent
aford afford
afraid
afray affray
afresh
afro
afront affront
aft
after
afterbirth
afterglow
afterlife
aftermath
afternoon
afters
afterthought
afterwards
again
against
agape
agate
age, aged, ageing or aging
agency, -cies
agenda, -das
agensy agency
agent
agghast aghast
aggrandise, -dised, -dising
aggrandisement

aggrandiser
aggravate, -vated, -vating
aggravation
aggravator
aggreeved   aggrieved
aggregate, -gated, -gating
aggregation
aggregative
aggreived   aggrieved
aggreshun   aggression
aggression
aggressive, -ly
aggressor
aggreved   aggrieved
aggrieved
aggro
agground   aground
aghast
agile, -ly
agility
agis   aegis
agist, -ed, -ing
agistment
agitate, -tated, -tating
agitater   agitator
agitation
agitative
agitator
agnostic
agnosticism
ago
agog
agonise, -nised, -nising
agonisingly
agony, -nies
agorafobia   agoraphobia
agoraphobia
agraculture   agriculture
agrarian
agravate   aggravate
agravation   aggravation
agree, agreed, agreeing
agreeabel   agreeable
agreeable, -bly
agreeableness
agreeabul   agreeable
agreement
agregate   aggregate
agression   aggression
agressive   aggressive
agressor   aggressor
agricultural, -ly
agriculturalist
agriculture
agrieved   aggrieved
agronomist
agronomy
aground
ahead
ahed   ahead
ahoy
aid (help)
aide (assistant)
ail, -ed, -ing
ail   ale (beer)
aileron
ailias   alias
ailment
aim, -ed, -ing
aimless, -ly
aimlessness
ain't (am not)
aint   ain't
air, -ed, -ing
air   hair
airate   aerate
airborn   airborne
airborne
air-brake
air-break   air-brake
airbus
air condishun   air-condition
air-condition, -ed, -ing
aircraft, -craft
airfeild   airfield
airfield
airforce
airgun
air hostess
aireal   aerial
airial   aerial
airily
airlift
airline

airliner	
airlock	
airmail	
airman, -men	
airobatics	aerobatics
airobics	aerobics
airodrome	aerodrome
airodynamics	aerodynamics
airoplane	aeroplane
airosol	aerosol
air-pocket	
airport	
air-pressure	
airship	
airspace	
airspeed	
airstream	
airstrip	
air terminal	
airtight	
airtite	airtight
airwaves	
airy, airier, airiest	
airy-fairy	
aisle (path)	
aitch	
ajar	
ajis	aegis
akimbo	
akin	
alabaster	
alabi	alibi
alacart	à la carte
à la carte	
alackrity	alacrity
alacritous	
alacritus	alacritous
alacrity	
Alah	Allah
alarm, -ed, -ing	
alarmist	
alas	
alaska	
albatros	albatross
albatross, albatrosses	
albeeit	albeit
albeit	

albino, -nos	
albinism	
album	
albumen (egg white)	
albumin (protein)	
albuminous	
albuminus	albuminous
alcali	alkali
alcaline	alkaline
alchemist	
alchemy	
alcohol	
alcoholic	
alcoholism	
alcove	
alderman, -men	
ale (beer)	
ale	ail (ill)
alege	allege
alert, -ed, -ing	
alfa	alpha
alfabet	alphabet
alfalfa	
alfresco	
alga, -gae	
algebra	
algebraic, -ally	
alias, aliases	
alibi, -bis	
alien	
alienate, -nated, -nating	
alienation	
alienator	
alight, alighted, alighting	
align, -ed, -ing	
alignment	
alike	
aliment (food)	
aliment	element (part)
alimentary (food)	
alimentary (basic)	elementary
alimony	
alive	
alkaholic	alcoholic
alkali, -lis, -lies	
alkaline	

alkalinity	
alkeline	alkaline
alkohol	alcohol
alkoholic	alcoholic
alkoholism	alcoholism
alkove	alcove
all (every)	
all	awl (tool)
allabaster	alabaster
Allah	
allay, -layed, -laying	
allbatross	albatross
alledge	allege
allegation	
allege, -leged, -leging	
allegiance	
allegianse	allegiance
allegorical, -ly	
allegory, -ries	
allegro	
alleluia	
allergic	
allergy, -gies	
allert	alert
alleviate, -ated, -ating	
alleviation	
alleviator	
alley, alleys	
alliance	
allied	
alliense	alliance
allies	
alligator	
all-in	
alliteration	
alliterative, -ly	
allmanac	almanac
allmost	almost
allocate, -cated, -eating	
allocation	
alloft	aloft
allone	alone
allot, -lotted, -lotting	
allotment	
all-out	
allow, -ed, -ing	
allowabel	allowable

allowable	
allowabul	allowable
allowance	
allowense	allowance
alloy	
all right	
allrite	all right
all-rounder	
allso	also
allude, -luded, -luding (refer)	
allude	elude (avoid)
allure, -lured, -luring	
allushun	allusion
allusion (mention)	
allusion	illusion (trick)
allusive, -ly (mentioned)	
allusive	elusive (avoid)
alluvial	
ally, -lies	
ally, -lied, -lying	
ally	alley
almanac	
almanack	
almightily	
almightiness	
almighty	
almond	
almoner	
almost	
alms (gifts)	
alocate	allocate
aloe	
aloft	
alone	
along	
alongside	
alood	allude
aloof	
alot	a lot (of)
alot	allot (give)
aloud (speak)	
aloud	allowed (permit)
alow	allow
alowable	allowable
alowance	allowance
aloy	alloy

Word	Correct spelling
alp	
alpaca	
alpacka	alpaca
alpha	
alphabet	
alphabetical, -ly	
alphebet	alphabet
alpine	
already	
alredy	already
Alsatian	
also	
altar (church)	
altatude	altitude
altenate	alternate
alter (change)	
alterable, -bly	
alteration	
altercation	
altercative	
alter ego	
alternate, -nated, -nating	
alternately	
alternation	
alternative, -ly	
alternator	
alterration	alteration
although	
altimeter	
altitude	
alto, -tos	
altogether	
altrooism	altruism
altrueism	altruism
altruism	
altruistic, -ally	
alturnate	alternate
alude	allude
alumina	
aluminium	
aluminum	aluminium
alumminum	aluminium
alure	allure
alurt	alert
alushun	allusion
alusive	allusive
always	

Word	Correct spelling
amaize	amaze
amalgam	
amalgamate, -mated, -mating	
amalgamation	
amalgum	amalgam
amass, -ed, -ing	
amassabel	amassable
amassable	
amassabul	amassable
amatcher	amateur
amatchur	amateur
amater	amateur
amateur	
amatory	
amaze, -mazed, -mazing	
amazement	
Amazon	
ambaguity	ambiguity
ambassader	ambassador
ambassador, -ial	
ambel	amble
amber	
ambiance	ambience
ambiant	ambient
ambidexterity	
ambidextrous, -ly	
ambience	
ambiense	ambience
ambient	
ambiguity, -ties	
ambiguous, -ly	
ambiguus	ambiguous
ambishen	ambition
ambishus	ambitious
ambit	
ambition	
ambitious, -ly	
ambivalence	
ambivalense	ambivalence
ambivalent	
amble, -bled, -bling	
ambul	amble
ambulance	
ambulanse	ambulance
ambush, -ed, -ing	
ame	aim
ameanable	amenable

ameba	amoeba
ameliorate, -rated, -rating	
amelioration	
amen	
amenabel	amenable
amenable, -bly	
amenabul	amenable
amend, -ed, -ing	
amendment	
amends	
amenity, -ties	
America	
ameter	ammeter
amethist	amethyst
amethyst	

For amf- words, look under **amph-** .

amiabel	amiable
amiability	
amiable, -bly	
amiabul	amiable
amicabel	amicable
amicability	
amicable, -bly	
amicabul	amicable
amid	
amidst	
amigo	
amiss	
amity, -ties	
ammeter	
ammonia	
ammunition	

For other amm- words, look under **am-** .

amnesia, -iac	
amnesty, -ties	
amnesty, -tied, -tying	
amoeba, -bae, -bas	
amoebic	
amok	
among	
amongst	
amoral, -ly	
amorfous	amorphous
amorous, -ly	
amorphism	
amorphous, -ly	
amorphus	amorphous
amortise, -tised, -tising	
amount, -ed, -ing	
amownt	amount
ampair	ampere
ampel	ample
amperage	
ampere	
amphetamine	
amphibian	
amphibious, -ly	
amphitheatre	
ample, -pler, -plest (enough)	
amplefy	amplify
amplification	
amplifier	
amplify, -fied, -fying	
amplitude	
amply	
ampoule (bottle)	
ampul	ample (enough)
ampul	ampoule (bottle)
amputate, -tated, -tating	
amputation	
amuck	
amuk	amok
amuk	amuck
amulet	
amung	among
amungst	amongst
amunition	ammunition
amuse, amused, amusing	
amusement	
anachronism	
anachronistic	
anackronism	anachronism
anackronistic	anachronistic
anaconda	
anaemia	
anaesthesia	
anaesthetic	
anaesthetisation	
anaesthetise, -tised, -tising	

anaesthetist
anagram
anaky — anarchy
anal
analgesia
analgesic
analise — analyse
analisis — analysis
analist — analyst
analog (electric)
analog — analogue (similar)
analogous, -ly
analogue (similar)
analogue — analog (electric)
analogy, -gies
analyse, -lysed, -lysing
analysis, -ses
analyst
analytical, -ly
anarchical, -ly
anarchism
anarchist
anarchy
anathema, -mas
anatomical, -ly
anatomist
anatomy, -mies
ancestor
ancestral, -ly
ancestry, -tries
anchor, -ed, -ing
anchorage
anchorman, -men
anchovy, -vies
ancient
ancillary, -aries
anecdotal
anecdote
anemia — anaemia
anemic — anaemic
anesthesia — anaesthesia
anesthetic — anaesthetic
anesthetise — anaesthetise
anesthetist — anaesthetist
aneurism
anew
anewity — annuity
angel (spirit)
angel — angle (fishing)
angelic
angellic — angelic
anger, -ed, -ing
angina
angle, angled, angling (fishing)
angle — angel (spirit)
angler
Anglican
Anglicanism
Anglo-Catholic
Anglo-Sacksen — Anglo-Saxon
Anglo-Saxon
angora
angree — angry
angrie — angry
angrily
angry, angrier, angriest
angsiety — anxiety
anguish, -ed, -ing
angular, -ity
anguler — angular
angwish — anguish
anigma — enigma
animal
animate, -mated, -mating
animatedly
animation
animel — animal
animosity, -ties
aniseed
aniversary — anniversary
anjel — angel
anjelic — angelic
anjina — angina
anker — anchor
ankerage — anchorage
ankeridge — anchorage
ankerije — anchorage
ankle
anklet
annals
anneal, -ed, -ing
annex, -ed, -ing (join)

annexation
annexe (building)
annialate — annihilate
annihilate, -lated, -lating
anniversary, -ries
Anno Domini
annotate, -tated, -tating
annotation
announce, announced, announcing
announcement
annoy, annoyed, annoying
annual, -ly
annuity, -ties
annul, annulled, annulling
annulment
annulus, -li, or -luses
annunciate, -ated, -ating
annunciation

For other ann- words, look under an- .

anode
anodine — anodyne
anodyne
anoint, -ed, -ing
anomaley — anomaly
anomaly, -lies
anon
anonimity — anonymity
anonimous — anonymous
anonymity
anonymous, -ly
anorak
anorecksia — anorexia
anorexia
another
anoynt — anoint
anser — answer
anserable — answerable
anserabul — answerable
ansestor — ancestor
ansestral — ancestral
ansestrul — ancestral
ansestry — ancestry
ansilary — ancillary
answer, -ed, -ing
answerabel — answerable
answerable, -bly
answerabul — answerable
antacid
antagonise, -nised, -nising
antagonism
antagonist
antagonistic, -ally
Antarctic
antasid — antacid
anteak — antique
anteater
antecedent
antechamber
anteclimax — anticlimax
antecyclone — anticyclone
antedate, -dated, -dating
antediloovian — antediluvian
antediluvian
anteek — antique
antelope, antelopes
antena — antenna
antenatal
antenatel — antenatal
antenatul — antenatal
antenna, -tennae, -tennas
anterior
anteroom
anthem
anthill
anthology, -gies
anthracite
anthracks — anthrax
anthrasite — anthracite
anthrax, -thraces
anthropoid
anthropologey — anthropology
anthropologist
anthropology
antibiotic
antibody, -bodies
antic
anticeptic — antiseptic
antichamber — antechamber
Antichrist
anticiclone — anticyclone
anticipate, -pated, -pating
anticipation

anticipatory	
anticlimacks	anticlimax
anticlimactic	
anticlimax	
anticlockwise	
anticyclone	
anticyclonic	
antidate	antedate
antidepressant	
antidotal	
antidote	
antifon	antiphon
antifreeze	
antigen	
antihisstamine	antihistamine
antihistamine	
antikwarian	antiquarian
antikwated	antiquated
antikwitey	antiquity
antilope	antelope
antimony	
antinatal	antenatal
antinatul	antenatal
antinewklear	antinuclear
antinuclear	
antipathy, -pathies	
antiperspirant	
antiphon	
antipodes	
antipodies	antipodes
antiquarian	
antiquary, -quaries	
antiquated	
antique	
antiquity, -quities	
antiroom	anteroom
anti-Semitic	
anti-Semitism	
antiseptic, -ally	
antisiclone	anticyclone
antisipation	anticipation
antisocial, -ly	
antithesis, -theses	
antithisis	antithesis
antitoksic	antitoxic
antitoksin	antitoxin
antler	
antonim	antonym
antonym	
anus	
anuther	another
anvil	
anvul	anvil
anxiety, -ties	
anxious, -ly	
any	
anybody	
anyhow	
anyone	
anything	
anyway	
anywear	anywhere
anywere	anywhere
anywhere	
Anzac	
aorta, -tas, -tae	
apace	
apart	
apartheid	
apartied	apartheid
apartite	apartheid
apartment	
apase	apace
apathetic, -ally	
apathy	
ape, aped, aping	
apeace	apiece
apease	apiece
apeice	apiece
apeks	apex
apercher	aperture
apergee	apogee
apergey	apogee
aperitif	
aperture	
apex, apexes, apices	
aphasia	
aphid	
aphorism	
aphrodisiac	
apiary, apiaries	
apiece	
apissul	epistle
apistle	epistle

aplom	aplomb
aplomb	
aply	apply
apocalipse	apocalypse
apocalypse	
apocalyptic	
apocrifal	apocryphal
apocryphal, -ly	
apogee	
apologetic, -ally	
apologey	apology
apologise, -gised, -gising	
apologist	
apology, -gies	
apoplectic	
apoplexy	
aposle	apostle
apostasy, -sies	
apostel	apostle
apostle	
apostolate	
apostolic	
apostrofy	apostrophe
apostrophe	
aposul	apostle
apothecary, -ries	
apoynt	appoint

For other ap- words, look under **app-** .

appal, -palled, -palling	
apparatus, -tus, -tuses	
apparel	
apparent, -ly	
apparishun	apparition
apparition	
appart	apart
appeal, -ed, -ing	
appealing, -ly	
appear, -ed, -ing	
appearance	
appearense	appearance
appease, -peased, -peasing	
appeasement	
appelant	appellant
appellant	
appellate	
appellation	
append, -ed, -ing	
appendacitis	appendicitis
appendage	
appendectomy, -mies	
appendicitis	
appendige	appendage
appendiks	appendix
apperatus	apparatus
appertain, -ed, -ing	
apperture	aperture
appetiser	
appetite	
applaud, -ed, -ing	
applause	
applawd	applaud
applaws	applause
apple	
appliance	
applianse	appliance
applicability	
applicable, -bly	
applicant	
application	
applie	apply
applied	
applique	
apply, -plied, -plying	
appoint, -ed, -ing	
appointment	
apporshun	apportion
apportion, -ed, -ing	
apportionment	
apposishun	apposition
apposite, -ly	
apposition	
appraisal	
appraise, -praised, -praising	
appraysal	appraisal
apprayse	appraise
appreciabel	appreciable
appreciable, -bly	
appreciabul	appreciable
appreciate, -ated, -ating	
appreciation	
appreciative, -ly	
apprehend, -ed, -ing	

Word	Correct spelling
apprehenshun	apprehension
apprehensibel	apprehensible
apprehensible	
apprehensibul	apprehensible
apprehension	
apprehensive, -ly	
apprentice	
apprenticeship	
apprentise	apprentice
appricot	apricot
apprise, -prised, -prising	
approach, -ed, -ing	
approachabel	approachable
approachable	
approbation	
approch	approach
approchabul	approachable
approove	approve
appropos	apropos
appropriate, -ated, -ating	
appropriation	
approval	
approve, -proved, -proving	
approvel	approval
approximate, -mated, -mating	
approximately	
approximation	
apricot	
April	
apron	
apropos	
apt, -ly	
aptitude	
aptley	aptly
aqualung	
aquamarine	
aquaplane	
aquarium	
Aquarius	
aquatic	
aqueduct	
aqueous	
aquiline	
arabel	arable
arabesk	arabesque
arabesque	
Arabic numerals	

Word	Correct spelling
arable	
arabul	arable
araign	arraign
arain	arraign
arange	arrange
aray	array
arber	arbour
arbiter	
arbitrary	
arbitrate, -trated, -trating	
arbitration	
arbor (axis)	
abor	arbour (shade)
arboreal	
arboricultural	
arboriculture	
arbour (shade)	
arbour	arbor (axis)
arc, arced, arcing (curve)	
arc	ark (boat)
arcade	
arcane	
arch	
archaeological, -ly	
archaeologist	
archaeology	
archaic	
archaism	
archangel	
archary	archery
archbishop	
archer	
archerfish	
archery	
archetypal	
archetype	
archipelago, -gos, -goes	
architect	
architectural, -ly	
architecture	
architrave	
archival	
archives	
archivist	
arcipelago	archipelago
arcipeligo	archipelago
arcitect	architect

arcitectural	architectural
arcitecture	architecture
arcives	archives
arc light	
arctic	
Arctic Circle	
ardent, -ly	
arder	ardour
ardour	
arduous, -ly	
arduus	arduous
are	
area	
arears	arrears
arena	
aren't	
arent	aren't
arest	arrest
argent	
argew	argue
argon	
arguabel	arguable
arguable, -bly	
arguabul	arguable
argue, -gued, -guing	
arguement	argument
argument	
argumentation	
argumentative, -ly	
argus	
arguw	argue
argy-bargy, -bargies	
aria (melody)	
aria	area (piece)
arial	aerial
arid, -ly	
aridity	
Aries	
arina	arena
arise, arose, arisen, arising	
aristocracy, -cies	
aristocrasy	aristocracy
aristocrat	
aristocratic	
arithmetic	
arithmetical, -ly	
arithmetician	
arival	arrival
arive	arrive
ark (boat)	
ark	arc (curve)

For other ark- words, look under **arc-**.

arm	
armacher	armature
armachur	armature
armada	
armadillo, -los	
Armageddon	
armament	
armature	
armchair	
armed	
armer	armour
armey	army
armistice	
armistise	armistice
armoner	almoner
armour	
armoured	
armourer	
armoury, -ries	
armpit	
arms (weapons)	
arms	alms (gifts)
army, -mies	
arogance	arrogance
aroganse	arrogance
arogant	arrogant
aroma	
aromatic	
arora	aurora
arose	
around	
arousal	
arouse, aroused, arousing	
arow	arrow
arownd	around
arowroot	arrowroot
arowse	arouse
arpeggio	
arpejio	arpeggio
arraign, -ed, -ing	

authorisation
authorise, -rised, -rising
authoritarian
authoritative, -ly
authority, -ties
autism
auto
autobiographical, -ly
autobiography, -phies
autocracy
autocrasy autocracy
autocrat
autocratic
autocue
autograf autograph
autograph
automatic
automation
automative
automobile
automotive
autonomee autonomy
autonomous, -ly
autonomus autonomous
autonomy
autopilot
autopsy, -sies
autum autumn
autumn
autumnal, -ly
auxiliary, -ries
avail, -ed, -ing
availabel available
availability
available
availabul available
avalable available
avalanch avalanche
avalanche
avale avail
avaliable available
avant-garde
avarey aviary
avarice
avaricious, -ly
avaris avarice
avarishus avaricious
avenew avenue
avenge, avenged, avenging
avenger
avenue
aver, averred, averring
average, -raged, -raging
avericious avaricious
averidge average
averige average
averishus avaricious
averiss avarice
averse, -ly
avershun aversion
aversion
avert, -ed, -ing
avery aviary
avgas
aviary, aviaries
aviater aviator
aviation
aviator
avid, -ly
avinue avenue
avlanch avalanche
avocado, avocados
avoid, -ed, -ing (evade)
avoid ovoid (egg)
avoidable, -ably
avow, -ed, -ing
avowal
avoyd avoid
avridge average
avrije average
avud avid
avur aver
avurse averse
avurshun aversion
avursion aversion
avurt avert
await, -ed, -ing
awake, awoke, awaking
awaken, -ed, -ing
award, -ed, -ing
aware
awareness
away
awayte await

awb orb
awe, awed, awing (fear)
awe oar (boat)
awear aware
awesome, -ly
awful, -ly
awgy orgy
awksilary auxiliary
awkward, -ly
awkwud awkward
awl (tool)
awl all (every)
awning
awoke
awry
axe, axes
axe, axed, axing
axel axle
axial, -ly
axident accident
axidental accidental
axiom
axiomatic
axis, axes
axle

axsede accede
axseed accede
axsel axle
axsellerate accelerate
axsent accent
axsentuate accentuate
axsept accept
axseptable acceptable
axseptabul acceptable
axseptance acceptance
axsesary accessary
axsesory accessory
axsess access
axsessable accessible
axsessabul accessible
axsessible accessible
axsessibul accessible
ay, ayes (yes)
ayatollah
aye (ever)
aysure azure
azalea
azalia azalea
azure
azury

Bb

babbel — babble (chatter)
babble, -led, -ling (chatter)
babboon — baboon
babbul — babble (chatter)
babe
babel (confusion)
babel — babble (chatter)
babey — baby
babie — baby
baboon
babul — babble (chatter)
baby, babies
baby-sitter
baccarat
bach — batch
bacheler — bachelor
bachelor
bacillus, bacilli
back, -ed, -ing
backbencher
backblocks
backbone
back-burn
backer
backfire, -fired, -firing
backgammon
background
backhand
backing
backlash
back-pedal, -alled, -alling
backroom
back-seat driver
backstage
backstitch, -ed, -ing
backstop, -stopped, -stopping
backstroke, -stroked, -stroking
back-to-back
backwards
backwash
backyard
bacon
bacteria
bad, worse, worst (not good)
bade (ask)
badge
badger
badly
badminton
baffel — baffle
baffle, -fled, -fling
bag, bagged, bagging
bagatelle
baggage
baggidge — baggage
baggy, baggier, baggiest
bagman, -men
bagpipes
baige — beige
bail (court)
bail — bale (bundle)
bailiff — bailiff
bailiff
bairn
bait (fishing)
bait — bate (hold)
baize, baized, baizing
baje — badge
bake, baked, baking
bakelite
baker
bakery
bakshee
balaclava
balad — ballad
balalaika
balance, -anced, -ancing
balanse — balance
balast — ballast
balay — ballet
balcony, -conies

bald (hairless)
  bald — bawled (cried)
balderdash
balding
baldness
bale, baled, baling (bundle)
  bale — bail (court)
baleful, -ly
  balefull — baleful
  balerina — ballerina
  balero — bolero
  balet — ballet
  baliff — bailiff
ball (round)
  ball — bawl (cry)
ballad
ballast
ball-bearing
ballerina
ballet
ballistics
balloon
balloonist
ballot, balloted, balloting
ballpoint
  balsa — balsa
  ballsam — balsam
ballyhoo
balm
balmy, balmier, balmiest (good)
  balmy — barmy (stupid)
  balonee — baloney
baloney
  baloon — balloon
  ballot — ballot
balsa
balsam
balustrade
  balyhoo — ballyhoo
bamboo
bamboozle, -zled, -zling
ban, banned, banning
banal, -ly
banana
  banana — republic
band, banded, banding (strip)
band (group)
  band — banned (forbidden)
bandage, -daged, -daging
bandanna
  bandey — bandy
bandicoot
  bandige — bandage
bandit
  bandoleer — bandolier
bandolier
bandsaw
bandwagon
bandy, -died, -dying
bandy-legged
  baner — banner
bangalow
  bangel — bangle
banger
bangle
bang-on
banish, -ed, -ing
banishment
banister
banjo, banjos
bank, -ed, -ing
bankbook
banker
banknote
  bankrupcy — bankruptcy
  bankrupsy — bankruptcy
bankrupt
bankruptcy
banksia
  bankwet — banquet
banned (forbidden)
  banned — band (strip)
banner
banns (notices)
banquet, -queted, -queting
bans (forbids)
  bans — banns (notices)
bantam
bantamweight
banter, -ed, -ing
  bantum — bantam
banyan
  baonet — bayonet

bap	
baptise, -tised, -tising	
baptism	
baptismal	
Baptist	
bar, barred, barring	
barack	barrack
baracouta	barracouta
barage	barrage
barb	
barbarian	
barbaric	
barbarism	
barbarous, -ly	
barbarus	barbarous
barbecue, -cued, -cuing	
barbed wire	
barbell	
barbeque, -qued, -quing	
barber	
barbiturate	
bard (poet)	
bard (stopped)	barred
bare, bared, baring (uncover)	
bare, barer, barest	
bare	bear (animal)
bareback	
barefaced	
barefoot	
bareheaded	
barel	barrel
barely	
baren	baron (noble)
baren	barren (sterile)
bareskin	bearskin
bargain, -ed, -ing	
bargainer	
bargan	bargain
barge, barged, barging	
bargee	
bargen	bargain
baricade	barricade
barier	barrier
baring (uncovering)	
baring	barring (stop)
baring	bearing (hold)

barister	barrister
baritone	
barium	
bark, -ed, -ing	
barley	
barlie	barley
barm	balm
barmade	barmaid
barmaid	
barman, -men	
barmy, barmier, barmiest (stupid)	
barmy	balmy (good)
barn	
barn	bairn
barnacel	barnacle
barnacle	
barnacled	
barnacul	barnacle
barney	
barnicul	barnacle
barnstorm	
barometer	
barometric	
baron (noble)	
baron	barren (sterile)
baronet	
baronial	
baroque	
barrow	barrow
barrack, -ed, -ing	
barracker	
barracouta	
barracuda	
barrage, -raged, -raging	
barramundi	
barrel, -relled, -relling	
barren (sterile)	
barren	baron (noble)
barrenness	
barricade, -caded, -cading	
barrier	
barring (stop)	
barring	baring (uncovering)
barrister	
barrow	
barrul	barrel

barter, -ed, -ing
  barul — barrel
basal, -ly
basalt
base, based, basing (support)
base, baser, basest
  base — bass (low tone)
baseball
basement
  baset — basset
bash, -ed, -ing
bashful, -ly
basic
basilica
  basillus — bacillus
basin
  basinette — bassinette
basis, bases
  basit — basset
bask, -ed, -ing (enjoy warmth)
  bask — basque (garb)
basketball
  baskit — basket
  basoon — bassoon
basque (garb)
bas-relief
bass (low tone)
  bass — base (support)
bass clef
basset
bassinette
bassoon
bastard
  bastardisashun — bastardisation
bastardisation
bastardry
baste, basted, basting
  basterd — bastard
bastion
bat, batted, batting
batch
bate, bated, bating (hold breath)
  bate — bait (fishing)
  baten — baton (stick)
  baten — batten (timber)
  bater — batter
  baterey — battery

bath
bathe, bathed, bathing
bathers
bathroom
batik
  battle — battle
  batler — battler
batman, -men
baton (stick)
  baton — batten (timber)
batsman, -men
batt (insulating)
  batt — bat (cricket)
battalion
  battaliun — battalion
  battle — battle
batten (timber)
batter
battering ram
battery, -ries
battle, battled, battling
battleaxe
battledress
battler
battleship
batty, battier, battiest
  batul — battle
  baty — batty
  baubel — bauble
bauble
  baubul — bauble
baulk, -ed, -ing
bauxite
  bawble — bauble
  bawdie — bawdy
bawdiness
bawdy, -dier, -diest
bawl, -ed, -ing (cry)
  bawl — ball (round)
  bawlsa — balsa
bay
  bayliff — bailiff
  baynet — bayonet
bayonet
  baythe — bathe
bazaar (market)
  bazaar — bizarre (odd)

bazaar — bazaar
bazooka
be, been, being (exist)
be — bee (insect)
beach, -ches (shore)
beach — beech (tree)
beachcomber
beachcomer — beachcomber
beacon
bead, -ed, -ing
beady, beadier, beadiest
beaf — beef
beafeater — beefeater
beafy — beefy
beagel — beagle
beagle
beak
beaker
beam, -ed, -ing
bean (vegetable)
bean — been (be)
beanie
beano
bear (animal)
bear, borne, bearing (carry)
bear — bare (uncover)
bearback — bareback
beard
bearer
bearfaced — barefaced
bearfoot — barefoot
bearheaded — bareheaded
bearing (hold)
bearing — baring (uncovering)
bearskin
beast
beastliness
beastly, beastlier, beastliest
beat, beaten, beating (strike)
beat — beet (food)
beatel — beetle
beater
beatific
beatify, -fied, -fying
beatitude
beatle — beetle
beatnik
beatroot — beetroot
beatul — beetle
beau, beaus, beaux (suitor)
beaut
beauteous, -ly
beautician
beautie — beauty
beautiful, -ly
beautify, -fied, -fying
beautishun — beautician
beauty, beauties
beaver
becalmed
became
becarmed — becalmed
because
beck
beckon, -ed, -ing
become, became, becoming
becon — beacon
becos — because
bed, bedded, bedding
bedeck, -ed, -ing
bedevel — bedevil
bedevil, -illed, -illing
bedevul — bedevil
bedlam
bedouin
bedowin — bedouin
bedpan
bedraggled
bedraguled — bedraggled
bedridden
bedriden — bedridden
bedrock
bedside
bed-sitting room
bedspread
bedspred — bedspread
bedstead
bedsted — bedstead
bed-wetting
bee (insect)
bee — be (exist)
beech (tree)
beech — beach (shore)

beechcomber	beachcomber
beechcomer	beachcomber
beecon	beacon
beed	bead
beef	
beefeater	
beefy, beefier, beefiest	
beegel	beagle
beegle	beagle
beehive	
beeline	
beem	beam
been (be)	
been	bean (food)
beenie	beanie
beep	
beer (ale)	
beer	bier (coffin)
beerd	beard
beest	beast
beeswaks	beeswax
beeswax	
beet (food)	
beet	beat (strike)
beetel	beetle
beetle	
beetle off	
beetroot	
beetul	beetle
beever	beaver
befall, -fell, -fallen, -falling	
befit, -fitted, -fitting	
befor	before
before	
beforehand	
befuddle, -dled, -dling	
befudul	befuddle
beg, begged, begging	
began	
begar	beggar
beger	beggar
beggar	
beggarly	
begger	beggar
begile	beguile
begin, began, begun, beginning	
beginner	

begone	
begonia	
begrudge, -grudged, -grudging	
begruge	begrudge
beguile, -guiled, -guiling	
begun	
behalf	
beharf	behalf
behave, -haved, -having	
behavior	behaviour
behaviour	
behavioural	
behead, -ed, -ing	
behed	behead
beheld	
behest	
behind	
behive	beehive
beige	
beije	beige
being	
bekos	because
bekweath	bequeath
bekwest	bequest
bel	bell (ring)
bel	belle (girl)
belabor	belabour
belabour, -ed, -ing	
belated, -ly	
belay, -layed, -laying	
bellbird	bellbird
belch, -ed, -ing	
beleaf	belief
beleavabul	believable
beleave	believe
beleif	belief
beleive	believe
belfrey	belfry
belfry, -fries	
Belgian	
beli	belie
belicose	bellicose
belie, -lied, -lying	
belief	
believable, -bly	
believe, -lieved, -lieving	
beligerence	belligerence

Word	Correct spelling
beligerency	belligerency
beligerense	belligerence
beligerent	belligerent
beline	beeline
belittel	belittle
belittle, -tled, -tling	
bell (ring)	
bellbird	
belle (girl)	
bellicose, -ly	
belligerence	
belligerency	
belligerent, -ly	
bellow, -ed, -ing (roar)	
bellow	below (under)
bellows	
belly, bellies	
belly, bellied, bellying	
bellyache	
belong, -ed, -ing	
belongings	
belose	bellows
beloved	
belovid	beloved
below (under)	
below	bellow (roar)
belows	bellows
belt, -ed, -ing	
belt-up, belted-up, belting-up	
bely	belly
bemoan, -ed, -ing	
bemused	
bench, benches	
benchmark	
bend, bent, bending	
bender	
beneath	
benediction	
benefactor	
benefactress	
benefice	
beneficence	
beneficent, -ly	
beneficial, -ly	
beneficiary, -aries	
benefis	benefice
benefisense	beneficence

Word	Correct spelling
benefisent	beneficent
benefishal	beneficial
benefisharey	beneficiary
benefit, -fited, -fiting	
benevolence	
benevolense	benevolence
benevolent, -ly	
benign, -ly	
benine	benign
bent	
benum	benumb
benumb	
benzene (coal tar)	
benzine (petroleum)	
bequeath	
bequeeth	bequeath
bequest	
berate, -rated, -rating	
beray	beret
bereave, -reaved, -reaving	
bereeve	bereave
bereft	
beret	
bereve	bereave
berglar	burglar
beri	berry (fruit)
beri	bury (in earth)
berial	burial
beri-beri	
berie	berry (fruit)
berley (bait)	
berley	burly (large)
berli	berley (bait)
berli	burly (large)
berry, berries (fruit)	
berry	bury (in earth)
berserk	
berth (ship)	
berth	birth (born)
bery	berry (fruit)
bery	bury (in earth)
beseach	beseech
beseech, -seeched, -seeching	
beseige	besiege
beset, -set, -setting	
beside	
besides	

besiege, -sieged, -sieging
besotted
best
bestial, -ly
bestiality
bestir, -stirred, -stirring
bestow, -ed, -ing
bestowal
bet, bet, betting
beta
beta particle
betel nut
  betel   beetle
  betle   beetle
betoken, -ed, -ing
betray, -ed, -ing
betrayal
betrayer
betrothal
better
betterment
  betul   beetle
between
betwixt
bevel, -elled, -elling
beverage
  beveridge   beverage
  bevarije   beverage
  bevie   bevy
bevy, bevies
bewail
beware
  bewayl   bewail
  bewear   beware
  bewhere   beware
  bewhich   bewitch
bewilder, -ed, -ing
bewilderment
bewitch
  bewty   beauty
beyond
  bezerk   berserk
biannual, -ly (twice a year)
  biannual   biennial (every two years)
bias, biased, biasing
bias binding
  biass   bias
  biassed   biased
  Bibel   Bible
Bible
  bibliografy   bibliography
bibliographer
bibliography, -phies
  Bibul   Bible
  became   became
bicameral
bicarbonate
  bicarmed   becalmed
bicentenary
bicentennial
biceps
  bich   bitch
  bicicle   bicycle
bicker, -ed, -ing
bicycle
bid, bade, bidding
  biday   bidet
biddy, -dies
bide, bided, biding
bidet
  bidevil   bedevil
biennial, -ly (every two years)
  biennial   biannual (twice a year)
bier (coffin)
  bier   beer (ale)
  bifell   befell
bifocal
bifurcate, -cated, -cating
big, bigger, biggest
bigamist
bigamy
  bigan   began
  bigot   bigot
bight (bay)
  bight   bite (cut)
  bight   byte (computer)
  bigile   beguile
  begin   begin
  biginer   beginner
  bigining   beginning
  bigon   begone

bigone bygone
bigot
bigoted, -ly
bigotry
bigrudge begrudge
bigun begun

For bih- words,
look under **beh-** .

bikameral bicameral
bike
bikini
bikweath bequeath
bikwest bequest
bil bill
bilaber belabour
bilated belated
bilateral, -ly
bilaw by-law
bilay belay
bild build
bilding building
bile
bileavabul believable
bileave believe
bileif belief
bilet billet
bilge
biliards billiards
bilief belief
bilingual, -ly
bilingwal bilingual
bilion billion
bilious, -ly
biliousness
bilittul belittle
bilius bilious
bilk, -ed, -ing
bill, -ed, -ing
billabong
billet, -eted, -eting
billiards
Billingsgate
billion
billit billet
billow (wave)
billy, billies
billycan
billygoat
bilong belong
bilow below (under)
bilow billow (wave)
bilyards billiards
bilyon billion
bilyus billious
bimoan bemoan
bimuse bemuse
bin, binned, binning
bin been
binary
bind, bound, binding
binder
bineath beneath
binevolent benevolent
binge
bingo
binine benign
binoculars
binomial, -ly
binumb benumb
biochemist
biochemistry
biodegradable
biografer biographer
biografical biographical
biografy biography
biographer
biographical, -ly
biography, -phies
biokemist biochemist
biologey biology
biological, -ly
biologist
biology
biopsey biopsy
biopsy
biorhythm
bipartisan
bipartite
bipartizen bipartisan
bipass by-pass
biped
biplane
biproduct by-product

birate	berate
birch	
bird	
birdie	
bird's-eye	
bireave	bereave
bireft	bereft
biro	
birth (born)	
birth	berth (ship)
birthday	
birthrate	
biscet	biscuit
biscuit	
biscut	biscuit
bisecshun	bisection
bisect, -ed, -ing	
bisection	
bisector	
biseech	beseech
biseege	besiege
biseige	besiege
biseksual	bisexual
bisen	bison
bisentenary	bicentenary
bisentenyal	bicentennial
biseps	biceps
biset	beset
bisexual, -ly	
bisexuality	
bishop	
bishopric	
bisicle	bicycle
biside	beside
bisier	busier
bisily	busily
biskit	biscuit
bismuth	
bisness	business
bison, -son	
bisotted	besotted
bistander	bystander
bistir	bestir
bistow	bestow
bistowal	bestowal
bistro	
bisun	bison

bisy	busy
bit	
bitch, -ches	
bitchiness	
bitchumen	bitumen
bitchy	
bite, bitten, bit, biting (cut)	
bite	bight (bay)
bite	byte (computer)
biter	bitter
bitoken	betoken
bitray	betray
bitrayal	betrayal
bitrothal	betrothal
bitser	
bitten (bite)	
bitten	bittern (bird)
bitter, -ly	
bittern (bird)	
bitterness	
bitters	
bitumen	
bituminous	
bitween	between
bitwixt	betwixt
biuld	build
bivalve	
bivouac, -acked, -acking	
bivuac	bivouac
biwail	bewail
biway	byway
biwear	beware
biwich	bewitch
biwilder	bewilder
biwitch	bewitch
biword	byword
bizar	bazaar (fair)
bizar	bizarre (odd)
bizarre, -ly (odd)	
bizier	busier
bizily	busily
bizmuth	bismuth
bizness	business
bizy	busy
blab, blabbed, blabbing	
blabber, blabbered, blabbering	

blabbermouth
blaber blabber
black
blackberry, -ries
blackbirding
blackboard
blackbord blackboard
blackbutt
blackcurrant
blackcurrent blackcurrant
blacken, -ed, -ing
blackfellow
blackguard
blackhead
blackjack
blackleg
blackmail
blackmale blackmail
blackout
blackshirt
blacksmith
blacktracker
bladder
blade
blader bladder
blaggard blackguard
blaid blade
blaim blame
blaimless blameless
blair blare
blaise blaze
blaiser blazer
blame, blamed, blaming
blameless, -ly
blameworthy
blamonge blancmange
blanch, -ed, -ing
blancmange
bland, -ly
blandish
blandishment
blank
blanket
blare, blared, blaring
blarney, -neyed, -neying
blarny blarney
blasay blasé
blasé
blasfeem blaspheme
blasfemus blasphemous
blasfemy blasphemy
blaspheme, -phemed, -pheming
blasphemous, -ly
blasphemy, -mies
blast, -ed, -ing
blast-off
blatancy
blatant, -ly
blather
blaze, blazed, blazing
blazer
blazon
bleach, -ed, -ing
bleachers
blead bleed
bleak, -ly
bleakness
blear, -ed, -ing
blearily
bleary, blearier, blearist
bleat, -ed, -ing
bleech bleach
bleed, bled, bleeding
bleeder
bleek bleak
bleep
bleer blear
bleet bleat
blemish, -ed, -ing
blench, -ed, -ing
blend, -ed, -ing
blender
blert blurt
bless, blessed, blessing
blew (to blow)
blew blue (colour)

For other blew- words, look under **blue-** .

blight, -ed, -ing
blighter
Blighty
blimey
blimp

blind, -ed, -ing
blind, -ly
blindfold
blindman's buff
blindness
blink, -ed, -ing
blinker
blip
bliss
blissful, -ly
blister, -ed, -ing
blistery
blite — blight
bliter — blighter
blithe, -ly
blithering
blits — blitz
blitz, -ed, -ing
blizard — blizzard
blizzard
blo — blow
bloat, -ed, -ing
bloater
blob
bloc (group)
block, -ed, -ing (stop)
blockade, -kaded, -kading
blockage
blockaid — blockade
blockbuster
blockidge — blockage
blok — bloke
bloke
blond, blonde
blone — blown
blood
bloodbath
bloodcurdling
blooded
bloodless
blood-poisoning
blood pressure
bloodshed
bloodshot
bloodstream
bloodthirsty
bloody, bloodied, bloodying
bloody, bloodier, bloodiest
bloom, -ed, -ing
bloomers
blosom — blossom
blossom
blot, blotted, blotting
blot — bloat
blotch, -ed, -ing
blotchy
bloting — blotting
blouse
blow, blew, blown, blowing
blower
blowfly
blowhole
blowlamp
blow-out
blowpipe
blowse — blouse
blow-up
blu — blue (colour)
blu — blew (to blow)
blubber
blubbery
bluber — blubber
bludge, bludged, bludging
bludger
bludgeon

> For all other blud- words, look under **blood-** .

blue (colour)
blue — blew (to blow)
blue, bluer, bluest
bluebird
bluebottle
blue-collar
blueprint
blue-ribbon
blues
blue-tongue
bluey
bluf — bluff
bluff, -ed, -ing
bluish
blummers — bloomers
blunder, -ed, -ing

blunt, -ed, -ing	
blur, blurred, blurring	
blurb	
blurt, -ed, -ing	
blush, -ed, -ing	
bluster, -ed, -ing	
blustery	
blustry	blustery
boa	
boa constrictor	
boar (pig)	
boar	boor (rude)
boar	bore (drill)
board, -ed, -ing	
board (wood)	
board	bored (drill)
boarder (lodger)	
boarder	border (edge)
boast, -ed, -ing	
boastful, -ly	
boat	
boater	
boat-house	
boating	
boat people	
boat-race	
boatswain	
bob, bobbed, bobbing	
bobbel	bobble
bobbie	bobby
bobbin	
bobble	
bobbul	bobble
bobby, -bies	
bobby-dazzler	
bobby pin, bobby pins	
bobcat	
bobie	bobby
bobin	bobbin
boble	bobble
bobslay	bobsleigh
bobsled	
bobsleigh	
boby	bobby
boch	botch
boddy	body
bodgie	

bodice	
bodie	body
bodigard	bodyguard
bodiley	bodily
bodily	
bodis	bodice
body, bodies	
body, bodied, bodying	
body corporate	
bodyguard	
body language	
bodywork	
boffin	
bog, bogged, bogging	
bogey, bogies (golf)	
bogey	bogy (evil)
boggel	boggle
boggle, -gled, -gling	
bogul	boggle
bogus	
bogy, bogies (evil)	
bogy	bogey (golf)
bohemian	
boi	boy (male)
boi	buoy (afloat)
boiancy	buoyancy
boiant	buoyant
boicot	boycott
boil, -ed, -ing	
boiler	
boilermaker	
boilersuit	
boisterous, -ly	
boisterus	boisterous
boks	box
bolairo	bolero
bolard	bollard
bolaro	bolero
bold, -ly (brave)	
bold	bowled (ball)
bolder (braver)	
bolder	boulder (rock)
bole (trunk)	
bole	bowl (ball)
bolero	
bollard	
Bolshevik	

Word	Correct spelling
Bolshevism	
bolshie	
bolster, -ed, -ing	
bolt	
bom	bomb
bomb, -ed, -ing	
bombardier	
bombardment	
bombastic	
bomber	
bomberdeer	bombardier
bombora	
bombshell	
bomer	bomber
bona fide	
bonanza	
bonbon	
bonce	
bond, -ed, -ing	
bondage	
bone, boned, boning	
bonet	bonnet
bonfire	
bonie	boney
bonie	bonny
bonit	bonnet
bonk, -ed, -ing	
bonny, bonnier, bonniest	
bonsai	
bonus	
bony, bonier, boniest	
bonzer	
boo, booed, booing	
boob	
boobie	booby
boo-boo	
booby, -bies	
boodwar	boudoir
boofant	bouffant
boogie-woogie	
book, -ed, -ing	
bookay	bouquet
bookcase	
bookeeping	bookkeeping
bookie	
bookish, -ly	
bookkeeping	

Word	Correct spelling
bookmaker	
bookstall	
bookworm	
boolevard	boulevard
boom, -ed, -ing	
boomer	
boomerang	
boon	
boor (rude)	
boor	boar (pig)
boor	bore (drill)
boorjwah	bourgeois
boorjwahzey	bourgeoisie
boost, -ed, -ing	
booster	
boot	
bootee (shoe)	
bootee	booty (plunder)
booteek	boutique
booth	
bootie	bootee (shoe)
bootie	booty (plunder)
bootik	boutique
bootleg, -legged, -legging	
bootlegger	
bootstrap	
booty, -ties (plunder)	
booty	bootee (shoe)
booze, boozed, boozing	
boozer	
bora	
boracic	
boraks	borax
borasic	boracic
borax	
borbon	bourbon
bord	board (plank)
bord	bored (tired)
border (edge)	
border	boarder (lodger)
border, -ed, -ing	
borderline	
bording	boarding
bordom	boredom
bordy	bawdy
bore, bored, boring (drill)	

Word	Correct spelling
bore	boar (pig)
bore	boor (rude)
boredom	
boree	
borer	
born (birth)	
born	borne (carry)
born	bourn (limit)
borne (carry)	
borne	born (birth)
borne	bourn (limit)
boronia	
borough (town)	
borough	burrow (hole)
borow	borrow
borrow, -ed, -ing	
borrower	
Borstal	
bort	bought
bos	boss
bosie	bossy
bosily	bossily
bosn	bosun
bosom	
boss, -ed, -ing	
bossom	bosom
bossy, bossier, bossiest	
bosun	
bosy	bossy
bot	boat
botaney	botany
botanical, -ly	
botanist	
botany	
botch, -ed, -ing	
botchy	
boter	boater
both	
bother	
bothersome	
bothersum	bothersome
botom	bottom
bottel	bottle
bottle, -tled, -tling	
bottlebrush	
bottleneck	
bottler	

Word	Correct spelling
bottom -ed, -ing	
bottomless	
botul	bottle
botulism	
boudoir	
bouffant	
bougainvillea	
bough (branch)	
bough	bow (bend)
bought	
bouillon	
boukay	bouquet
boulder (rock)	
boulder	bolder (braver)
boulevard	
bounce, bounced, bouncing	
bouncer	
bound, -ed, -ing	
boundary, -ries	
boundry	boundary
bounteous, -ly	
bountiful, -ly	
bountious	bounteous
bounty, -ties	
bouquet	
bourbon	
bourgeois	
bourgeoisie	
bourgwah	bourgeois
bourgwahzey	bourgeoisie
bourn (limit)	
bourn	born (birth)
bourn	borne (carry)
bout	
bouteek	boutique
boutique	
bovine	
bow, -ed, -ing (bend)	
bow	bough (branch)
bow	beau (dandy)
bowel	
bower	
bowerbird	
bowie knife	
bowl (ball)	
bowl	bole (trunk)
bowleg	

bowler
bowline
bownce bounce
bownd bound
bowndary boundary
bownse bounce
bouwnser bouncer
bownteous bounteous
bowntiful bountiful
bowt bout
bowyang
box, -ed, -ing
boxer
box-frame
boy (child)
boy buoy (float)
boyansy buoyancy
boyant buoyant
boycot boycott
boycott, -ed, -ing
boykot boycott
boyle boil
boysterus boisterous
bra, bras (brassiere)
brace, braced, bracing (clamp)
bracelet
bracken
bracket, -ed, -ing
brackish
brackit bracket
braclete bracelet
brade braid
brag, bragged, bragging
bragart braggart
braggart
bragger
Brahma
Brahman, -mans
braid
brail braille
braille
brain
brainstorm
brainwash, -ed, -ing
brainy, brainier, brainiest
braise, braised, braising (cook)
braise braze (solder)
braisen brazen
brakage breakage
brakaway breakaway
brakdown breakdown
brake, braked, braking (stop)
brake break (divide)
braken bracken
brakeneck breakneck
braker breaker
brakewater breakwater
brakidge breakage
braking breaking
brakish brackish
brale braille
brambel bramble
bramble
brambly
brambul bramble
bramin Brahman
bran
branch, -ches
branch, -ed, -ing
brand, -ed, -ing
brandish, -ed, -ing
brand-new
brandy, -dies
brane brain
braney brainy
bras (brassieres)
bras brass (metal)
brase brace (clamp)
brash
brasier brassiere (bra)
brasier brazier (burner)
braslet bracelet
brass
brassiere (bra)
brassy, brassier, brassiest
brasy brassy
brat
bravado, -does, -dos
brave, braver, bravest
bravely
bravery, -ries
bravly bravely
bravo, -voes, -vos
bravrey bravery

brawd — broad
brawl, -ed, -ing
brawn
brawny, brawnier, brawniest
bray, -ed, -ing
brayd — braid
brayn — brain
braze, brazed, brazing (solder)
braze — braise (cook)
brazen, -ly
brazenness
brazier (burner)
brazier — brassiere (bra)
brazil nut
breach, -ed, -ing (break)
breach — breech (gun)
bread (food)
bread — bred (produced)
breadline
breadth
breadwinner
break, broke, broken, breaking (divide)
break — brake (stop)
breakabel — breakable
breakable
breakabul — breakable
breakage
breakaway
breakdown
breaker
breakfast
break-in
breakthrough
breakwater
bream (fish)
breast
breastbone
breastfeed, -fed, -feeding
breastplate
breast stroke
breath (air)
breath — breadth (wide)
breathaliser — breathalyser
breathalyser
breathe, breathed, breathing
breather
breathless, -ly
breathtaking
bred (produced)
bred — bread (food)
bredth — breadth
bree — brie
breech, -ches (gun)
breech — breach (break)
breed, bred, breeding
breeder
breeding
breef — brief
breeze, breezed, breezing
breezily
breezy, breezier, breeziest
breif — brief
brest — breast
brest stroke — breast stroke
breth — breath (air)
breth — breadth (wide)
brethalyser — breathalyser
brethless — breathless
brethren
brethtaking — breathtaking
breve
brevity, -ties
brew, -ed, -ing (beer)
brewed — brood (worry)
brewer
brewery, -ries
brews — bruise (hurt)
breze — breeze
brezy — breezy
briar
bribe, bribed, bribing
bribery, -ies
bric-a-brac
brick, -ed, -ing
brickbat
brickette — briquette
bricklayer
brick veneer
brickyard
bridal (marry)
bridal — bridle (horse)
bride

bridegroom	
bridel	bridal (marry)
bridel	bridle (horse)
bridesmade	bridesmaid
bridesmaid	
bridge, bridged, bridging	
bridle, -dled, -dling (horse)	
bridle	bridal (marry)
brie	
brief, -ly	
briefcase	
briefs	
brig	
brigade, -gaded, -gading	
brigadeer	brigadier
brigadier	
brigalow	
brigand	
brige	bridge
bright, -ly	
brighten, -ed, -ing	
brightness	
brilliance	
brilliant, -ly	
brilliantine	
brilyanse	brilliance
brilyansy	brilliancy
brilyant	brilliant
brim, brimmed, brimming (edge)	
brim	bream (fish)
brimstone	
brindled	
brine, brined, brining	
briney	briny
bring, brought, bringing	
brink	
brinkmanship	
briny, brinier, briniest	
bri-nylon	
briquette	
brisel	bristle
brisk, -ly	
brisket	
brisle	bristle
bristle, -tled, -tling	
bristly	
Britain	
brite	bright
briten	brighten
British	
britle	brittle
brittle, brittler, brittlest	
brittleness	
broach, -ed, -ing (mention)	
broach	brooch (pin)
broad, -ly	
broadcast, -cast, -casting	
broadcaster	
broaden, -ed, -ing	
broad-minded	
broadsheet	
brocade, -caded	
broccoli	
broch	broach (mention)
broch	brooch (pin)
brochure	
brocoli	broccoli
brog	brogue
brogue	
broil, -ed, -ing	
broken, -ly	
broken-hearted	
broker	
brokerage	
brokeridge	brokerage
brolly, -lies	
bromide	
bromine	
bronchial	
bronchitis	
bronco, -cos	
bronkial	bronchial
bronkitis	bronchitis
bronze, bronzed, bronzing	
brooch, -ches (pin)	
brood (worry)	
brood	brewed (beer)
broody, broodier, broodiest	
brook, -ed, -ing	
broom	
broonette	brunette
broose	bruise
broot	brute

brootal brutal
brootality brutality
brootish brutish
brorn brawn
brort brought
broshure brochure
brosure brochure
broth
brothel
brother
brotherhood
brother-in-law, brothers-in-law
brotherliness
brotherly
brow, brows (eyebrow)
browbeat, -beat, -beaten, -beating
brown
brownee brownie
brownie
brows browse (read)
browse, browsed, browsing
browser
bruise, bruised, bruising (hurt)
bruise brews (beer)
bruiser
brumby, brumbies
brunch
brunet brunette
brunette
bruse brews (beer)
bruse bruise (hurt)
brush, -ed, -ing
brushwood
brushwork
brusk brusque
brusque, -ly
brusqueness
brutal, -ly
brutality, -ties
brute
brutish
bubbel bubble
bubble, -bled, -bling
bubble-and-squeak
buble bubble
bubly bubbly
bubonic plague

bubul bubble
bucaneer buccaneer
buccaneer
buccaneering
bucher butcher
buck, -ed, -ing
buckaneer buccaneer
buckel buckle
bucket, -ed, -ing
bucketful, bucketfuls
buckjump, -ed, -ing
buckjumper
buckle, -led, -ling
buckshot
buckskin
bucktooth, -teeth
buckul buckle
bucolic
bud, budded, budding
Buddhism
Buddhist
buddy, -dies
budge, budged, budging
budgereegar budgerigar
budgerigar
budget, -eted, -eting
budgetary
budgie
budgrigar budgerigar
Budhism Buddhism
Budhist Buddhist
buf buff
bufalo buffalo
bufay buffet
bufer buffer
buff
buffalo, -loes, -los
buffay buffet
buffer
buffet (food)
buffet, -ed, -ing (hit)
buffoon
buffoonery, -eries
bufit buffet
bufoon buffoon
bufoonery buffoonery
bug, bugged, bugging

bugbare	bugbear
bugbear	
bugel	bugle
bugerigar	budgerigar
buget	budget
buggy, -gies	
bugie	buggy
bugle, -gled, -gling	
bugler	
bugy	buggy
build, built, building	
builder	
build-up	
buisness	business
bukshee	

For buk- words, look under buc- .

bul	bull
bulb	
bulbar	bull-bar
bulbous	
bulbul	
buldog	bulldog
buldoze	bulldoze
bulet	bullet
buletin	bulletin
bulfight	bullfight
bulfrog	bullfrog
bul-headed	bull-headed
bulion	bullion
bulk	
bulkhead	
bulky, bulkier, bulkiest	
bull-bar	
bulldog	
bulldoze, -dozed, -dozing	
bulldozer	
bullet	
bulletin	
bullfight	
bullfrog	
bull-headed	
bullion	
bullock	
bullring	
bullroarer	
bullrush	
bullseye	
bull-terrier	
bullwark	bulwark
bully, -lies	
bully, -lied, -lying	
bulock	bullock
bulring	bullring
bulroarer	bullroarer
bulrush	
bulseye	bullseye
bulwalk	bulwark
bulwark	
buly	bully
bulyun	bullion
bum, bummed, bumming	
bumbel	bumble
bumble, bumbled, bumbling	
bumf	
bump, -ed, -ing	
bumper	
bumpey	bumpy
bumpiness	
bumpkin	
bumpshus	bumptious
bumptious, -ly	
bumptiousness	
bumpy, bumpier, bumpiest	
bumshus	bumptious
bunch, -ches	
bunch, -ed, -ing	
buncum	bunkum
bundel	bundle
bundle, -dled, -dling	
bundul	bundle
bundy	
buney	bunny
bung, -ed, -ing	
bungaloe	bungalow
bungalow	
bungel	bungle
bunger	
bunghole	
bungkum	bunkum
bungle, -gled, -gling	
bungler	
bungul	bungle

bunie	bunny
bunion	
bunk, -ed, -ing	
bunker, -ed, -ing	
bunkum	
bunny, -nies	
bunnyip	bunyip
Bunsen burner	
bunt	
bunting	
buny	bunny
bunyip	
bunyon	bunion
buoy, -ed, -ing (float)	
buoy	boy (child)
buoyancy	
buoyansy	buoyancy
buoyant, -ly	
burbel	burble
burble, -bled, -bling	
burbul	burble
burch	birch
burd	bird
burden, -ed, -ing	
burdensome	
burdensum	burdensome
burdie	birdie
burdseye	bird's-eye
bureau, -eaus, -eaux	
bureaucracy, -cies	
bureaucrasy	bureaucracy
bureaucrat	
bureaucratic	
buret	burette
burette	
burgandy	burgundy
burgel	burgle
burgeon, -ed, -ing	
burger	burgher
burgess	
burgher	
burglar	
burglary, -ries	
burgle, -gled, -gling	
burgler	burglar
burgul	burgle
burgundy	
burial	
burke, burked, burking	
burl, -ed, -ing	
burlap	
burlesk	burlesque
burlesque, -lesqued, -lesquing	
burlie	burly (large)
burly, -lier, -liest (large)	
burly	berley (bait)
burn, burnt, burned, burning	
burnable	
burn-back	
burner	
burnish, -ed, -ing	
buro	bureau
buro	burro
burocrasy	bureaucracy
burocrat	bureaucrat
burow	bureau
burow	burrow (hole)
burr, burred, burring	
burra	borough (town)
burro, -ros (donkey)	
burro	bureau
burrocracy	bureaucracy
burrocrat	bureaucrat
burrow, -ed, -ing (hole)	
burrow	borough (town)
burrow	burro (donkey)
bursar	
bursary, -ries	
burser	bursar
bursery	bursary
burst, burst, bursting	
burth	berth (ship)
burth	birth (born)
bury, buried, burying (cover)	
bury	berry (fruit)
bus, buses, busses	
bus, bused, busing or bussed, bussing	
busbie	busby
busby, -bies	
busel	bustle
bush, -ed, -ing	
bushcraft	
bushel	
bushfire	

bushie (farmer)
bushie — bushy
bush-lawyer
bushman, -men
bushranger
bushranging
bushwalk
bushy, bushier, bushiest
busier
busily
business
businesslike
businessman, -men
businesswoman, -women
busk, -ed, -ing
busker
bust, -ed, -ing
bustard
busted — bustard
bustel — bustle
buster
bustle, -tled, -tling
bust-up
busul — bustle
busy, busied, busying
busy, busier, busiest
busybody, -bodies
but (contrary)
but — butt (end)
butane
butcher, -ed, -ing
buteek — boutique
buten — button
buter — butter
buterfly — butterfly
butey — beauty
butician — beautician
butify — beautify
butique — boutique
butishun — beautician
butler
butock — buttock
buton — button
butress — buttress
butt, -ed, -ing (end)
butt — but (contrary)
butter, -ed, -ing
butter-fingers
butterfly, -flies
butterscotch
buttock
button
buttonhole, -holed, -holing
buttress, buttresses
buxom, -ly
buy, bought, buying (purchase)
buy — by (near to)
buy — bye (sport)
buyer
buz — buzz
buzard — buzzard
buzer — buzzer
buz-saw — buzz-saw
buzz, -ed, -ing
buzz, -es
buzzard
buzzer
buzz-saw
by (near to)
by — bye (sport)
by — buy (purchase)
bye (sport)
bye — by (near to)
bye — buy (purchase)
bye-bye, bye-byes
by-election
byennial — biennial
byer — buyer
byer — byre (shed)
byfocal — bifocal
bygone
bying — buying
byke — bike
by-law
byle — bile
bylore — by-law
bymetallic — bimetallic
bymonthly — bimonthly
bynominal — binominal
byopsey — biopsy
bypartisan — bipartisan
bypartite — bipartite
bypass
byped — biped

byplane	biplane
by-product	
byre (shed)	
bysecshun	bisection
bysect	bisect
byseksual	bisexual
bystander	
byte (computer)	
byte	bite (chew)
byway	
byword	
Byzantine	

Cc

cab
cabal, -balled, -balling
  cabaray   cabaret
cabaret
cabbage
  cabbidge   cabbage
cabby, cabbies
  cabel   cable
  cabey   cabby
  cabie   cabby
  cabige   cabbage
cabin
cabinet
cable, -bled, -bling
caboose
  cabul   cable
cacao, -caos
  cach   cache
  cach   catch
  cachay   cachet
cache, cached, caching (hide)
  cache   cash (money)
cachet
  cachou   cashew
  cachword   catchword
  cackel   cackle
cackle, -led, -ling
  cacktus   cactus
  cackul   cackle
  cacofony   cacophony
cacophony, -nies
cactoblastis
cactus, -ti, -tuses
  cacul   cackle
cad
cadaver
cadaverous, -ly
  caddey   caddie (golf)
  caddey   caddy (tea)
caddie, -died, -dying (golf)
  caddie   caddy (tea)
caddy, -ies (tea)
  caddy   caddie (golf)
cadence
  cadense   cadence
cadenza
cadet
cadetship
cadge, cadged, cadging
  cadjole   cajole
cadmium
Caesar
caesarean section
  cafay   cafe
cafe
  cafeen   caffeine
cafeteria
caffeine
  caffeteria   cafeteria
  cafiene   caffeine
  cafiteria   cafeteria
caftan
cage, caged, caging
cagey, cagier, cagiest
  cagy   cagey
cahoots
  cain   cane
cairn
caisson
  caje   cage
cajole, -joled, -joling
cake, caked, caking
calabash
calamari
calamine
calamitous, -ly
calamity, -ties
  calarie   calorie
calcareous
  calcarious   calcareous
calcification
calcify, -fied, -fying
calcium
calculable
  calculabul   calculable

calculate, -lated, -lating
calculation
calculative
calculator
calculaytor calculator
calculus, -luses
Caledonian
calendar (time)
calender (roll)
calendula
calf, calves
calfskin
caliber calibre
calibrate, -brated, -brating
calibration
calibrator
calibre
calicks calyx
calico, -coes, -cos
calif caliph
caligraphy calligraphy
caling calling
caliper
caliph
calipso calypso
calisthenics
calix calyx
calk caulk
call, -ed, -ing (cry out)
call caul (membrane)
callamity calamity
calldron cauldron
caller
callgirl
calligrapher
calligraphy
calliper
callistemon
callisthenics
callosity, -ties
callous, -ly (cruel)
callous callus (skin)
callousness
callow
callus, calluses (skin)
callus callous (cruel)
calm, -ly
calmness
calorie
calorific
calorimeter
calory calorie
calow callow
calsify calcify
calsium calcium
calumniate, -ated, -ating
calumniation
calumnious, -ly
calumnius calumnious
calumny, -nies
calus callous (cruel)
calus callus (skin)
Calvary
calve, calved, calving (give birth)
calve carve (cut)
Calvinism
Calvinist
calypso, -sos
calyx, calyces, calyxes
cam
camaflage camouflage
camaraderie
camber
cambric
came
camel
camelhair
camellia
camelya camellia
camember camembert
camembert
cameo, -os
camera
cameraman
camerardery camaraderie
camfer camphor
camio cameo
camisole
camle camel
camouflage, -flaged, -flaging
camp, -ed, -ing
campaign
campain campaign

campanology
camper
campervan
campher — camphor
camphor
campus, -es
camshaft
camul — camel
can, could (able to)
can, canned, canning (tinned)
canabis — cannabis
Canadian
canal
canape
canary, -ries
canasta
cancan
cancel, -celled, -celling
cancelation — cancellation
cancellation
cancer
cancerous
cancerus — cancerous
candel — candle
candelabrum
candellight — candlelight
candelstick — candlestick
cander — candour
candey — candy
candid (open)
candid — candied (sugar)
candidate
candied (sugar)
candied — candid (open)
candle
candlelight
candlestick
candour
candul — candle
candulstick — candlestick
candy, -dies
candy, candied, candying (sugar)
cane, caned, caning (hit)
caned — canned (tinned)
canee — canny
canery — cannery
cane-sugar

canibal — cannibal
canibalism — cannibalism
canie — canny
canine
canister
cannabis
cannary — canary
canned (tinned)
canned — caned (hit)
cannelloni
cannery, -ries
cannibal
cannibalism
canniness
cannon (gun)
cannon — canon (law)
cannot
canny, -nier, -niest

For other cann- words, look under can- .

canoe, -es
canoe, -noed, -noeing
canoeist
canon (law)
canon — cannon (gun)
canonical
canonisation
canonise, -nised, -nising
canoo — canoe
canoodle, -dled, -dling
canooist — canoeist
canopy, -pies
cansel — cancel
canser — cancer
canserous — cancerous
cant (insincere)
can't (cannot)
cantaloup
cantaloupe
cantankerous, -ly
cantankerus — cantankerous
cantata
canteen
canter, -ed, -ing
cantilever
canto, -tos

canton
cantor

canue	canoe

canvas, -es (tent)

canvas	canvass (gather)

canvass, -ed, -ing (gather)

canvass	canvas (tent)
cany	canny

canyon
cap, capped, capping
capability, -ties
capable, -bly

capabul	capable

capacious, -ly
capacitor
capacity, -ties

capasitor	capacitor
capasity	capacity
capchure	capture

cape
caper, -ed, -ing

capilary	capillary

capillary, -laries
capital
capitalisation
capitalise, -lised, -lising
capitalism
capitalist
capitalistic
capitulate, -lated, -lating
capitulation
capon
cappuccino

For all other capp- words, look under cap- .

caprice
capricious, -ly
capriciousness
Capriçorn

caprise	caprice
caprishus	capricious
capshulate	capsulate
capshun	caption
capshus	captious

capsicum
capsize, -sized, -sizing
capstan
capsule
captain, -ed, -ing
captaincy

capter	captor
captin	captain

caption
captious, -ly
captiousness

captius	captious

captivate, -vated, -vating
captivation
captive
captivity, -ties
captor
capture, -tured, -turing

caracter	character
caracteristic	characteristic

carafe

caraffe	carafe

caramel

caramul	caramel

carat (weight)

carat	carrot (food)
carate	karate

caravan, -vanned, -vanning
caraway
carbine
carbohydrate
carbon
carbonate, -nated, -nating
carbon dioxide
carbonise, -nised, -nising
carbon monoxide
carbuncle

carbuncul	carbuncle

carburettor
carcase
carcass
carcinogen
carcinogenic
carcinoma, -mata, -mas
card, -ed, -ing

cardagan	cardigan

cardboard

cardbord	cardboard

cardiac
cardigan
cardinal, -ly
cardiograf cardiograph
cardiologist
cardiology
cardiovascular
cardsharp
care, cared, caring
careen
career, -ed, -ing
carefree
careful, -ly
careless, -ly
carelessness
caress, -ed, -ing
caressingly
caret (mark)
caret carat (weight)
caretaker
cargo, -goes
caribou, -bou
caricature, -tured, -turing
caricaturist
caricter character
caricteristic characteristic
caridge carriage
carie carry (bear)
carier carrier
caries (decay)
caries carries (bear)
carillion carillon
carillon
carillyon carillon
carion carrion
carisma charisma
carkey khaki
carki khaki
carm calm
carmine
carnage
carnal, -ly
carnality
carnation
carnidge carnage
carnije carnage
carnival

carnivore
carnivorous, -ly
carol, -rolled, -rolling (song)
carol carrel (study)
carol corral (yard)
caroller
carot carat (weight)
carousal (feast)
carousal carousel (merry-go-round)
carouse, -roused, -rousing
carousel (merry-go-round)
carousel carousal (feast)
carp, -ed, -ing
carpenter
carpentry
carpet, -ed, -ing
carrel (study)
carrel carol (song)
carrel corral (yard)
carriage
carriageway
carrier
carries (bears)
carries caries (decay)
carrion
carrot (food)
carrot carat (weight)
carry, -ried, -rying
carryon carrion
carsinoma carcinoma
cart, -ed, -ing
carte blanche
cartel
cartilage
cartilege cartilage
cartilidge cartilage
cartografy cartography
cartographer
cartographic
cartography
carton
cartoon, -ed, -ing
cartoonist
cartridge
cartrige cartridge

cartrije	cartridge
cartwheel	
carve, carved, carving (cut)	
carve	calve (give birth)
cary	carry
casava	cassava
cascade, -caded, -cading	
case, cased, casing	
caseen	casein
casein	
casement	
caserole	casserole
casette	cassette
casock	cassock
casowary	cassowary
cash, -ed, -ing (money)	
cash	cache (hide)
cashay	cachet
casheer	cashier
cashew	
cashier	
cashmear	cashmere
cashmere	
cashoo	cashew
casia	cassia
casing	
casino, -nos	
cask	
caskade	cascade
casket	
caskit	casket
casock	cassock
cassava	
cassel	castle
casserole, -roled, -roling	
casset	cassette
cassette	
cassia	
cassock	
cassowary, -ries	
cast, cast, casting (fling)	
cast	caste (class)
castanet	
castaway	
caste (class)	
caster or castor (sugar)	

caster	castor (oil)
castigate, -gated, -gating	
castigation	
cast-iron	
castle, -tled, -tling	
castor (oil)	
castrait	castrate
castrate, -trated, -trating	
castration	
castrayte	castrate
casual, -ly	
casuality	casualty
casualty, -ties	
casuarina	
casuistic	
casuistry, -tries	
casulty	casualty
catachism	catechism
cataclysm	
cataclysmic	
catacomb	
catalise	catalyse
catalist	catalyst
catalitic	catalytic
catalog	catalogue
catalogue, -logued, -loguing	
cataloguer	
catalyse, -lysed, -lysing	
catalyst	
catalytic	
catamaran	
catapiler	caterpillar
catapult	
catar	catarrh
catarrh	
cataract	
catarh	catarrh
catarrhal	
catastrofic	catastrophic
catastrofy	catastrophe
catastrophe	
catastrophic, -ally	
catcall, -ed, -ing	
catch, caught, catching	
catcher	
catchment	
catchword	

catchy, catchier, catchiest
catechise, -chised, -chising
catechism
catechist
categorical, -ly
categorise, -rised, -rising
categorist
category, -ries
catel   cattle
cater, -ed, -ing
caterer
caterpillar
caterpiller   caterpillar
caterwall   caterwaul
caterwaul
catfish, -fishes, -fish
catgut
catharsis
cathartic
cathedral
catheter
cathode
catholic (universal)
Catholic (religion)
Catholicism
Catholicity
caticise   catechise
catigoric   categoric
catigorise   categorise
catigory   category
catikism   catechism
catish   cattish
catkin
catle   cattle
catnap, -ed, -ing
cat-o'-nine-tails
cattel   cattle
catterpillar   caterpillar
cattle
cattlegrid
cattle, -run
cattish, -ly
catty, -ier, -iest
catul   cattle
catwalk
Caucasian
caucus, -ed, -ing

caught (did catch)
caught   court (law)
cauk   caulk
caul (membrane)
caul   call (cry)
cauldron
cauliflour   cauliflower
cauliflower
caulk, -ed, -ing
causal, -ly
causal   casual
causality, -ties
causation
causative, -ly
cause, caused, causing
causeway
caustic, -ally
cauterise, -rised, -rising
caution, -ed, -ing
cautionary
cautious, -ly
cavalcade, -caded, -cading
cavaleer   cavalier
cavalier
cavalry, -ries
cavalryman, -men
cave, caved, caving
caveman, -men
cavern
cavernous
caviar
cavil, -illed, -illing
cavity, -ties
caw   core (heart)
caw   corps (group)
cawcas   caucus
Cawcasian   Caucasian
cawcus   caucus
cay
cayenne
cease, ceased, ceasing
cease-fire
ceaseless, -ly
cedar
cede, ceded, ceding (yield)
cede   seed (plant)
ceder   cedar

ceeling	ceiling (roof)
ceese	cease
cefalic	cephalic
ceiling (roof)	
ceiling	sealing (close)
celebrant	
celebrate, -brated, -brating	
celebration	
celebrity, -ties	
celerity	
celery (food)	
celery	salary (wage)
celestial, -ly	
celibacy, -cies	
celibasy	celibacy
celibate	
celibrant	celebrant
celibrate	celebrate
cell (prison)	
cell	sell (goods)
cellar (basement)	
cellar	seller (goods)
cellarman, -men	
celler	seller (goods)
cellist	
cello, -los	
cellofane	cellophane
cellophane	
cellular	
celluler	cellular
celluloid	
cellulose	
celofane	cellophane
Celsius	
cement, -ed, -ing	
cemetary	cemetery
cemetery, -teries	
cemical	chemical
cemist	chemist
cemistry	chemistry
cenotaf	cenotaph
censer (incense)	
censer	censor (books)
censership	censorship
censhure	censure
censor (books)	
censor	censer (incense)

censorious, -ly	
censorship	
censurable	
censurabul	censurable
censure, -sured, -suring	
census	
cent (coin)	
cent	scent (perfume)
cent	sent (away)
centaur	
centenarian	
centenary, -ries	
centenery	centenary
centennial, -ly	
center	centre
Centigrade	
centimeter	centimetre
centimetre	
centipede	
centor	centaur
central, -ly	
Centralia	
centralisation	
centralise, -lised, -lising	
centralism	
centralist	
centrality	
centre, -tred, -tring	
centreboard	
centrefold	
centrepiece	
centrifugal, -ly	
centrifuge	
centripetal, -ly	
centupel	centuple
centuple, -pled, -pling	
centupul	centuple
centurion	
century, -ries	
cephalic	
ceramic	
ceramicist	
ceramics	
ceramist	

For any cerc- words, look under **circ-** .

cereal (grain)
cereal serial (part)
cerebelum cerebellum
cerebellum, -bella
cerebral
cerebrate, -brated, -brating
cerebration
cerebrum, -bra
ceremonial, -ly
ceremonious, -ly
ceremonius ceremonious
ceremony, -monies
cerial cereal (grain)
cerial serial (part)
ceribellum cerebellum
ceribrum cerebrum
cerise

> For any cerk- words, look under circ- .

certain, -ly
certainty, -ties
certanty certainty
certen certain
certenty certainty
certifiable, -fiably
certifiabul certifiable
certificate, -cated, -cating
certification
certifier
certify, -fied, -fying
certinty certainty
certitude
cervical
cervicul cervical
cerviks cervix
cervix, cervixes, cervices
cesation cessation
ceshun session (time)
cesion cession (yield)
cespit cesspit
cespool cesspool
cessation
cession(yield)
cession session (time)
cesspit
cesspool

chablis
cha-cha
chacoal charcoal
chafe, chafed, chafing (rub)
chafe chaff (straw)
chaff (straw)
chaffinch, -es
chagrin, -ed, -ing
chain
chain-drive
chain-reaction
chainsaw
chain-smoke, -smoked, -smoking
chain-stitch, -ed, -ing
chain-store
chair, -ed, -ing
chairlift
chairman, -men
chairperson
chairwoman, -women
chaise chase
chalet
chalice
chalinge challenge
chalis chalice
chalk, -ed, -ing
challenge, -lenged, -lenging
challenger
chamba chamber
chamber
chamberlain
chamberlin chamberlain
chambermade chambermaid
chambermaid
chameleon
chamee chamois
chamfer, -ed, -ing
chamie chamois
chamois
champ, -ed, -ing
champagne
champaign champagne
champers
champignon
champion, -ed, -ing
championship
champiun champion

chance, chanced, chancing
chancel
chanceler chancellor
chancelery chancellery
chanceller chancellor
chancellery, -ries
chancellor
chancellorship
chancery, -ceries
chancy, chancier, chanciest
chandeleer chandelier
chandelier
chandler
chane chain
chane-drive chain-drive
chanel channel
chane-reaction chain-reaction
chanesaw chainsaw
change, changed, changing
changeable, -bly
changeabul changeable
changeling
changeover
channel, -nelled, -nelling
chanse chance
chansel chancel
chanseler chancellor
chanselery chancellery
chansey chancy
chant, -ed, -ing
chaos
chaotic, -ally
chap, chapped, chapping
chapel
chaperone
chaple chapel
chaplain
chaplaincy
chaplet
chaplin chaplain
chapter
char, charred, charring
character
characterise, -rised, -rising
characteristic, -ally
charade
charaid charade

charcoal
chare chair
chareman chairman
chareperson chairperson
charewoman chairwoman
charey chary
charge, charged, charging
charger
chariot
charioteer
charisma
charismatic
charitable
charitableness
charitably
charitabul charitable
charity, -ties
charlady, -ladies
charlatan
charleston
charm, -ed, -ing
charmer
chart, -ed, -ing
charter, -ed, -ing
chartreuse
chartroos chartreuse
chary, charier, chariest
chase, chased, chasing
chased (follow)
chased chaste (pure)
chasen chasten
chaser
chasis chassis
chasm
chassie chassis
chassis, chassis
chaste (pure)
chaste chased (follow)
chasten, -ed, -ing
chastener
chastise, -tised, -tising
chastisement
chastiser
chastity
chat, chatted, chatting
chateau, -teaus, -teaux
chatel chattel

chater	chatter
chatily	chattily
chatiness	chattiness

chattel
chatter, -ed, -ing
chatterbox, -boxes
chattily
chattiness
chatty, -tier, -tiest

chaty	chatty
chauffer	chauffeur

chauffeur
chauvinism
chauvinist
chauvinistic, -ally
cheap (price)

cheap	cheep (sound)

cheapen, -ed, -ing
cheapish, -ly
cheapskate

chear	cheer
chearful	cheerful
chease	cheese

cheat, -ed, -ing
cheater
check, -ed, -ing (stop)

check	cheque (money)
Check	Czech (person)

checkers
checkmate, -mated, -mating
checkout
checkpoint
checkup

chedar	cheddar

cheddar

cheder	cheddar
cheef	chief
cheeftan	chieftain

cheekily
cheekiness
cheeky, cheekier, cheekiest
cheep, -ed, -ing (sound)

cheep	cheap (price)

cheer, cheered, cheering

cheerey	cheery

cheerful, -ly
cheerfulness

cheerie	cheery

cheerily
cheeriness
cheerio, -os
cheery, -rier, -riest
cheese
cheesecake
cheesecloth
cheesed-off
cheeseparing
cheesy, -sier, -siest

cheet	cheat
cheeta	cheetah

cheetah

cheeter	cheetah

chef
chef-d'oeuvre, chefs-d'oeuvre

cheif	chief
cheiftan	chieftain
chelist	cellist
chelo	cello

chemical, -ly
chemise
chemist

chemistrey	chemistry

chemistry, -tries
chemotherapist
chemotherapy
chenille
cheongsam
cheque (money)

cheque	check (stop)
Cheque	Czech (person)

cheque-book
chequer
chequered

cherie	cherry
cherio	cheerio

cherish, -ed, -ing
cheroot

cherp	chirp

cherry, -ries
cherub, cherubim, cherubs
cherubic, -ally

chery	cheery
chery	cherry
ches	chess

chesbord	chessboard
chess	
chessboard	
chessnut	chestnut
chest	
chesterfield	
chestnut	
chevalier	
chevon (goat meat)	
chevron (stripe)	
chew, -ed, -ing (eat)	
chewie	
chewing gum	
chews	choose (select)
chewy	
chiack, -ed, -ing	
chic (stylish)	
chicanery, -ries	
chick (young bird)	
chickenfeed	
chickenpox	
chickpea	
chickweed	
chicle	
chicory, -ries	
chide, chided, chiding	
chidingly	
chief, chiefs	
chiefly	
chieftain	
chieftaincy	
chiffon	
chiffonier	
chifon	chiffon
chignon	
chihuahua	
chil	chill
chilblain	
chilblane	chilblain
child, children	
childbaring	childbearing
childbearing	
childberth	childbirth
childbirth	
childhood	
childish, -ly	
childlike	

childproof	
chili, -ies (fruit)	
chili	chilly (cold)
chill, -ed, -ing	
chilli, -ies (fruit)	
chilli	chilly (cold)
chilliness	
chilly, -ier, -iest (cold)	
chilly	chilli (fruit)
chimbly	chimney
chime, chimed, chiming	
chimera, -ras	
chimeric, -ally	
chimnee	chimney
chimney, -neys	
chimpanzee	
chin	
china	
chinchilla	
Chinese	
chink, -ed, -ing	
chintz, chintzes	
chintzy	
chip, chipped, chipping	
chipboard	
chipmonk	chipmunk
chipmunk	
chipolata	
chiropodey	chiropody
chiropodist	
chiropody	
chiropracter	chiropractor
chiropractic	
chiropractor	
chirp, -ed, -ing	
chirpily	
chirpy, -pier, -piest	
chisel, -elled, -elling	
chiseller	
chit	
chitchat	
chivalrous, -ly	
chivalrus	chivalrous
chivalry	
chive	
chivvy, -ied, -ying	
chloride	

chlorinate, -nated, -nating
chlorination
chlorine
  chlorofill   chlorophyll
chloroform, -ed, -ing
chlorophyll
chock, -ed, -ing
chock-a-block
chock-full
chocks
  choclat   chocolate
chocolate
choice, choicer, choicest
choir (singers)
  choir   quire (measure)
  choise   choice
choke, choked, choking
choker
choko
choler (anger)
  choler   collar (neck)
cholera
choleric
cholesterol
  choo   chew
chook
choose, chose, chosen, choosing (select)
  choose   chews (eats)
choosy
chop, chopped, chopping
chopper
choppy, -pier, -piest
  chopsooey   chop suey
chopstick
  chopy   choppy
choral, -ly (sing)
  choral   chorale (tune)
chorale (tune)
  chorale   choral (sing)
chord (music)
  chord   cord (string)
chore
  choreograf   choreograph
choreograph, -ed, -ing
choreographer
choreographic

choreography
chorister
chortle, -tled, -tling
  chortul   chortle
chorus, -ruses
chorus, -rused, -rusing
chose
chosen
chow
chowder
chow mein
  chrisalis   chrysalis
chrism
  Chrismas   Christmas
Christ
  Christain   Christian
christen, -ed, -ing
Christendom
Christian
Christianity
Christmas
chromatic, -ally
chrome
chromium
chromosome
  chronalogical   chronological
chronic, -ally
  chronical   chronicle
chronicle, -cled, -cling
chronicler
chronologer
chronological, -ly
chronology, -gies
chronometer
chrysalis, chrysalises
chrysanthemum
chubbily
chubbiness
chubby, -bier, -biest
  chubier   chubbier
  chuby   chubby
chuck, -ed, -ing
  chuckel   chuckle
chuckle, chuckled, chuckling
chuckler
chuff, -ed, -ing
chug, chugged, chugging

chum, chummed, chumming
chummy, -mier, -miest
chump
chunk
chunkiness
chunky, -kier, -kiest
church, -es
churinga
churl
churlish, -ly
churn, -ed, -ing
  churp   chirp
chute (drop)
  chute   shoot (gun)
chutney, -neys
  chutney   chutney
chutzpah
  cianide   cyanide
  cibernetics   cybernetics
cicada, -dae, -das
  cicatriss   cicatrix
cicatrix, cicatrices, cicatrixes

For all other cic- words, look under cyc- .

cider
  cifer   cipher
cigar
  cigaret   cigarette
cigarette
  cignet   cygnet (swan)
  cignet   signet (ring)
  cilestial   celestial
cilium, cilia
  cilinder   cylinder
  cilindrical   cylindrical
  cimbal   cymbal (music)
  cimbal   symbol (sign)
  ciment   cement
  cinamon   cinnamon
cinch, -ches
cincture
cinder
cinderella
cinema
cinemascope
cinematic, -ally
cinematograph
cineraria
  cinic   cynic
  cinical   cynical
  cinicul   cynical
  cinima   cinema
  cinimatograf   cinematograph
  cinimatograph   cinematograph
  cinimon   cinnamon
cinnamon
  cinosure   cynosure
cipher
  cipress   cypress
circa
  circel   circle
  circit   circuit
circle, -cled, -cling
circlet
circuit, -ed, -ing
circuit-breaker
circuitous, -ly
circuitry
  circul   circle
circular, -ly
circularise, -rised, -rising
circularity
circulate, -lated, -lating
circulation
circulator
circulatory
circumcise, -cised, -cising
circumcision
circumference
  circumferense   circumference
circumnavigate, -gated, -gating
circumnavigation
circumnavigator
circumscribe, -ribed, -ribing
circumscription
circumspect
circumspection
circumstance
  circumstanse   circumstance
  circumstanshul   circumstantial
circumstantial, -ly
circumvent, -ed, -ing
circumvention

circus, circuses
cirrhosis
cirriculum curriculum
cirrosis cirrhosis
cirrus
cissy, cissies
cist cyst
cistern
cistitis cystitis
citadel
citation
cite, cited, citing (quote)
cite sight (see)
cite site (place)
citie city
citizen
citric acid
citris citrus
citron
citronella
citros citrus
citrous
citrus
city, cities
civet
civic
civies civvies
civik civic
civil, -ly
civilian
civilisation
civilise, -lised, -lising
civility, -ties
civit civet
civvies
clad
cladding
claim, -ed, -ing
claimable
claimabul claimable
claimant
claimer
clairvoyance
clairvoyant
clam, clammed, clamming
clamber, -ed, -ing
clame claim
clamer clamour
clamerus clamorous
clammily
clamminess
clammy, -mier, -miest
clamorous, -ly
clamour, -ed, -ing
clamp, -ed, -ing
clamy clammy
clan
clandestine, -ly
clang, -ed, -ing
clanger (error)
clangour (loud sound)
clangourous, -ly
clank, -ed, -ing
clannish, -ly
clap, clapped, clapping
clapper
clapperboard
claptrap
claret
clarify, -fied, -fying
clarification
clarifier
clarinet
clarinettist
clarion
clarionet
clarity
clark clerk
claryon clarion
clash, -ed, -ing
clasify classify
clasp, -ed, -ing
clasroom classroom
class, classes
classable
classabul classable
classer
classic
classical, -ly
classicism
classicist
classifiable
classifiabul classifiable
classification

classify, -fied, -fying	
classroom	
classy, classier, classiest	
clatter, -ed, -ing	
clause (grammar)	
clause	claws (animal)
claustrofobia	claustrophobia
claustrophobia	
claves	
clavicel	clavicle
clavichord	
clavicord	clavichord
clavier	
claw, -ed, -ing	
claws (animal)	
claws	clause (grammer)
clay	
clayey	
clayie	clayey
clayish	
claym	claim
clean, -ed, -ing	
cleanliness	
cleanse, cleansed, cleansing	
cleanskin	
clear, -ed, -ing	
clearance	
clearly	
clearness	
clearway	
cleat	
cleavage	
cleave, cleaved, cleaving	
cleaver	
cleavidge	cleavage
cleek	clique
cleeshay	cliché
cleet	cleat
cleeve	cleave
cleevage	cleavage
cleever	cleaver
cleevidge	cleavage
clef	
cleft	
clematis	
clemency	

clemensy	clemency
clement	
clench, -ed, -ing	
clenliness	cleanliness
clense	cleanse
cleptomania	
clergy, -gies	
clergyman, -men	
cleric	
clerical, -ly	
clerk	
clever, cleverer, cleverest	
cleverly	
cleverness	
clew (ball)	
clew	clue (hint)
clianthus	
clichay	cliché
cliché, -chés	
click, -ed, -ing (sound)	
click	clique (group)
clicker	
clidesdale	clydesdale
client	
clientele	
clientell	clientele
cliff	
cliff-hanger	
climacteric (crucial)	
climactic (climax)	
climaks	climax
climate (weather)	
climatic, -ally	
climatology	
climax, -maxes	
climb, -ed, -ing (upward)	
clime (region)	
clinch, -ed, -ing	
clincher	
cling, clung, clinging	
clinger	
clinic	
clinical, -ly	
clink, -ed, -ing	
clinker, -ed, -ing	
clip, clipped, clipping	
clipper	

clique (group)
clique   click (sound)
clitoris
clitris   clitoris
cloak
cloak-and-dagger
cloakroom
clobber, -ed, -ing
clock, -ed, -ing
clockwise
clockwork
clod
cloddish
clodhopper
clog, clogged, clogging
cloggy
cloister, -ed, -ing
cloistral
cloke   cloak
clone, cloned, cloning
cloride   chloride
clorinate   chlorinate
clorine   chlorine
clorofil   chlorophyll
cloroform   chloroform
clorophyll   chlorophyll
close, closed, closing
close, closer, closest
closed-circuit
closeness
closet, -ed, -ing
closure
clot, clotted, clotting
cloth, cloths (fabric)
clothe, clothed, clothing
clothes (garments)
clothier
cloud, -ed, -ing
cloudbank
cloudburst
cloudless, -ly
cloudy, cloudier, cloudiest
clout, -ed, -ing
clove
cloven
cloven-hoofed
clover
cloverleaf, -leaves
clowd   cloud
clowdless   cloudless
clowdy   cloudy
clown, -ed, -ing
clownery
clownish, -ly
clowt   clout
cloy, -ed, -ing
cloyster   cloister
club, clubbed, clubbing
clubhouse
cluch   clutch
cluck, -ed, -ing
clucky
clue, clued, cluing (hint)
clue   clew (ball)
clump, -ed, -ing
clumpish
clumpy
clumsily
clumsiness
clumsy, -sier, -siest
clung
clurgy   clergy
cluster, -ed, -ing
clutch, -ed, -ing
clutch-start
clutter, -ed, -ing
Clydesdale
coach, -ed, -ing
coachman, -men
coacksial   coaxial
coagulate, -lated, -lating
coagulation
coagulator
coaks   coax
coal
coaldust
coalesce, -lesced, -lescing
coalescence
coalescent
coaless   coalesce
coalessence   coalescence
coalessent   coalescent
coalface
coalfield

coalishun	coalition
coalition	
coalitionist	
coalmine	
coalminer	
coalmining	
coarse, coarser, coarsest (rough)	
coarse	course (path)
coarsen, -ed, -ing	
coast, -ed, -ing	
coastal	
coaster	
coastgard	coastguard
coastguard	
coastline	
coat, -ed, -ing	
coat-hanger	
coatless	
coax, -ed, -ing	
coaxial	
coaxingly	
coaxiul	coaxial
cobalt	
cobber	
cobble, -bled, -bling	
cobbler	
cobblestone	
cober	cobber
coble	cobble
cobler	cobbler
coblestone	cobblestone
cobulstone	cobblestone
cobra	
cobweb	
cocain	
cocaine	
cocane	cocaine
cocanut	coconut
cocatoo	cockatoo
coccix	coccyx
coccyx, -coccyges	
coch	coach
cochineal	
cochineel	cochineal
cock, -ed, -ing	
cockade	
cockatoo	
cockatrice	
cockatriss	cockatrice
cockcrow	
cockelshell	cockleshell
cockerel	
cocker spaniel	
cocket	coquette
cocketry	coquetry
cockeyed	
cockfight	
cockily	
cockiness	
cockle	
cockleshell	
cockney, -neys	
cockpit	
cockroach, -es	
cockroch	cockroach
cockscomb	
cockshure	cocksure
cocksure	
cocktail	
cocktale	cocktail
cockul	cockle
cocky, cockier, cockiest	
coco, -cos (palm tree)	
cocoa (drink)	
coconut	
cocoon	
coddle, -dled, -dling	
code, coded, coding	
codecks	codex
codeen	codeine
codeine	
codex, codices	
codger	
codicil	
codiene	codeine
codification	
codifier	
codify, -fied, -fying	
codisil	codicil
codle	coddle
codswallop	
codul	coddle
co-ed	
coeducashun	coeducation

coeducation
coeducational
coefficient
coefishent — coefficient
coegsist — coexist
coequal, -ly
coequality
coerce, -erced, -ercing
coercible
coercibul — coercible
coercion
coercive, -ly
coerse — coerce
coershun — coercion
coersible — coercible
coersive — coercive
coeval, -ly
coevil — coeval
coevul — coeval
coexist, -ed, -ing
coexistence
coexistense — coexistence
coexistent
cofee — coffee
cofer — coffer
cofey — coffee
coff — cough
coffee
coffer
coffin
cofin — coffin
cog
cogency
cogenital — congenital
cogent, -ly
coger — codger
cogitate, -tated, -tating
cogitation
cogitative
cognac
cognate
cognisance
cognisanse — cognisance
cognisant
cognishun — cognition
cognition
cognitive

cohabit, -ed, -ing
cohabitation
cohearent — coherent
cohere, -hered, -hering
coherence
coherense — coherence
coherent, -ly
coheshun — cohesion
cohesion
cohesive, -ly
cohort
coiffure
coifur — coiffure
coil, -ed, -ing
coin, -ed, -ing
coinage
coincide, -cided, -ciding
coincidence
coincident, -ly
coinidge — coinage
coinsidence — coincidence
coinsident — coincident
coir
coishun — coition
coition
coitus
coke, coked, coking
coket — coquette
cokoon — cocoon
col
cola
colander
colapse — collapse
cold, -er, -est
cole — coal
colender — colander
coler — choler (anger)
colera — cholera
coleric — choleric
colesterol — cholesterol
coleus
colic
colicky
colitis
collaborate, -rated, -rating
collaboration
collaborator

collage
collapsable
collapse, -lapsed, -lapsing
collapsible
collar, -ed, -ing (neck)
collar — choler (anger)
collarbone
collate, -lated, -lating
collateral
collation
collator
colleague
collect, -ed, -ing
collectable
collection
collective, -ly
collectivism
collector
college
collegian
collegiate
coller — choler (anger)
coller — collar (neck)
collide, -lided, -liding
collie
collier
colliery, -ries
collinear, -ly
collision
collocate, -cated, -cating
collocation
collonial — colonial
colloquial, -ally
colloquialism
colloquy, -quies
collusion
collusive, -ly
cologne
colon
colonade — colonnade

> For other col- words, look under **coll-**.

colonel
colonial, -ly
colonisation
colonise, -nised, -nising
coloniser
colonnade
colony, -nies
color — colour
coloratura
colorful — colourful
colossal, -ly
colossus, -lossuses
colour, -ed, -ing
colour-bar
colour-blindness
colourful, -fully
colt
coltish, -ly
colum — column
columbine
column

> For other col- words, look under **coll-**.

columnist
coma (sleep)
coma — comma (mark)
comatose, -ly
comb, -ed, -ing
combat, -bated, -bating
combatant
combative, -ly
comber
combination
combine, -bined, -bining
combustible
combustibility
combustibul — combustible
combustion
come, came, come, coming
comeback
comedian
comedienne
comedy, -dies
comeliness
comely, -lier, -liest
commend — commend
comestible
comestibul — comestible
comet
comeuppance

comfert	**comfort**
comfortable	**comfortable**
comferter	**comforter**

comfort, -ed, -ing
comfortable, -bly
comforter
comfortless, -ly
comfy
comic
comical, -ly
comicality

> **Look under** comm- **if the word is not under com- .**

comma (mark)

comma	**coma (sleep)**

command, -ed, -ing
commandant
commander
commandment
commando, -dos, -does
commemorate, -rated, -rating
commemoration
commemorative, -ly
commence, -menced, -mencing
commencement
commend, -ed, -ing
commendable, -bly

commendabul	**commendable**

commendation
commendatory

commense	**commence**

commensurable, -bly

commensurabul	**commensurable**

commensurate
comment, -ed, -ing
commentary, -aries

commentater	**commentator**

commentator

commentry	**commentary**
commer	**comma**

commerce
commercial, -ly
commercialisation
commercialise, -lised, -lising
commercialism

commershal	**commercial**
commershalise	**commercialise**
commisar	**commissar**
commisariat	**commissariat**
commisary	**commissary**

commiserate, -rated, -rating
commiseration

commishun	**commission**
commision	**commission**
commisionaire	**commissionaire**
commisioner	**commissioner**

commissar
commissariat
commissary, -saries
commission
commissionaire
commissioner
commit, -mitted, -mitting
commitment
committal
committee

commitul	**committal**

commo

commodaty	**commodity**

commode
commodious, -ly
commodity, -ties

commodius	**commodious**
commodoor	**commodore**

commodore
common, -ly
commonality, -ties
commoner
commonplace
Commons
commonsense
commonsensical
Commonwealth

Commonwelth	**Commonwealth**
commoshun	**commotion**

commotion
communal, -ly
commune, -muned, -muning
communicable

communicabul	**communicable**

communicate, -cated, -cating
communication
communicative

communicator
communikay — communique
communion
communique
communism
communist
communistic
community, -ties
commutation
commute, -muted, -muting
commuter

Look under com- if the word is not under comm- .

compact
compair — compare (liken)
compair — compere (stage)
companion
companionable, -bly
companionship
company, -nies
companyun — companion
comparable, -bly
comparabul — comparable
comparative, -ly
compare, -pared, -paring (liken)
compare — compere (stage)
comparison
compartment
compartmentalise, -ised, -ising
compass — compass
compashun — compassion
compashunate — compassionate
compass, -es
compass, -ed, -ing
compassion
compassionate, -nated, -nating
compatibility
compatible, -bly
compatibul — compatible
compatition — competition
compatriot
compel, -pelled, -pelling
compendium, -diums, -dia
compensate, -sated, -sating
compensation
compensator
compensatory
compensatory — compensatory
company — company
compere, -pered, -pering (stage)
compere — compare (liken)
competent — competent
competitive — competitive
compete, -peted, -peting
competency
competense — competence
competent, -ly
competishun — competition
competition
competitive, -ly
competitor
compilation
compile, -piled, -piling
compiler
compinsation — compensation
complacency, -cies
complacent, -ly (smug)
complain, -ed, -ing
complainant
complaint
complaisant (obliging)
complanant — complainant
complane — complain
complant — complaint
complasense — complacence
complasent — complacent
complement, -ed, -ing (complete)
complement — Compliment (praise)
complementary (completing)
complementary — Complimentary (free)
complete, -pleted, -pleting
completion
complex, -ly
complexion
complexity, -ties
compliable
compliabul — compliable
compliance
compliant, -ly
complicate, -cated, -cating
complication

complicity
  complient compliant
compliment, -ed, -ing (praise)
  compliment Complement (completely)
complimentary (free)
  complimentary complementary
  complissity complicity
comply, -plied, -plying
compo
component
comport
comportment
compose, -posed, -posing
composedly
  composhure composure
  composishun composition
composite, -ly
composition
compositor
compost
composure
  compot compote
compote
compound, -ed, -ing
compoundable
  compoundabul compoundable
comprehend, -ed, -ing
comprehendingly
  comprehenshun comprehension
comprehensible, -bly
comprehension
comprehensive, -ly
comprehensiveness
compress, -ed, -ing
compressibility
compressible
  compressibul compressible
compression
compressor
comprisal
comprise, -prised, -prising
compromise, -mised, -mising
comptroller
  compulsory compulsory
  compulshun compulsion
compulsion
compulsive, -ly
compulsorily
compulsory
  compulsrey compulsory
compunction
computability
computation
compute, -puted, -puting
computer
computerisation
computer program
computer terminal
  comrad comrade
comrade
comradeship

Look under comm- if the word is not under com-.

con, conned, conning
  conbine combine
concave, -ly
concavity, -ties
conceal, -ed, -ing
concealable
  concealabul concealable
concealment
concede, -ceded, -ceding
conceit
conceited, -ly
conceivable
conceivably
  conceivabul conceivable
conceive, -ceived, -ceiving
  concensus consensus
concentrate, -trated, -trating
concentration
concentric
concentricity
  concepshun conception
concept
conception
conceptual, -ly
conceptualise, -lised, -lising
concern, -ed, -ing
concert, -ed, -ing
concertina
concertmaster

concerto, -tos, -ti
concession
conch, conchs, conches

concherto	concerto
conciet	conceit
concieted	conceited
concievable	conceivable
concieve	conceive

conciliate, -ated, -ating
conciliation
conciliator
conciliatory
concise, -ly

> Look under **cons-** if the word is not under **conc-** .

conciseness
conclave
conclude, -cluded, -cluding

conclushun	conclusion

conclusion
conclusive, -ly
concoct, -ed, -ing
concoction
concomitance
concomitancy
concomitant, -ly
concord
concordance

concordanse	concordance

concordant

concorse	concourse

concourse

concreet	concrete

concrete, -creted, -creting
concretely
concreteness
concubinage
concubine
concupiscence
concupiscent

concupissense	concupiscence
concupissent	concupiscent

concur, -curred, -curring

concurence	concurrence
concurent	concurrent

concurrence
concurrent, -ly

concus	concuss
concushun	concussion

concuss, -ed, -ing
concussion
concussive

condament	condiment
condaminium	condominium
condansation	condensation
condem	condemn

condemn, -ed, -ing
condemnation
condemnatory

condence	condense
condencer	condenser

condensation
condense, -densed, -densing
condenser

condensor	condenser

condescend, -ed, -ing
condescension
condiment

condisend	condescend
condisension	condescension
condishun	condition
condishunal	conditional

condition, -ed, -ing
conditional, -ly
condolatory
condole, -doled, -doling
condolence

condolense	condolence

condolingly
condominium
condonation
condone, -doned, -doning
condor
conducive

conducshun	conduction

conduct, -ed, -ing

conducter	conductor

conductible
conductibility

conductibul	conductible

conduction
conductivity, -ties
conductor

conductress	
conduit	
condusive	conducive
cone	
conecshun	connection
connect	connect
connective	connective
confection	
confectionary, -aries (factory)	
confectionery, -eries (sweets)	
confedence	confidence
confederacy, -cies	
confederacy	confederacy
confederate, -rated, -rating	
confederation	
confer, -ferred, -ferring	
conference	
conferm	confirm
confess, -ed, -ing	
confesser	
confession	
confessional	
confessor	
confetti	
confidant (trusted man)	
confidant	confident (sure)
confidante (trusted woman)	
confide, -fided, -fiding	
confidence	
confidenshul	confidential
confident (sure)	
confident (trusted man)	confidant
confidential, -ly	
confidentiality	
configeration	configuration
configuration	
confine, -fined, -fining	
confinement	
confirm, -ed, -ing	
confirmable	
confirmation	
confiscate, -cated, -cating	
confiscation	
conflagration	
conflict, -ed, -ing	
confluence	

confluent	
conform, -ed, -ing	
conformable, -bly	
conformabul	conformable
conformist	
conformity, -ties	
confound, -ed, -ing	
confownd	confound
confrence	conference
confront, -ed, -ing	
confrontation	
confurm	confirm
confuse, -fused, -fusing	
confusion	
confutation	
confute, -futed, -futing	
conga (dance)	
conga	conger (eel)
congeal, -ed, -ing	
congeel	congeal
congenial	congenial
congenial, -ly	
congeniality	
congenital, -ly	
conger (eel)	
conger	conga (dance)
congest, -ed, -ing	
congestion	
congestive	
conglomerate, -rated, -rating	
conglomeration	
congradulation	congratulation
congragation	congregation
congratulate, -lated, -lating	
congratulation	
congratulatory	
congregate, -gated, -gating	
congregation	
congregational	
congress	
congressional	
congrewent	congruent
congrewus	congruous
congruence	
congruent	
congruity, -ties	
congruous, -ly	

conic
conical, -ly
conifer
coniferous
conjeckture conjecture
conjecturable, -bly
conjecture, -tured, -turing
conjenial congenial
conjestion congestion
conjoin, -ed, -ing
conjoint, -ly
conjuce conduce
conjugal, -ly
conjugality
conjugate, -gated, -gating
conjugation
conjugal conjugal
conjuice conduce
conjuncshun conjunction
conjunct, -ly
conjunction
conjunctional, -ly
conjunctive, -ly
conjunctivitis
conjuncture
conjuration
conjure, -jured, -juring
conjurer
conjuror
conk, -ed, -ing
conker (nut)
conker conquer (win)
conkwest conquest
con man, -men
connect, -ed, -ing
connectedly
connecter
connection
connective, -ly
connector
connesser connoisseur
connewbial connubial
conning tower
connivance
connivanse connivance
connive, -nived, -niving
connoisseur
connotation
connote, -noted, -noting
connubial, -ly
connubial connubial
conosseur connoisseur
connote connote
conquer, -ed, -ing
conquerable
conquerabul conquerable
conquerer conqueror
conqueror
conquest
conquistador
consanguine
consanguineous, -ly
consanguinity
consceintious conscientious
conscience
conscienshus conscientious
conscientious, -ly
conscious, -ly
consciousness
conscripshun conscription
conscript, -ed, -ing
conscription
conseal conceal
conseat conceit
consecrate, -crated, -crating
consecration
consecutive
consede concede
consekwence consequence
consensus
consent, -ed, -ing
consequence
consequent
consequential, -ly
conservatery conservatory
conservation
conservational
conservationist
conservative, -ly
conservatism
conservatoire
conservatorium
conservatory, -tries
conservatry conservatory

conserve, -served, -serving	
conserver	
consession	concession
consicrate	consecrate
consider, -ed, -ing	
considerable, -ably	
considerabul	considerable
considerate, -ly	
consideration	
consign, -ed, -ing	
consignable	
consignabul	consignable
consignee	
consigner	
consignible	consignable
consignment	
consignor	
consiliate	conciliate
consine	consign
consinee	consignee
consinement	consignment
consinor	consignor
consise	concise
consist, -ed, -ing	
consistence	
consistency, -cies	
consistense	consistence
consistensy	consistency
consistent, -ly	
consolable	
consolabul	consolable
consolation	
console, -soled, -soling	
consoler	
consolingly	
consolidate, -dated, -dating	
consolidated revenue	
consolidation	
consolidator	
consommé	
consonance	
consonant, -ly	
consort, -ed, -ing	
consortium, -tia	
conspicuous, -ly	
conspicuousness	
conspiracy, -cies	

conspirasy	conspiracy
conspirater	conspirator
conspirator	
conspiratory	
conspiratry	conspiratory
conspire, -spired, -spiring	
constable	
constabul	constable
constabulary, -ries	
constancy	
constansy	constancy
constant, -ly	
constapation	constipation
constellation	
consternation	
constipate, -pated, -pating	
constipation	
constituency, -cies	
constituensy	constituency
constituent	
constitute, -tuted, -tuting	
constitution	
constitutional, -ly	
constrain, -ed, -ing	
constraint	
constrickshun	constriction
constrict, -ed, -ing	
constriction	
construct, -ed, -ing	
construction	
constructive, -ly	
constructor	
construe, -strued, -struing	
consul	
consular	
consulate	
consuler	consular
consult, -ed, -ing	
consultant	
consultation	
consultative	
consultent	consultant
consulter	
consumable	
consumabul	consumable
consume, -sumed, -suming	
consumer	

consumerism
consummate, -mated, -mating
consummation
consummative
consummé consommé
consumpshun consumption
consumption
consumptive, -ly
contact, -ed, -ing
contact lenses
contageous contagious
contagion
contagious, -ly
contagus contagious
contajus contagious
contain, -ed, -ing
container
containment
contaminate, -nated, -nating
contamination
contane contain
contanement containment
contaner container
contemplate, -plated, -plating
contemplation
contemplative, -ly
contemporaneous, -ly
contemporary, -raries
contempt
contemptable contemptible
contemptible, -bly
contemptibul contemptible
contemptuous, -ly
contend, -ed, -ing
contender
contenshun contention
contenshus contentious
content
contented, -ly
contention
contentious, -ly
contentment
contest, -ed, -ing
contestant
contestent contestant
context
contextual, -ly

contiguity
contiguous, -ly
continence
continense continence
continent
continental
contingency, -cies
contingensy contingency
contingent, -ly
continnuation continuation
continual, -ly
continuance
continuanse continuance
continuation
continue, -ued, -uing
continuity, -ties
continuous, -ly
continuum, -tinuums, -tinua
contorshun contortion
contort, -ed, -ing
contortion
contortionist
contour
contraband
contraception
contraceptive, -ly
contrackshun contraction
contract, -ed, -ing
contraction
contractor
contractual
contradickshun contradiction
contradict, -ed, -ing
contradiction
contradictory, -ries
contralto, -ti
contrapshun contraption
contraption
contrarily
contrariness
contrariwise
contrary, -ries
contrasepshun contraception
contraseptive contraceptive
contrast, -ed, -ing
contravene, -vened, -vening
contravenshun contravention

  contribushun — contribution
contribute, -buted, -buting
contribution
contributor
contributory
  contributry — contributory
  contrishun — contrition
contrite, -ly
contrition
contrivance
  contrivanse — contrivance
contrive, -trived, -triving
control, -trolled, -trolling
controllable
  controllabul — controllable
controller
  controvershal — controversial
controversial, -ly
controversy, -sies
contumely, -lies
contuse, -tused, -tusing
  contushun — contusion
contusion
contusive
conurbation
convalesce, -lesced, -lescing
convalescence
  convalescense — convalescent
convalescent
  convaless — convalesce
  convalessence — convalescence
convection
convective, -ly
convector
convene, -vened, -vening
convenience
  conveniense — convenience
convenient, -ly
convenor
  convenshun — convention
  convenshunal — conventional
convent
convention
conventional, -ly
conventionalism
converge, -verged, -verging
conversant, -ly
conversation
conversational, -ly
conversationalist
converse, -versed, -versing
conversely
  conversent — conversant
  convershun — conversion
conversion
convert, -ed, -ing
  convertabul — convertible
converter
convertible, -ly
  convertibul — convertible
convex, -ly
convexity, -ties
convey, -ed, -ing
conveyance
conveyancer
conveyancing
  conveyanse — conveyance
conveyor belt
  convickshun — conviction
convict, -ed, -ing
conviction
  convienence — convenience
convince, -vinced, -vincing
convincible
  convincibul — convincible
convincingly
convivial, -ly
convivialty
convocation
convoke, -voked, -voking
  convolushun — convolution
convolute, -luted, -luting
convolution
convoy, -ed, -ing
convulse, -vulsed, -vulsing
  convulshun — convulsion
convulsion
convulsive, -ly
  conyac — cognac
coo, cooed, cooing
cooee, cooeed, cooeeing
  cooger — cougar
cook, -ed, -ing
cookery, -eries

cookhouse
cookie, cookies
cookoo cuckoo
cool, -ed, -ing
coolabah
coolabar coolabah
coolamon
coolant
coolie (labourer)
coolly (calmly)
coop, -ed, -ing
co-op
cooper
cooperage
cooperate, -rated, -rating
cooperation
cooperative, -ly
coopon coupon
co-opt, -ed, -ing
coordinate, -nated, -nating
coordination
coordinator
cop, copped, copping (accept)
coparison comparison
cope, coped, coping (put up with)
coper copper
copha
copier
co-pilot
copious, -ly
cop-out
copper
copperhead
copperplate
coppy copy
copra
cops copse
copse
cop shop
copula, -lae
copulate, -lated, -lating
copulation
copulative, -ly
copy, copies
copy, copied, copying
copybook
copycat, -catted, -catting
copyer copier
copyist
copyright, -ed, -ing (licence)
copyrite copyright
copywriter
coquet, -quetted, -quetting
coquetry
coquette
coquettish, -ly
coral (reef)
coral choral (sing)
coral corral (yard)
coralfish
corcus caucus
cord (rope)
cord chord (music)
cordage
corded
cordial, -ly
cordiality
cordige cordage
cordon, -ed, -ing
cordon bleu
cords (trousers)
corduroy
core, cored, coring (centre)
core caw (cry)
core corps (group)
corecshun correction
corect correct
corection correction
corective corrective
corelate correlate
corella
coreografy choreography
corespond correspond
corespondence correspondence
corespondense correspondence
co-respondent (divorce)
corespondent correspondent
coriander
coridoor corridor
coridor corridor
Corinthian
coriografy choreography
corispond correspond
corispondence correspondence

corispondent	correspondent
corister	chorister
cork, -ed, -ing	
corkage	
corker	
corkscrew, -ed, -ing	
corm	
cormorant	
corn	
corncob	
cornea, -neas, -neae	
corneal	
corned beef	
corneel	corneal
corner, -ed, -ing	
cornerstone	
cornet	
cornflour	
cornia	cornea
cornice, -niced, -nicing	
cornstalk	
cornucopia	
corny, -nier, -niest	
coroborate	corroborate
coroborator	corroborator
coroboree	corroboree
corode	corrode
corola	corolla
corolary	corollary
corolla	
corollary, -ries	
corona, -nas, -nae	
coronary	
coronary thrombosis	
coronation	
coroner	
coronet	
coroshun	corrosion
corosive	corrosive
corparation	corporation
corperal	corporal
corporal, -ly	
corporate, -ly	
corporation	
corporeal, -ly	
corps (group)	
corps	corpse (body)

corpse (body)	
corpse	corps (group)
corpulence	
corpulense	corpulence
corpulent, -ly	
corpus, -pora	
corpuscle	
corpuscular	
corpusle	corpuscle
corpussel	corpuscle
corral, -ralled, -ralling (yard)	
Corral	choral (sing)
correckshun	correction
correct, -ed, -ing	
correction	
correctional	
corrective, -ly	
correlate, -lated, -lating	
correlation	
correlative, -ly	
correlativity	
correspond, -ed, -ing	
correspondence	
correspondent	
corridor	
Corriedale	
corroborate, -rated, -rating	
corroboration	
corroborative, -ly	
corroborator	
corroboree	
corrode, -roded, -roding	
corrodible	
corrodibul	corrodible
corrollary	corollary
corroshun	corrosion
corrosion	
corrosive, -ly	
corrugate, -gated, -gating	
corrugated iron	
corrugation	
corrupshun	corruption
corrupt, -ed, -ing	
corruptabul	corruptible
corruptible, -bly	
corruptibility	
corruptibul	corruptible

Word	Correct spelling
corruption	
corsage	
corsair	
corsashun	causation
corse	coarse (rough)
corse	course (path)
corsen	coarsen
corset	
corsetry	
corshun	caution
corshus	cautious
corsit	corset
cort	caught (held)
cort	court (law)
cort marshal	court martial
cortage	cortege
cortege	
corterise	cauterise
cortex, -tices	
cortier	courtier
cortion	caution
cortious	cautious
cortisan	courtesan
cortisone	
cortly	courtly
cortroom	courtroom
cortship	courtship
cortyard	courtyard
corugate	corrugate
corupt	corrupt
coruptible	corruptible
coruption	corruption
corus	chorus
corvet	corvette
corvette	
cos	
cosh	
cosmetic	
cosmetically	
cosmografy	cosmography
cosmography, -phies	
cosmology	
cosmonaut	
cosmonort	cosmonaut
cosmopolitan	
cosmos	
Cossack	

Word	Correct spelling
cost, cost, costed, costing	
cost	coast
co-star, -starred, -starring	
coster	
costguard	coastguard
costliness	
costly, -lier, -liest	
costume, -tumed, -tuming	
costume jewellery	
cosy, -sies	
cosy, -sier, -siest	
cot	
cotage	cottage
cotchineal	cochineal
cote (shelter)	
cote	coat (garment)
coterie	
cotige	cottage
coton	cotton
cotoneaster	
cotonwool	cottonwool
cottage	
cotter pin	
cotton	
cottonbush	
cottonwood	
cottonwool	
cottony	
cou daytar	coup d'état
couch	
cougar	
cough, -ed, -ing	
could	
couldn't (could not)	
couldnt	couldn't
coulter	
councel	council (meeting)
councel	counsel (advice)
council (meeting)	
councel	counsel (advice)
counciller	councillor
councillor (member)	
councillor	counselor (adviser)

counsel, -selled, -selling (advice)

counsel	council (meeting)
counseller	counsellor

counsellor (adviser)

counsellor (member)	councillor

count, -ed, -ing
countdown
countenance, -nanced, -nancing

countenanse	countenance

counter
counteract, -ed, -ing
counteraction
counteractive, -ly
counterattack, -ed, -ing
counterbalance, -anced, -ancing
counter culture
counterespionage

counterfeet	counterfeit

counterfeit, -ed, -ing
counterfeiter
counterintelligence
countermand, -ed, -ing
counterpane
counterpart
counterpoint
counterproductive
counter-revolution
counter-revolutionary, -aries
countersign, -ed, -ing
countersignature

countersine	countersign
counterwait	counterweight

counterweight
countess

countie	county

countless
country, -tries
countryman, -men
countryside
county, -ties
coup, -coups

coupay	coupé

coup de grace
coup d'état
coupé
couple, -led, -ling
couplet
coupon
courage
courageous, -ly
courier
course (path)

course	coarse (rough)
coursen	coarsen

court, -ed, -ing (law)

court	caught (held)

courtesan
courtesy, -sies
courthouse
courtier
courtly, -lier, -liest

court marshal	court martial

court martial
courtroom
courtyard
cousin
couture
couturier
covenant
cover, -ed, -ing
coverage
covert, -ly
cover-up
covet, -ed, -ing
covetous, -ly
covey, -eys
coward (scared)

coward (cringed)	cowered

cowardice

cowardiss	cowardice

cowardly
cowboy
cower, -ed, -ing (cringe)

cowerd	coward
cowered	coward (scared)

cowl, -ed, -ing
cowlick
cowling

For cown- words, look under **coun-**.

cowslip
cox
coxcomb
coxe coax
coxswain
coy, -ly
coyn coin
coyote
crab, crabbed, crabbing
crab-apple
crabby, -bier, -biest
crablouse
crack, -ed, -ing
crackdown
cracker
crackle, -led, -ling
crackpot
crackul crackle
cradle, -dled, -dling
cradle-snatcher
cradul cradle
craft
craftily
craftiness
craftsman, -men
craftsmanship
crafty, -tier, -tiest
crag
cragged
craggy, -gier, -giest
crain crane
crake
cram, crammed, cramming
cramp, -ed, -ing
cranberry, -ries
crane, craned, craning
cranial, -ly
cranium, -nia
crank, -ed, -ing
crankcase
crankiness
crankshaft
cranky, -kier, -kiest
cranny, -nies
craps
crapulous
crash, -ed, -ing
crasher
crass
crate, crated, crating
crater
cravat
crave, craved, craving
craven, -ly
craw
crawl, -ed, -ing
crawler
crayfish, -fishes, -fish
crayon, -ed, -ing
craype crepe
craypot
craysh crèche
craze, crazed, crazing
crazily
craziness
crazy, -zier, -ziest
creacher creature
creak, -ed, -ing (squeak)
creak creek (stream)
cream, -ed, -ing
creaminess
creamy, -mier, -miest
creap creep
crease, creased, creasing
create, -ated, -ating
creater creator
creation
creative, -ly
creativeness
creativity
creator
creature
crèche
creecher creature
credence
credense credence
credenshul credential
credential
credibility
credible
credibly
credibul credible
credit, -ed, -ing
creditable, -bly

creditabul	creditable
credit card	
crediter	creditor
creditor	
credo, -dos	
credulity	
credulous, -ly	
credulousness	
creed	
creek (stream)	
creek	creak (squeak)
creel	
creem	cream
creep, crept, creeping	
creeper	
creepiness	
creeps	
creepy, -pier, -piest	
cremate, -mated, -mating	
cremation	
crematorium	
creme	
crenellate, -lated, -lating	
creole	
creosote, -soted, -soting	
crepe, creped, creping	
crept	
crepuscular	
crescendo, -dos	
crescent	
cresh	crèche
creshendo	crescendo
cress	
cressent	crescent
crest, -ed, -ing	
crestfallen, -ly	
cretin	
cretinism	
cretinous	
creture	creature
crevase	crevasse
crevase	crevice
crevasse, -vassed, -vassing	
crevice	
creviss	crevice
crew, -ed, -ing	
crewel (yarn)	
crewel	cruel (harsh)
crewl	cruel
crew neck	
crews (sailors)	
crews	cruise (ship)
crib, cribbed, cribbing	
cribage	cribbage
cribbage	
cribbidge	cribbage
crick	
cricket	
cricketer	
crier	
crime	
criminal, -ly	
criminality, -ties	
criminologist	
criminology	
crimp, -ed, -ing	
crimpy, -pier, -piest	
crimson	
cringe, cringed, cringing	
crinkle, -kled, -kling	
crinkul	crinkle
crinkly	
crinoline	
cripple, -pled, -pling	
cript	crypt
criptic	criptic
criptograf	cryptograph
criptogram	cryptogram
criptograph	cryptograph
cripul	cripple
crisalis	chrysalis
crisalus	chrysalis
criscros	crisscross
crisen	christen
Crisendom	Christendom
crisis, -ses	
crisp, -ed, -ing	
crispness	
crispy	
crisscross	
Crist	Christ
cristal	crystal
cristaline	crystalline
cristalise	crystallise

Cristian	Christian
Cristianity	Christianity
criteek	critique
criterion, -teria	
critic	
critical, -ly	
criticise, -cised, -cising	
criticism	
critique	
critisise	criticise
croak, -ed, -ing	
croaky	
crochet, -ed, -ing	
crock	
crockadile	crocodile
crockery	
crocodile	
crocus, crocuses	
croft	
crofter	
croissant	
crokay	croquet
cromatic	chromatic
crome	chrome
cromosome	chromosome
crone	
crony, -nies	
crood	crude
crook	
crooked, -ly	
crookedness	
croon, -ed, -ing	
crooner	
crop, cropped, cropping	
crop-dust, -ed, -ing	
crop-duster	
cropper	
croquet (sport)	
croquette (food)	
crosier	
cross, -ed, -ing	
crossbar	
crossbench	
crossbencher	
crossbones	
crossbow	
crossbreed, -bred, -breeding	
crosscheck	
cross-country	
crosscut, -cut, -cutting	
cross-examination	
cross-examine, -ined, -ining	
cross-examiner	
cross-eyed	
cross-fertilisation	
cross-fertilise, -lised, -lising	
crossover	
cross-pollinate, -nated, -nating	
cross-purpose	
cross-reference, -renced, -rencing	
crossroad	
cross-section	
cross-stitch, -ed, -ing	
crosswise	
crossword puzzle	
crotch	
crotchet	
crotchetiness	
crotchety	
crouch, -ed, -ing	
croup	
croupier	
crouton	
crow, crowed, crowing	
crowbar	
crowd, -ed, -ing	
croweater	
crown, -ed, -ing	
crown-of-thorns	
crow's-foot, -feet	
crow's-nest	
crucial, -ly	
crucibel	crucible
crucible	
crucibul	crucible
crucifix	
crucifixion	
cruciform, -ly	
crucify, -fied, -fying	
crude, cruder, crudest	
crudeness	
crudity, -ties	
cruel, cruelled, cruelling	
cruelty, -ties	

cruet
cruise, cruised, cruising (ship)
  cruise — crews (sailors)
cruiser
  crum — crumb
crumb, -ed, -ing
crumble, -bled, -bling
crumbly, -blier, -bliest
  crumbul — crumble
crummy, -mier, -miest
crumpet
crumple, -pled, -pling
  crumpul — crumple
  crumy — crummy
crunch, -ed, -ing
crunchy, -chier, -chiest
crusade, -saded, -sading
crusader
crush, -ed, -ing
  crushal — crucial
crusher
  crusibul — crucible
crust
crustacean
  crustashun — crustacean
crustiness
crusty, crustier, crustiest
crutch, -ed, -ing
crux, cruxes, cruces
  cruze — cruise
cry, cries
cry, cried, crying
crypt
cryptic, -ally
cryptogram
cryptograph
cryptographer
cryptographic
cryptography
  crysalis — chrysalis
crystal
crystalline
crystallisation
crystallise, -lised, -lising
cub
cubby, -bies
cubbyhole

cubbyhouse
cube, cubed, cubing
cubic
cubical, -ly (cube-shaped)
cubicle (room)
cubism
cubist
cubmaster
  cuboard — cupboard
  cuby — cubby
  cubyhole — cubbyhole
  cubyhouse — cubbyhouse
cuckold, -ed, -ing
cuckoldry
cuckoo
cucumber
cud
  cuddel — cuddle
cuddle, -dled, -dling
cuddlesome
cuddly
cuddy, -dies
cudgel, -elled, -elling
cudgerie
  cudly — cuddly
  cudos — kudos
cue, cued, cuing (billiards)
  cue — queue (line)
cuff, -ed, -ing
cuisine
  culcher — culture
cul-de-sac
  culer — colour
culinary
cull, -ed, -ing
culminate, -nated, -nating
culmination
  culots — culottes
culottes
culpability
culpable, -bly
  culpabul — culpable
culprit
cult
cultism
cultist
cultivate, -vated, -vating

Word	Correct spelling
cultivater	cultivator
cultivation	
cultivator	
cultural, -ly	
culture, -tured, -turing	
cultured pearl	
culture shock	
culvert	
cumbasome	cumbersome
cumbersome, -ly	
cumbersum	cumbersome
cumfurt	comfort
cumin	
cummerbund	
cumpass	compass
cumquat	
cumulative, -ly	
cumulus	
cuning	cunning
cunning, -ly	
cuntry	country
cup, cupped, cupping	
cupboard	
cupbord	cupboard
cupful, cupfuls	
cupid	
cupidity	
cupola	
cuppa	
cur	
curable, -bly	
curacao	
curacy, -cies	
curage	courage
currant	currant (fruit)
curare	
curate	
curater	curator
curative, -ly	
curator	
curatorial	
curb, -ed, -ing (control)	
curb	kerb (gutter)
curcuit	circuit
curd	
curdle, -dled, -dling	
curdul	curdle
cure, cured, curing	
curency	currency
curent	current (flow)
curette, -retted, -retting	
curfew	
curiculum	curriculum
curio, curios	
curiosity, -ties	
curious, -ly	
curiousness	
curius	curious
curl, -ed, -ing	
curler	
curlew	
curly, -lier, -liest	
curnel	colonel
currage	courage
curragus	courageous
currajong	
currant (fruit)	
currant	current (flow)
currawong	
currency, -cies	
currensy	currency
current (flow)	
current	currant (fruit)
current account	
currently	
curriculum, -lums, -la	
curriculum vitae	
curry, -ries	
curry, -ried, -rying	
curse, cursed, cursing	
cursive, -ly	
cursor	
curt, -ly	
curtail, -ed, -ing	
curtailment	
curtain, -ed, -ing	
curtale	curtail
curtsy, -sies	
curtsy, -sied, -sying	
curvaceous	
curvachure	curvature
curvashus	curvaceous
curvature	
curve, curved, curving	

curvilinear	
cushion, -ed, -ing	
cushon	cushion
cushy, cushier, cushiest	
cusp	
cuspid	
cuss	
cussed, -ly	
custard	
custard-apple	
custodial	
custodian	
custodiul	custodial
custodiun	custodian
custom	
customarily	
customary, -aries	
custom-built	
customer	
custom-made	
cut, cut, cutting	
cutback	
cute, cuter, cutest	
cuteness	
cutical	cuticle
cuticle	
cuticul	cuticle
cutlass	
cutlery	
cutlet	
cut-off	
cut-out	
cut-price	
cutter	
cutthroat	
cuttlebone	
cuttlefish, -fishes, -fish	
cuttulbone	cuttlebone
cutworm	

cuvenant	covenant
cuver	cover
cuvet	covet
cuvey	covey
cyanide	
cybernetics	
cyclamate	
cyclamen	
cycle, cycled, cycling	
cyclic	
cyclist	
cycloid	
cyclone	
cyclonic	
cyclostyle, -led, -ling	
cyder	
cygnet (swan)	
cygnet	signet (ring)
cylinder	
cymbal (instrument)	
cymbal	symbol (sign)
cymbalist	
cymbidium	
cynic	
cynical, -ly	
cynicism	
cynoshure	cynosure
cynosure	
cypher	
cypress	
cyst	
cystitis	
cytology	
czar	
czarina	
czarist	
Czech	
Czechoslovak	
Czechoslovakia	

Dd

dab, dabbed, dabbing	
dabble, -bled, -bling	
dabed	dabbed
dabing	dabbing
dable	dabble
dabul	dabble
dachshund	
dacks	daks
dacor	decor
dad	
daddy-long-legs	
daemon	
daffodil	
daffodill	daffodil
daffy, daffier, daffiest	
dafny	daphne
dafodil	daffodil
daft	
dager	dagger
dagger	
dahlia	
dail	dale
daily	
daim	dame
daintie	dainty
daintily	
dainty, -tier, -tiest	
dair	dare
dairy, -ries (milk)	
dairy	diary (book)
dais	
daisie	daisy
daisy	
daks	
dalee	dally
dalia	dahlia
dally, -lied, -lying	
Dalmatian	
daly	daily
dam, dammed, damming (water)	
dam	damn (swear)
damage, -aged, -aging	
damageable	
damask	
dame	
damedge	damage
damestic	domestic
damn, -ed, -ing (swear)	
damn	dam (water)
damnable, -bly	
damnabul	damnable
damnation	
damp	
dampcourse	
dampen, -ed, -ing	
damper	
damsel	
damsil	damsel
damsul	damsel
dance, danced, dancing	
dancer	
dandelion	
dandilion	dandelion
dandle, -dled, -dling	
dandruff	
dane	deign
dangel	dangle
danger	
dangerous, -ly	
dangerus	dangerous
dangle, -gled, -gling	
dangul	dangle
danjer	danger
danjerus	dangerous
daper	dapper
dapple	dapple
dapper, -ly	
dapple, -pled, -pling	
darby	derby
dare, dared, daring	
daredevil	
darey	dairy
dark, -ly	
darken, -ed, -ing	
darkin	darken

darkness
darkroom
  darlin — darling
darling
darn, -ed, -ing
dart, -ed, -ing
  darta — data
  dartabase — database
darter
dash, -ed, -ing
dashboard
  dashbord — dashboard
  dashound — dashshund
dastard, -ly
  dastid — dastard
  dastud — dastard
data
database
date, dated, dating
  dater — data
  datim — datum
datum
daub
  daufin — dauphin
daughter
daunt, -ed, -ing
dauphin
  dauter — daughter
  dawb — daub
dawdle, -dled, -dling
  dawdul — dawdle
dawn, -ed, -ing
  dawnt — daunt
  dawter — daughter
day
  daybrake — daybreak
daybreak
daydream
  daycor — decor
  dayify — deify
  dayis — dais
  dayity — deity
  daylia — dahlia
daylight
  daylite — daylight
  dayly — daily
  dayn — deign
  daysy — daisy
daze, dazed, dazing (stun)
  daze — days (time)
dazzle, -zled, -zling
dazzler
deacon
deactivate, -ated, -ating
dead, -ly
dead centre
deaden, -ed, -ing
dead heart
dead heat
deadline
deadlock
deadly, -lier, -liest
deadpan
dead reckoning
dead weight
deadwood
deaf
deafen, -ed, -ing
  deaft — deft
deal, dealt, dealing
dealer
  deam — deem
dean
deanery
dear, -ly (loved)
  dear — deer (animal)
dearth
death
death adder
deathly
death-wish

> Look under di- if the word is not under **de-**.

debacle
  debacul — debacle
debar, -barred, -barring
debase, -based, -basing
debasement
debatable, -bly
  debatabul — debatable
debate, -bated, -bating
  debatible — debatable
debauch, -ed, -ing

debauchery, -ries
debbit debit
debensher debenture
debenshure debenture
debenture
debilitate, -tated, -tating
debilitation
debility, -ties
debit, -ed, -ing
debonair
deboo debut
debree debris
debrief, -ed, -ing
debris
debt
debter debtor
debtor
debug, -bugged, -bugging
debunk, -ed, -ing
debut
debutante
decade
decadence
decadense decadence
decadent, -ly
decamp, -ed, -ing
decant, -ed, -ing
decanter
decapitate, -tated, -tating
decapitation
decathalon decathlon
decathlon
decay, -ed, -ing
decease, -ceased, -ceasing
deceit
deceitful, -ly
deceive, deceived, deceiving
decelerate, -rated, -rating
December
decency, -cies
decent, -ly
decentralisation
decentralise, -lised, -lising
decepshun deception
deception
deceptive, -ly
decibel
decibell decibel
decide, -cided, -ciding
decidedly
deciduous
decieve deceive
decifer decipher
decimal
decimate, -mated, -mating
decipher, -ed, -ing
decishun decision
decision
decisive, -ly
deck, -ed, -ing
deckade decade
deckchair
deckchare deckchair
deckerate decorate
deckhand
deckle
deckul deckle
declaim, -ed, -ing
declamation
declarable
declarabul declarable
declaratory
declaratry declaratory
declare, -clared, -claring
declassify, -fied, -fying
decline, -clined, -clining
decode, -coded, -coding
decompose, -posed, -posing
decomposishun decomposition
decomposition
decompreshun decompression
decompress, -ed, -ing
decompression
decongestant
decor
decorate, -rated, -rating
decoration
decorative, -ly
decorous, -ly
decorum
decorus decorous
decoy, -ed, -ing
decrease, -creased, -creasing
decree, -creed, -creeing

decreese — decrease
decrepit
decrepitude
decrese — decrease
decry, -cried, -crying
ded — dead
deden — deaden

> Look under di- if the word is not under **de-**.

dedicate, -cated, -cating
dedication
dedly — deadly
deduce, -duced, -ducing
deduct, -ed, -ing
deductible
deductibul — deductible
deduction
deed
deel — deal
deem, -ed, -ing
deen — dean
deep, -ly
deepen, -ed, -ing
deep freeze, -frozen, -freezing
deepwater
deer (animal)
deer — dear (loved)
de-escalate, -lated, -lating
def — deaf
deface, -faced, -facing
defacit — deficit
de facto
defamation
defamatory
defamatry — defamatory
defame, -famed, -faming
default, -ed, -ing
defaulter
defeat, -ed, -ing
defeatism
defeatist
defecate, -cated, -cating
defeckshun — defection
defect, -ed, -ing
defection
defective, -ly
defector
defeet — defeat
defen — deafen
defence
defend, -ed, -ing
defendant
defendent — defendant
defensable — defensible
defensible
defensibul — defensible
defensive, -ly
defer, -ferred, -ferring
deferance — deference
deference
deferense — deference
deferenshul — deferential
deferential, -ly

> For deff- words, look under **def-**.

defiance
defianse — defiance
defiant, -ly
deficiency, -cies
deficit
defience — defiance
defile, -filed, -filing
definate — definite
define, -fined, -fining
definishun — definition
definit — definite
definite, -ly
definition
definitive, -ly
defishency — deficiency
defishent — deficient
defisit — deficit
deflate, -flated, -flating
deflation
deflationary
defleckshun — deflection
deflect, -ed, -ing
deflection
defnite — definite
defoliant
defoliate, -ated, -ating
defoliation

deform, -ed, -ing
deformity, -ies
defraud, -ed, -ing
defrauder
defray, -ed, -ing
defreeze, -frozen, -freezing
defrord — defraud
defrost, -ed, -ing
deft, -ly
deftness
defunct
defuse, -fused, -fusing
defy, -fied, -fying
defyance — defiance
defyant — defiant

> Look under **di-** if the word is not under **de-**.

degeneracy
degenerasy — degeneracy
degenerate, -rated, -rating
degeneration
degradation
degrade, -graded, -grading
degree
degridation — degradation
dehidrate — dehydrate
dehydrate, -drated, -drating
dehydration
deifie — deify
deify, -fied, -fying
deign
deisel — diesel
deitee — deity
deity, -ties
dejeckshun — dejection
dejection
dekay — decay
delay, -ed, -ing
delecate — delicate
delectable, -bly
delectabul — delectable
delegate, -gated, -gating
delegation
delerious — delirious
deleshun — deletion
delete, -leted, -leting
deleterious, -ly
deletion
delfinium — delphinium
deli
deliberate, -rated, -rating
deliberately
deliberation
deliberative, -ly
delicacy, -cies
delicate, -ly
delicatessen
delicious, -ly
deliciouse — delicious
deligate — delegate
delight, -ed, -ing
delightful, -ly
delineate, -ed, -ing
delineation
deliniate — delineate
delinkwency — delinquency
delinkwent — delinquent
delinquancy — delinquency
delinquency
delinquent
delirious, -ly
delirium
delirius — delirious
delishus — delicious
delite — delight
deliteful — delightful
deliver, -ed, -ing
deliverance
deliverence — deliverance
delivery, -eries
dell
dellie

> For other **dell-** words, look under **del-**.

delood — delude
delphinium
delt — dealt
delta
delude, -luded, -luding
deluge, -uged, -uging
deluks — de luxe
delushun — delusion

delusion
delusive, -ly
delusory
delve, delved, delving
demagogue
demagogy
demand, -ed, -ing
demarcate, -cated, -cating
demarcation
demean, -ed, -ing
demeaner — demeanour
demeanour
demensha — dementia
demented, -ly
dementia
demerara
demerit
demigod
demilitarised zone
demise
demister
demo
demob
demobilisation
demobilise, -lised, -lising
democracy, -cies
democrasy — democracy
democrat
democratic, -ally
democratisation
demografy — demography
demographic, -ally
demography
demolish, -ed, -ing
demolishun — demolition
demolition
demolitionist
demon
demonic
demonology
demonstrable, -bly
demonstrabul — demonstrable
demonstrate, -strated, -strating
demonstrater — demonstrator
demonstration
demonstrator
demoralise, -lised, -lising

demote, -moted, -moting
demur, -murred, -murring (object)
demur — demure (coy)
demure, -murer, -murest (coy)
demure — demur (object)
den
dence — dense
dencher — denture
dencity — density
denem — denim
dengue
deni — deny
denial
denigrate, -grat.d, -grating
denigration
denim
denizen

> For denn- words, look under **den-**.

denominate, -nated, -nating
denomination
denominational, -ly
denominator
denotable
denotabul — denotable
denote, -noted, -noting
denounce, -nounced, -nouncing
denouncement
denownse — denounce
dense, denser, densest
densely
densitee — density
density
dent, -ed, -ing
dental
dentist
dentistry
denture
denude, -nuded, -nuding
denunciate, -ated, -ating
deny, denied, denying
deoderant — deodorant
deoderise — deodorise
deodorant
deodorise, -rised, -rising
deparcher — departure

depart, -ed, -ing
department
departmental, -ly
departure
depen — deepen
depend, -ed, -ing
dependable, -bly
dependabul — dependable
dependant (noun)
dependence
dependency, -cies
dependensy — dependency
dependent, -ly (adjective)
dependible — dependable
depickshun — depiction
depict, -ed, -ing
depiction
depilatery — depilatory
depilatory, -ries
depilatry — depilatory
depleshun — depletion
deplete, -pleted, -pleting
depletion
deploi — deploy
deplorable, -bly
deplorabul — deplorable
deplore, -plored, -ploring
deploy, -ed, -ing
deployment
depo — depot
deport, -ed, -ing
deportation
deportee
depose, -posed, -posing
deposit, -ed, -ing
deposishun — deposition
depositer — depositor
deposition
depositor
depository, -ries
depositry — depository
depot

> For **depp-** words, look under **dep-** .

depraved
depravity, -ties
deprecate, -cated, -cating
deprecation
depreciate, -ated, -ating
depreciation
depredation
depresherise — depressurise
depreshiate — depreciate
depreshun — depression
depresive — depressive
depresor — depressor
depress, -ed, -ing
depressant
depressent — depressant
depresshun — depression
depression
depressive, -ly
depressor
depressurise, -ised, -ising
depricate — deprecate
deprive, -prived, -priving
depth
deputation
depute, -puted, -puting
deputey — deputy
deputise, -tised, -tising
deputy, -ties

> Look under **di-** if the word is not under **de-** .

derail, -ed, -ing
derailment
derale — derail
derange, -ranged, -ranging
derby, -bies
deregister, -ed, -ing
derelickshun — dereliction
derelict
dereliction
derick — derrick
deride, -rided, -riding
derigible — dirigible
derishun — derision
derision
derisive, -ly
derivation
derivative
derive, -rived, -riving

dermatitis
dermatologist
dermatology

derogatery	derogatory

derogatory

derogatry	derogatory

derrick

For other **derr-** words, look under **der-**.

dert	dirt
derth	dearth
derty	dirty

dervish
desalination

desastrous	disastrous

descant
descend, -ed, -ing
descendant (noun)
descendent (adjective)
descent (down)

descent	dissent (differ)
desciple	disciple

describe, -scribed, -scribing

descripshun	description

description
descriptive, -ly
descry, -cried, -crying

desease	disease
deseat	deceit
deseave	deceive

desecrate, -crated, -crating
desecration
desegregate, -gated, -gating
desegregation

desel	diesel
deselerate	decelerate
Desember	December
desency	decency
desend	descend

desensitise, -tised, -tising

desent	decent
desent	descent
desentralise	decentralise
desershun	desertion

desert, deserts
desert, -ed, -ing (leave)

desert	dessert (food)

deserter
desertion
deserve, -served, -serving

desese	disease
desibel	decibel

de-sex, -sexed, -sexing

desicate	desiccate
desication	desiccation

desiccate, -cated, -cating
desiccation

deside	decide
desiduous	deciduous

design, -ed, -ing
designate, -nated, -nating
designation

desimal	decimal
desimate	decimate
desimul	decimal
desine	design
desipher	decipher

desirability
desirable, -bly

desirabul	desirable

desire, -sired, -siring
desirous

desirus	desirous

desist, -ed, -ing
desk

deskant	descant

Look under **di-** if the word is not under **de-**.

desolate, -lated, -lating
desolation

despach	despatch

despair, -ed, -ing

despare	despair

despatch, -ed, -ing

despensable	dispensable

desperado, -does, -dos
desperate, -ly
desperation
despicable, -bly

despicabul	despicable

despise, -spised, -spising
despite

despoil, -ed, -ing
despoliation
despondency
despondensy — despondency
despondent, -ly
despot
despotic
despotism
desprate — desperate
dessert (food)
dessert — desert (leave)
dessertspoon
destination
destine, -tined, -tining
destiny, -nies
destitushen — destitution
destitute
destitution
destroy, -ed, -ing
destroyer
destruckshun — destruction
destruct, -ed, -ing
destructible
destructibul — destructible
destruction
destructive, -ly
desultory
det — debt
detach, -ed, -ing
detachable
detachabul — detachable
detail, -ed, -ing
detain, -ed, -ing
detainee
detainment
detale — detail
detane — detain
deteckshun — detection
detect, -ed, -ing
detectable
detectabul — detectable
detection
detective
detector
detektive — detective
detenshun — detention
detention
deter, -terred, -terring
deter — debtor
deterent — deterrent
detergent
deterjent — detergent
deteriorate, -rated, -rating
deterioration
determinant
determination
determine, -mined, -mining
determinism
deterrence
deterrent
detest, -ed, -ing
detestable, -bly
detestabul — detestable
detestation
deth — death
detonate, -nated, -nating
detonation
detonator
detour, -ed, -ing
detrackshun — detraction
detract, -ed, -ing
detraction
detractor
detramental — detrimental
detriment
detrimental, -ly
detterent — deterrent
dettor — debtor
deuce
deutschmark
devaluation
devalue, -valued, -valuing
devastate, -tated, -tating
devastation
devel — devil
develop, -ed, -ing
develope — develop
developement — development
developer
development
developmental, -ly
deviance
deviancy
devianse — deviance

deviansy deviancy
deviant, -ly
deviate, -ated, -ating
deviation
device (thing)
device devise (plan)
devide divide
devil
devilish, -ly
devilment
devilry
devil's advocate
devious, -ly
devise, -vised, -vising (plan)
devise device (thing)
devius devious
devoid
devolushun devolution
devolution
devolutionary
devolve, -volved, -volving
Devonshire tea
devoshun devotion
devote, -voted, -voting
devotee
devotion
devour, -ed, -ing
devout, -ly
dew (water)
dew due (payable)
dewdrop
dewey dewy
dewy, dewier, dewiest
dexterity
dexterous, -ly
dexterus dexterous

Look under **de-** if the word is not under **di-**.

diabeetes diabetes
diabetes
diabetic
diabolic
diabolical, -ly
diadem
diafanus diaphanous
diafram diaphragm
diagnose, -nosed, -nosing
diagnosis, -ses
diagnostic
diagnostician
diagnostishun diagnostician
diagonal, -ly
diagram
diagrammatic, -ally
dial, dialled, dialling
dialect
dialectic
dialectician
dialectishun dialectician
dialise dialyse
dialisis dialysis
dialog dialogue
dialogue
dialyse, -lysed, -lysing
dialysis, -ses
diamante
diameter
diametrical, -ly
diamond
diaper
diaphanous, -ly
diaphanus diaphanous
diaphragm
diarea diarrhoea
diarist
diarrhoea
diary, -ries (book)
diary dairy (milk)
diatonic, -ally
diatribe
dibase debase
dibate debate
dibs
dice, diced, dicing
dicey
dichotomy, -mies
dicipul disciple
dick
dickens
dicky
dicotomy dichotomy
dicshun diction
dicshunry dictionary

dictate, -tated, -tating
dictation
dictator
dictatorial, -ly
  dictatoriul — dictatorial
  dictayshun — dictation
diction
dictionary, -aries
dictum, -ta, -tums
did
didactic, -ally
  diddel — diddle
diddle, -dled, -dling
diddler
  didel — diddle
didgeridoo
  didgit — digit
  didgitalis — digitalis
didn't (did not)
  didnt — didn't
  didul — diddle
die (singular of dice)
die, dies (tool)
die, died, dying (death)
  die — dye (colour)
dieback
die-casting
diehard
  dieing — dying (death)
  dieing — dyeing (colour)
  diernal — diurnal
diesel
diet, dieted, dieting
dietary
dietician
  dietishen — dietician

For dif- words,
look under diff-

differ, -ed, -ing
difference
  differense — difference
  differenshul — differential
different, -ly
differential, -ly
differentiate, -ated, -ating
differentiation

difficult
difficulty, -ties
diffidence
diffident, -ly
diffuse, -fused, -fusing
  diffushun — diffusion
diffusion
  diflect — deflect
dig, dug, digging
  diger — digger
digest, -ed, -ing
digestible
  digestibul — digestible
digestion
digger
diggings
digit
digital
digital computer
digitalis
dignify, -fied, -fying
dignitary, -taries
  dignitry — dignitary
dignity, -ties
digress, -ed, -ing
  digresshun — digression
digression
digs
dike
  dil — dill
dilapidated
dilapidation
dilate, -lated, -lating
dilation
dilatory
  dilatry — dilatory
  dilema — dilemma
dilemma
  dilatent — dilettante
dilettante, -ti
  dilibag — dillybag
  dilidali — dilly dally
diligence
  diligense — diligence
diligent, -ly
dill
dillybag

dilly dally
dilushen	dilution
dilution
diluvial
diluvian

> Look under de- if the word is not under di-.

dim, dimmed, dimming
dim, dimmer, dimmest
dime
dimenshun	dimension
dimension
dimensional, -ly
dimer	dimmer
diminish, -ed, -ing
diminishing returns
diminushen	diminution
diminution
diminutive, -ly
dimmer
dimple, -pled, -pling
dimpul	dimple
dim sim
dimwit
dimwitted, -ly
dinamic	dynamic
dinamite	dynamite
dinamo	dynamo
dinasty	dynasty
dine, dined, dining (eat)
dine	dyne (unit)
diner (eating)
diner	dinner (food)
ding
dingbats
ding-dong
dinghy, -ghies (boat)
dingie	dinghy
dingo, -goes, -gos
dingy, -gier, -giest (dull)
dingy	dinghy (boat)
dink, -ed, -ing
dinkum
dinky, dinkier, dinkiest
dinky-di
dinner (food)
dinner	diner (eating)
dinosaur
dinosoar	dinosaur
dinosore	dinosaur
dint, -ed, -ing
diocese
diode
diokside	dioxide
dioxide
dip, dipped, dipping
diper	diaper
diper	dipper
diphtheria
diphthong
diploma
diplomacy, -cies
diplomasy	diplomacy
diplomat
diplomatic, -ally
dipper
dipsomania
dipsomaniac
diptych
dire, direr, direst
direckshun	direction
direct, -ed, -ing
direct current
directer	director
direct evidence
direction
directional
direction-finder
directive
directly
director
directory, -ries
directry	directory
direct tax
dirge
dirigible
dirigibul	dirigible
dirk
dirt
dirtily
dirty, dirtied, dirtying
dirty, dirtier, dirtiest
disable, -bled, -bling

disabul disable
disabuse, -bused, -busing
disadvantage, -taged, -taging
disadvantageous, -ly
disadvantige disadvantage
disadvantij disadvantage
disafect disaffect
disaffect, -ed, -ing
disaffection
disagree, -greed, -greeing
disagreeable, -bly
disagreeableness
disagreeabul disagreeable
disagreement
disallow, -ed, -ing
disalow disallow
disapear disappear
disapoint disappoint
disappear, -ed, -ing
disappearance
disappearanse disappearance
disappoint, -ed, -ing
disappointment
disapproval
disapprove, -proved, -proving
disaprove disapprove
disaray disarray
disarray
disasociate disassociate
disassociate, -ated, -ating
disassociation
disaster
disastrous, -ly
disastrus disastrous
disatisfy dissatisfy
disavow, -ed, -ing
disavowal
disband, -ed, -ing
disbandment
disbeleif disbelief
disbeleive disbelieve
disbelief
disbelieve, -lieved, -lieving
disc
discard, -ed, -ing
disc brake
discern, -ed, -ing
discernible, -bly
discernibul discernible
discernment
discharge, -charged, -charging
disciple
disciplinarian
disciplinary
discipline, -plined, -plining
discipul disciple
disc jockey
disclaim, -ed, -ing
disclaimer
disclaym disclaim
disclose, -closed, -closing
disclosure
disco
discolor discolour
discolour, -ed, -ing
discolouration
discomfert discomfort
discomfit, -ed, -ing (thwart)
discomfit discomfort
discomfort, -ed, -ing (pain)

> Look under **de-** if the word is not under **di-**.

discompose, -posed, -posing
discomposhur discomposure
discomposure
disconcert, -ed, -ing
disconneckshun disconnection
disconnection
disconsert disconcert
disconsolate, -ly
discontent
discontinue, -tinued, -tinuing
discontinuity
discontinuous, -ly
discord
discordance
discordanse discordance
discordant, -ly
discotheque
discount, -ed, -ing
discourage, -raged, -raging
discouragement
discourse, -coursed, -coursing

discourteous, -ly
discourtesy
discourtius discourteous
discover, -ed, -ing
discoverer
discovery, -eries
discownt discount
discredit, -ed, -ing
discreditable, -bly
discreditabul discreditable
discreet (prudent)
discreet discrete (apart)
discrepancy
discrepansy discrepancy
discreshun discretion
discreshunry discretionary
discrete (apart)
discretion
discretionary
discribe describe
discriminate, -nated, -nating
discrimination
discriminator
discriminatory
discriminatry discriminatory
discripshun description
discriptive descriptive
discuridge discourage
discursive, -ly
discurtious discourteous
discus (sport)
discushun discussion
discuss, -ed, -ing (talk)
discussion
disdain, -ed, -ing
disdainful, -ly
dise dice
disease
diseased
diseave deceive
diseckshun dissection
disect dissect
disembark, -ed, -ing
disembarkation
disemble disembowel
disembodied
disembowel, -elled, -elling
diseminate disseminate
disenchant, -ed, -ing
disenchantment
disenshun dissension
disentangle, -gled, -gling
disentanglement
disentry dysentery
disern discern
disernibul discernible
disertation dissertation
disservise disservice
disesed diseased
disfaver disfavour
disfavour, -ed, -ing
disfiger disfigure
disfigure, -ed, -ing
disfranchise, -chised, -chising
disfranchisement
disgise disguise
disgorge, -gorged, -gorging
disgrace, -graced, -gracing
disgraceful, -ly
disgracefull disgraceful
disgruntled
disguise, -guised, -guising
disgust, -ed, -ing
disgustedly
dish, -ed, -ing
disharmoney disharmony
disharmony
disharten dishearten
dishcloth
dishearten, -ed, -ing
dishevelled
dishonest, -ly
dishonesty
dishonor dishonour
dishonour, -ed, -ing
dishonourabel dishonourable
dishonourable, -bly
dishonourabul dishonourable
disidence dissidence
disident dissident
disign design
disillusion, -ed, -ing
disillusionment
disilushun disillusion

disimilar dissimilar
disimulate dissimulate
disinclination
disincline, -clined, -clining
disinfect, -ed, -ing
disinfectant
disinfectent disinfectant
disinherit, -ed, -ing
disinheritance
disintegrate, -grated, -grating
disintegration
disinter, -terred, -terring
disinterment
disinterested, -ly
disintigrate disintegrate
disipate dissipate
disipation dissipation
disiple disciple
disiplinary disciplinary
disipline discipline
disjoint, -ed, -ing
disk
diskwalify disqualify
diskwiet disquiet
diskwolify disqualify
dislexia dyslexia
dislike, -liked, -liking
dislocate, -cated, -cating
dislocation
dislodge, -lodged, -lodging
disloge dislodge
disloyal, -ly
disloyalty, -ties
dismal, -ly
dismantel dismantle
dismantle, -tled, -tling
dismantul dismantle
dismay, -ed, -ing
dismember, -ed, -ing
dismemberment
dismisal dismissal
dismiss, -ed, -ing
dismissal
dismount, -ed, -ing
dismownt dismount
disobay disobey
disobedience
disobediense disobedience
disobedient, -ly
disobey, -ed, -ing
disoblige, -bliged, -bliging
disoloot dissolute
disoluble dissoluble
disolute dissolute
disolution dissolution
disolve dissolve
disonance dissonance
disonanse dissonance
disonant dissonant
disone disown
disoner dishonour
disonerable dishonourable
disonest dishonest

Look under de- if the word is not under **di-**.

disorder
disorderliness
disorderly
disorganisation
disorganise, -nised, -nising
disorientate, -tated, -tating
disown, -ed, -ing
dispair despair
disparage, -raged, -raging
disparagement
disparagingly
disparate, -ly
disparidge disparage
disparige disparage
disparity, -ties
dispashonate dispassionate
dispashunate dispassionate
dispassionate, -ly
dispatch, -ed, -ing
dispel, -pelled, -pelling
dispencable dispensable
dispencary dispensary
dispence dispense
dispensable
dispensabul dispensable
dispensary, -saries
dispensry dispensary
dispensation

dispenser
dispepsia dyspepsia
dispersal
disperse, -persed, -persing
dispershun dispersion
dispersion
dispicable despicable
dispirit, -ed, -ing
dispite despite
displace, -placed, -placing
displaceable
displaceabul displaceable
displacement
displacment displacement
displase displace
display, -ed, -ing
displease, -pleased, -pleasing
displeasure
displese displease
displeshur displeasure
displesure displeasure
disport, -ed, -ing
disposable
disposable income
disposabul disposable
dispose, -posed, -posing
disposeshun dispossession
disposess dispossess
disposishun disposition
disposition
dispossess, -ed, -ing
dispossession
disprin
disproporshun disproportion
disproportion
disproportionate, -ly
disprove, -proved, -proving
dispursal dispersal
dispurse dispurse
dispurshun dispersion
disputable, -bly
disputabul disputable
disputation
disputatious
dispute, -puted, -puting
disqualification
disqualify, -fied, -fying

disquiet, -ed, -ing
disquietude
disquite disquiet
disregard, -ed, -ing
disreguard disregard
disrepair
disrepare disrepair
disreputable, -bly
disreputible disreputable
disrespect
disrespectful, -ly
disrespectfull disrespectful
disrigard disregard
disrispect disrespect
disrobe, -robed, -robing
disrupshun disruption
disrupt, -ed, -ing
disruption
disruptive, -ly
dissapate dissipate
dissapear disappear
dissapoint disappoint
dissaprove disapprove
dissatisfaction
dissatisfy, -fied, -fying
disscord discord
dissect, -ed, -ing
dissemble, -bled, -bling
disseminate, -nated, -nating
dissemination
dissenshun dissension
dissension
dissent, -ed, -ing
dissenter
dissertation
disservicabul disserviceable
disservice
disserviceable
dissidence
dissidense dissidence
dissident, -ly
dissimilar, -ly
dissimilarity
dissimulate, -lated, -lating
dissimulation
dissipate, -pated, -pating
dissipation

dissociate, -ated, -ating
dissociation
disoloot — dissolute
dissoluble
dissolubul — dissoluble
dissolushun — dissolution
dissolute, -ly
dissolution
dissolvable
dissolvabul — dissolvable
dissolve, -solved, -solving
dissonance
dissonanse — dissonance
dissonant, -ly
disstil — distil
dissuade, -suaded, -suading
distaff
distance, distanced, distancing
distanse — distance
distant, -ly
distaste
distasteful, -ly
distastefull — distasteful
distemper, -ed, -ing
distend, -ed, -ing
distenshun — distention
distent — distant
distention
disterb — disturb
disterbance — disturbance
distil, -tilled, -tilling
distillate
distillation
distillery, -eries
distillry — distillery
distincshun — distinction
distinct, -ly
distinction
distinctive, -ly
distinguish, -ed, -ing
distinguishable, -bly
distingwish — distinguish
distink — distinct
distorshun — distortion
distort, -ed, -ing
distortion
distrackshun — distraction
distract, -ed, -ing
distraction
distraught, -ly
distrawt — distraught
distress, -ed, -ing
distressful, -ly
distressfull — distressful
distressingly
distress signal
distribushun — distribution
distribution
distributive, -ly
distributor
district
distrust, -ed, -ing
disturb, -ed, -ing
disturbance
disturbanse — disturbance
disunion
disunite, -nited, -niting
disunity, -ties
disurn — discern
disurnible — discernible
disuse, -used, -using
diswade — dissuade
diswashun — dissuasion
diswasive — dissuasive
ditch, -ed, -ing
ditch, -ditches
dither
dithering
dithery
dito — ditto
ditto
ditty, -ties
dity — ditty
divan
dive, dived, diving
dive-bomb
diver
diverge, -verged, -verging
divergence
divergense — divergence
divergent, -ly
diverse, -ly
divershun — diversion
diversification

diversify, -fied, -fying

Look under de- if the word is not under di-.

diversion
diversionary
diversionry diversionary
diversity, -ties
divert, -ed, -ing
divest, -ed, -ing
divestible
divide, -vided, -viding
dividend
divider
divination
divinatory
divine, -vined, -vining
divinely
diviner
divinitey divinity
divinity, -ties
diviser divisor
divishun division
divisible, -bly
divisibul divisible
divisif divisive
division
divisional, -ly
divisive, -ly
divisor
divorce, -vorced, -vorcing
divorcee
divorse divorce
divorsee divorcee
divulge, -vulged, -vulging
divulgence
divulgense divulgence
divvy, -vies
divvy, -vied, -vying
dixie
dizier dizzier
diziest dizziest
dizmal dismal
dizolve dissolve
dizy dizzy
dizzily
dizziness

dizzy, dizzied, dizzying
dizzy, dizzier, dizziest
do, did, done, doing
do doe (animal)
dob, dobbed, dobbing
dobbin
docile, -ly
docility
dock, -ed, -ing
docker
docket
dockit docket
dockyard
docter doctor
doctor, -ed, -ing
doctoral
doctorate
doctrin doctrine
doctrinair doctrinaire
doctrinaire
doctrinal, -ly
doctrine
doctrinul doctrinal
doctrut doctorate
document, -ed, -ing
documentary, -ries
documentation
documentry documentary
dodder, -ed, -ing
doddery
doddle
doder dodder
dodge, dodged, dodging
dodgem
dodger
dodgy, dodgier, dodgiest
dodje dodge
dodjy dodgy
dodo, -does, -dos
doe (animal)
doe dough (bread)
doer
does
doesn't (does not)
doesnt doesn't
dof doff
doff, -ed, -ing

doffin dauphin
dog, dogged, dogging
dogbox
dogerul doggerel
dogfight
dogfish
dogfite dogfight
doggerel
doggo
doghouse
dogleg
doglegged
dogma, -mas, -mata
dogmatic
dogmatical, -ly
dogmatism
dogmatist
dog paddle
dog paddul dog paddle
dog watch
doilie doily
doily, -lies
doings
dol dole (pay)
dol doll (toy)
dolar dollar
Dolby system
doldrums
dole, doled, doling (pay)
dole doll (toy)
doler dollar
dolerus dolorous
dolfin dolphin
doll, -ed, -ing (toy)
doll dole (pay)
dollar
doller dollar
dollop
dolly, dollies
dolomite
dolorous, -ly
dolorus dolorous
dolour
dolphin
dolt
doltish, -ly
domain
domane domain
dome
domed
domestic, -ally
domesticate, -cated, -cating
domestication
domesticity
domestisity domesticity
domicile, -ciled, -ciling
domiciliary
dominance
dominanse dominance
dominant, -ly
dominate, -nated, -nating
dominater dominator
domination
dominative
dominator
dominear domineer
domineer, -ed, -ing
dominent dominant
dominion
domino, -noes
domino theory
dominyun dominion
domisile domicile
domminate dominate
don, donned, donning
donate, -nated, -nating
donater donator
donation
donator
done
doner donor
dong, -ed, -ing
donkey, -keys
donkey vote
donkey's years
donky donkey
donnybrook
donor
don't (do not)
dont don't
donut
dooch douche
doodad
doodah

doodle, -dled, -dling
 doodul doodle
doom, -ed, -ing
doomsday
door
 door dour
doorjamb
doorknock, -ed, -ing
 doornock doorknock
 doosh douche
dope, doped, doping
dopey, dopier, dopiest
 dophin dauphin
 dore door
dormancy
 dormansy dormancy
dormant
 dormitery dormitory
 dormitry dormitory
 dorn dawn
dorsal
 dorsul dorsal
 dorter daughter
dory, -ries
dosage
dose, dosed, dosing
 dosier dossier
 dosige dosage
 dosije dosage
 dosile docile
 dosility docility
doss, -ed, -ing
dossier
dot, dotted, dotting
dotage
dote, doted, doting
 dotidge dotage
 dotije dotage
dotterel
dottle
dotty, dottier, dottiest
 doubel double
double, -led, -ling
double agent
double-barrelled
double bass
double-breasted
doublecross, -ed, -ing
double-dealing
double dissolution
double-dutch
double exposure
double-jointed
double standard
doublet
doublethink
double time
doubloon
doubt, -ed, -ing
doubtful, -ly
 doubtfull doubtful
doubtingly
doubtless, -ly
douche, douched, douching
 douel dowel
dough
doughnut
doughty, -tier, -tiest
dour, -ly
dourness
douse, doused, dousing
 dout doubt
 doutful doubtful
 doutless doubtless
 douty doughty
dove
dover
dovetail
 dovetale dovetail
 dow dhow (boat)
 dow doe (animal)
 dow dough (bread)
dowager
 dowdie dowdy
dowdily
dowdiness
dowdy, -dier, -diest
 dowery dowry
 dowey doughy
down, -ed, -ing
down-and-out
downcast
 downey downy
downfall

downfallen
downgrade, -graded, -grading
downhearted, -ly
downhill
down payment
downpipe
  downpore   downpour
downpour
downright, -ly
  downrite   downright
downstairs
downstream
down-to-earth
downtown
downtrodden
down-under
downward, -ly
downwards
  downwerds   downwards
downwind
downy, downier, downiest
  dowrie   dowry
dowry, -ries
dowse, dowsed, dowsing
  dowt   doubt
  dowtey   doughty
  dowtful   doubtful
  dowtless   doubtless
doxology, -gies
doyen
doze, dozed, dozing (sleep)
  doze   does
dozen, dozen, dozens
dozily
doziness
drab, drabber, drabbest
  draconean   draconian
draconian
draft, -ed, -ing (plan)
  draft   draught (air)
draft dodger
  draftey   draughty
  draftiness   draughtiness
  drafts   draughts
draftsman, -men
  drafty   draughty
drag, dragged, dragging

dragnet
dragonfly, -flies
dragoon, -ed, -ing
drag race
dragster
drain, -ed, -ing
drainage
  drainige   drainage
drainpipe
drake
dram
drama
dramatic, -ally
dramatics
dramatisation
dramatise, -tised, -tising
dramatist
drank
drape, draped, draping
draper
drapery, -eries
drastic, -ally
draught (air)
  draught   draft (plan)
draughtboard
draughthorse
draughts
draughtsman, -men
draughty, -tier, -tiest
draw, drew, drawn, drawing
drawback
drawbridge
  drawbrije   drawbridge
drawcard
drawer
drawing-pin
drawl, -ed, -ing
drawn
dray
dread, -ed, -ing
dreadful, -ly
  dreadfull   dreadful
  dreadnort   dreadnought
dreadnought
dream, dreamed, dreamt, dreaming
dreamer
dreamily

dreamless, -ly
dreamy, dreamier, dreamiest
drearily
dreariness
dreary, drearier, dreariest
dred — dread
dredful — dreadful
dredger
drednort — dreadnought
dreem — dream
drege — dredge
dregs
dreje — dredge
dremt — dreamt
drench, -ed, -ing
drerie — dreary
drery — dreary
dres — dress
dresie — dressy
dresige — dressage
dresmaker — dressmaker
dress, -ed, -ing
dressage
dress circle
dress down
dresser
dressmaker
dressmaking
dressy
drew
dri — dry
dribble, -bled, -bling
dribbler
dribbul — dribble
dribs and drabs
dribul — dribble
dried
drier
driest
drift, -ed, -ing
drifter
driftwood
drill, -ed, -ing
drily
drink, drunk, drinking
drinkable
drinkabul — drinkable

drink-driving
drive-in
drivel, -elled, -elling
driver
driveway
drizzle, -zled, -zling
drizzly
drizzul — drizzle
droll
drollery, -cries
drolly
dromedary, -daries
drone, droned, droning
drongo, -gos
drool, -ed, -ing
droop, -ed, -ing
droopy, -ier, -iest
drop, dropped, dropping
droplet
drop-out
dropper
dropsey — dropsy
dropsy
dross
drought
drousy — drowsy
drout — drought
drove, droved, droving
drover
drown, -ed, -ing
drowse, drowsed, drowsing
drowsey — drowsy
drowsily
drowsy, drowsier, drowsiest
drowt — drought
drub, drubbed, drubbing
drudge, drudged, drudging
drudgery, -cries
drug, drugged, drugging
druge — drudge
drugery — drudgery
drugstore
drum, drummed, drumming
drummer
drumstick
drunk
drunkard

drunken, -ly
drunkenness
dry, dried, drying
dry, drier, driest
dry cell
dry-clean
dryer
dryly
dryness
dual, -ly (two)
  dual   duel (fight)
dualism
duality
dub, dubbed, dubbing
  dubel   double
dubious, -ly
  dubius   dubious
  duble   double
  dubly   doubly
ducal, -ly
  duce   deuce
duck, -ed, -ing
duckbill
duckling
  ducktile   ductile
duco
duct
ductile
dud
dudgeon
due (owing)
  due   dew (water)
  duedrop   dewdrop
duel, -ed, -ing (fight)
  duel   dual (two)
  duelist   duellist
duellist
duet
duettist
  dufel   duffle
duffer
duffle
  dufful   duffle
dugong
dugout
duke
  dul   dull

dulcet
  duler   duller
  dulie   duly
dull
dullard
dullness
dully
  dulset   dulcet
duly
  dum   dumb
dumb, -ly
dumbbell
  dumbell   dumbbell
dumbfound, -ed, -ing
dumbness
  dumfound   dumbfound
dummy, -mies
dummy, -mied, -mying
  dumness   dumbness
dump, -ed, -ing
dumper
dumpling
  dumy   dummy
dun, dunned, dunning (demand)
  dun   done
dunce
dunderhead
dune
dung
dungaree
  dungen   dungeon
dungeon
  dunjun   dungeon
dunk, -ed, -ing
dunny
  dunse   dunce
duodenal
duodenum
dupe, duped, duping
  duplacate   duplicate
  duplecks   duplex
duplex
duplicate, -cated, -cating
duplication
duplicity, -ties
  duplisity   duplicity
durable, -bly

durability
durabul — durable
duration
duress
durge — dirge
durible — durable
during
durt — dirt
durtie — dirty
durty — dirty
dusk
duskiness
dusky, duskier, duskiest
dust, -ed, -ing
dustbin
duster
dustman, -men
dustpan
dust-up
dusty, dustier, dustiest
Dutch courage
Dutch curije — Dutch courage
duteous, -ly
dutiable
dutiabul — dutiable
dutifree — duty-free
dutiful, -ly
duty, -ties
duty-free
duv — dove
duvet
duvtail — dovetail
duvtale — dovetail

dux
duzen — dozen
dwarf, dwarfs, dwarves
dwarf, -ed, -ing
dwarfish, -ly
dwell, dwelt, dwelled, dwelling
dwindle, -dled, -dling
dworf — dwarf
dworves — dwarfs
dye, dyed, dyeing (colour)
dye — die (dead)
dyed — died (dead)
dyehard — diehard
dyeing — dying (death)
dyer
dyke, dyked, dyking
dynamic, -ally
dynamics
dynamism
dynamite, -mited, -miting
dynamo, -mos
dynasty, -ties
dyne (unit)
dyne — dine (eat)
dysentery
dysentry — dysentery
dysfunction
dyslectic
dyslexia
dyslexic
dyspepsia
dyspeptic
dystrophy

Ee

each
eagel eagle
eager
eagle
eaglehawk
eaglet
eal eel
ear
earache
eardrum
earfone earphone
earie eerie (weird)
earie eyrie (nest)
earing earring
early, -lier, -liest
earmark, -ed, -ing
earmuf earmuff
earmuff
earn, -ed, -ing
earner
earnest, -ly
earnestness
earnings
earphone
earring
earshot
earth, -ed, -ing
earthbound
earthen
earthenware
earthiness
earthling
earthly, -lier, -liest
earthquake
earthworm
earthy, earthier, earthiest
earwig
ease, eased, easing
easel
easement
easily
east
easten eastern
East End
Easter
easterly
eastern
eastward, -ly
eastwards
easiness
easy, easier, easiest
eat, ate, eaten, eating
eatable
eatabul eatable
eater
eau-de-Cologne
eaves
eavesdrop, -dropped, -dropping
eavesdropper
ebb, -ed, -ing
ebbony ebony
ebonie ebony
ebony, -onies
ebuliense ebullience
ebulient ebullient
ebullience
ebullient, -ly
eccentric, -ally
eccentricity, -ties
ecclesiastic
ecclesiastical, -ly
ecentric eccentric
ech each
echelon
echidna
echo, echoes
echo, echoed, echoing
eclair
eclare eclair
eclectic, -ally
eclesiastic ecclesiastic
eclipse, eclipsed, eclipsing
ecliptical, -ly
ecologey ecology
ecological, -ly

ecologist
ecology
economic
economical, -ly
economics
economise, -mised, -mising
economist
economy, -mies
ecosphere
ecosystem
 ecsema — eczema
 ecsentric — eccentric
ecstasy, -sies
ecstatic, -ally
ecumenical, -ly
ecumenism
eczema
edam
 edem — edam
eddy, eddies
eddy, eddied, eddying
edelweiss
edge, edged, edging
edger
edgeways
 edgey — edgy
edginess
edgy, -ier, -iest
edible
edibility
 edibul — edible
edict
 edie — eddy
edify, -fied, -fying
edit, -ed, -ing
 editer — editor
edition (book)
 edition — addition (add)
editor
editorial, -ly
educable
 educabul — educable
educate, -cated, -cating
education
educational, -ly
educationalist
educative
educator
Edwardian
 edy — eddy
 eeger — eager
 eegle — eagle
eel
 eenin — oenin
 eer — ear
eerie, eerier, eeriest (weird)
 eerie — eyrie (nest)
eerily
eeriness
 eermark — earmark

For ef- words, look under eff- .

efface, -faced, -facing
effect, -ed, -ing
effective, -ly
effectual, -ly
effeminacy
 effeminasy — effeminacy
effeminate, -ly
effervesce, -vesced, -vescing
effervescence
effervescent, -ly
 effervesent — effervescent
 effervess — effervesce
 effervessence — effervescence
efficacious, -ly
efficacy, -cies
 efficayshus — efficacious
efficiency, -cies
 efficiensy — efficiency
efficient, -ly
effigy, -gies
effloresce, -resced, -rescing
efflorescence
efflorescent
effluent
effluvium, -via, -viums
effort
effortless, -ly
effrontery, -teries
 effrontrey — effrontery
 effushun — effusion
effusion

effusive, -ly
efigy — effigy
eg — egg
egalitarian
egalitarianism
egg, -ed, -ing
eggcup
egghead
eggplant
eggshell
eggwhite
eggwite — eggwhite
Egipshun — Egyptian
Egipt — Egypt
egis — aegis
ego, egos
egocentric
egocentricity
egoism
egoist
egoistical, -ly
egosentric — egocentric
egotism
egotist
egotistical, -ly
egress
egret

> For egs- words, look under ex- .

Egypt
Egyptian
eiderdown
eight
eighteen
eighth
eightieth
eighty, eighties
eisteddfod
either
ejaculate, -lated, -lating
ejaculation
ejeckshun — ejection
eject, -ed, -ing
ejection
ejector
eke, eked, eking
eklipse — eclipse
eko — echo

> For eks- words, look under ex- .

ekumenical — ecumenical

> For ekw- words, look under eq- .

elaborate, -rated, -rating
elaborately
elaboration
elan
eland
elapse, elapsed, elapsing
elastic, -ally
elasticity
elastisitey — elasticity
elate, elated, elating
elbow, -ed, -ing
elbowroom
elder, -ly
elderberry, -ries
eldest
elecshun — election
elect, -ed, -ing
election
electioneer, -ed, -ing
elective
elector
electoral, -ly
electorate
electric
electrical, -ly
electrician
electricity
electrification
electrishun — electrician
electrisity — electricity
electrocardiogram
electrocardiograph
electrocushun — electrocution
electrocute, -cuted, -cuting
electrode
electrolysis
electromagnet
electromagnetic

electromotive
electron
electronic
electronic data processing
electronics
electroplate, -plated, -plating
electrostatic
elegance
  eleganse — elegance
elegant, -ly
  elegey — elegy
elegy, -gies
element
elemental, -ly
elementary
  elementry — elementary
  elementul — elemental
elephant
elephantine
  elevan — eleven
elevate, -vated, -vating
  elevater — elevator
elevation
elevator
eleven
eleventh
elf, elves
elfin
elfish
  elfs — elves
elicit, -ed, -ing (draw)
  elicit — illicit (wrong)
  elifant — elephant
  eliganse — elegance
  eligant — elegant
eligible, -bly
eligibility
  eligibul — eligible
  elikser — elixir
  eliment — element
  elimentry — elementary
eliminate, -nated, -nating
eliminator
  elipse — ellipse
  elipsis — ellipsis
  elishun — elision
elision
elite
elitism
elitist
  elivate — elevate
elixir
Elizabethan
elk
ellipse
ellipsis, -ses
elliptical, -ly
  ellite — elite
elm
  elocushun — elocution
elocution
elocutionist
  elokwence — eloquence
elongate, -gated, -gating
elongation
elope, eloped, eloping
elopement
eloper
  eloquant — eloquent
eloquence
  eloquense — eloquence
eloquent, -ly
else
  elsewere — elsewhere
elsewhere
  elswhere — elsewhere
elucidate, -dated, -dating
elucidation
elucidatory
elude, eluded, eluding (evade)
  elude — allude (say)
  elusidate — elucidate
elusive, -ly
elves
emaciate, -ated, -ating
emaciation
emanate, -nated, -nating
emanation
emancipate, -pated, -pating
emancipation
emancipator
emancipist
  emanent — eminent
  emansipate — emancipate

emasculate, -lated, -lating
emasculation
emasiate emaciate
embalm, -ed, -ing
embankment
embarass embarrass
embargo, -goes
embargo, -goed, -going
embark, -ed, -ing
embarkation
embarrass, -ed, -ing
embarrassment
embassy, -sies
embed, -bedded, -bedding
embellish, -ed, -ing
embellishment
ember
embezel embezzle
embezzle, -zled, -zling
embezzlement
embitter, -ed, -ing
emblazon, -ed, -ing
emblem
emblematic, -ally
embodie embody
embodiment
embody, -bodied, -bodying
embolism
embos emboss
emboss, -ed, -ing
embrace, -braced, -bracing
embraceable
embrase embrace
embrio embryo
embroider, -ed, -ing
embroidery, -deries
embroil, -ed, -ing
embryo, -os
embryonic
emend, -ed, -ing
emerald
emerey emery
emerge, emerged, emerging
emergence
emergency
emergense emergence
emergensy emergency

emergent
emerie emery
emeritus
emery
emetic
emfasema emphysema
emfasise emphasise
emfatic emphatic
emigrant
emigrate, -grated, -grating
eminence (high)
eminense eminence
eminent, -ly (known)
eminent imminent
(near)
emisary emissary
emishun emission
emissary, -saries
emission
emit, emitted, emitting
emitter
emollient
emolument
emoshun emotion
emotion
emotional, -ly
emotionalism
emotionless, -ly
emotive, -ly
empanel, -elled, -elling
empathy
emperer emperor
emperor
emphasis, -ses
emphasise, -sised, -sising
emphatic, -ally
emphysema
empire
empirical, -ly
empiricism
empiricist
empirisism empiricism
employ, -ed, -ing
employable
employabul employable
employee
employer

employment
emporium, -poriums, -poria
empower, -ed, -ing
empress
emptie empty
emptiness
empty, -tied, -tying
empty, -tier, -tiest
emrald emerald
emu
emulate, -lated, -lating
emulation
emulshun emulsion
emulsion
enable, -bled, -bling
enabul enable
enact, -ed, -ing
enactment
enamel, -elled, -elling
enameller
enamer enamour
enamour, -ed, -ing
encapsulate, -lated, -lating
encephalitis
encephalogram
enchant, -ed, -ing
enchantment
enciclical encyclical
enciclopedia encyclopaedia
encircle, -cled, -cling
encirclement
encircul encircle
enclave
enclose, -closed, -closing
encloshur enclosure
enclosure
encode, -coded, -coding
encompass, -ed, -ing
encore, -cored, -coring
encounter
encownter encounter
encourage, -raged, -raging
encouragement
encroach, -ed, -ing
encumber, -ed, -ing
encumbrance
encumbranse encumbrance

encyclical
encyclopaedia
encyclopaedic
end, -ed, -ing
endanger, -ed, -ing
endear, -ed, -ing
endearment
endeavour, -ed, -ing
endeer endear
endemic, -ally
endever endeavour
endive
endless, -ly
endorse, -dorsed, -dorsing
endorsement
endow, -ed, -ing
endowment
endurable, -bly
endurance
enduranse endurance
endure, -dured, -during
endurible endurable
endways
enema
enemy, -mies
energetic, -ally
energy, -gies
enervate, -vated, -vating
enervative
enfeeble, -bled, -bling
enfeebul enfeeble
enfold, -ed, -ing
enforce, -forced, -forcing
enforceable
enforceabul enforceable
enforcement
enforcer
enforse enforce
enforsibul enforceable
enfranchise, -chised, -chising
engage, -gaged, -gaging
engagement
engajment engagement
engender, -ed, -ing
engine
enginear engineer
engineer, -ed, -ing

English
engrave, -graved, -graving
engraver
engross, -ed, -ing
engulf, -ed, -ing
enhance, -hanced, -hancing
enhancement
enhanse enhance
enigma
enigmatic, -ally
enima enema
enimy enemy
enithing anything
eniwhere anywhere
enjender engender
enjin engine
enjineer engineer
enjoi enjoy
enjoiabul enjoyable
enjoiment enjoyment
enjoin, -ed, -ing
enjoy, -ed, -ing
enjoyable, -bly
enjoyabul enjoyable
enjoyment
enlarge, -larged, -larging
enlargement
enlarger
enlighten, -ed, -ing
enlightenment
enlist, -ed, -ing
enlistment
enliten enlighten
enliven, -ed, -ing
en masse
enmity, -ties
ennoble, -bled, -bling
enoblement
ennui
enobul ennoble
enormity, -ties
enormous, -ly
enormus enormous
enough
enquire, -quired, -quiring
enquirer
enquiry, -ries

enrage, -raged, -raging
enrap enwrap
enrapcher enrapture
enrich, -ed, -ing
enrichment
enrol, -rolled, -rolling
enrolment
en route
ensconce, -ed, -ing
ensconse ensconce
ensemble
ensembul ensemble
ensercul encircle
enshure ensure
ensign
ensine ensign
ensue, -sued, -suing
en suite
ensure, -sured, -suring
ensweet en suite
entail, -ed, -ing
entale entail
entangle, -gled, -gling
entanglement
entangul entangle
entente
enter, -ed, -ing
enteritis
enterprise
enterprising, -ly
entertain, -ed, -ing
entertainer
entertainment
entertane entertain
enthral, -led, -ling
enthuse, -thused, -thusing
enthusiasm
enthusiast
enthusiastic, -ally
entice, -ticed, -ticing
entire, -ly
entirety
entise entice
entitel entitle
entitey entity
entitle, -tled, -tling
entitlement

Word	Correct spelling
entity, -ties	
entourage	
entouraje	entourage
entrails	
entrance	
entranse	entrance
entrant	
entre	entree
entreat, -ed, -ing	
entreaty, -treaties	
entree	
entreet	entreat
entreprener	entrepreneur
entrepreneur	
entrepreneurial	
entrust, -ed, -ing	
entry, -tries	
enuff	enough
enumerable	
enumerabul	enumerable
enumerate, -rated, -rating	
enumeration	
enunciate, -ated, -ating	
enunciation	
enunsiate	enunciate
enuresis	
envelop, -ed, -ing (wrap up)	
envelope (letter)	
enviable, -bly	
enviabul	enviable
envie	envy
envious, -ly	
envirament	environment
environment	
environmental, -ly	
environmentalism	
environmentalist	
environs	
envisage, -aged, -aging	
envisidge	envisage
envius	envious
envoi	envoy
envoy	
envy, -vies	
envy, envied, envying	
enwrap, enwrapped, enwrapping	
enzime	enzyme

Word	Correct spelling
enzyme	
epaulet	
epawlet	epaulet
ephemeral, -ly	
epic	
epical, -ly	
epicenter	epicentre
epicentre	
epicure	
epicurean	
epidemic	
epidemical, -ly	
epidermal	
epidermis	
epigraf	epigraph
epigram	
epigrammatic, -ally	
epigraph	
epilepsy	
epileptic	
epilog	epilogue
epilogue	
episcopacy, -cies	
episcopal	
Episcopalian	
episode	
episodic, -ally	
epissel	epistle
epitaph	
epitarf	epitaph
epithet	
epitome	
epitomise, -mised, -mising	
epoch	
epochal	
epok	epoch
eppigram	epigram
equable, -bly	
equal, equalled, equalling	
equalise, -lised, -lising	
equality, -ties	
equanimity, -ties	
equate, equated, equating	
equater	equator
equation	
equator	
equatorial	

Word	Correct spelling
equestrian	
equidistant, -ly	
equilateral	
equilibrium	
equine	
equinocks	equinox
equinoctial	
equinox	
equip, equipped, equipping	
equipment	
equitable, -bly	
equitabul	equitable
equity, -ties	
equivalence	
equivalense	equivalence
equivocal, -ly	
equivocate, -cated, -cating	
equivocation	
era	
eradicable, -bly	
eradicate, -cated, -cating	
eradication	
erand	errand
erant	errant
erase, erased, erasing	
eraser	
erasion	
erata	errata
eratic	erratic
erayshure	erasure
erban	urban
erbane	urbane
erbanise	urbanise
erbanity	urbanity
erchun	urchin
erecshun	erection
erect, -ed, -ing	
erection	
erer	error
erge	urge
ergent	urgent
ergonomics	
erie	eerie (weird)
erie	eyrie (nest)
erk (rank)	
erk	irk (bore)
erksome	irksome

Word	Correct spelling
erl	earl
erly	early
ermine	
ern	earn (money)
ern	urn (vessel)
ernest	earnest
erode, eroded, eroding	
erogenous	
eroneous	erroneous
eror	error
Eros	
eroshun	erosion
erosion	
erotic, -ally	
erotica	
eroticism	
erotisism	eroticism
err, -ed, -ing	
errand	
erratic, -ally	
erratum, -ta	
erroneous, -ly	
erronius	erroneous
error	
errupt	erupt
ersatz	
erstwhile	
erth	earth
erthen	earthen
erthly	earthly
erudishun	erudition
erudition	
erupt, -ed, -ing	
eruption	
erwing	earwig
esay	essay
escalate, -lated, -lating	
escalater	escalator
escalation	
escalator	
escapade	
escape, -caped, -caping	
escapee	
escaper	
escapement	
escapism	
escapist	

escarpment
eschew, -ed, -ing
  eschue   eschew
escort, -ed, -ing
escutcheon
  escutshun   escutcheon
  esel   easel
  esence   essence
  esenshul   essential
Eskimo, -mos
  eskwire   esquire
esky
  esophagus   oesophagus
esoteric, -ally
especial, -ly
  espeshul   especial
espionage
esplanade
  esplanaid   esplanade
espousal
espouse, -poused, -pousing
  espowse   espouse
espresso
esprit
espy, -pied, -pying
esquire
essay, -ed, -ing (try)
  essay   assay (analyse)
essayist
essence
  essense   essence
  essenshul   essential
essential, -ly
establish, -ed, -ing
establishment
estate
esteem, -ed, -ing
  Ester   Easter
  estern   eastern
estimable, -bly
  estimabul   estimable
estimate, -mated, -mating
estimation
estimator
estrange, estranged, estranging
  estrogen   oestrogen
estuary, -aries

et cetera
etch, -ed, -ing
etcher
eternal, -ly
eternity, -ties
ether
  ether   either
ethereal, -ly
ethic
ethical, -ly
ethics
ethnic, -ally
ethnology
ethos
  etiket   etiquette
  etimology   etymology
  etiquet   etiquette
etymology, -gies
eucalyptus, -tuses, -ti
euchre, -chred, -chring
Euclid

For euf- words,
look under **euph-** .

eugenics
  Euklid   Euclid
eulogise, -gised, -gising
eulogy, -gies
eunuch
euphemism
euphemistic, -ally
euphony, -nies
euphoria
euphoric
  Eurapean   European
  Eurashun   Eurasian
Eurasian
eureka flag
eurhythmics
  eurithmics   eurhythmics
European
euthanasia
evacuate, -uated, -uating
evacuation
evacuee
evade, evaded, evading
evaluate, -ated, -ating

evaluation
evangalist evangelist
evangelical, -ly
envangelicul evangelical
evangelism
evangelist
evaperate evaporate
evaporate, -rated, -rating
evaporation
evasion
evasive, -ly
eve
evedence evidence
even, -ed, -ing
evenly
evenness
event
eventual, -ly
eventuality, -ties
eventuate, -ated, -ating
ever
evergreen
everlasting, -ly
every
everybody
everyday
everyone
everything
everywhere
eves eaves
evict, -ed, -ing
eviction
evictor
evictshun eviction
evidence, -denced, -dencing
evident, -ly
evil, -ly
evince, evinced, evincing
evinse evince
eviscerate, -rated, -rating
evocative
evoke, evoked, evoking
evolushun evolution
evolution
evolve, evolved, evolving
evolvement
evry every
ewe (sheep)
ewe yew (tree)
exacerbate, -bated, -bating
exacerbation
exackly exactly
exact, -ed, -ing
exactitude
exactly
exactness
exagerate exaggerate
exaggerate, -rated, -rating
exaggeration
exalt, -ed, -ing
exaltation
examination
examine, -ined, -ining
examiner
example
exampul example
exaserbate exacerbate
exasperate, -rated, -rating
exasperation
excavate, -vated, -vating
excavation
excavator
exceed, -ed, -ing (surpass)
exceed accede (agree)
exceedingly
excel, -celled, -celling
excell excel
excellence
excellency, -cies
excellense excellence
excellent, -ly
excepshun exception
except, -ed, -ing
exception
exceptional, -ly
excerpt
excess
excessive, -ly
exchange, -changed, -changing
exchangeable
exchequer
excise, -cised, -cising
excishun excision
excision

excitable, -bly
excitabul excitable
excite, -cited, -citing
excitement
exclaim, -ed, -ing
exclamation
exclamatory
exclamatry exclamatory
exclude, -luded, -luding
exclushun exclusion
exclusion
exclusive, -ly
excommunicate, -cated, -cating
excommunication
excrement
excrescence
excreshun excretion
excressense excrescence
excreta
excrete, -creted, -creting
excretion
excretory
excruciating, -ly
excursion
excusable, -bly
excuse, -cused, -cusing
execrable, -bly
execrate, -crated, -crating
execushun execution
execute, -cuted, -cuting
execution
executioner
executive
executor
exemplary
exemplify, -fied, -fying
exempshun exemption
exempt
exemptible
exemptibul exemptible
exemption
exercise, -cised, -cising
exershun exertion
exert, -ed, -ing
exertion
ex gratia
exhalation
exhale, -haled, -haling
exhaust, -ed, -ing
exhaustion
exhaustive, -ly
exhibishun exhibition
exhibit, -ed, -ing
exhibition
exhibitionism
exhibitionist
exhibitor
exhilarate, -rated, -rating
exhilaration
exhort, -ed, -ing
exhortation
exhume, -humed, -huming
exhumation
exibit exhibit
exigency, -cies
exigensy exigency
exile, -iled, -iling
exist, -ed, -ing
existence
existense existence
existenshul existential
existent
existential, -ly
existentialism
existentialist
exit
exodus
exonerate, -rated, -rating
exorbitant, -ly
exorcise, -cised, -cising
exorcism
exorcist
exorsism exorcism
exorst exhaust
exort exhort
exortashun exhortation
exoteric, -ally
exotic, -ally
expand, -ed, -ing
expanse
expanshun expansion
expansion
expansive, -ly
expansiveness

expatiate, -ated, -ating
expatriate, -ated, -ating
expatriation
expect, -ed, -ing
expectancy, -cies
expectant, -ly
expectation
expectorant
expectorate, -rated, -rating
expediency
expediensy — expediency
expedient, -ly
expedishun — expedition
expedite, -dited, -diting
expedition
expeditionary
expeditious, -ly
expeditiousness
expel, -pelled, -pelling
expend, -ed, -ing
expendable
expendicher — expenditure
expenditure
expense
expensive, -ly
experience, -enced, -encing
experiment, -ed, -ing
experimental, -ly
experimentation
expert, -ly
expertise
expiate, -ated, -ating
expiation
expiration
expire, -pired, -piring
expiry, -ries
explain, -ed, -ing
explanation
explanatory
explane — explain
explanetry — explanatory
expletive
explicable, -bly
explicabul — explicable
explicate, -cated, -cating
explicit, -ly
explisit — explicit
explode, -ploded, -ploding
exploit, -ed, -ing
exploitation
exploration
exploratory
explore, -plored, -ploring
explorer
explosion
explosive, -ly
exponent
exponential, -ly
export, -ed, -ing
exporter
exposay — exposé
expose, -posed, -posing
exposé
exposhur — exposure
expostulate, -lated, -lating
exposure
expound, -ed, -ing
expreshun — expression
expresive — expressive
express, -ly
express, -ed, -ing
expression
expressionism
expressionist
expressive, -ly
expresso — espresso
expressway
expropriate, -ated, -ating
expropriation
expulsion
expunction
expunge, -punged, -punging
expurgate, -gated, -gating
expurgation
exquisite, -ly
exquisiteness
exseed — exceed
exsel — excel
exselence — excellence
exserpt — excerpt
ex-serviceman, -men
extant
extasy — ecstasy
extatic — ecstatic

extemporaneous, -ly
extempore
extend, -ed, -ing
extendible
  extendibul — extendible
  extenshun — extension
extension
extensive, -ly
extent
extenuate, -ated, -ating
extenuation
  exterier — exterior
exterior
exterminate, -nated, -nating
extermination
exterminator
external, -ly
extinct
extinction
  extingshun — extinction
extinguish, -ed, -ing
extinguisher
extol, -tolled, -tolling
  extorshun — extortion
extort, -ed, -ing
extortion
extortionate, -ly
extortioner
extortionist
extra
  extracshun — extraction
extract, -ed, -ing
extractable
extraction
extracurricular
  extradishun — extradition
extradite, -dited, -diting
extradition
extramarital
extraneous, -ly
extraordinary
extrapolate, -ated, -ating
extrapolation
extrasensory
extraterrestrial
extravagance
extravagancy
extravagant, -ly
extravaganza
  extravert — extrovert
  extremast — extremist
extreme, -tremer, -tremest
extremely
extremism
extremist
extremity, -ties
extricate, -cated, -cating
extrication
extrovert
extrude, -truded, -truding
extrusion
exuberance
  exuberanse — exuberance
exuberant, -ly
exude, -uded, -uding
exult, -ed, -ing
exultant, -ly
exultation
  exume — exhume
eye, eyed, eyeing
eyeball
eyebrow
eyelash
eyelet
eyelid
eyesight
eyesore
eyetooth, -teeth
eyewash
eyewitness, -nesses
eyrie (nest)
  eyrie — eerie (weird)
  eze — ease
  ezel — easel
  ezy — easy

Ff

fable, -bled, -bling
fabric
fabricate, -cated, -cating
fabrication
fabulous, -ly
fabulus fabulous
facade
face, faced, facing
faceless
facelift
faceshus facetious
facet, -eted, -eting
facetious, -ly
facia (panel)
facia fascia (band)
facial, -ly
facile, -ly
facilitate, -tated, -tating
facility, -ties
facist fascist
facsimile, -led, -leing
fact
faction
factionalism
factor
factory, -ries
factotum
factual, -ly
faculty, -ties
fad
faddish, -ly
fade, faded, fading
faeces
fag, fagged, fagging
faggot
fagot faggot
Fahrenheit
fail, -ed, -ing
fail-safe
failure
failyer failure
faim fame
faimus famous
fain (gladly)
fain feign (pretend)
faint, -ed, -ing (weak)
faint feint (pretend)
fair, -ly (honest)
fair fare (price)
fair game
fairway
fair-weather
fairwell farewell
fairy, -ries
fairytale
fait fate
faitful fateful
fait accompli
faith
faithful, -ly
faith-healing
fake, faked, faking
faker (fraud)
fakir (holy)
falacy fallacy
falanx phalanx
falasius fallacious
falasy fallacy
falcon
falconry
fale fail
falesy fallacy
falible fallible
falic phallic
fall, fell, fallen, falling
fallacious, -ly
fallacy, -cies
fallible, -bly
fallibul fallible
fallout
fallow
fallus phallus
falow fallow
false, falser, falsest
falsehood

falsetto, -tos
falsification
falsify, -fied, -fying
falt — fault
falter, -ed, -ing
falteringly
falure — failure
falus — phallus
fame, famed, faming
familial
familiar, -ly
familiarisation
familiarise, -rised, -rising
familiarity, -ties
familier — familiar
family, -lies
famine
famished
famous, -ly
famus — famous
fan, fanned, fanning
fanatic
fanatical, -ly
fanaticism
fancier
fanciful, -ly
fancy, -cies
fancy, -cied, -cying
fancy, -cier, -ciest
fane — fain (glad)
fane — feign (pretend)
fanfair — fanfare
fanfare
fang
fanlight
fansie — fancy
fansiful — fanciful
fansy — fancy
fantam — phantom
fantasey — fantasy
fantasia
fantasise, -sised, -sising
fantastic, -ally
fantasy, -ies
fantom — phantom
far, farther, farthest
far, further, furthest

faranyx — pharynx
faraway
farce
fare, fared, faring (get on)
fare — fair (honest)
farenhite — Fahrenheit
farewell
far-fetched
farm, -ed, -ing
farmacist — pharmacist
farmacy — pharmacy
farmasist — pharmacist
farmer
farmstead
farrago, -goes
farrier
farrow, -ed, -ing
far-sighted
farther (away)
farther — father (parent)
farthing
faryngitis — pharyngitis
farytale — fairytale
fascia, fasciae (band)
fascia — facia (panel)
fascinate, -nated, -nating
fascination
fascism
fascist
fase — face
fase — phase
fasen — fasten
faset — facet
fasetious — facetious
fasha — facia (panel)
fasha — fascia (band)
fashal — facial
fashion, -ed, -ing
fashionable, -bly
fashism — fascism
fashist — fascist
fashon — fashion
fashonabul — fashionable
fasilitate — facilitate
fasility — facility
fasinate — fascinate
fasination — fascination

fast, -ed, -ing
fasten, -ed, -ing
fastener
fastidious, -ly
fastidiousness

fastidius	fastidious

fat, fatted, fatting
fat, fatter, fattest
fatal, -ly
fatalism
fatalist
fatalistic, -ally
fatality, -ties
fate (destiny)

fate	fete (fair)

fated
fateful, -ly

faten	fatten

father, -ed, -ing (parent)

father	farther (away)

Father Christmas
fatherhood
father-in-law, fathers-in-law
fatherland
fatherly
fathom, -ed, -ing
fathomable
fatigue, -tigued, -tiguing
fatten, -ed, -ing
fattener
fatty, -tier, -tiest
fatuous, -ly
faucet
fault, -ed, -ing
faultless, -ly
faulty, faultier, faultiest
faun (god)

faun	fawn (deer)

fauna
faux pas

faver	favour
faverite	favourite
faveritism	favouritism
favorite	favourite

favour, -ed, -ing
favourable, -bly
favourite
favouritism
fawn, -ed, -ing (deer)

fawn	faun (god)
fawna	fauna
faysha	facia (panel)
faysha	fascia (band)
fayshal	facial

faze, fazed, fazing

feacher	feature

fealty, -ties
fear, -ed, -ing
fearful, -ly

fearfull	fearful

fearless, -ly
fearsome, -ly
feasible, -bly
feasibility

feasibul	feasible

feast, -ed, -ing
feat (act)

feat	feet (body)

feather, -ed, -ing
featherbed, -bedded, -bedding
featherweight
feathery
feature, -tured, -turing
febrile
February

Febuary	February
feces	faeces
fech	fetch

feckless, -ly
fecund
fecundity

fedaration	federation

federal, -ly
federalism
federalist
federate, -rated, -rating
federation
fee
feeble, -bler, -blest

feebul	feeble

feebleness
feebly
feed, fed, feeding
feedback

feeder	
feel, felt, feeling	
feeld	field
feeler	
feend	fiend
feest	feast
feet (body)	
feet	feat (act)
feetul	foetal
feetus	foetus
feign, -ed, -ing (pretend)	
feign	fain (glad)
feild	field
feind	fiend
feint, -ed, -ing (pretend)	
feint	faint (weak)
fekund	fecund
fekundity	fecundity
felicitate, -tated, -tating	
felicitation	
felicitous, -ly	
felicity, -ties	
feline, -ly	
felisitous	felicitous
felisity	felicity
fell	
fellow	
fellowship	
felon	
felonious, -ly	
felony, -nies	
felow	fellow
felt	
female	
feminine, -ly	
femininity	
feminism	
femme fatale	
femur	
fence, fenced, fencing	
fend, -ed, -ing	
fender	
fenix	phoenix
fennel	
fenomenon	phenomenon
fenominal	phenomenal
fense	fence

fer	fir (tree)
fer	fur (pelt)
feral	
feret	ferret
ferie	ferry
ferl	furl
ferlong	furlong
ferment, -ed, -ing	
fermentation	
fern	
fernery, -ries	
ferny	
fernice	furnace
fernish	furnish
ferniture	furniture
ferocious, -ly	
ferocity	
feroshus	ferocious
ferret, -ed, -ing	
ferrous	
ferrule, -ruled, -ruling (tip)	
ferrule	ferule (rod)
ferry, -ries	
ferry, -ried, -rying	
ferryboat	
ferther	further
ferthest	furthest
fertile, -ly	
fertilisation	
fertilise, -lised, -lising	
fertiliser	
fertility	
ferule, -ruled, -ruling (rod)	
ferule	ferrule (tip)
fervency	
fervent, -ly	
ferver	fervour
fervid, -ly	
fervour	
fery	ferry
fesant	pheasant
fesible	feasible
festal, -ly	
fester, -ed, -ing	
festival	
festive, -ly	
festivity, -ties	

Entry	Correct spelling
festoon, -ed, -ing	
feta	fetta (cheese)
fetch, -ed, -ing	
fete, feted, feting (fair)	
fete	fate (destiny)
feter	fetter (chain)
fether	feather
fetid, -ly	
fetish	
fetishism	
fetlock	
fetta (cheese)	
fetter, -ed, -ing (chain)	
fettle	
fettler	
feud, -ed, -ing	
feudal, -ly	
feudalism	
fever	
fevered	
feverish, -ly	
few	
fewd	feud
fewdal	feudal
fey, -ly	
fez, fezzes	
fezant	pheasant
fial	file (papers)
fial	phial (tube)
fiance (man)	
fiancee (woman)	
fiansey	fiancee
fiasco, -cos	
fib, fibbed, fibbing	
fibber	
fiber	fibber
fiber	fibre
fibre	
fibreglass	
fibro	
fibrositis	
fibrous, -ly	
fibrus	fibrous
fibula	
fickle, -kly	
fickleness	
ficshun	fiction
fiction	
fictional, -ly	
fictishus	fictitious
fictitious, -ly	
fiddle, -dled, -dling	
fiddler	
fiddlesticks	
fiddly	
fidelity, -ties	
fidget, -ed, -ing	
fidgety	
fiddle	fiddle
field, -ed, -ing	
fielder	
fieldsman, -men	
fiend	
fiendish, -ly	
fierce, fiercer, fiercest	
fiercely	
fierceness	
fierey	fiery
fierse	fierce
fiery, fierier, fieriest	
fiesta	
fife	
fifteen	
fifteenth	
fifth	
fiftieth	
fifty	
fifty-fifty	
fig	
figer	figure
figerative	figurative
figet	fidget
fight, fought, fighting	
fighter	
figment	
figuration	
figurative, -ly	
figure, -ured, -uring	
figurehead	
figurine	
Fiji	
Fijian	
fiksation	fixation
fiksative	fixative

fikscher	fixture

> For other fila- words, look under **phila-** .

filch, -ed, -ing
filcher
file, filed, filing (paper)

file	phial (tube)
filet	fillet

filial, -ly
filibuster

filie	filly

filigree

filip	fillip

Filipino

Filippines	Philippines
filistine	philistine

fill, -ed, -ing
filler
fillet
fillip
filly, -lies
film, -ed, -ing
filmy, filmier, filmiest

> For filo- words, look under **philo-** .

filter, -ed, -ing
filth
filthily
filthiness
filthy, filthier, filthiest
filtrate, -trated, -trating
filtration

fily	filly

fin, finned, finning
final, -ly (end)
finale (last part)
finalisation
finalise, -lised, -lising
finalist
finality, -ties
finance, -nanced, -nancing
financial, -ly
financier

finanse	finance

finch, -ches
find, found, finding
finder
fine, fined, fining
fine, finer, finest
finely
fineness
finery, -ries
finesse, -nessed, -nessing
finetuner
finger
fingernail
fingerprint
fingertip
finical, -ly
finicky
finis (conclusion)
finish, -ed, -ing
finisher
finite, -ly
fiord
fir (tree)

fir	fur (pelt)

fire, fired, firing
firearm
firebreak
fire-escape
fire-extinguisher
firefly, -flies
fireman, -men
fireplace
fireproof
firescreen
fireworks
firm, -ed, -ing
firmament
first, -ly
first-hand
first-past-the-post
fiscal, -ly
fish, fishes, fish
fisherman, -men
fishery, -ries
fish-eye lens
fishmonger
fish-net
fishplate

fishun	fission

fishy, fishier, fishiest
fisile fissile
fision fission

> For other fisi- words, look under **physi-**.

fiskle fiscal
fissile
fission
fissure, -sured, -suring
fist
fisticuff
fistula, -las, -lae
fit, fitted, fitting
fit, fitter, fittest
fite fight
fitful, -ly
fitfull fitful
fitness
fitter
five
fiver
fix, fixed, fixing
fixated
fixation
fixative
fixcher fixture
fixity, -ties
fixture
fizz, -ed, -ing
fizzer
fizzle, -zled, -zling
fizzul fizzle
fizzy, -zier, -ziest
fjord
flabbergast, -ed, -ing
flabbily
flabbiness
flabby, -bier, -biest
flabergast flabbergast
flaby flabby
flaccid, -ly
flaccidity
flag, flagged, flagging
flagellate, -lated, -lating
flagon
flagrant, -ly
flagship
flagstone
flail, -ed, -ing
flair (talent)
flair flare (blaze)
flak
flake, flaked, flaking
flakily
flaky, flakier, flakiest
flamboyance
flamboyancy
flamboyant, -ly
flame, flamed, flaming
flamenco, -cos
flamethrower
flame-tree
flamingo, -gos, -goes
flammable
flammabul flammable
flan
flanel flannel
flange, flanged, flanging
flanje flange
flank, -ed, -ing
flannel, -elled, -elling
flannelette
flanul flannel
flap, flapped, flapping
flapjack
flapper
flare, flared, flaring (blaze)
flare flair (talent)
flash, -ed, -ing
flashback
flashbulb
flashgun
flashlight
flashpoint
flashy, flashier, flashiest
flask
flat, flatted, flatting
flat, flatter, flattest
flaten flatten
flater flatter
flatette
flatfoot, -feet
flat-footed, -ly

flathead	
flatten, -ed, -ing	
flatter, -ed, -ing	
flatterer	
flattery, -teries	
flatulence	
flatulense	flatulence
flatulent, -ly	
flaunt, -ed, -ing	
flautist	
flaver	flavour
flavour, -ed, -ing	
flaw, -ed, -ing (fault)	
flaw	floor (room)
flax	
flaxen	
flay, -ed, -ing	
flea (insect)	
flea	flee (escape)
flea-bitten	
fleat	fleet
fleck, -ed, -ing	
flecks (spots)	
flecks	flex (bend)
fledge, fledged, fledging	
flee, fled, fleeing (escape)	
flee	flea (insect)
fleece, fleeced, fleecing	
fleeciness	
fleecy, fleecier, fleeciest	
fleese	fleece
fleet, -ly	
fleeting, -ly	
fleetness	
flegling	fledgling
flegmatic	phlegmatic
fleks	flecks (spots)
fleksible	flexible
flem	phlegm
flert	flirt
flesh	
fleshy, fleshier, fleshiest	
fleur-de-lis, fleurs-de-lis	
flew (fly)	
flew	flu (ill)
flew	flue (passage)
flex, -ed, -ing (bend)	
flex	flecks (spots)
flexible, -bly	
flexitime	
fli	fly
flibbertigibbet	
flick, -ed, -ing	
flicker, -ed, -ing	
flick-knife, flick-knives	
flier	
flight	
flightiness	
flighty, -tier, -tiest	
flimsily	
flimsiness	
flimsy, -sies	
flimsy, -sier, -siest	
flinch, -ed, -ing	
flinchingly	
fling, flung, flinging	
flint	
flinty, flintier, flintiest	
flip, flipped, flipping	
flipansy	flippancy
flipant	flippant
fliper	flipper
flippancy	
flippant, -ly	
flipper	
flirt, -ed, -ing	
flirtation	
flirtatious, -ly	
flit, flitted, flitting	
flite	flight
flo	floe (ice)
flo	flow (pour)
float, -ed, -ing	
floatation	
floater	
flock, -ed, -ing	
flocks (groups)	
flocks	phlox (plant)
floe (ice)	
floe	flow (pour)
flog, flogged, flogging	
flood, -ed, -ing	
floodgate	
floodlight, -lit, -lighting	

floor, -ed, -ing (room)	
floor	flaw (fault)
floorboard	
flooride	fluoride
floot	flute
flop, flopped, flopping	
floppily	
floppy, -pier, -piest	
floppy disc	
flora, floras, florae	
floral, -ly	
florescence (flowering)	
florescence (giving light)	fluorescence
florescent	
florescent	fluorescent
florid, -ly	
floridate	fluoridate
florin	
florish	flourish
florist	
floss	
flossy, flossier, flossiest	
flotation	
flote	float
flotilla	
flotsam and jetsam	
flounce, flounced, flouncing	
flounder, -ed, -ing	
flounse	flounce
flour (grain)	
flour	flower (plant)
flourish, -ed, -ing	
floury	
flout, -ed, -ing	
flow, -ed, -ing	
flower, -ed, -ing (plant)	
flower	flour (grain)
flowerbed	
flowery, -rier, -riest	
flown	
flownder	flounder
flownse	flounce
flow-on	
flowt	flout
flox	phlox
flu (ill)	
flu	flew (fly)
flu	flue (passage)
fluctuate, -ated, -ating	
fluctuation	
flue (passage)	
flue	flew (fly)
flue	flu (ill)
fluency	
fluensy	fluency
fluent, -ly	
fluff, -ed, -ing	
fluffily	
fluffiness	
fluffy, fluffier, fluffiest	
fluid, -ly	
fluidity	
fluke, fluked, fluking	
fluks	flux
fluky, flukier, flukiest	
flunk, -ed, -ing	
fluoresce, -resced, -rescing	
fluorescence (giving light)	
fluoridate, -dated, -dating	
fluoridation	
flurish	flourish
flurry, -ries	
flurry, -ried, -rying	
flurt	flirt
flurtation	flirtation
flury	flurry
flush, -ed, -ing	
fluster, -ed, -ing	
flute, fluted, fluting	
flutter, -ed, -ing	
fluvial	
flux	
fly, flies	
fly, flew, flown, flying	
flyblown	
flycatcher	
flyleaf, -leaves	
flyover	
flytrap	
flyweight	
flywheel	
foal, -ed, -ing	
foam, -ed, -ing	

fob, fobbed, fobbing
fobia phobia
focal, -ly
focus, -ci or -cuses
focus, -cused, -cusing or -cussed, -cussing
focuser
fodder
foe
foe pas faux pas
foetal
foetus
fog, fogged, fogging
fogey, fogeys
fogginess
foggy, -gier, -giest
foghorn
fogy, -gies
foible
foier foyer
foil, -ed, -ing
foist, -ed, -ing
foks fox
fold, -ed, -ing
folder
fole foal
foliage
foliaged
foliaje foliage
foliation
folie folly
folio, -lios
folk
folk dance
folklaw folklore
folklore
follicle
follicul follicle
follow, -ed, -ing
follower
folly, -lies
folow follow
foly folly
fome foam
foment, -ed, -ing
fond, -ly
fondant
fondle, -dled, -dling
fondness
fondue
fondul fondle
fone phone
fonetic phonetic
fonograf phonograph
font
fony phony
food
foodstuff
fool, -ed, -ing
foolery, -eries
foolhardiness
foolhardy, -dier, -diest
foolish, -ly
foolishness
foolproof
foolscap
foot, feet
football
footballer
foothill
foothold
footie
footing
footlights
footloose
footman, -men
footnote
footpath
footprint
footsore
footstep
footwork
fop
foppish, -ly
for (with the purpose of)
for fore (front)
for four (number)
forage, -raged, -raging
foray
forbarance forbearance
forbear, -bore, -borne, -bearing
forbearance
forbid, -bad, -bidden, -bidding
forbode forebode

forcasle forecastle
forcast forecast
forcastle forecastle
force, forced, forcing
forceful, -ly
forceps, -ceps, -cipes
forcible, -bly
forcibul forcible
forclose foreclose
ford, -ed, -ing
fordable
fore (front)
fore four (number)
forearm
forebear
forebode, -boded, -boding
forecast, -ed, -ing
forecaster
forecastle
foreclose, -closed, -closing
forefather
forefinger
forego, -gone, -going (go before)
forego forgo (give up)
foreground
forehand
forehead
foreign
foreigner
foreknow, -knew, -knowing
foreknowledge
foreman, -men
foren foreign
forener foreigner
forerunner
foresee, -saw, -seeing
foreshadow, -ed, -ing
foreshore
foresight
foreskin
forest, -ed, -ing
forestall, -ed, -ing
forester
forestry
foretaste, -tasted, -tasting
foretell, -told, -telling
forethought
forever
forewarn, -ed, -ing
foreword (book)
foreword forward (ahead)
forfeit, -ed, -ing
forfeiture
forfit forfeit
forfiture forfeiture
forgary forgery
forge, forged, forging
forgery, -eries
forget, -got, -gotten, -getting
forgetful, -ly
forget-me-not
forgettable
forgive, -gave, -given, -giving
forgiveness
forgo, -went, -gone, -going (give up)
forgo forego (go before)

> For for- words, also look under **fore-** .

forige forage
forin foreign
fork, -ed, -ing
fork-lift
forlorn, -ly
form, -ed, -ing
formal, -ly
formalise, -lised, -lising
formality, -ties
format
formation
formative, -ly
former, -ly
formica
formidable, -bly
formidabul formidable
formula, -las, -lae
formulate, -lated, -lating
formulation
formulator
forn faun (god)
forn fawn (deer)
fornicate, -cated, -cating

fornication	
forsable	forcible
forsake, -sook, -saken, -saking	
forse	force
forseps	forceps
forsful	forceful
forsible	forcible
forsight	foresight
fort (soldiers)	
fort	fought (fight)
forte (strong)	
forth (away)	
forth (number)	fourth.
forthcoming	
forthright	
forthwith	
fortieth	
fortification	
fortify, -fied, -fying	
fortitude	
fortnight	
fortnightly	
fortnite	fortnight
fortress	
fortuitous, -ly	
fortuitus	fortuitous
fortunate, -ly	
fortune	
fortune-teller	
forty, -ties	
forum, forums, fora	
forward (ahead)	
forward (book)	foreword
forwards	
fosfate	phosphate
fosforesent	phosphorescent
fosforus	phosphorus
fosil	fossil
fossick, -ed, -ing	
fossil	
foster, -ed, -ing	

For foto- words, look under **photo-** .

foul, -ed, -ing (dirt)	
foul	fowl (bird)
found, -ed, -ing	
foundation	
founder, -ed, -ing	
foundling	
foundry, -dries	
fount	
fountain	
four (number)	
four	fore (ahead)
four-stroke	
fourt	fort (soldiers)
fourt	fought (fight)
fourteen	
fourteenth	
fourth, -ly	
fourty	forty
fowl (bird)	
fowl	foul (dirt)
fownd	found
fowndation	foundation
fowndry	foundry
fownt	fount
fowntain	fountain
fox, foxes	
foxhole	
fox-hunting	
foxtrot	
foxy, foxier, foxiest	
foyble	foible
foyer	
fracas	
fracshun	fraction
fracshus	fractious
fraction	
fractional, -ly	
fractious, -ly	
fracture, -tured, -turing	
fragile, -ly	
fragility, -ties	
fragment, -ed, -ing	
fragmentary	
fragmentation	
fragmented	
fragmentry	fragmentary
fragrance	
fragranse	fragrance

fragrant, -ly
frail, -ly
frailty, -ties
frame, framed, framing
frame-up
framework
franc (money)
  franc — frank (mark)
franchise
frangipanni, -nies
frank, -ed, -ing (mark)
  frank — franc (money)
frankfurt
frankincense
frantic, -ally
  frase — phrase
  frate — freight
fraternal, -ly
fraternisation
fraternise, -nised, -nising
fraternity, -ties
fraud
fraudulence
  fraudulense — fraudulence
fraudulent, -ly
fraught
  fraut — fraught
  frawd — fraud
  frawdulence — fraudulence
  frawdulent — fraudulent
  frawt — fraught
fray, -ed, -ing
frazzle, -zled, -zling
  frazzul — frazzle
freak
freakish, -ly
freckle, -led, -ling
free, freed, freeing
free, freer, freest
freeborn
freedom
freehand
freehold
freelance, -lanced, -lancing
freelancer
freeload, -ed, -ing
freeloader
freely
freeman, -men
Freemason
Freemasonry
free-range
freesia
freestanding
freestyle
freeway
freewheel, -ed, -ing
freeze, froze, frozen, freezing (cold)
  freeze — frieze (band)
freezer
freight, -ed, -ing
freighter
  freind — friend
  frekwency — frequency
  frekwent — frequent
French
  frend — friend
  frendly — friendly
  frendship — friendship
frenetic, -ally
  frenzie — frenzy
frenzied
frenzy, -zies
frenzy, -zied, -zying
frequency, -cies
  frequensy — frequency
frequent, -ly
fresco, -coes
fresco, -coed, -coing
fresh, -ly
freshen, -ed, -ing
freshener
fresher
freshness
freshwater
  fresko — fresco
fret, fretted, fretting
fretful, -ly
fretwork
Freudian
  fri — fry
friable
  friabul — friable
friar

fricassee, -seed, -seeing
  fricshun — friction
friction
frictional, -ly
Friday
fridge
friend
friendliness
friendly, -lier, -liest
friendship
  frier — friar
Friesian
frieze (band)
  frieze — freeze (cold)
frigate
fright
frighten, -ed, -ing
frightener
frightful, -ly
  frightfull — frightful
frigid, -ly
frigidity, -ties
frigidness
frill, -ed, -ing
frill-necked lizard
fringe, fringed, fringing
frippery, -ries
frisk, -ed, -ing
friskily
frisky, friskier, friskiest
  frite — fright
  friteful — frightful
  friten — frighten
  friter — fritter
fritter, -ed, -ing
frivolity, -ties
frivolous, -ly
  frivolus — frivolous
frizz, frizzes
frizz, frizzed, frizzing
frizzle, -zled, -zling
frizzy
  frizzul — frizzle
fro
frock, -ed, -ing
frog
frogman, -men
frogmarch, -ed, -ing
frogmouth
  Froidian — Freudian
frolic, -icked, -icking
frolicsome, -ly
frond
front, -ed, -ing
frontage
frontal, -ly
frontbencher
frontier
  frontige — frontage
  froogal — frugal
  frooishun — fruition
  froot — fruit
  frootful — fruitful
frost, -ed, -ing
frostbite, -bit, -bitten, -biting
frostily
frosty, -tier, -tiest
froth, -ed, -ing
frothiness
frothy, frothier, frothiest
frown, -ed, -ing
frowzy, -zier, -ziest
froze
frozen, -ly
fructose
frugal, -ly
frugality, -ties
  fruishun — fruition
fruit, -ed, -ing
fruiterer
fruit-fly
fruitful, -ly
fruition
fruitless, -ly
fruity, -tier, -tiest
frump
frumpish, -ly
  frunt — front
  fruntal — frontal
  fruntier — frontier
frustrate, -trated, -trating
frustration
  frut — fruit
  fruterer — fruiterer

frutful fruitful
frutie fruity
fry, fried, frying
fry, fries
fucher future
fucheristic futuristic
fuchsia
fudal feudal
fudalism feudalism
fuddle, -dled, -dling
fuddul fuddle
fude feud
fudge, fudged, fudging
fuel, fuelled, fuelling
fuel-injection
fuel-injector
fugitive
fugue
ful full
fulcrum, -crums, -cra
fulfil, -filled, -filling
fulfilment
full
full-back
full-blooded
fullfil fulfil
fully
fully-fledged
fulminate, -ated, -ating
fulscap foolscap
fulsome, -ly
fulsomeness
fumble, -bled, -bling
fumbler
fumbul fumble
fume, fumed, fuming
fumigant
fumigate, -gated, -gating
fumigation
fumigator
fun
funcshun function
function
functional, -ly
functionalism
functionary, -ries
fund, -ed, -ing
fundamental, -ly
funnel funnel
funeral
funereal, -ly
funfair
fungicide
fungus, fungi
funicular
funnily funnily
funk, -ed, -ing
funnel, -nelled, -nelling
funnel-web
funnily
funny, -nier, -niest
fur, furred, furring (pelt)
fur fir (tree)
furbish, -ed, -ing
furie furry (fur)
furie fury (anger)
furrier furrier
furious, -ly
furius furious
furl, -ed, -ing
furlong
furlough
furm firm
furmament firmament
furment ferment
furmentation fermentation
furn fern
furnace
furnish, -ed, -ing
furnisher
furnishings
furniture
furore
furphy, -phies
furrier
furrow, -ed, -ing
furry, -rier, -riest (fur)
furst first
further
furtherance
furthest
furtive, -ly
fury, -ries (anger)
fus fuss

fuse, fused, fusing
fuselage

fusha	fuchsia
fusier	fussier
fusiest	fussiest
fusilade	fusillade
fusilage	fuselage

fusilier
fusillade
fusion
fuss, -ed, -ing
fusspot
fussy, -sier, -siest
futile, -ly
futility, -ties
future
futurism
futuristic
futurology
fuzz
fuzzily
fuzziness
fuzzy, -zier, -ziest

fyord	fiord
fyord	fjord

For fysi- words,
look under **physi-** .

Gg

gab, gabbed, gabbing
gabardine
gabble, -bled, -bling (talk)
gable (roof)
gabul gabble (talk)
gabul gable (roof)
gadget
Gaelic
gaf gaff (hook)
gaf gaffe (mistake)
gaff (hook)
gaffe (mistake)
gag, gagged, gagging
gaga
gage gauge
gaget gadget
gaggle
gagit gadget
gagul gaggle
gaiety, -ties
gail gale
gaily
gain, -ed, -ing
gainful, -ly
gainsay, -said, -saying
gait (walk)
gait gate (opening)
gaiter
gaitey gaiety
gala (festival)
gala galah (bird)
galah (bird)
galaksey galaxy
galant gallant
galantry gallantry
galaw galore
galaxy, -axies
gale
galery gallery
galey galley
galivant gallivant
gall, -ed, -ing
gallant, -ly
gallantry, -tries
galleon
gallery, -leries
galley, -leys
gallivant, -vanted, -vanting
gallon
gallop, galloped, galloping (pace)
gallows
gallstone
gallup poll (survey)
galon gallon
galop gallop (pace)
galore
galoshes
galows gallows
galup poll gallup poll
galvanise, -nised, -nising
galvanised iron
galy galley
gambit
gamble, -bled, -bling (chance)
gambol, -bolled, -bolling (frolic)
game, gamed, gaming
gamesmanship
gamin (urchin)
gamma
gammon (bacon)
gammy, -mier, -miest
gamut
gander
gang
gangling
ganglion, -glia, -glions
gangplank
gangreen gangrene
gangrene
gangrenous
gangrenus gangrenous
gangster
gangway
gannet
gantry, -tries

Word	Correct spelling
gaol (prison)	
gaol	goal (aim)
gaolbird	
gaoler	
gap	
gape, -ed, -ing	
garage, -raged, -raging	
garantee	guarantee
garantee	guaranty
garantor	guarantor
garb, -ed, -ing	
garbage	
garbige	garbage
garble, -bled, -bling	
garbul	garble
gard	guard
garden, -ed, -ing	
gardener	
gardenia	
gardian	guardian
garfish, -fish, -fishes	
gargle, -gled, -gling	
gargoil	gargoyle
gargoyle	
gargul	gargle
garish, -ly	
garison	garrison
garland, -landed, -landing	
garlic	
garment	
garner, -ed, -ing	
garnet	
garnish, -ed, -ing	
garnishee, -sheed, -sheeing	
garnit	garnet
garrison, -ed, -ing	
garrot	garrotte
garrotte, -rotted, -rotting	
garrulity	
garrulous, -ly	
garter	
garulus	garrulous
gas, gases	
gas, gassed, gassing	
gasbag, -bagged, -bagging	
gasebo	gazebo
gaselene	gasoline
gaseous	
gash, gashed, gashing	
gasious	gaseous
gasket	
gasmask	
gasolene	
gasoline	
gasometer	
gasp, -ed, -ing	
gassey	gassy
gassy, -sier, -siest	
gastley	ghastly
gastric	
gastritis	
gastroenteritis	
gastronome	
gastronomy	
gate (opening)	
gate	gait (walk)
gateau, -teaux	
gatecrash, -crashed, -crashing	
gater	gaiter
gateway	
gather, -ed, -ing	
gauche	
gaudie	gaudy
gauge, gauged, gauging	
gaunt, -ly	
gauntlet	
gauze	
gave	
gavel	
gavot	gavotte
gavotte	
gawdie	gaudy
gawk, -ed, -ing	
gawky, -kier, -kiest	
gawl	gall
gawnt	gaunt
gawntlet	gauntlet
gawse	gauze
gay, gayer, gayest	
Gaylic	Gaelic
gayn	gain
gaysha	geisha
gaze, -ed, -ing	
gazebo, -bos, -boes	

gazel	gazelle
gazelle	
gazette, -etted, -etting	
gazump, -ed, -ing	
gear, -ed, -ing	
gearbox, -boxes	
gear-ratio	
gearstick	
gearwheel	
gecko, -os, -oes	
geebung	
geek	
gees	geese
geese	
geezer	
Geiger counter	
geisha, -shas	
gel, gelled, gelling	
gelatin	gelatine
gelatine	
gelatinous, -ly	
gelatinus	gelatinous
gelato	
geld, gelded, gelding	
gelignite	
gem, gemmed, gemming	
gemfish, -fish, -fishes	
Gemini	
gen, genned, genning	
gendarme, -darmes	
gender	
gene	
genealogist	
genealogy, -gies	
genee	genie
general, -ly	
generalise, -ised, -ising	
generality, -ties	
generate, -ed, -ing	
generation	
generation-gap	
generator	
generic	
generical, -ly	
generosity, -ties	
generous, -ly	
generus	generous
genesis, -ses	
genetic	
genetical, -ly	
genetics	
geney	genie
genial, -ly	
genie	
geniology	genealogy
genital	
genius, geniuses	
genocide	
genoside	genocide
genre	
gent	
genteel, -ly (proper)	
genteel	gentle
gentile (Christian)	
gentility, -ties	
gentle, -tler, -tlest	
gentleman, -men	
gentlewoman, -women	
gentrey	gentry
gentrification	
gentry	
gentul	gentle
gentulman	gentleman
genuflect, -ed, -ing	
genuin	genuine
genuine, -ly	
genuineness	
genus, genera	
geny	genie
geofysics	geophysics
geografey	geography
geography, -phies	
geologist	
geology, -gies	
geometrey	geometry
geometric	
geometrical, -ly	
geometry, -tries	
geophysicist	
geophysics	
georgette	
geranium	
gerd	gird
gerder	girder

gerdle	girdle
gerdul	girdle
geriatric	
gerilla	gorilla
gerilla	guerilla
gerkin	gherkin
gerl	girl
germ	
German	
germane	
germinal	
germinate, -nated, -nating	
gerontology	
gerth	girth
gerund	
gerymander	gerrymander
gescha	gesture
geser	geyser
gess	guess
gest	guest
gestate, -tated, -tating	
gestation	
gesticulate, -lated, -lating	
gesture, -tured, -turing	
get, got, getting	
getaway	
getto	ghetto
geyser	
ghastly, -lier, -liest	
gherkin	
ghetto, ghettos, ghettoes	
ghost, -ly	
ghoul	
ghoulish, -ly	
ghoulishness	
giant	
gibber	
gibberish	
gibbet, -beted, -beting	
gibe, gibed, gibing (mock)	
gibe	jibe (sail)
giber	gibber
giberish	gibberish
gibet	gibbet
giblet	
gidance	guidance
gidanse	guidance
giddy, -dier, -diest	
gide	guide
gidgee	
gidgie	gidgee
gidie	giddy
gidy	giddy
gift	
gig, gigged, gigging	
gigantic, -ally	
giggle, -gled, -gling	
gigolo, -los	
gigul	giggle
gil	gill
gild, gilded, gilding (gold)	
gild	guild (union)
gile	guile
gilgai	
gilgy	gilgai
gill	
giloteen	guillotine
gilotine	guillotine
gilt (gold)	
gilt	guilt
giltey	guilty
gilty	guilty
gim	gym
gimick	gimmick
gimkana	gymkhana
gimlet	
gimmick	
gimnasium	gymnasium
gimnastics	gymnastics
gin, ginned, ginning	
ginecology	gynaecology
giney	guinea
gineypig	guineapig
gingam	gingham
ginger	
gingerley	gingerly
gingerly	
gingham	
gingivitis	
ginie	guinea
giniepig	guineapig
ginjer	ginger
ginjivitis	gingivitis
ginseng	

gip gyp
gipsey gipsy
gipsie gipsy
gipsum gypsum
gipsy, -sies
giraf giraffe
gird, -ed, -ing
girder
girdle, -dled, -dling
girdul girdle
girl
girocompass gyrocompass
giroscope gyroscope
girth
gise guise
gismo
gist
gitar guitar
give, gave, given, giving
giy guy
gizerd gizzard
gizzard
glacial, -ly
glacier
glad, gladded, gladding
glad, gladder, gladdest
glade
gladen gladden
gladiater gladiator
gladiator
glamer glamour
glamorous, -ly
glamour
glance, -ed, -ing
gland
glandular
glanduler glandular
glanse glance
glare, glared, glaring
glas glass
glashal glacial
glasier glacier
glass, glasses
glasshouse
glassy, -sier, -siest
glaucoma
glawcoma glaucoma

glaze, glazed, glazing
glazier
glea glee
gleam, -ed, -ing
glean, -ed, -ing
glee
gleem gleam
gleen glean
glib, glibber, glibbest
glicerine glycerine
glide, glided, gliding
glider
glimmer, -ered, -ering
glimpse, glimpsed, glimpsing
glimse glimpse
glint, -ed, -ing
glisen glisten
gliserin glycerine
glisten, -ed, -ing
glitter, -ed, -ing
glo glow
gloat, -ed, -ing
glob
global, -ly
globe, globed, globing
globule
gloo glue
gloocose glucose
gloom
gloomily
gloomy, -mier, -miest
glooten gluten
glorie glory
glorify, -fied, -fying
glorious, -ly
glorius glorious
glory, glories
glory, gloried, glorying
glos gloss
glosary glossary
gloss, glossed, glossing
glossary, -ries
glossie glossy
glossy, glossier, glossiest
glote gloat
glove
glow, -ed, -ing

glower, -ered, -ering
glucose
glue, glued, gluing
glum, -ly
glut, glutted, glutting
gluten (glue)
glutten glutton
glutton (eat)
gluv glove
glycerine
gnarled
gnash, -ed, -ing
gnat
gnaw, gnawed, gnawing
gnome
gnu, gnus
go, gone, going
goad, -ed, -ing
goal (aim)
goal gaol (prison)
goalkeeper
goanna
goat
goatee
gob
gobbel gobble
gobble, -bled, -bling
gobbledegook
gobbler
go-between
goblet
goblin
gobul gobble
go-cart
God
godchild, -children
goddess
godforsaken
godly, -lier, -liest
godparent
godsend, -sent, -sending
godspeed
goer
goes
goggle, -gled, -gling
gogul goggle
goiter goitre
goitre
go-kart
gold
golden, -ly
goldfield
goldfish
goldmine
gole goal (aim)
golf (game)
golf gulf (bay)
golliwog
gollywog
gon gone
gondola
gondolier
gone
goner
gong
goo
good, better, best
gooda gouda
goodbye, -byes
goodnight
goodwill
gooey, gooier, gooiest
goof, goofed, goofing
googly
gool ghoul
goolash goulash
goormand gourmand
goormay gourmet
goose, geese
gooseberie gooseberry
gooseberry, -ries
goosestep, -stepped, -stepping
gopher
gore, gored, goring
gorge, gorged, gorging
gorgeous, -ly
gorgus gorgeous
gorilla (ape)
gorilla guerilla (soldier)
gormandise, -dised, -dising
gorse
gory, gorier, goriest
gosamer gossamer

goshawk	
gosip	gossip
gosling	
go-slow	
gospel	
gospeller	
gossamer	
gossip, -ed, -ing	
gost	ghost
gote	goat
Gothic	
gouda	
gouge, gouged, gouging	
goul	ghoul
goulash	
gourd	
gourmand	
gourmet	
gout	
goven	govern
govern, -ed, -ing	
governer	governor
governess	
government	
governmental, -ly	
governor	
governor-general, governors-general.	
govner	governor
gowge	gouge
gawt	gout
grab, grabbed, grabbing	
grace, graced, gracing	
graceful, -ly	
gracious, -ly	
gradation	
grade, graded, grading	
grader	
gradient	
gradual, -ly	
graduate, -ated, -ating	
graduation	
graf	graph
graffiti	
grafic	graphic
grafics	graphics
grafite	graphite
grafiti	graffiti
graft, grafted, grafting	
grail	
grain	
graling	grayling
gram	
gramar	grammar
gramarian	grammarian
gramatical	grammatical
gramer	grammar
gramerfone	gramophone
grammar	
grammarian	
grammatical, -ly	
gramophone	
grampus	
gran	
granary, -ries	
grand	
grandeur	
grandiloquent, -ly	
grandiose, -ly	
grandiosity	
grandparent	
grandstand	
grane	grain
grange	
granie	granny
granit	granite
granite	
granny, grannies	
grant, -ed, -ing	
granular	
granulate, -lated, -lating	
granule	
grany	granny
grape	
grapefruit, grapefruit	
grapevine	
graph, -ed, -ing	
graphic	
graphical, -ly	
graphics	
graphite	
graple	grapple
grapnel	
grapple, -pled, -pling	
grappul	grapple

Word	Correct spelling
gras	grass
grase	grace
grashoper	grasshopper
grashus	gracious
grasp, -ed, -ing	
grass	
grasshopper	
glassland	
grassroots	
grassy, -sier, -siest	
grate (fireplace)	
grate, grated, grating (rub)	
grate	great (large)
grateful, -ly	
gratification	
gratify, -fied, -fying	
gratingly	
gratis	
gratitude	
gratuitey	gratuity
gratuitous, -ly	
gratuitousness	
gratuitus	gratuitous
gratuity	
grave	
gravel, gravelled, gravelling	
gravelly	
gravie	gravy
gravitashun	gravitation
gravitate, -tated, -tating	
gravitation	
gravity, -ties	
gravure	
gravvity	gravity
gravy, -vies	
grayhownd	greyhound
grayl	grail
grayling	
grayn	grain
graze, grazed, grazing	
grazier	
grease, greased, greasing	
greasepaint	
great (large)	
great	grate (rub)
greatful	grateful
grede	greed

Word	Correct spelling
greed	
greedily	
greedy, greedier, greediest	
greef	grief
green	
greenery, -eries	
greengrocer	
greenhorn	
greenhouse	
greese	grease
greet, -ed, -ing	
gregarious, -ly	
gregarius	gregarious
greif	grief
greive	grieve
greivus	grievous
gremlin	
grenade	
grenadier	
grene	green
grenery	greenery
grengroser	greengrocer
grenhorn	greenhorn
grenhous	greenhouse
grese	grease
grete	greet
grevance	grievance
grevanse	grievance
greve	grieve
grevillea	
grevus	grievous
grew	
grey	
greyhound	
greyness	
grid	
griddle, -dled, -dling	
griddul	griddle
gridiron	
grief	
grief-stricken	
grievance	
grievanse	grievance
grieve, -ed, -ing	
griever	
grievous, -ly	
griffin	

grill, -ed, -ing (cook)
grille (screen)
griller (barbeque)
griller gorilla
griller guerilla
grim, grimmer, grimmest
grimace, -maced, -macing
grimase grimace
grime, grimed, griming
grimy, grimier, grimiest
grin, grinned, grinning
grind, ground, grinding
grinder
grindstone
grined grind
grip, gripped, gripping (hold)
gripe, griped, griping (pain)
grippe (flu)
grisel gristle (fibre)
grisel grizzle (whine)
grisly, -lier, -liest
grissle gristle (fibre)
grissle grizzle (whine)
grist
gristle (fibre)
grit, gritted, gritting
grizzle, -zled, -zling (whine)
grizzle gristle (fibre)
grizzleguts
gro grow
groan, groaned, groaning (moan)
groan grown (mature)
grocer
grocery, -ceries
grog
groggy, -gier, -giest
groin (body)
groin groyne (jetty)
grone groan
grone grown
groo grew
grool gruel
groop group
groosum gruesome
groove, grooved, grooving
groovey groovy
groovy, -vier, -viest
grooyere gruyere
grope, groped, groping
groper
gros gross
groser grocer
gross, grosses
grotesk grotesque
grotesque, -ly
groto grotto
grotto, -toes, -tos
grotty, -tier, -tiest
groty grotty
grouch, -ed, -ing
groun grown
ground, -ed, -ing
groundsheat groundsheet
groundsheet
groundsman, -men
group, -ed, -ing
grouse, groused, grousing
grout, -ed, -ing
grove
grovel, -elled, -elling
grovle grovel
grow, grew, grown, growing
grower
growl, -ed, -ing
grown (mature)
grown groan (moan)
grownd ground
growse grouse
growth
groyne (jetty)
groyne groin (body)
grub, grubbed, grubbing
grubber
grubby, -bier, -biest
grudge, -ed, -ing
gruel, gruelled, gruelling
gruesome, -ly
gruesomeness
gruf gruff
gruff, -ly
gruge grudge
grumble, -led, -ling
grumbul grumble
grummet

grumpie grumpy
grumpy, -pier, -piest
grunt, -ed, -ing
grunter
grusome gruesome
grusum gruesome
gruyaire gruyère
gruyare gruyère
gruyère
G-string
guano, -nos
guarantee, -teed, -teeing
guarantor
guaranty, -tied, -tying
guaranty, -ties
guard, -ed, -ing
guardian
guava
gudgeon
guerilla (soldier)
guerilla gorilla (ape)
guernsey, -seys
guess, -ed, -ing
guest
guesthouse, -houses
gufaw guffaw
guffaw, -awed, -awing
guidance
guide, guided, guiding
guideline
guild (union)
guild gild (gold)
guile
guileless, -ly
guillotine, -tined, -tining
guiloteen guillotine
guilotine guillotine
guilt
guiltily
guilty, -tier, -tiest
guinea
guineapig
guise, guised, guising
guitar
gul gull
gulash goulash
gulch
gulet gullet
guley gully
gulf (bay)
gulf golf (game)
gulible gullible
gulie gully
gull, -ed, -ing
gullet
gullible, -bly
gullibility
gullibul gullible
gully, gullies
gulp, -ed, -ing
guly gully
gum, gummed, gumming
gumboil
gumboot
gummy, -mier, -miest
gumnut
gumption
gumshun gumption
gun, gunned, gunning
gung ho
gunk
gunl gunwale
gunman, -men
gunmetal
gunnel gunwale
gunner
gunnery, -eries
gunny, -nies
gunnysack
gunpowder
gunsmith
gunwale
guppy, -pies
gurdle girdle
gurgle, -gled, -gling
gurgul gurgle
gurnard, -nards
gurnerd gurnard
gurth girth
guru, gurus
gush, gushed, gushing
gusset
gussit gusset
gust, -ed, -ing

Word	Correct spelling
gusto	
gut, gutted, gutting	
guter	gutter
guteral	guttural
gutersnipe	guttersnipe
gutless, -ly	
gutsa	gutser
gutser	
gutsie	gutsy
gutsy	
gutter	
guttersnipe	
guttural, -ly	
guvern	govern
guverness	governess
guvernment	government
guvner	governor
guy	
guzul	guzzle
guzzle, guzzled, guzzling	
gwano	guano
gwava	guava
gybe	gibe
gym	
gymkana	gymkhana
gymkhana	
gymnasium, -nasiums, -nasia	
gymnastics	
gynaecological	
gynaecologist	
gynaecology	
gyp, gypped, gypping	
gypsum	
gypsy, -sies	
gyrate, -ed, -ing	
gyrocompass	
gyroscope	

Hh

Word	Correct spelling
habeas corpus	
haberdasher	
haberdashery, -ries	
habet	habit
habias corpus	habeas corpus
habichual	habitual
habichuate	habituate
habit	
habitable, -bly	
habitabul	habitable
habitat	
habitation	
habitual, -ly	
habituate, -ated, -ating	
hach	hatch
hachery	hatchery
hachett	hatchet
hacienda	
hack, -ed, -ing	
hackle, -led, -ling	
hackney, -neyed, -neying	
hacksaw	
hackul	hackle
hackwork	
haddock	
hades	
hadn't (had not)	
hadnt	hadn't
haematology	
haemefilia	haemophilia
haemoglobin	
haemophilia	
haemorage	haemorrhage
haemorrhage, -haged, -haging	
haemorrhoid	
haemorroid	haemorrhoid
haft, -ed, -ing	
hag	
hagard	haggard
hagerd	haggard
haggard, -ly	
haggis	
haggle, -gled, -gling	
hagiography, -phies	
hagis	haggis
hagul	haggle
haiku	
hail (ice)	
hail	hale (robust)
hailstone	
hailstorm	
hair (head)	
hair	hare (animal)
hair	heir (inherit)
hairdo, -dos	
hairdresser	
hairline	
hairpiece	
hairpin	
hairspring	
hair-trigger	
hairy, -rier, -riest	
haka	
hake, hake, hakes	
hakea	
halcion	halcyon
halcyon	
hale, haler, halest (robust)	
hale	hail (ice)
haleluya	hallelujah
halestone	hailstone
halestorm	hailstorm
half	
half-back	
half-baked	
half-blood	
half-breed	
half-brother	
half-caste	
half-cock	
half-forward	
half-hearted, -ly	
half-life	
half-mast	
half-measure	

half-mesure	half-measure
half-moon	
half-sister	
half-time	
half-truth	
halfway	
halfway house	
halfwit	
halibut, -buts	
halilooya	hallelujah
halitosis	
hall (room)	
hall	haul (carry)
hallelujah	
halleluyah	hallelujah
hallmark	
hallo (greet)	
hallow, -ed, -ing (holy)	
Halloween	
hallucinate, -nated, -nating	
hallucination	
hallucinogen	
halmark	hallmark
halo, -loes, -los (light)	
halo	hallo (greet)
halo	hallow (holy)
halogen	
Haloween	Halloween
halsiun	halcyon
halt, -ed, -ing	
halter	
halusinate	hallucinate
halusinogen	hallucinogen
halve, -ed, -ing	
halyard	
halyerd	halyard
ham, hammed, hamming	
hamburger	
hamer	hammer
ham-fisted	
hamlet	
hammer, -ed, -ing	
hammerhead	
hammock	
hamper, -ered, -ering	
hamster	
hamstring, -strung, -stringing	
hand, handed, handing	
handbag	
handball	
handbill	
handbook	
handbrake	
handclap, -clapped, -clapping	
handcuff, -cuffed, -cuffing	
handey	handy
handeywork	handiwork
handicap, -capped, -capping	
handicraft	
handie	handy
handiwork	
handkerchief, -chiefs, -chieves	
handle, -dled, -dling	
handlebar	
handler	
handmade (article)	
handmaid (servant)	
hand-me-down	
handout	
hand-pick, -picked, -picking	
handpiece	
handrail	
handriting	handwriting
handset	
handshake	
handsome, -somer, -somest (fine)	
handspring	
handstand	
hand-to-mouth	
handul	handle
handwriting	
handy, -dier, -diest	
handyman	
hang, hung or hanged, hanging	
hangar (shed)	
hangar (clothes)	hanger
hangdog	
hanger (clothes)	
hanger	hangar (shed)
hanger-on, hangers-on	
hang-glider	
hangi	
hangkerchief	handkerchief

hangman	
hangover	
hang-up	
hank	
hanker, -ed, -ing	
hankerchief	handkerchief
hankie	
hankuff	handcuff
hanky, hankies	
hanky-panky	
Hansard	
hansom (cab)	
hansom (fine)	handsome
hansum	handsome
hapen	happen
haphazard, -ly	
hapie	happy
hapless, -ly	
happen, -ended, -ening	
happily	
happy, happier, happiest	
happy-go-lucky	
hapy	happy
harang	harangue
harangue, -rangued, -ranguing	
haras	harass
harass, -ed, -ing	
harassment	
harber	harbour
harbinger	
harbour, -ed, -ing	
hard, -ly	
hardback	
hard-bitten	
hardboard	
hard-core	
hard-court	
harden, -ed, -ing	
hard-hearted, -ly	
hardie	hardy
hard-hit	
hardihood	
hardiness	
hardlie	hardly
hardline	
hardness	
hardnose	
hard-pressed	
hardship	
hardtop	
hardware	
hardwear	hardware
hardwood	
hardy, hardier, hardiest	
hare (animal)	
hare	hair (head)
hare	heir (inherit)
harebrained	
harelip	
harem	
harico	haricot
haricot	
hark, -ed, -ing	
harlot	
harm, -ed, -ing	
harmonic	
harmonica	
harmonious, -ly	
harmonise, -nised, -nising	
harmonium	
harmonius	harmonious
harmony, -nies	
harness, -ed, -ing	
harow	harrow
harp, -ed, -ing	
harpoon	
harpsichord	
harpsicord	harpsichord
harpy	
harrier	
harrow, -ed, -ing	
harry, -ried, -rying	
harsh, -ly	
hart (deer)	
hart	heart (body)

For all other **hart-** words, look under **heart-**.

harum-scarum	
harve	halve
harvest, -ed, -ing	
harvester	
harvist	harvest

Word	Correct spelling
hary	hairy
has-been	
hasen	hasten
hash, -ed, -ing	
hashish	
hasn't (has not)	
hasnt	hasn't
hasock	hassock
hasp	
hassel	hassle
hassle, -led, -ling	
hassock	
haste, -tily	
hasten, -ed, -ing	
hasty, hastier, hastiest	
hatch, -ed, -ing	
hatchback	
hatcherey	hatchery
hatchery, -eries	
hatchet	
hatchway	
hate, -ed, -ing	
hateful, -ly	
hatred	
hatrid	hatred
hatstand	
hatter	
hat-trick	
haughty, -tier, -tiest	
haul, -ed, -ing, (carry)	
haul	hall (room)
haulage	
haulier	
haulige	haulage
haunch	
haunt, -ed, -ing	
haute cuisine	
hav	have
have	
haven	
haven't (have not)	
havent	haven't
haversack	
havoc, -ocked, -ocking	
hawk, -ed, -ing	
hawker	
hawl	haul
hawlidge	haulage
hawlige	haulage
hawlier	haulier
hawnch	haunch
hawnet	hornet
hawnt	haunt
hawse (ship)	
hawse	horse (animal)
hawser	
hawthorn	
hawticulcher	horticulture
hawticulture	horticulture
hawtie	haughty
hawty	haughty
hay (grass)	
hay	hey (cry)
hayday	heyday
hayfever	
haystack	
haywire	
hazard	
hazardous, -ly	
haze, hazed, hazing	
hazel	
hazerd	hazard
head, -ed, -ing	
headache	
headcount, -ed, -ing	
headdress	
header	
headfirst	
headfone	headphone
head-hunting	
headlamp	
headland	
headlight	
headline, -lined, -lining	
headlite	headlight
headlong	
headman	
headmaster	
headmistress	
head-on	
headphone	
headquarters	
headset	
headshrinker	

headspring
headstand
head start
headstone
headstream
headstrong
headwaters
headway
headwind
headword
heady, -dier, -diest
heal (health)
  heal — heel (shoe)
health
healthy, -thier, -thiest
heap, -ed, -ing
hear, heard, hearing (listen)
  hear — here (place)
heard (listen)
  heard — herd (animals)
hearer
hearing aid
hearsay
hearse
heart (body)
heartache
heart attack
heartbeat
heartbreak
heartbroken, -ly
heartburn
hearten, -ed, -ing
heartfelt
hearth
heartless, -ly
heart-rending, -ly
heartstring
heart-throb
hearty, -tily
heat, -ed, -ing
heater
heath
heathen, -then, -thens
heather
heatwave
heave, -ed, -ing
heave-ho
heaven, -ly
heavy, -ily
heavy-duty
heavy-handed, -ly
heavy-hearted, -ly
heavy-laden
heavyweight
Hebrew
  Hebroo — Hebrew
heck
heckle, -led, -ling
hectare
hectic, -ally
hector, -ed, -ing
he'd (he would)
  hed — head (body)
  hed — he'd (he would)
hedge, hedged, hedging
hedgehog
hedonism
heed, -ed, -ing
heedless, -ly
heehaw
heel (shoe)
  heel — heal (health)
heeler
  heematology — haematology
  heemoglobin — haemoglobin
  heemophilia — haemophilia
  heep — heap
  heer — hear (listen)
  heer — here (place)
  heet — heat
  heeth — heath
  hefer — heifer
  heftie — hefty
heft, -ed, -ing
hefty, -tier, -tiest
  hege — hedge
hegemony, -nies
heifer
height
heighten, -ed, -ing
  heighth — height
heinous, -ly
  heinus — heinous
heir (inherit)

heir	hair (head)
heir	here (place)
heir apparent, heirs apparent	
heiress	
heirloom	
heist, -ed, -ing	
heith	height
hel	hell
held	
helicopter	
heliograf	heliograph
heliograph	
heliotrope	
helipad	
heliport	
helium	
hell	
he'll (he will)	
hell	he'll
hell-bent	
hellcat	
Hellenic	
hellfire	
hello, -los	
hello, -loed, -loing	
hell's angel	
helm	
helmet	
helmsman, -men	
helo	hello
helot	
help, -ed, -ing	
helpless, -ly	
helpmate	
helter-skelter	
helth	health
helthy	healthy
hemerige	haemorrhage
hemeroid	haemorrhoid
hem, hemmed, hemming	
hemisfare	hemisphere
hemisfear	hemisphere
hemisphere	
hemlock	
hemp	
hemstitch, -stitched, -stitching	
hen	
hena	henna
hence	
henchman, -men	
henge	
henna	
henpeck, -pecked, -pecking	
hens	hence
henus	heinous
hepatic	
hepatitis	
heptagon	
herald, -ed, -ing	
heraldic, -ally	
heraldrey	heraldry
heraldry, -dries	
herb	
herbaceous	
herbage	
herbalist	
herbashus	herbaceous
herbicide	
herbiside	herbicide
herbivore	
herbivorous	
herbivorus	herbivorous
herculean	
herd (animals)	
herd	heard (listen)
herdsman, -men	
here (place)	
here	hear (listen)
hereafter	
hereby	
hereditary	
hereditey	heredity
hereditrey	hereditary
heredity, -ties	
Hereford	
herein	
hereof	
heresay	hearsay
heresie	heresy
heresy, -sies	
heretic	
hereto	
hereunder	
hereupon	

herewith
hering herring
heritable, -ly
heritage
heritige heritage
herl hurl
hermafrodite hermaphrodite
hermaphrodite
hermaphroditism
hermatage hermitage
hermetic
hermetical, -ly
hermit
hermitage
hermitige hermitage
hernia, -nias
hero, -roes
heroic
heroical, -ly
heroicle heroical
heroin (drug)
heroine (female hero)
heroism
heron
hero-worship, -shipped, -shipping
herpeas herpes
herpes
herring, -rings, -ring
herringbone
hers
herse hearse
herself
hert hurt
hertle hurtle
hertul hurtle
hertz
he's (he is, or he has)
hes he's
hesian hessian
hesitancy
hesitansey hesitancy
hesitant, -ly
hesitate, -tated, -tating
hesitation
hessian
heterogeneity
heterogeneous, -ly
heterogenius heterogeneous
heterosexual, -ly
hethen heathen
hether heather
het-up
heuristic, -ally
heve heave
heven heaven
hevenly heavenly
hevie heavy
hevily heavily
heviwait heavyweight
hevy heavy
hew, hewed, hewn, hewing (cut)
hew hue (colour)
hex
hexagon
hexagonal, -ly
hexameter
hey (cry)
hey hay (grass)
heyday

For other hi- words, look under hy-.

hi (cry)
hi high (up)
hiasinth hyacinth
hiatus, -tuses
hiatus hernia
hibernate, -nated, -nating
hibiscus
hibrid hybrid
hiccup, -ed, -ing
hich hitch
hichhike hitchhike
hick
hickory, -ries
hicup hiccup
hidden
hide, hid, hiding
hideaway
hidebound
hideous, -ly
hide-out
hidius hideous
hidy-hole

hier	hire
hierarchy, -chies	
hierarkey	hierarchy
hieroglific	hieroglyphic
hieroglyphic, -ally	
hi-fi	
high, -ly	
highborn	
highbrow	
high-class	
higher (up)	
higher	hire (rent)
highfalutin	
high-fidelity	
high-grade	
high-handed, -ly	
highland	
highlight	
highly-wrought	
high-minded, -ly	
highness	
high-pitched	
high-powered	
high-pressure	
high-rise	
high-speed	
high-spirited	
hight	height
high-tension	
highway	
highwayman, -men	
hijack, -ed, -ing	
hike, -ed, -ing	
hil	hill
hiland	highland
hilarious, -ly	
hilarius	hilarious
hilight	highlight
hilite	highlight
hill	
hillbilly, -lies	
hillock	
hilly, hillier, hilliest	
hilt	
him (he)	
him	hymn (song)
himself	

hind	
hinder, -ed, -ing	
hinderanse	hindrance
Hindoo, -doos	
Hindooism	
hindquarter	
hindrance	
hindranse	hindrance
hindsight	
hindsite	hindsight
Hindu	
Hinduism	
hiness	highness
hinge, -ed, -ing	
hint, -ed, -ing	
hinterland	
hip, hipped, hipping	
hipbath	
hipie	hippie
hipopotamus	hippopotamus
hippie, -ies	
Hippocratic oath	
hippopotamus, -muses, -mi	
hipster	
hipy	hippie
hire, hired, hiring (rent)	
hire	higher (up)
hireling	
hire-purchase	
hiroglific	hieroglyphic
hiss, -ed, -ing	
histerey	history
histeria	hysteria
histogram	
historian	
historic	
historiography	
history, -ries	
histrey	history
histrionic, -ally	
hit, hit, hitting	
hitch, -ed, -ing	
hitchhike, -hiked, -hiking	
hite	height
hither	
hitherto	
hive, -ed, -ing	

hiway highway

For other hi- words, look under hy-.

ho hoe
hoaks hoax
hoard, -ed, -ing (gather)
hoard horde (mob)
hoarding
hoare whore
hoarse, hoarser, hoarsest (voice)
hoarse hawse (ship)
hoarse horse (animal)
hoary, hoarier, hoariest (old)
hoax, -ed, -ing
hob
hobbel hobble
hobble, -bled, -bling
hobby, -bies
hobbyhorse
hobie hobby
hobnail
hobnob, -nobbed, -nobbing
hobo, -bos, -boes
hochpoch hotchpotch
hock, -ed, -ing
hockey
hockie hockey
hocus-pocus, -cussed, -cussing
hod
hoe, hoed, hoeing (tool)
hoes hose (water)
hog, hogged, hogging
hogget
hogshead
hogshed hogshead
hogwash
hoi polloi
hoist, -ed, -ing
hokem hokum
hokey pokey
hokum
hold, held, holding
holdfast
hold-up
hole, holed, holing (opening)
hole whole (all)
holey wholly
holiday
holie holly (plant)
holie holy (saint)
holie wholly (all)
holihock hollyhock
holiness
holland
holler, -ed, -ing (shout)
hollow, -ly (hole)
holly, -lies (plant)
holly holy (saint)
holly wholly (all)
hollyhock
holocaust
holocost holocaust
holow hollow
holster
holus-bolus
holy, -lier, -liest (saint)
holy holly (plant)
holy wholly (all)
homage
homburg
home, -ed, -ing
home-brew
homeland
homely, -lier, -liest
homeopathy
homesick
homespun
homestead
homeward
homework
homicide
homige homage
homiley homily
homily, -lies
homiopathy homeopathy
homiside homicide
homogeneous, -ly
homogenise, -nised, -nising
homogenius homogeneous
homonim homonym
homonym
homophone
Homo sapiens

homoseksual	homosexual
homoseksuality	homosexuality
homosexual	
homosexuality	
hone, honed, honing	
honest, -ly	
honesty	
honey, honeys	
honeybee	
honeycomb	
honeydew	
honeyeater	
honeymoon	
honeysuckle	
hongi	
honie	honey
honk, -ed, -ing	
honky, -tonk	
honorarium, -rariums, -raria	
honorary	
honorific, -ally	
honour, -ed, -ing	
honourable, -bly	
hony	honey
hood, -ed, -ing	
hoodlum	
hoodwink, -ed, -ing	
hoof, hoofs, hooves	
hook, -ed, -ing	
hookah	
hooker	
hookie	hooky
hook-up	
hookworm	
hooky	
hoola-hoola	hula-hula
hooligan	
hoop	
hooping coff	whooping cough
hoopla	
hooray	
hooroo	
hoot, -ed, -ing	
hooter	
hoover	
hop, hopped, hopping	
hope, hoped, hoping	
hopeful	
hopefull	hopeful
hopeless, -ly	
hopper	
hopping-mouse	
hopsack	
hopscotch	
horde, horded, hording (animals)	
horde	hoard (gather)
hore	whore
horendus	horrendous
horer	horror
horible	horrible
horid	horrid
horific	horrific
horify	horrify
horizon	
horizontal, -ly	
hormone	
horn, -ed, -ing	
hornbill	
hornpipe	
horn-rimmed	
horny, -nier, -niest	
horology	
horor	horror
horoscope	
horrendous, -ly	
horrible, -bly	
horribul	horrible
horrid, -ly	
horrific	
horrify, -fied, -fying	
horror	
hors d'oeuvre	
horse, horses (animal)	
horse, horsed, horsing	
horse	hawse (ship)
horse	hoarse (voice)
horseflesh	
horseplay	
horsepower	
horserace	
horseradish	
horseshoe, -shoed, -shoeing	
horsy, -sier, -siest	

Word	Correct spelling
hortative, -ly	
hortatory	
horthorn	hawthorn
horticulcher	horticulture
horticulture	
hortie	haughty
hose, hosed, hosing (water)	
hose	hoes (tools)
hosiery	
hospice	
hospitable, -bly	
hospitabul	hospitable
hospital	
hospitality, -ties	
host, -ed, -ing	
hostage	
hostaple	hospital
hostel	
hostess	
hostige	hostage
hostile, -ly	
hostility, -ties	
hot, hotted, hotting	
hot, hotter, hottest	
hot-blooded	
hotchpotch	
hotel	
hotelier	
hoter	hotter
hotest	hottest
hotfoot	
hothead	
hot-headed, -ly	
hothed	hothead
hotheded	hotheaded
hothouse	
hotplate	
hotpot	
hot rod	
hot seat	
hot-shot	
hot-water bottle	
hound, -ed, -ing	
hound's-tooth	
hour (time)	
hour	our
hourglass	

Word	Correct spelling
houri, -ris	
hourly	
house, houses	
house, housed, housing	
houseboat	
housebreaker	
housebroken	
housecoat	
housefly, -flies	
household	
housekeeper	
housemaid	
House of Commons	
houseproud	
house-train	
house-warming	
housewife, -wives	
housey-housey	
housie-housie	
housing	
hovel, -elled, -elling	
hover, -ed, -ing	
hovercraft	
how	
however	
howl, -ed, -ing	
howler	
hownd	hound
howse	house
howsoever	
hoy	
hoyden	
hu	hew (cut)
hu	hue (colour)
hubbub	
huch	hutch
huckster	
huddle, -dled, -dling	
hue (colour)	
hue	hew (cut)
huf	huff
huff, -ed, -ing	
hug, hugged, hugging	
huge, huger, hugest	
hul	hull
hula-hula	
hulabaloo	hullabaloo

hulk
hull, -ed, -ing
hullabaloo
hullo
hum, hummed, humming
human
humane, -ly
humanism
humanist
humanitarian
humanity, -ties
humanly
humanoid
humble, -bled, -bling
humble, -bler, -blest
humble pie
humbug, -bugged, -bugging
humbul — humble
humdinger
humdrum
humer — humour
humerist — humorist
humerus, -meri (bone)
humerus (funny) — humorous
humid, -ly
humidifier
humidity
humiliate, -ated, -ating
humiliation
humility, -ties
hummingbird
hummock
humock — hummock
humorist
humorous, -ly (funny)
humorous — humerus (bone)
humour, -ed, -ing
hump, -ed, -ing
humpback
humpy, -pier, -piest
humus
hunch, -ed, -ing
hunchback
hundred, -dreds
hundredfold
hundredth
huney — honey
hunger
hungrie — hungry
hungry, -grier, -griest
hunie — honey
hunk
hunt, -ed, -ing
hunter
huntress
huntsman, -men
Huon pine
huray — hurray
hurd — heard (listen)
hurd — herd (animals)
hurdiegurdie — hurdy-gurdy
hurdle, -dled, -dling
hurdul — hurdle
hurdy-gurdy, -dies
huricane — hurricane
hurie — hurry
hurl, -ed, -ing
hurlie-burlie — hurly-burly
hurly-burly, -burlies
hurmit — hermit
hurnia — hernia
hurray
hurricane
hurry, -ried, -rying
hurse — hearse
hurt, hurt, hurting
hurtel — hurtle
hurtle, -tled, -tling
hurtul — hurtle
hurtz — hertz
hury — hurry
husband
husbandry
hush, -ed, -ing
husie — hussy
husk
huskie — husky
husky, -kier, -kiest (hoarse)
husky, -kies (dog)
hussar
hussel — hustle
hussey — hussy
hussul — hustle

hussy, -sies
hustings
hustle, -tled, -tling
hut, hutted, hutting
hutch
hutkeeper
hyacinth
hybrid
hydatids
hydra, -dras, -drae
hydrangea
hydranja — hydrangea
hydrant
hydrate, -drated, -drating
hydration
hydraulic, -ally
hydrocarbon
hydrochloric acid
hydro-electric
hydrofobia — hydrophobia
hydrofoil
hydrogen
hydrologist
hydrology
hydrolic — hydraulic
hydrolysis, -ses
hydrometer
hydroplane, -planed, -planing
hydroponics
hydrous
hydroxide
hyena
hygene — hygiene
hygiene
hygienic, -ally
hygroscopic
hym — hymn
hymen
hymn (song)
hymnal
hype, hyped, hyping
hyperactive
hyperbola, -las (curve)
hyperbole (overstatement)
hypersensitive
hypertension
hyphen
hyphenate, -nated, -nating
hypnosis, -ses
hypnotherapy
hypnotise, -tised, -tising
hypnotism
hypo
hypochondria
hypocrisy, -sies
hypocrite
hypodermic
hypodermic syringe
hypotenuse
hypothesis, -ses
hypothesise, -sised, -sising
hypothetical, -ly
hysterectomy, -mies
hysteria
hysteric
hysterical, -ly

Ii

ibis
ice, iced, icing
iceberg
icebound
icebox
icebreaker
ice-cream
icepack
icepick
ich — itch
icicle
iclesiastic — ecclesiastic
iclipse — eclipse
icon, icons
iconoclast
iconomey — economy
iconomist — economist
icy, icier, iciest
idea
ideal, -ly
idealise, -ised, -ising
idealism
idem
identical, -ly
identicul — identical
identification
identify, -fied, -fying
identikit
identity, -ties
ideology, -gies
iderdown — eiderdown
ides
idilic — idyllic
idill — idyll
idiocy, -cies
idiologey — ideology
idiom
idiomatic, -ally
idiosincrasy — idiosyncrasy
idiosyncrasy, -sies
idiot
idium — idiom
idle, idled, idling (not busy)
idle — idol (statue)
idler
idol (statue)
idol — idle (not busy)
idolatry, -tries
idolise, -lised, -lising
idyl — idyll
idyll
idyllic, -ally
iface — efface
ifect — effect
ifel — eiffel
ifeminite — effeminate
ificiency — efficiency
igalitarian — egalitarian
igloo, -loos
igneous
ignishun — ignition
ignite, -nited, -niting
ignition
ignition coil
ignius — igneous
ignoble, -bly
ignominy, -minies
ignor — ignore
ignoramus, -muses
ignorant, -ly
ignore, -nored, -noring
iguana
iguarna — iguana
ijaculation — ejaculation
ijection — ejection
ikon, ikons
ikuip — equip
ikwivocal — equivocal
ikwivocate — equivocate
il — I'll (I will)
il — ill (sick)
ilaberate — elaborate
iland — island
ilapse — elapse
ilation — elation

ilastic	elastic
ilate	elate
ile	aisle (passage)
Ile	I'll (I will)
ile	isle (island)
ilect	elect
ilection	election
ilectorate	electorate
ilectrocute	electrocute
ilectronic	electronic
ilegal	illegal
ilegibul	illegible
ilegitimate	illegitimate
ileven	eleven
ilicit	elicit
ilicit	illicit
ilikser	elixir
iliminate	eliminate
ilimination	elimination
ilipse	ellipse
iliptic	elliptic
ilisit	elicit
ilisit	illicit
iliteracy	illiteracy
iliterate	iliterate
ilixir	elixir

ilk
I'll (I will)
ill, worse, worst(sick)
ill-advised, -ly
ill-assorted
ill-bred
ill-defined
illegal, -ly
illegal, -bly

illegibul	illegible

illegitimate, -ly
ill-fated
ill-gotten
ill health
illberal, -ly
illicit, -ly (unlawful)

illicit	elicit (evoke)

illiteracy
illiterate
ill-mannered, -ly
ill-natured, -ly
illness
illogical, -ly
ill-treat, -ed, -ing
illuminate, -nated, -nating
illumination
illumine, -mined, -mining
ill-use, -used, -using
illusion (deception)

illusion	allusion (brief reference)
illusion	elusion (evade)

illusive (deceptive)

illusive	allusive
illusive	elusive

illusory
illustrate, -strated, -strating
illustration
illustrative, -ly
illustrator
illustrious, -ly
ill will

ilogical	illogical
ilope	elope
ilucidate	elucidate
ilude	elude
iluminate	illuminate
ilumination	illumination
ilusidate	elucidate
ilusion	allusion
ilusion	elusion
ilusion	illusion
ilusive	allusive
ilusive	elusive
ilusive	illusive
ilustrate	illustrate
ilustration	illustration
ilustrator	illustrator
ilustrius	illustrious

I'm (I am)

Im	I'm
imaciate	emaciate
imaculate	immaculate

image, -aged, -aging
imagery, -ries

imagin	imagine

imaginary, -ries
imagination

imaginative
imagine, -ined, -ining
imancipate emancipate
imansipation emancipation
imashiate emaciate
imaterial immaterial
imature immature
imaturity immaturity
imbalance
imbalancse imbalance
imbarrass embarrass
imbecile, -ly
imbeseal imbecile
imbibe, -bibed, -bibing
imbroglio, -os
imbue, -bued, -buing
imerge emerge
imergence emergence
imergency emergency
imergent emergent
imetic emetic
imission emission
imit emit

For other im- words, look under imm-.

imitate, -tated, -tating
imitation
immaculate, -ly
immanent (inherent)
immanent (known) eminent
immanent (near) imminent
immaterial, -ly
immature, -ly
immeasurable, -bly
immediate, -ly
immemorial, -ly
immense, -ly
immerse, -mersed, -mersing
immershun immersion
immersion
immesurable immeasurable
immigrant
immigrate, -grated, -grating
imminent (near)
imminate (known) eminent
imminent herent) immanent (inherent)
immobile
immobility
immimmoderate, -ly
immodest, -ly
immolate, -lated, -lating
immoral, -ly
immortal, -ly
immoratalise, -lised, -lising
immortality, -ties
immovable, -bly
immune, -ly
immunise, -nised, -nising
immunology
immure, -mured, -muring
immutable, -bly
imolient emollient
imolument emolument
imoshen emotion
imoshun emotion
imoshunal emotional
imotion emotion
imotive emotive
imp
impact, -ed, -ing
impair, -ed, -ing
impale, -paled, -paling
impalpable, -bly
impare impair
imparshal impartial
impart, -ed, -ing
impartial, -ly
impasable impassable
impashent impatient
impasioned impassioned
impassive impassive
impassable, -bly
impasse
impassioned, -ly
impassive, -ly
impatient, -ly
impeach, -ed, -ing
impecabul impeccable
impeccable, -bly

impecunious, -ly
impecunius impecunious
impede, -peded, -peding
impediment, -ary
impeech impeach
impel, -pelled, -pelling
impentrable, -bly
impenge impinge
imperative, -ly
imperceptibel imperceptible
imperceptible, -bly
imperfect, -ly
imperial, -ly
imperialism
imperil, -rilled, -rilling
imperious, -ly
imperius imperiou
impermeable, -bly
impermeabul impermeable
imperseptibul imperceptible
impersonal, -ly
impersonate, -nated, -nating
impertinence
impertinense impertinence
imperturbable, -bly
impervious, -ly
impervius impervious
impetuous, -ly
impetus, -tuses
impiety, -ties
impinge, -pinged, -pinging
impious, -ly
impish, -ly
impius impious
implacable, -bly
implacabul implacable
implant, -ed, -ing
implausible, -bly
imlausibul implausible
implement, -ed, -ing
implicate, -cated, -cating
implication
implicit, -ly
implie imply
implied
implisit implicit
implode, -ploded, -ploding
implore, -plored, -ploring
imply, -plied, -plying
impolite, -ly
impolitic, -ly
import, -ed, -ing
importance
importanse importance
important, -ly
importunate, -ly
importune, -tuned, -tuning
imposcher imposture
impose, -posed, -posing
imposibul impossible
imposishun imposition
imposition
impossible, -bly
imposter impostor
impostor
imposture
impotence
impotent, -ly
impound, -ed, -ing
impoverish, -ed, -ing
impracticability
impracticable, -bly
impracticabul impracticable
impractical, -ly
imprecate, -cated, -cating
imprecise, -ly
imprecise, -bly
impregnabul impregnable
impregenate, -nated, -nating
impres impress
impresario, -os
impreshun impression
impreshunable impressionable
imprehunism impressionism
impresise imprescise
impresive impressive
impress, -pressed, -pressing
impression
impressionable, -bly
imressionism
impressive, -ly
imprimature
imprint, -ed, -ing
imprison, -ed, -ing

Entry	Correct spelling
improbable, -bly	
impromptu	
improper, -ly	
impropriety, -ties	
improve, -proved, -proving	
improvement	
improvident, -ly	
improvise, -vised, -vising	
imprudent, -ly	
impruve	improve
impudent, -ly	
impugn, -ed, -ing	
impulse	
impune	impugn
impunity	
impure, impurer, impurist	
impute, -puted, -puting	
imulshun	emulsion
imune	immune
imunologey	immunlolgy
imurge	emerge
in	
in	inn (hotel)
inability	
in absenshia	in absentia
in absentia	
inaccessabul	inaccessible
inaccessible, -bly	
inaccuracy, -cies	
inactive, -ly	
inacurascy	inaccuracy
inacurasey	inaccuracy
inadekwat	inadequate
inadequate, -ly	
inadvertent, -ly	
inalienable, -bly	
inalienabul	inalienable
inane, -ly	
inanimate, -ly	
inappreciable, -bly	
inappreciabul	inappreciable
inappropriate, -ly	
inapropriate	inappropriate
inapt, -ly	
inaptitude	
inarticulate, -ly	
inasmuch as	

Entry	Correct spelling
inate	innate
inatentive	inattentive
inattentive, -ly	
inaugural	
inaugurate, -rated, -rating	
inausoicious, -ly	
inawmus	enormous
inawspishus	inauspicious
inborn	
inbreed, -bred, -bredding	
incalculable, -bly	
in camera	
incandescence	
incandescent, -ly	
incandescence	incandescence
incantation	
incapable, -bly	
incapabul	incapable
incapacitate, -tated, -tating	
incapacity, -ties	
incapasitate	incapacitate
incaoasitey	incapacity
incarcerate, -rated, -rating	
incarnate, -nated, -nating	
incarserate	incarcerate
incendiary, -aries	
incense (perfume)	
incense, -censed, -censing (angry)	
incentive	
inception	
incessant, -ly	
incessent	incessant
incest	
incestuous, -ly	
inch, -ed, -ing	
incidence	
incident	
incidental, -ly	
incinerate, -rated, -rating	
incinerator	
incipient, -ly	
incise, -cised, -cising	
incision	
incisive, -ly	
incisor	
incite, -cited, -citing (urge)	
incite	insight (see)

incivility, -ties
inclement, -ly
inclination
incline, -clined, -clining
inclose enclose
include, -cluded, -cluding
inclusion
inclusive, -ly
incognito, -tos
incoherent, -ly
income
incommensurable, -bly
incommensurate, -ly
incommode, -moded, -moding
incommodity, -ties
incommunicability
incommunicable, -bly
incommunicado
incommunicative, -ly
incomparable, -bly
incompatible, -bly
incompatibul incompatible
incompetent, -ly
incomplete, -ly
incomprehensible, -bly
incomprehnsion
incomunicado incommunicado
inconceivable, -bly
inconcievable inconceivable
inconclusive, -ly
incongruous, -ly
incongruus incongruous
inconseavable inconceivable
inconsequent, -ly
inconsequential, -ly
inconsiderate, -ly
inconsistant inconsistent
inconsistent, -ly
inconsolable, -bly
inconsolabul inconsolable
inconspicuous, -ly
inconstant, -ly
incontestable, -bly
incontestabul incontestable
incontinet, -ly
incontrovertible, -bly
inconvenience, -ienced, -iencing
inconvenient, -ly
incorect incorrect
incorigibul incorrigible
incorporate, -raed, -rating
incorporation
incorrect, -ly
incorrigible, -bly
incorrupt, -ly
incorruptible, -bly
increase, -creased, -creasing
incredible, -bly
incredibul incredible
incredulity
incredulous, -ly
incredulus incredulous
increment
incremental
increse increase
incriminate, -nated, -nating
incubate, -bated, -bating
incubator
incubate, -cated, -cating
incum income
incumbent, -ly
incumbrance
incur, -curred, -curring
incurable, -bly
incurabul incurable
incurshun incursion
incursion
indebted
indecent, -ly
indecipherable
indecishun indecision
indecision
indecisive, -ly
indeclinable
indeclinabul indeclinable
indecorous, -ly
indecorus indecorous
indeed
indefatigable, -bly
indefatigabul indefatigable
indefensibe, -bly
indefeasibul indefeasible
indefensible, -bly
indefensibul indefensible

Entry	Misspelling	Correct spelling
indefinable, -bly		
	indefinabul	indefinable
indefinite, -ly		
	indeks	index
indelible, -bly		
	indelibul	indelible
indelicate, -ly		
	indemnifie	indemnify
indemnify, -fied, -fying		
indemnity, -ties		
	indencher	indenture
indent, -ed, -ing		
indenture, -tured, -turing		
independent, -ly		
in-depth		
indescribable, -bly		
	indescribabul	indescribable
	indesent	indecent
	indesiferable	indecipherable
	indespensable	indispensable
indestructible, -bly		
	indestructibul	indestructible
	indeted	indebted
indeterminate, -ly		
index, -dexes, -dices		
indexation		
Indian		
indiarubber		
indicate, -cated, -cating		
indicative, -ly		
indicator		
indices		
indict, -ed, -ing		
indictment		
	indiferent	indifferent
indifferent, -ly		
indigenous, -ly		
indigent, -ly		
indigestible, -bly		
	indigestibul	indigestible
indigestion		
indignant, -ly		
indignation		
indignity, -ties		
indigo, -gos		
	indipendent	independent
indirect, -ly		

Entry	Misspelling	Correct spelling
indiscreet, -ly		
	indiscreshun	indiscretion
	indiscrete	indiscreet
indiscretion		
indiscriminate, -ly		
	indisishun	indecision
	indisisive	indecisive
	indisoluble	indissoluble
indispensable, -bly		
	indispensabul	indispensable
indisposed		
indisposition		
indisputable, -bly		
	indisputabul	indisputable
indissoluble, -bly		
indistinct, -ly		
indistinguishable, -bly		
indite, -dited, -diting (write)		
	indite	indict (accuse)
individual, -ly		
individualism		
individualist		
individuality, -ties		
indivisible, -bly		
	indivisibul	indivisible
indoctrinate, -nated, -nating		
indolent, -ly		
indomitable, -bly		
	indomitabul	indomitable
indoor		
indubitable, -bly		
	indubitabul	indubitable
induce, -duced, -ducing		
	inducshion	induction
	inducshun	induction
induct, -ed, -ing		
induction		
inductive, -ly		
inductor		
indulge, -dulged, -dulging		
indulgence		
	indulgense	indulgence
indulgent, -ly		
	industrey	industry
industrial, -ly		
industrialise, -lised, -lising		
industrialism		

industrialist
industrious, -ly
industrius   industrious
industry, -tries
inebriate, -ated, -ating
inebriation
inedible
inedibul   inedible
inefable   ineffable
inefective   ineffective
inefectual   ineffectual
ineffable, -bly
ineffective, -ly
ineffectual, -ly
inefficient, -ly

For ineks- words, look under **inex-** .

inelegant, -ly
ineligible, -bly
ineligibul   ineligible
inept, -ly
inequality, -ties
inequitable, -bly
inequitabul   inequitable
inequity, -ties
ineradicable, -bly
ineradicabul   ineradicable
inersha   inertia
inert, -ly
inertia
inescapable, -bly
inescapabul   inescapable
inesenshul   inessential
inessential, -ly
inestimable, -bly
inestimabul   inestimable
inevitable, -bly
inevitabul   inevitable
inexact, -ly
inexcusable, -bly
inexhaustible, -bly
inexorable, -bly
inexorabul   inexorable
inexpedient, -ly
inexpensive, -ly
inexperienced
inexperiense   inexperience
inexpert, -ly
inexplicable, -bly
inexplicit, -ly
inexpressible, -bly
in extremis
inextricable, -bly
infalible   infallible
infalibul   infallible
infallible, -bly
infamey   infamy
infamous, -ly
infamus   infamous
infamy, -mies
infancy, -cies
infansey   infancy
infant
infanticide
infantiside   infanticide
infantile
infantrey   infantry
infantry
infatuate, -ated, -ating
infatuation
infecshun   infection
infect, -ed, -ing
infection
infectious, -ly
infelicity, -ties
infer, -ferred, -ferring
inference
inferense   inference
inferier   inferior
inferior
inferiority complex
inferm   infirm
infermarey   infirmary
infernal, -ly
inferno, -nos
infertile
infest, -ed, -ing
infidel
infidelity, -ties
infighting
infiltrate, -trated, -trating
infinite, -ly
infinitesimal, -ly

infinitey	**infinity**
infinitive, -ly	
infinity, -ties	
infirior	**inferior**
infirm, -ly	
infirmary, -ries	
inflamabul	**inflammable**
inflamatry	**inflammatory**
inflame, -flamed, -flaming	
inflammable, -bly	
inflammation	
inflammatory	
inflatable	
inflate, -flated, -flating	
inflation	
inflect, -ed, -ing	
inflection	
inflexible, -bly	
inflict, -ed, -ing	
infliction	
inflow	
influence, -enced, -encing	
influense	**influence**
influenshul	**influential**
influential, -ly	
influenza	
influks	**influx**
inform, -ed, -ing	
informal, -ly	
informant	
information	
informer	
infracshun	**infraction**
infraction	
infra-red	
infrastructure	
infrekwency	**infrequency**
infrekwent	**infrequent**
infrequency	
infrequent, -ly	
infringe, -fringed, -fringing	
infuriate, -ated, -ating	
infurnal	**infernal**
infuse, -fused, -fusing	
infusion	
infusun	**infusion**
ingenious, -ly (clever)	
ingenius	**ingenious**
ingenue	
ingenuity, -ties	
ingenuous, -ly (innocent)	
ingenuus	**ingenuous**
ingest, -ed, -ing	
ingestion	
Inglish	**English**
ingot	
ingrain, -ed, -ing	
ingrashiate	**ingratiate**
ingrate	
ingratiate, -ated, -ating	
ingratitude	
ingrave	**engrave**
ingredient	
ingress	
in-groop	**in-group**
in-group	
ingrown	
inhabit, -ed, -ing	
inhalant	
inhalation	
inhale, -haled, -haling	
inhear	**inhere**
inhere, -hered, -hering	
inherent, -ly	
inherit, -ed, -ing	
inheritance	
inheritanse	**inheritance**
inhibishun	**inhibition**
inhibit, -ed, -ing	
inhospitable, -bly	
inhospitabul	**inhospitable**
inhospitality	
inhuman, -ly	
inhumane, -ly	
inhumanity, -ties	
inikwality	**inequality**
inikwity	**iniquity**
inikwitus	**iniquitous**
inimical, -ly	
inimitable, -bly	
inimitability	
inimitabul	**inimitable**
inings	**innings**
iniquitey	**iniquity**

iniquitous, -ly	
iniquitus	iniquitous
iniquity, -ties (sin)	
iniquity	inequity (unfair)
inishal	initial
inishative	initiative
inishiate	initiate
initial, -ialled, -ialling	
initiate, -ated, -ating	
initiation	
initiative	
inject, -ed, -ing	
injection	
injenue	ingenue
injere	injure
in-joke	
injudicious, -ly	
injudishus	injudicious
injunction	
injunkshun	injunction
injure, -jured, -juring	
injurey	injury
injurius	injurious
injury, -ries	
injustice	
injustise	injustice
ink	
inkeeper	innkeeper
inkling	
inkwest	inquest
inkwire	enquire
inkwisitive	inquisitive
inkwisitor	inquisitor

For other ink- words, look under **inc-**.

inlade	inlaid
inland	
in-law	
inlay, -laid, -laying	
inlet	
in loco parentis	
inmate	
in memoriam	
inmost	
inn (hotel)	
innards	
innate, -ly	
inner	
innerject	interject
innermost	
innings	
innkeeper	
innocence	
innocent, -ly	
innocuous, -ly	
innovate, -vated, -vating	
innovation	
innovative, -ly	
innovatory	
innuendo, -dos	
innumerable, -bly	
innumerate	
inocent	innocent
inoculate, -lated, -lating	
inoculation	
inocuus	innocuous
inofensive	inoffensive
inoffensive, -ly	
inoperable, -bly	
inoperative, -ly	
inoportune	inopportune
inopportune, -ly	
inordible	inaudible
inordibul	inaudible
inordinate, -ly	
inorganic, -ally	
inorgural	inaugural
inorgurate	inaugurate
inormity	enormity
inormous	enormous
inorspishus	inauspicious
inosence	innocence
inosent	innocent
inough	enough
inovate	innovate
in-patient	
in-payshent	in-patient
input	
inquest	
inquietude	
inquire, -quired, -quiring	
inquiry, -ries	

inquisitive, -ly	
inrage	enrage
inroad	
inrode	inroad
insalubrious, -ly	
insalubrious	insalubrious
insaine	insane
insane, -ly	
insanitary	
insanitey	insanity
insanitry	insanitary
insanity, -ties	
insatiable, -bly	
insayshabul	insatiable
inscribe, -scribed, -scribing	
inscription	
inscrutable, -bly	
inscrutability	
insect	
insecticide	
insectiside	insecticide
insecure, -ly	
insecurity, -ties	
inseminate, -nated, -nating	
insemination	
insendiary	incendiary
insensate, -ly	
insense	incense
insensible, -bly	
insensibility, -ties	
insensibul	insensible
insensitive, -ly	
insensitivity	
insentive	incentive
inseparable, -bly	
inseperabul	inseparable
inseprabul	inseparable
insepshun	inception
insert, -ed, -ing	
insertion	
insertitude	incertitude
in-service	
insesent	incessant
insest	incest
insestuous	incestuous
inset, -set, -setting	
inshoranse	insurance
inshore	ensure (certain)
inshore	insure (protect)
inshorense	insurance
inside	
insidense	incidence
insident	incident
insidentul	incidental
insidious, -ly	
insidius	insidious
insight, (see)	
insight	incite (urge)
insignia	
insignificance	
insignificant, -ly	
insincere, -ly	
insincerity, -ties	
insinerate	incinerate
insinerater	incinerator
insinsere	insincere
insinserity	insincerity
insinuate, -ated, -ating	
insipid, -ly	
insipient	incipient
insiser	inciser
insision	incision
insisive	incisive
insist, -ed, -ing	
insistence	
insistent, -ly	
insite	incite (urge)
insite	insight (see)
insivility	incivility
insobriety	
insofar	
insolence	
insolense	insolence
insolent, -ly	
insolubility	
insoluble, -bly	
insolubul	insoluble
insolvency	
insolvensy	insolvency
insolvent	
insomnia	
inspechun	inspection
inspect, -ed, -ing	
inspecter	inspector

inspection	
inspector	
inspiration	
inspire, -spired, -spiring	
instability	
instagate	**instigate**
instal	**install**
install, -ed, -ing	
installment	**instalment**
instalment	
instance, -stanced, -stancing	
instanse	**instance**
instant, -ly	
instantaneous, -ly	
instantanius	**instantaneous**
instatution	**institution**
instead	
insted	**instead**
instep	
instigate, -gated, -gating	
instigater	**instigator**
instigation	
instigator	
instil	**instill**
instilashun	**instillation**
instill, -stilled, -stilling	
instillation	
instinct	
instinctive, -ly	
institushen	**institution**
institute, -tuted, -tuting	
institution	
institutional, -ly	
institutionalise, -lised, -lising	
instremunt	**instrument**
instruct, -ed, -ing	
instruction	
instructive, -ly	
instrument	
instrumental, -ly	
instrumentalist	
instrumentation	
instrument panel	
insubordinate, -ly	
insubordination	
insubstanshul	**insubstantial**
insubstantial, -ly	
insue	**ensue**
insufferable, -bly	
insufficiency	
insufficient, -ly	
insuffishency	**insufficiency**
insufrabul	**insufferable**
insular, -ly	
insularity	
insulate, -lated, -lating	
insulation	
insulin	
insult, -ed, -ing	
insuperable, -bly	
insuperabul	**insuperable**
insurance	
insuranse	**insurance**
insure, -sured, -suring	
insurecshun	**insurrection**
insurgence	
insurgency	
insurgense	**insurgence**
insurgent	
insurmountable, -bly	
insurrection	
insurshun	**insertion**
insurt	**insert**
intact	
intaglio, intaglios, intagli	
intail	**entail**
intake	
intangible, -bly	
intangibul	**intangible**
integer	
integral, -ly	
integrate, -grated, -grating	
integrated circuit	
integration	
integrity	
intelect	**intellect**
intelectual	**intellectual**
inteligense	**intelligence**
inteligensia	**intelligentsia**
inteligent	**intelligent**
inteligibul	**intelligible**
intellect	
intellectual, -ly	
intelligence	

intelligent, -ly
intelligentsia
intemperance
intemperanse intemperance
intemperate, -ly
intend, -ed, -ing
intense, -ly
intenshun intention
intensify, -fied, -fying
intensive, -ly
intent, -ly
intention
intentional, -ly
inter, -terred, -terring
interact, -ed, -ing
interaction
inter alia
intercede, -ceded, -ceding
intercept, -ed, -ing
interception
interceptor
interceshun intercession
intercession
intercessor
interchange, -changed, -changing
interchangeable, -bly
intercom
intercontinental
intercorse intercourse
intercourse
interdependence
interdependency
interdependent, -ly
interdict
interdisciplinary
interelate interrelate
interest, -ed, -ing
interface, -faced, -facing
interfear interfere
interfere, -fered, -fering
interference
interfuse, -fused, -fusing
intergalactic
interier interior
interim
interior
interject, -ed, -ing
interjection
injector
interlace, -laced, -lacing
interline, -lined, -lining
interlock, -ed, -ing
interloap interlope
interlood interlude
interlope, -loped, -loping
interloper
interlude
intermarie intermarry
intermarry, -ried, -rying
intermediary, -aries
intermediate, -ly
interment
intermesh, -ed, -ing
intermezzo, -zos, -zi
interminable, -bly
interminabul interminable
intermishun intermission
intermission
intermittent, -ly
intern
internal, -ly
internal-combustion engine
internalise, -lised, -lising
internashunal international
international, -ly
internationale
internationalism
internecine
internee
internisine internecine
interogate interrogate
interpersonal, -ly
interplay, -ed, -ing
interpolate, -lated, -lating
interpose, -posed, -posing
interpret, -ed, -ing
interpretation
interpreter
interracial, -ly
interregnum, -nums
interrelate, -lated, -lating
interrogate, -gated, -gating
interrogation
interrogative, -ly

interrogator
interrupt, -ed, -ing
interruption
intersect, -ed, -ing
intersection
intersede   intercede
intersepshun   interception
intersept   intercept
interseshun   intercession
intersperse, -spersed, -spersing
interspurse   intersperse
interstate
interstice, -tices
intertwine, -twined, -twining
interupshun   interruption
interurban
interval
interveiw   interview
intervene, -vened, -vening
intervener
intervenor   intervener
intervenshun   intervention
intervention
interview, -ed, -ing
interviewer
intervue   interview
interweave, -woven, -weaving
interweaver
intestate
intestine
intice   entice
intiger   integer
intigral   integral
intigrate   integrate
intimacy, -cies
intimasy   intimacy
intimate, -ly
intimate, -mated, -mating
intimation
intimidate, -dated, -dating
intimidation
intimidator
intoksicate   intoxicate
intolerable, -bly
intolerabul   intolerable
intolerance
intoleranse   intolerance
intolerant, -ly
intonation
intone, -toned, -toning
in toto
intoxicant
intoxicate, -cated, -cating
intoxication
intractable, -bly
intractabul   intractable
intransigence
intransigency
intransigense   intransigence
intransigensy   intransigency
intransigent, -ly
intransitive, -ly
intrastate
intra-uterine device
intravenous, -ly
intravenus   intravenous
in-tray
intreege   intrigue
intrepid, -ly
intricacy, -cies
intricasey   intricacy
intricate, -ly
intrigue, -trigued, -triguing
intriguer
intrinsic, -ally
introduce, -duced, -ducing
introducshun   introduction
introduction
introductory
introduse   introduce
introode   intrude
introosive   intrusive
introspection
introvert, -ly
intrude, -truded, -truding
intruder
intrushun   intrusion
intrusion
intrusive, -ly
intrust   entrust
intuishun   intuition
intuition
intuitive, -ly
inturn   intern

inturnal	internal
inuendo	innuendo
inumerabul	innumerable
inumerate	enumerate
inumeration	enumeration
inunciate	enunciate
inundate, -dated, -dating	
inundation	
inunsiate	enunciate
inure, inured, inuring	
inursha	inertia
inurt	inert
invade, -vaded, -vading	
invalid, -ly	
invalidate, -dated, -dating	
invalidation	
invaluable, -bly	
invaluabul	invaluable
invaluble	invaluable
invariability	
invariable, -bly	
invariabul	invariable
invasion	
invatation	invitation
invay	inveigh
invaygul	inveigle
invective, -ly	
inveigh, -ed, -ing	
inveigle, -gled, -gling	
inveigul	inveigle
invenshun	invention
invent, -ed, -ing	
invention	
inventive, -ly	
inventor	
inventory, -tories	
inventry	inventory
inverse, -ly	
invershun	inversion
inversion	
invert, -ed, -ing	
invertebrate	
invest, -ed, -ing	
investagation	investigation
investichure	investiture
investigate, -gated, -gating	
investigation	
investigator	
investiture	
investment	
inveterate	
invidios	invidious
invidious, -ly	
invidiousness	
inviegh	inveigh
inviegle	inveigle
invigorate, -rated, -rating	
invincible, -bly	
invinsibul	invincible
inviolable, -bly	
inviolabul	inviolable
inviolate, -ly	
invisibility	
invisible, -bly	
invisibul	invisible
invitation	
invite, -vited, -viting	
in vitro	
invocation	
invoice, -voiced, -voicing	
invoise	invoice
invoke, -voked, -voking	
involuntary, -tarily	
involuntrey	involuntary
involushun	involution
involution	
involve, -volved, -volving	
involvement	
invulnerable, -bly	
invulnerabul	invulnerable
inverce	inverse
invirt	invert
inward, -ly	
inwardness	
inwards	
inwood	inward
inyure	inure
iodene	iodine
iodine	
ion (atom)	
ion	iron (metal)
ionesfere	ionosphere
ionise, -nised, -nising	
ionosphere	

Word	Correct spelling
iony	irony
iota	
IOU	
iradiate	irradiate
iradicate	eradicate
irascibility	
irascible, -bly	
irascibleness	
irascibul	irascible
irase	erase
irate, -ly	
irational	irrational
ire	

For other ir- words, look under irr-.

Word	Correct spelling
iridesense	iridescence
iridesent	iridescent
iridescence	
iris, irises	
Irish	
irk (bore)	
irk	erk (rank)
irksome, -ly	
irksum	irksome
iron, -ed, -ing (metal)	
iron	ion (atom)
ironbark	
ironeus	erroneous
ironic, -ally	
ironmonger	
ironmongery	
ironware	
irony, -nies	
iroshun	erosion
irosion	erosion
irotic	erotic
irradiashun	irradiation
irradiate, -ated, -ating	
irradiation	
irrashionul	irrational
irrational, -ly	
irreconcilable, -bly	
irrecoverable, -bly	
irrecoverabul	irrecoverable
irredeemable, -bly	
irredeemabul	irredeemable
irreducibility	
irreducible, -bly	
irreducibul	irreducible
irrefutable, -bly	
irrefutabul	irrefutable
irregardless	
irregular, -ly	
irregularity, -ties	
irrelevance	
irrelevancy	
irrelevansey	irrelevancy
irrelevant, -ly	
irreligious, -ly	
irreligus	irreligious
irreparable, -bly	
irreparabul	irreparable
irreplacabul	irreplaceable
irreplaceable, -bly	
irrepresibul	irrepressible
irrepressible, -bly	
irreproachable, -bly	
irreprochabul	irreproachable
irresistabul	irresistible
irresistible, -bly	
irresolute, -ly	
irrespective, -ly	
irresponsibility	
irresponsible, -bly	
irresponsibul	irresponsible
irretraceable, -bly	
irretraseabul	irretraceable
irretrievable, -bly	
irretrievabul	irretrievable
irreverant	irreverent
irreverence	
irreverent, -ly	
irreverint	irreverent
irreversibility	
irreversible, -bly	
irreversibul	irreversible
irrevocable, -bly	
irrevocabul	irrevocable
irridescent	iridescent
irrigate, -gated, -gating	
irrigation	
irrisistabel	irresistible
irrisistabul	irresistible

irritability	
irritable, -bly	
irritabul	irritable
irritancy	
irritansey	irritancy
irritant	
irritate, -tated, -tating	
irritation	
irrupshun	irruption
irrupt, -ed, -ing	
irruption	
irruptive, -ly	
isalate	isolate
isatope	isotope
ise	ice
ishue	issue
isicul	icicle
isight	eyesight
Islam	
Islamic	
island	
islander	
isle (island)	
isle	aisle (passage)
isn't (is not)	
isnt	isn't
isobar	
isolate, -lated, -lating	
isolation	
isolationism	
isolationist	
isosceles	
isosilese	isosceles
isotope	
Israeli	
Isralie	Israeli
issue, issued, issuing	
isthmus, -muses	
istmus	isthmus
italic	
itch, -ed, -ing	
item	
itemise, -mised, -mising	
iterate, -rated, -rating	
iteration	
iternal	eternal
iternally	eternally
iternity	eternity
itinerant, -ly	
itinerary, -ries	
it'll (it will)	
itll	it'll
it's (it is)	
its (possessive)	
its	it's (it is)
itself	
ivacuate	evacuate
ivacuation	evacuation
ivade	evade
ivaluate	evaluate
ivaluation	evaluation
ivaporate	evaporate
ivaporation	evaporation
ivasion	evasion
ivasive	evasive
I've (I have)	
Ive	I've
ivent	event
iventual	eventual
ivery	ivory
ivey	ivy
ivict	evict
iviction	eviction
ivoke	evoke
ivolve	evolve
ivory, -ries	
ivory tower	
ivry	ivory
ivy, ivies	
Ivy League	

Jj

jab, jabbed, jabbing
jabber
jabiru
jacana
jacaranda
jack
jackal
jackass
jackdaw
  jackdoor   jackdaw
jackeroo
jacket
jackhammer
jack-in-the-box
jackknife, -knives
jack-of-all-trades
jackpot, -potted, -potting
Jacobean
jade, jaded, jading
jaffle
  jafful   jaffle
jag, jagged, jagging
jaguar
jail
jake
jalopy, -lopies
jam, jammed, jamming
jam (food)
  jam   jamb (door)
jamb (door)
jamboree
  jamborie   jamboree
jangle, -gled, -gling
  jangul   jangle
  janiter   janitor
janitor
January
  Janurey   January
Japanese, -nese
japonica
jar, jarred, jarring
jargon
jarrah
  jarrar   jarrah
  jasmin   jasmine
jasper
jaundice, -diced, -dicing
  jaundise   jaundice
jaunt, -ed, -ing
  jauntie   jaunty
jaunty, -tier, -tiest
javelin
  javlin   javelin
jaw
  jawndise   jaundice
  jawnt   jaunt
jay
jaywalk, -ed, -ing
jaywalker
  jaz   jazz
jazz
jazzy, -zier, -ziest
jealous, -ly
jealousy, -ousies
  jealus   jealous
jeans
jeep
jeer, -ed, -ing
Jehovah
Jehovah's Witness
jejune
  jelie   jelly
jelly, -lies
jelly, -lied, -lying
jellyfish, -fish, -fishes
  jelous   jealous
  jelus   jealous
  jely   jelly
  jemey   jemmy
  jemie   jemmy
jemmy, -mies
jemmy, -mied, -mying
  jemy   jemmy
jeopardise, -dised, -dising
jeopardy

Word	Correct spelling
jepardise	jeopardise
jepardy	jeopardy
jerboa	
jeribilt	jerry-built
jerk, -ed, -ing	
jerkin	
jerky, -kily	
jerry, -ries	
jerry-build, -built, -building	
jerry can	
jersey	
jersie	jersey
jest, -ed, -ing	
jester	
Jesuit	
Jesus	
jet, jetted, jetting	
jetie	jetty
jetison	jettison
jet lag	
jettison, -ed, -ing	
jetty, -ties	
jety	jetty
Jew	
Jewish	
jewel, -elled, -elling (cut gem)	
jewel	dual (two)
jewel	duel (fight)
jewel	joule (unit)
jeweler	jeweller
jeweller	
jewellery	
jewelrey	jewellery
jewfish	
Jewry (Jewish people)	
jewry	jury (court)
jew's harp	
jib, jibbed, jibbing	
jibe, jibed, jibing (sail)	
jibe	gibe (scoff)
jiffy, -fies	
jifie	jiffy
jify	jiffy
jig, jigged, jigging	
jigger	
jiggle, -gled, -gling	
jiggul	jiggle

Word	Correct spelling
jigsaw	
jillaroo	
jilt, -ed, -ing	
jim	gym
jimkana	gymkhana
jin	gin
jingel	jingle
jingle, -gled, -gling	
jingoism	
jingul	jingle
jinks	jinx
jinx, -es	
jirashun	gyration
jiration	gyration
jiro	gyro
jiroscope	gyroscope
jist	gist
jiter	jitter
jitter, -ed, -ing	
jittery	
jive, jived, jiving	
job, jobbed, jobbing	
jobber	
jockey, -eys	
jockey, -eyed, -eying	
jockie	jockey
jockstrap	
jocky	jockey
jocose, -ly	
jocosity, -ties	
jocular, -ly	
jocularity, -ties	
jocund, -ly	
jocundity, -ties	
jodhpurs	
jodpurs	jodhpurs
joey, -eys	
jog, jogged, jogging	
jogger	
jogtrot, -trotted, -trotting	
johnnycake	
joi	joy
join, joined, joining	
joiner	
joinery	
joint, -ly	
joist	

joke, joked, joking	
joker	
jollitey	jollity
jollity, -ties	
jolly, -lier, -liest	
jolt, -ed, -ing	
joly	jolly
jonah	
jonathan	
jonquil	
Joo	Jew
Jooish	Jewish
jool	joule (unit)
Joone	June
joopiter	Jupiter
joose	deuce (two)
joose	juice (liquid)
joote	jute
jostle, -tled, -tling	
josul	jostle
jot, jotted, jotting	
jotter	
joule (unit)	
joule	dual (two)
joule	duel (fight)
joule	jewel (gem)
journal	
journalese	
journalism	
journalist	
journel	journal
journey, -neys	
journey, -neyed, -neying	
joust, -ed, -ing	
Jove	
jovial, -ly	
joviality	
jowl	
joy	
joyful, -ly	
joyous, -ly	
joy-ride, -rode, -riding	
joystick	
joyus	joyous
ju	Jew
jube	
jubilant, -ly	

jubilate, -lated, -lating	
jubilation	
jubilee	
jubilie	jubilee
juce	deuce (two)
juce	juice (liquid)
Judaism	
judas	
judge, judged, judging	
judgement	
judgment	
judicacher	judicature
judicachur	judicature
judicature	
judicial, -ly	
judiciary, -aries	
judicious, -ly	
judishul	judicial
judisharey	judiciary
judishous	judicious
judishus	judicious
judo	
juel	dual (two)
juel	duel (fight)
juel	jewel (gem)
juel	joule (unit)
jug, jugged, jugging	
juge	judge
juggement	judgement
juggernaut	
juggle, -gled, -gling	
juggler	
jugul	juggle
jugular	
juice (liquid)	
juice	deuce (two)
juiciness	
juicy, -cier, -ciest	
Juish	Jewish
jujitsu	
jukebox	
jukstapose	juxtapose
julep	
Juli	July
July	
jumble, -bled, -bling	
jumbo, -bos	

jumbuck
  jumbul — jumble
jump, -ed, -ing
jumper
jump-start
jump suit
jumpy, jumpier, jumpiest
junction
juncture
June
jungle
  jungul — jungle
  junier — junior
junior
juniper
junk
  junkcher — juncture
junket
junkie
  junkshere — juncture
  junkshun — junction
  junkshure — juncture
junta
Jupiter
  jurer — juror
  juri — jury
juridical, -ly
  jurisdickshion — jurisdiction
  jurisdickshun — jurisdiction
jurisdiction
jurisprudence
  jurisprudense — jurisprudence
  jurisprudunse — jurisprudence
jurist
  jurnal — journal
  jurney — journey
juror
jury, -ries
  juse — juice
  jusie — juicy
jussive
just, -ly
justice
justice of the peace
  justifiabel — justifiable
justifiable, -bly
justification
justify, -fied, -fying
  justise — justice
jut, jutted, jutting
jute
juvenile, -ly
  juwel — dual (two)
  juwel — duel (fight)
  juwel — jewel (gem)
  juwel — joule (unit)
  juxapose — juxtapose
  juxaposition — juxtaposition
juxtapose, -posed, -posing
juxtaposition
  jym — gym
  jyroscope — gyroscope

Kk

Look under	if the word is not under k
kadaicha man	
kaleidoscope	
kalidascope	kaleidoscope
kalidescope	kaleidoscope
kalsomine, -mined, -mining	
kamikaze	
kampong	
kanaka	
kangaroo	
kaolin	
ka pai	
kapok	
kaput	
karate	
karkey	khaki
karki	khaki
karma	
karri, -ris (tree)	
karri	carry (bring)
kauri, -ris	
kayak	
kebab	
kedgeree	
keel, -ed, -ing	
keen, -ly	
keenness	
keep, kept, keeping	
keeper	
keg	
kelp	
kelpey	kelpie
kelpie	
kelt	Celt
keltic	Celtic
ken, kenned, kenning	
kenel	kennel
kennel, -nelled, -nelling	
kept	
keratin	
kerb (gutter)	
kerb	curb (check)
kerchief	
kerfuffle	
kernel (core)	
kernel	colonel (army)
kero	
keropody	chiropody
keroseen	kerosene
kerosene	
kerosine	
kestrel	
ketch	
ketchup	
ketle	kettle
kettle	
kettledrum	
kettul	kettle
kew	cue
kew	queue (line)
kewpie	
key, keys (lock)	
key, keyed, keying	
key	quay (wharf)
keyboard	
keystone	
khaki, -kis	
kibble, -bled, -bling	
kibbul	kibble
kiak	kayak
kibbutz	
kick, kicked, kicking	
kick-off	
kid, kidded, kidding	
kidnap, -napped, -napping	
kidney, -neys	
kikuyu	
kill, killed, killing	
killer	
killjoy	
kiln	
kilo	
kilogram	

Word	Correct spelling
kilojoule	
kilometer	kilometre
kilometre	
kilowatt	
kilowatt-hour	
kilt	
kilter	
kimono, -nos	
kin	
kina	
kind, -ly	
kindness	
kindergarten	
kindle, -dled, -dling	
kindly, -lier, -liest	
kindred	
kindrid	kindred
kindrud	kindred
kindul	kindle
kinetics	
king	
kingdom	
kingly	
kingfish	
kingfisher	
kingpin	
kink, kinked, kinking	
kinkiness	
kinky, -kier, -kiest	
kinsfolk	
kinship	
kinsman, -men	
kiosk	
kip, kipped, kipping	
kipper	
kirk	
kiropody	chiropody
kismet	
kiss, kissed, kissing	
kissable	
kit, kitted, kitting	
kitbag	
kitchen	
kite	
kiten	kitten
kith	
kitie	kitty
kitsch	
kitten	
kittenish, -ly	
kitty, -ties	
kity	kitty
kiwi	
kiyak	kayak
klaxon	
kleptomania	
knack	
knacker	
knapsack	
knave (rogue)	
knave	nave (church)
knead, -ed, -ing, (dough)	
knead	need (want)
knee, kneed, kneeing	
kneecap	
kneel, knelt, kneeling	
knell, -ed, -ing	
knew	
knew	gnu (animal)
knew	new
knickerbockers	
knick-knack	
knife, knives	
knife, knifed, knifing	
knight (lord)	
knight	night (time)
knighthood	
knit, knitted, knitting	
knitwear	
knob, knobbed, knobbing (handle)	
knobbly	
knobby, -bier, -biest	
knock, -ed, -ing	
knockabout	
knock-back	
knockdown	
knocker	
knock-knee	
knockout	
knoll	
knot, knotted, knotting (tie)	
knot	not (denial)
knothole	
knotty, -tier, -tiest	

know, knew, known, knowing
know-all
know how
knowledge
knowledgeable, -bly
knuckle, -led, -ling
knuckle-duster
koala
 kola koala
kookaburra
koori
korodji
Koran
korowai
 koroway korowai
kosher
kowtow, -ed, -ing
Kremlin
kris
Krishna
kudos
kumquat
kung-fu
kurrajong

For kw - words, look under **qu** -.

kylie

Ll

label, -belled, -belling
  laber labour
labial, -ly
labiate
  labirinth labyrinth
labium, -bia
  lable label
  labor labour
laboratory, -ries
  laboratrey laboratory
laborious, -ly
  laborius laborious
labour, -ed, -ing
labourer
labour-intensive
Labrador
  labratory laboratory
  labrinth labyrinth
  laburnem laburnum
laburnum
labyrinth
labyrinthine
lace, laced, lacing
lacebark
lacerate, -rated, -rating
laceration
  lach latch
lack, -ed, -ing
lackadaisical, -ly
  lacker lacquer
lackey, -eys
lackey, -eyed, -eying
  lacky lackey
laconic, -ally
lacquer, -ed, -ing
  lacross lacrosse
lacrosse
lactate, -tated, -tating
lactation
lacteal, -ly
lactic
lactose
lad
ladder
lade, laded, laden, lading (load)
  lade laid (placed)
  ladel ladle
  lader ladder
  ladie lady
ladle, -dled, -dling
  ladul ladle
lady, -dies
ladybird
lag, lagged, lagging
  lagard laggard
lager
laggard, -ly
  laghable laughable
lagoon
laid (placed)
  laid lade (load)
laid-back
  laim lame
lain (did lie)
  lain lane (passage)
lair (den)
  lair layer
  laissay fair laissez faire
laissez faire
  laitie laity
laity
lake
  lakross lacrosse
  laks lax
  laksative laxative
lam, lammed, lamming (spike)
  lam lamb (sheep)
lama
lamb (sheep)
  lamb lam (spike)
lambaste, -basted, -basting
lame, lamed, laming
lame, lamer, lamest
lament, -ed, -ing
lamentable, -bly

Word	Correct spelling
lamentation	
laminate, -nated, -nating	
lamington	
lamp	
lampoon, -ed, -ing	
lampoonist	
lamp-post	
lampray	lamprey
lamprey, -reys	
lance, lanced, lancing	
lancet	
land, -ed, -ing	
landfall	
landform	
landlady, -dies	
landlocked	
landlord	
landlubber	
landmark	
landmass	
landmine	
land rights	
landscape, -scaped, -scaping	
landslide	
lane (passage)	
lane	lain (did lie)
language	
languid, -ly	
languish, -ed, -ing	
languer	languor
languorous, -ly	
langwid	languid
langwidge	language
langwish	languish
lank, -ly	
landladie	landlady
lanladie	landlady
lanlady	landlady
lanlord	landlord
lanolin	
lanoline	
lanse	lance
lanser	lancer
lanset	lancet
lantana	
lantern	
lanyard	
lap, lapped, lapping	
lapel	
lapelled	
lapidary, -ries	
lapis lazuli	
lap-lap	
lapse, lapsed, lapsing	
larceny, -nies	
larcenous, -ly	
larconic	laconic
lard	
larder	
large, -ly	
largess	
lariat	
laringitis	laryngitis
larinx	larynx
lark	
larrikin	
larseny	larceny
larva, -vae (insect)	
larva	lava (rock)
laryngitis	
larynx, larynxes	
lascivious, -ly	
lase	lace
laser	
laserate	lacerate
lash, -ed, -ing	
lasitude	lassitude
lasivious	lascivious
lasivius	lascivious
lasoo	lasso
lasor	laser
lass	
lassitude	
lasso, -sos, -soes	
lasso, -soed, -soing	
last, lasted, lasting	
last-ditch	
lastly	
latch, -ed, -ing	
latchkey	
late, later, latest	
lately	
latency	
latensey	latency

latent, -ly
lateral, -ly
latex, latexes
lath (strip)
lathe (machine)
lather, -ed, -ing
lathery
Latin
  latise   lattice
latitude
latrine
latter
lattice
laud, lauded, lauding (praise)
  laud   lord (ruler)
laudable, -bly
laudanum
laudation
laudatory
laugh, laughed, laughing
laughable, -bly
laughter
  laun   lawn
launch, launched, launching
launder, -ed, -ing
  laundrey   laundry
laundromat
laundry, -dries
laureate
laurel, -relled, -relling
  lauyer   lawyer
lava (rock)
  lava   larva (insect)
lavatory, -ries
  lavatree   lavatory
  lavatrey   lavatory
lave, laved, laving
lavender
lavish, lavished, lavishing
law (rule)
  law   lore (learn)
  lawd   laud (praise)
  lawd   lord (ruler)
  lawdabul   laudable
lawful, -ly
lawless, -ly
lawn
  lawnch   launch
  lawnder   launder
  lawndrey   laundry
  lawndromat   laundromat
  lawndry   laundry
lawsuit
  lawsute   lawsuit
lawyer
lax, -ly
  lax   lacks
  laxadasical   lackadaisical
laxative
laxity
lay, laid, laying (rest)
  lay   lei (flowers)
  laybie   lay-by
lay-by
layer
layette
layman, -men
layout
laze, lazed, lazing
lazily
lazy, -zier, -ziest
lea (meadow)
  lea   lee (shelter)
leach, -ed, -ing (filter)
  leach   leech (worm)
lead, led, leading (show)
lead (metal)
  lead   led (shown)
leaden, -ly
leader
leadership
leaf, leaves
leaflet
league
leak (hole)
  leak   leek (food)
leakage
lean, leant or leaned, leaning (bend)
  leant   Lent (season)
  leant   lent (did lend)
lean-to
leap, leapt or leaped, leaping
leapfrog, -frogged, -frogging
learn, learnt or learned, learning

Word	Correct spelling
learner	
lease, leased, leasing	
leasehold	
leash, -ed, -ing	
leashur	leisure
leason	liaison
least	
leasure	leisure
leasurely	leisurely
leather	
leatherjacket	
leave, left, leaving	
leaven, -ed, -ing	
leaver	lever
lecher (man)	
lecher	lecture (talk)
lecherous, -ly	
lecherus	lecherous
lechery	
lectern	
lector	
lecture, -tured, -turing	
lecturer	
led (shown)	
led	lead (metal)
ledge	
ledger (book)	
ledger	leger (stand)
lee (shelter)	
lee	lea (meadow)
leeason	liaison
leech (worm)	
leech	leach (filter)
leed	lead
leef	leaf
leeflet	leaflet
leege	liege
leegue	league
leek (food)	
leek	leak (hole)
leen	lean
leep	leap
leer, -ed, -ing	
lees	
leese	lease
leesh	leash
leesion	lesion
leesiun	lesion
leeward	
leeway	
leewood	leeward
left	
leftenant	lieutenant
leftenent	lieutenant
left-footer	
left-handed	
leftist	
leftward	
left-winger	
leg, legged, legging	
legacy, -cies	
legal, -ly	
legalese (language)	
legalisation	
legalise, -lised, -lising (authorise)	
legalism	
legality, -ties	
legand	legend
legasey	legacy
legashen	legation
legate	
legation	
legend	
legendary, -ries	
legendrey	legendary
leger (stand)	
leger	ledger (book)
leghorn	
legibel	legible
legibility	
legible, -bly	
legion	
legionary, -ries	
legionnaire	
legislachur	legislature
legislate, -lated, -lating	
legislation	
legislative, -ly	
legislator	
legislature	
legitimacy	
legitimasey	legitimacy
legitimate, -mated, -mating	
legume	

Word	Correct spelling
lei, leis (flowers)	
lei	lay (rest)
leisure	
leisurely	
lejun	legion
lejunry	legionary
leksicografer	lexicographer
leksicografey	lexicography
leksicographer	lexicographer
leksicon	lexicon
leming	lemming
lemming	
lemon	
lemonade	
lemur	
lend, lent, lending	
lender	
length	
lengthen, -ed, -ing	
lengthily	
lengthways	
lengthwise	
lengthy, -thier, -thiest	
lenience	
leniency	
leniense	lenience
leniensy	leniency
lenient, -ly	
lenity, -ties	
lens, lenses	
lense	lens
Lent (season)	
lent	leant (bent)
lenth	length
lentil (pea)	
lentil	lintel (beam)
Leo	
leonine	
leopard	
leotard	
lepard	leopard
leper	
leperd	leopard
leprechaun	
leprechorn	leprechaun
leprosy	
lept	leapt
lerch	lurch
lerk	lurk
lern	learn
lesen	lessen (reduce)
lesen	lesson (study)
lesbian	
lesbianism	
leishur	leisure
lesion	
leson	lessen (reduce)
leson	lesson (study)
less	
lessee	
lessen (reduce)	
lesson (study)	
lessor	
lest	
lesure	leisure
let, let, letting	
letdown	
leter	letter
leter	litre
lethal, -ly	
lethargey	lethargy
lethargic, -ally	
lethargy, -gies	
lether	leather
letice	lettuce
letise	lettuce
letre	litre
letter	
lettered	
letterhead	
letterpress	
lettuce	
let-up	
letuse	lettuce
leucosis	
leukaemia	
leve	leave
levee (bank)	
levee	levy (tax)
level, -elled, -elling	
leveller	
level-headed	
levelheded	level-headed
leven	leaven

Word	Correct spelling
lever, -ed, -ing	
leverage	
leviathan	
levie	levee (bank)
levie	levy (tax)
levitate, -tated, -tating	
levitation	
levity, -ties	
levrage	leverage
levy, levies (tax)	
levy, levied, levying (tax)	
levy	levee (bank)
lewd, -ly	
lexicografer	lexicographer
lexicografey	lexicography
lexicographer	
lexicography	
lexicon	
lezbian	lesbian
li	lie
liability, -ties	
liable (legal)	
liabul	libel (crime)
liabul	liable (legal)
liaise, -aised, -aising	
liaison	
liana	
liar (tell lies)	
liar	lyre (music)
liason	liaison
libarian	librarian
libary	library
libel, -belled, -belling (crime)	
libel	liable (legal)
libelus	libellous
libul	liable
libellous, -ly	
liberal, -ly	
liberalism	
liberate, -rated, -rating	
liberation	
liberator	
libertey	liberty
libertine	
liberty, -ties	
libidinal	
libidinous, -ly	

Word	Correct spelling
libido	
Libra	
libralism	liberalism
librarian	
library, -ries	
libretto, -tos, -ti	
librian	librarian
lice	
licee	lychee
licence (noun)	
license, -censed, -censing	
licensee	
licenshiate	licentiate
licenshius	licentious
licenshus	licentious
licentiate	
licentious, -ly	
lichee	lychee
lichen	
lichenis	lichenous
lichenous	
lichenus	lichenous
lick, -ed, -ing	
licker	liqueur
licker	liquor
licorice	
licorish	licorice
licoriss	licorice
lickrish	licorice
lid	
lie, lied, lying (untruth)	
lie, lay, lain, lying (recline)	
lie	lye (solution)
liege	
lien	
liesure	leisure
lieu (instead)	
lieu	loo (toilet)
lieutenant	
life, lives	
lifebelt	
lifeboat	
lifeboy	lifebuoy
lifebuoy	
lifeguard	
lifeless, -ly	
lifelike	

lifelong
lifesaver
lifestyle
lifetime
lift, -ed, -ing
lift-off
  ligacher   ligature
  ligachur   ligature
ligament
light, lighted, lighting
lighten, -ed, -ing
light-fingered
light-headed
light-hearted, -ly
lighthouse
lightly
lightning
lightweight
ligneous
lignite
like, liked, liking
likeable
likelihood
likely, -lier, -liest
  likelyhood   likelihood
liken, likened, likening
likeness
likewise
  likorish   licorice
  likoriss   licorice
  likrish   licorice

For likw- words, look under **liqu-** .

lilac
  lilak   lilac
  lile   lisle
  lilie   lily
Lilliputian
lilly pilly
lilt, -ed, -ing
lily, -ies
lily-livered
limb
limber, limbered, limbering
limbo, -bos
lime, limed, liming
limelight
  limelite   limelight
limerick
  limersene   limousine
limestone
limey, -meys
  limf   lymph
  limfatic   lymphatic
limit, -ed, -ing
limitation
limousine
limp, -ed, -ing
limpet
  limph   lymph
  limphatic   lymphatic
limpid, -ly
linchpin
  linch   lynch
linctus
line, lined, lining (mark)
  line   lion (cat)
lineage
lineal, -ly
lineament (detail)
linear, -ly
  lineige   lineage
linen
liner
linesman, -men
line-up
ling, lings
linger, -ed, -ing
lingerie
lingo, -goes
lingual, -ly
linguist
linguistic, -ally
  lingwal   lingual
  lingwist   linguist
  linier   linear
liniment (oil)
  liniment   lineament (detail)
link, linked, linking
linkage
linnet
linocut

Word	Correct spelling
linoleum	
linolium	linoleum
linotype, -typed, -typing	
linseed	
lint	
lintel (beam)	
lintel	lentil (pea)
linx	lynx
lion (cat)	
lion	line (mark)
lioness	
lion-hearted, -ly	
lionisation	
lionise, -nised, -nising	
liotard	leotard
lip	
lip-read, -read, -reading	
lip-salve	
lip-service	
lipstick	
liquefier	
liquefy, -fied, -fying	
liquer	liqueur
liquer	liquor
liqueur (drink)	
liqueur	liquor (spirits)
liquid	
liquidambar	
liquidate, -dated, -dating	
liquidation	
liquidator	
liquidity	
liquor (spirits)	
liquor	liqueur (drink)
liquorice	
liquoris	liquorice
liquorish	liquorice
lire	lyre
lirebird	lyrebird
liric	lyric
lirical	lyrical
lise	lice
lisen	listen
lisence	licence (noun)
lisence	license (verb)
lisen	listen
lisensee	licensee
lisentiate	licentiate
lisentius	licentious
lisle	
lisp, -ed, -ing	
lissom	
lissum	lissom
list, -ed, -ing	
listen, -ed, -ing	
listless, -ly	
lit	
litany, -nies	
lite	light
litel	little
liter	litre
liter	litter
literacher	literature
literachur	literature
literacy	
literal, -ly	
literary, -ily	
literasy	literacy
literat	literate
literate	
literati	
literature	
litergy	liturgy
litewait	light-weight
lithe, -ly	
lithesome	
lithium	
lithograf	lithograph
lithograph	
lithographic, -ally	
lithography	
litigant	
litigation	
litigator	
litle	little
litmus	
litening	lightning
litracher	literature
litrachur	literature
litre	
litter, -ed, -ing	
litterbug	
little, less, least	
litul	little

liturgey	liturgy
liturgical, -ly	
liturgy, -gies	
liv	live
livary	livery
live, lived, living	
livelihood	
lively, -lier, -liest	
livelyhood	livelihood
liven, -ed, -ing	
liver	
liverish	
liverwurst	
livery, -ries	
livestock	
livewire	
livid, -ly	
livlie	lively
livrey	livery
liying	lying
lizard	
lizerd	lizard
llama	
lo	low
load, -ed, -ing (burden)	
load	lode (ore)
loaf, loaves	
loam, -ed, -ing	
loan (lend)	
loan	lone (alone)
loath (unwilling)	
loathe, loathed, loathing (hate)	
loathsome, -ly	
lob, lobbed, lobbing	
lobby, -bies	
lobby, -bied, -bying	
lobe	
lobie	lobby
lobotomy	
lobster	
loby	lobby
local, -ly	
locale	
localise, -lised, -lising	
locality, -ties	
locate, -cated, -cating	
location	
loch (lake)	
lock (door)	
locker	
locket	
lockjaw	
locksmith	
lockup	
locomoshun	locomotion
locomotion	
locomotive	
locum	
locust	
lode (ore)	
lode	load (burden)
lodestar	
lodestone	
lodge, lodged, lodging	
lodger	
lofe	loaf
loft, lofted, lofting	
loftily	
lofty, -tier, -tiest	
log, logged, logging	
loganberie	loganberry
loganberry, -ries	
logarithm	
logbook	
loge	lodge
loger	logger
logerithm	logarithm
loggerhead	
logic	
logical, -ly	
logicality	
logistics	
loier	lawyer
loin	
loincloth	
loiter, -ed, -ing	
loiterer	
lol	loll
lolipop	lollipop
loll, -ed, -ing	
lollipop	
lolly, -lies	
lome	loam
lone (alone)	

lone	loan (lend)
loneliness	
lonely, -lier, -liest	
loner	
lonesome, -ly	
lonesum	lonesome
long, -ed, -ing	
longevity	
longhand	
longing, -ly	
longitude	
longitudinal, -ly	
long-playing	
long-sighted	
longstanding	
long-suffering	
long-term	
longwinded, -ly	
loo (toilet)	
loo	lieu (instead)
loobricant	lubricant
loobricate	lubricate
loocid	lucid
loocrative	lucrative
loodicrous	ludicrous
loodicrus	ludicrous
loofah	
look, -ed, -ing	
lookemia	leukaemia
looker	lucre
lookout	
lookwarm	lukewarm
loom, -ed, -ing	
loominus	luminous
loon	
loona	luna
loonatic	lunatic
loony, loonier, looniest	
loop, -ed, -ing	
loophole	
loose, loosed, loosing (free)	
loose, looser, loosest	
loose	lose (fail)
loose-leaf	
loosen, -ed, -ing	
loosing	losing
loot (booty)	

loot	lute (music)
lop, lopped, lopping (cut)	
lope, loped, loping (run)	
lopsided, -ly	
loquacious, -ly	
loquacity	
loquashius	loquacious
loquashus	loquacious
loquat	
lord (ruler)	
lord	laud (praise)
lordly, -lier, -liest	
lord mayor	
lore (learn)	
lore	law (rule)
lorel	laurel
lorgnette	
loriat	laureate
lorie	lorry
lorikeet	
lornch	launch
lornyet	lorgnette
lorry, lorries (truck)	
lory, lories (bird)	
los	loss
lose, lost, losing (fail)	
lose	loose (free)
loser	
loshion	lotion
loshun	lotion
loss	
lot, lotted, lotting	
lotery	lottery
lothe	loathe
lothsum	loathsome
lotion	
lotry	lottery
lots	
lottery, -teries	
lotto	
lotus	
loud, -ly	
loudhailer	
loudspeaker	
lounge, lounged, lounging	
louse, lice	
louse, loused, lousing	

Word	Correct spelling
lousy, lousier, lousiest	
lout	
louver	louvre
louvre	
love, loved, loving	
loveliness	
lovelorn	
lovely, -lier, -liest	
lover	
loves	loaves
low, lower, lowest	
lowboy	
lowbrow	
lowd	loud
low-down (mean)	
lowdown (truth)	
lower, -ed, -ing	
low-key	
lowland	
lowly, -lier, -liest	
lownge	lounge
low-pressure	
lowse	louse
lowt	lout
low-voltage	
loyal, -ly	
loyalty, -ties	
loyle	loyal
lozenge	
lozinge	lozenge
lu	lieu (instead)
lu	loo (toilet)
lubber, -ly	
luber	lubber
lubricant	
lubricate, -cated, -cating	
lubrication	
lucer	lucre
lucerne	
lucid, -ly	
Lucifer	
luck, -ily	
lucky, -ier, -iest	
lucky dip	
lucrative, -ly	
lucre	
lude	lewd
ludicrous, -ly	
ludo	
luff, -ed, -ing	
lug, lugged, lugging	
lugage	luggage
luggage	
lugger	
lugige	luggage
lugsuriant	luxuriant
lugubrious, -ly	
lukemia	leukaemia
lukewarm	
luksuriant	luxuriant
luksuriate	luxuriate
luksurius	luxurious
luksury	luxury
lul	lull
lulabie	lullaby
lull, -ed, -ing	
lullaby, -bies	
lullaby, -bied, -bying	
lumbago	
lumbar (back)	
lumber (timber)	
lumberjack	
luminance	
luminary, -naries	
luminescence	
luminescent	
luminessence	luminescence
luminessent	luminescent
luminosity, -ties	
luminous, -ly	
luminus	luminous
lump, -ed, -ing	
lunacy, -cies	
lunar	
lunasey	lunacy
lunatic	
lunch, -ed, -ing	
luncheon	
lung	
lunge, lunged, lunging	
lungfish	
lupin	
lupus	
lurch, lurched, lurching	

lure, lured, luring
lurex
lurid, -ly
lurk, lurked, lurking
  lurn — learn
luscious, -ly
lush, -ly
  lushes — luscious
  lushious — luscious
  lushus — luscious
  lused — lucid
  lusid — lucid
lust, lusted, lusting
  luster — lustre
lustful, -ly
  lustie — lusty
lustre
lustrous, -ly
lusty, -tier, -tiest
lute, luted, luting (music)
  lute — loot (booty)
Lutheran
  luv — love
  luve — love
  luver — lover
  luvley — lovely
  luvlier — lovelier
lux
  luxery — luxury
luxuriance
luxuriant, -ly
luxuriate, -ated, -ating
luxurious, -ly
luxury, -ries
lyceum
lychee
lye (solution)
  lye — lie (untruth)
  lye — lie (recline)
lying-in
lymph
lymphatic
lynch, -ed, -ing
lynx, lynxes (wildcat)
  lynx — links
lyre (musical instrument)
  lyre — liar (tell lies)
lyrebird
lyric
lyrical, -ly
lyricist

Mm

macabre
macadam
macadamia nut
macaroni, -nis, -nies
macaw
mace
  mach — match
machete
machinate, -nated, -nating
machination
machine, -chined, -chining
machinery, -ries
mackerel
mackintosh, mackintoshes
macramé
mad, madder, maddest
mad, madded, madding
madam
madcap
made (produced)
  made — maid (girl)
madeira
mademoiselle
  maden — madden
  madera — madeira
madness
madonna
madrigal
maelstrom
maestro
mafia
magazine
maggot
magic
magical, -ly
magician
  magishion — magician
  magishun — magician
magisterial, -ly
magistrate
  magizine — magazine
  magnanimis — magnanimous
magnanimity
magnanimous, -ly
  magnanimus — magnanimous
  magnat — magnate
  magnat — magnet
magnate (wealth)
magnesium
magnet (attract)
magnetic, -ally
magnetisation
magnetise, -tised, -tising
magnetism
magnetite
magneto, -tos
magnification
magnificence
magnificent, -ly
magnifier
  magnifisense — magnificence
  magnifisent — magnificent
  magnifisunt — magnificent
magnify, -fied, -fying
magnitude
magnolia
magnum, -nums
  magot — maggot
magpie
  mahem — mayhem
mah-jong
mahogany, -nies
maid (girl)
  maid — made
maiden
mail (letters)
  mail — male (man)
mailbox, mailboxes
maim, -ed, -ing
main (chief)
  main — mane (hair)
mainland
mainline, -lined, -lining
mainliner
mainstay

mainstream	
maintain, -ed, -ing	
maintenance	
maintenanse	maintenance
maisonette	
maize (corn)	
maize	maze (puzzle)
majer	major
majestey	majesty
majestic, -ally	
majesty, -ties	
majong	mah-jong
major	
majority, -ties	
makaber	macabre
makadam	macadam
make, made, making	
makeshift	
make-up	
mako	
maladey	malady
maladjusted	
maladjustment	
malady, -dies	
malaise	
malapropism	
malard	mallard
malaria	
malase	malaíse
male (man)	
male	mail (letters)
maleable	malleable
malefacshun	malefaction
malefaction	
malefactor	
malet	mallet
malevolence	
malevolense	malevolence
malevolent, -ly	
malformation	
malformed	
malfuncshion	malfunction
malfuncshun	malfunction
malfunction, -ed, -ing	
maliable	malleable
malice	
malicious, -ly	

malign, -ed, -ing	
malignance	
malignancy	
malignansey	malignancy
malignant, -ly	
maline	malign
malinger, -ed, -ing	
malingerer	
malise	malice
malishus	malicious
mall	
mallard, -lards, -lard	
malleability	
malleable	
malleabul	malleable
mallee	
mallet	
mallow	mellow
malnutrishun	malnutrition
malnutrition	
malpractice	
malpractise	malpractice
malstrom	maelstrom
malt (liquor)	
malt	moult (lose)
Malthusian	
maltreat, -ed, -ing	
maltreet	maltreat
maluka	
mamal	mammal
mamarey	mammary
mame	maim
mamilla, -millae	
mamma, mammae	
mammal	
mammary	
mammon	
mammoth	
mamon	mammon
mamoth	mammoth
man, men	
man, manned, manning	
manacle, -cled, -cling	
manacul	manacle
manage, -aged, -aging	
manageability	
manageable, -bly	

management
manager
manageress
managerial, -ly
manana
manchester
mandarin (bureaucrat)
mandarine (fruit)
mandate, -dated, -dating
mandatory, -ries
  mandatry — mandatory
mandolin
mandrax
mane (hair)
  mane — main (chief)
  maner — manner (way)
  maner — manor (house)
mange
  mangel — mangle
manger
mangle, -gled, -gling
mango, -goes, -gos
mangrove
  mangul — mangle
mangy, -gier, -giest
  manhandel — manhandle
manhandle, -dled, -dling
  manhandul — manhandle
manhole
manhood
mania
maniacal, -ly
manic
manic-depression
manic-depressive
manicure, -cured, -curing
  manidge — manage
manifest, -ed, -ing
manifestation
manifesto, -tos
manifold
  manige — manage
manikin (dwarf)
  manikin — mannequin (model)
manila
  manipulashun — manipulation
manipulate, -lated, -lating
manipulation
manipulative
manipulator
manipulatory
  manje — mange
  manjer — manger
  manjy — mangy
mankind
manly, -lier, -liest
manna (food)
  manna — manner (way)
  manna — manor (house)
mannequin
manner (way)
  manner — manna (food)
  manner — manor (house)
mannered
mannerism
manoeuvrability
manoeuvrable
manoeuvre, -vred, -vring
  manoover — manoeuvre
  manoovrabul — manoeuvrable
manor (house)
  manor — manna (food)
  manor — manner (way)
manpower
manse
  manshun — mansion
mansion
manslaughter
  manslorter — manslaughter
mantel (shelf)
  mantel — mantle (cloak)
mantelpiece
mantilla
mantis, -tises
mantissa
mantle (cloak)
  mantle — mantel (shelf)
  mantul — mantel (shelf)
  mantul — mantle (cloak)
manual, -ly
  manufacsher — manufacture
manufacture, -tured, -turing
manure, -nured, -nuring

manuscript
many, more, most
  maonaise — mayonnaise
Maori, -ris
map, mapped, mapping
  mapel — maple
maple
mar, marred, marring
marathon
maraud, -ed, -ing
  marawed — maraud
marble, -bled, -bling
  marbul — marble
marcasite
March
march, -ed, -ing
marcher
marchioness
mare (horse)
  mare — mayor (chief)
  mareene — marine
margarine
margin
marginal, -ly
  mariage — marriage
  marie — marry
marijuana
marina
marinade, -naded, -nading
marinate, -nated, -nating
marine
mariner
  marionet — marionette
marionette
marital, -ly
maritime
  maritul — marital
  mariwana — marijuana
marjoram
mark, marked, marking
marker
market, -ed, -ing
marketeer
  markey — marquee
  markey — marquis
marksman, -men
marksmanship
  markuis — marquis
marlin
marlock
marmalade
  marone — maroon
maroon
  marow — marrow
marquee (tent)
marquis (nobleman)
marri (tree)
  marri — marry (unite)
marriage
marrow
marry, -ried, -rying (unite)
  marry — marri (tree)
Mars
marsh
marshal, -shalled, -shalling (officer)
  marshal — martial (brave)
marshland
marshmallow
  marshul — marshal
  marshul — martial
marshy, -shier, -shiest
marsupial
mart
  marter — martyr
martial (brave)
  martial — marshal (officer)
martinet
martini
martyr
martyrdom
marvel, -velled, -velling
marvellous, -ly
Marxism
Marxist
  mary — marry
marzipan
  mas — mass
  masacer — massacre
  masacre — massacre
  masage — massage
mascara
mascot
masculine, -ly

masculinity	
mase	mace
mash, -ed, -ing	
mashene	machine
mashine	machine
mashinry	machinery
masive	massive
mask, -ed, -ing	
maskerade	masquerade
masochism	
masochist	
masocism	masochism
mason	
masonic	
masonite	
masonry, -ries	
masquerade, -raded, -rading	
mass, -ed, -ing	
massacer	massacre
massacre, -cred, -cring	
massage, -saged, -saging	
masseur	
massif (mountain)	
massive, -ly (large)	
mass media	
mass-produce, -duced, -ducing	
massur	masseur
mast	
mastectomy, -mies	
master	
masterbate	masturbate
masterful, -ly	
mastermind	
masterpeace	masterpiece
masterpiece	
masthead	
mastiff	
masturbate, -bated, -bating	
masturbation	
mat, matted, matting (rug)	
mat	matt (dull)
matador	
match, -ed, -ing	
matchmaker	
mate, mated, mating	
mater	matter
material, -ly	
materialisation	
materialise, -lised, -lising	
materialism	
materialist	
maternal, -ly	
maternity	
mateship	
matey	
mathematical, -ly	
mathematician	
mathematics	
mathematisian	mathematician
maths	
matilda	
matinay	matinee
matinee	
mating	matting
matress	mattress
matriarch	
matriarchal	
matriarchic	
matriarchy, -chies	
matriculant	
matriculate, -lated, -lating	
matriculation	
matrimony, -nies	
matrix, matrices	
matron, -ly	
matt (dull)	
matter	
matting	
mattock	
mattress	
maturation	
mature, -tured, -turing	
maturity	
maudlin, -ly	
maul, -ed, -ing	
mausoleum, -leums, -lea	
mauve	
maverick	
mawgage	mortgage
mawkish, -ly	
mawl	maul
mawsoleum	mausoleum
maxi	
maxim	

Word	Correct spelling
maximisation	
maximise, -mised, -mising	
maximum, -ma, -mums	
maybe	
May Day	
mayhem	
mayonnaise	
mayor (chief)	
mayor	mare (horse)
mayoralty, -ties	
mayoress	
maypole	
maze (puzzle)	
maze	maize (corn)
mazurka	
mead	
meadow	
meager	meagre
meagre, -ly	
meak	meek
meal	
mean, meant, meaning (intend)	
mean	mien (show)
meander, -ed, -ing	
meantime	
meanwhile	
measels	measles
measles	
measure, -ured, -uring	
measurement	
meat (flesh)	
meat	meet (contact)
meat	mete (measure)
mecanic	mechanic
mecanise	mechanise
mecanism	mechanism
mechanic	
mechanical, -ly	
mechanisation	
mechanise, -nised, -nising	
mechanism	
medal, -alled, -alling (award)	
medallion	
medcine	medicine
meddle, -dled, -dling (interfere)	
meddler	
medeval	mediaeval
media	
mediaeval	
median	
mediashun	mediation
mediate, -ated, -ating	
mediation	
meditator	
medic	
medical, -ly	
medicate, -cated, -cating	
medication	
medicinal, -ly	
medicine	
medieval, -ly	
mediocer	mediocre
mediocre	
mediocrity, -ties	
medisinal	medicinal
medisine	medicine
meditate, -tated, -tating	
meditation	
meditator	
medium, -dia, -diums	
medle	meddle
medler	meddler
medley, -leys	
medly	medley
medow	meadow
medsine	medicine
medul	meddle
meed	mead
meek, -ly	
meel	meal
meen	mean (intend)
meen	mien (show)
meening	meaning
meerschaum	
meershum	meerschaum
meesels	measles
meet, met, meeting (contact)	
meet	meat (flesh)
meet	mete (measure)
megafone	megaphone
megalomania	
megalomaniac	
megaphone	
meger	meagre

mekanic	mechanic
mekanical	mechanical
mekanise	mechanise
mekanism	mechanism
melaleuca	
melancholia	
melancholic, -ally	
melancholy, -cholies	
Melanesian	
melee	
meliflous	mellifluous
meliorate, -rated, -rating	
melioration	
meliorator	
mellifluous, -ly	
mellow, -ly	
melodey	melody
melodic, -ally	
melodious, -ly	
melodius	melodious
melodrama	
melodramatic, -ally	
melody, -dies	
melon	
melow	mellow
melt, melted, melting	
member	
membership	
membrain	membrane
memento, -tos	
memo, memos	
memoir	
memorabel	memorable
memorabilia	
memorable, -bly	
memorabul	memorable
memorandum, -dums	
memorey	memory
memorial, -ly	
memorise, -rised, -rising	
memory, -ries	
memrable	memorable
menace, -aced, -acing	
menagerie	
menajery	menagerie
menase	menace
mend, -ed, -ing	
mendacious, -ly	
mendacity, -ties	
mendashus	mendacious
mendasity	mendacity
mendicant	
menial, -ly	
meningitis	
meninjitis	meningitis
meniscus, -nisci	
menopause	
menopaws	menopause
menshion	mention
menshun	mention
menstruate, -ated, -ating	
menstruation	
mensuration	
ment	meant
mental, -ly	
mentalitey	mentality
mentality, -ties	
menthol	
mentholated	
mention, -ed, -ing	
mentor	
menu	
merang	meringue
mercantile	
mercenary, -naries	
mercenrey	mercenary
mercer	
mercerise, -rised, -rising	
mercery, -ries	
merchandise, -dised, -dising	
merchant	
merchantman, -men	
merciful, -ly	
merciless, -ly	
mercurial, -ly	
mercury, -ries	
mercy, -cies	
mere, -ly	
meretricious, -ly	
meretrishious	meretricious
meretrishus	meretricious
merge, merged, merging	
merger	
meridian	

merie	merry
meringue	
merino, -nos	
merit, -ed, -ing	
meritories	meritorious
meritorious, -ly	
meritorius	meritorious
mermade	mermaid
mermaid	
merriment	
merry, -rier, -riest	
merry-go-round	
merrymaker	
mersenry	mercenary
mersy	mercy
mery	merry
mesa	
mescalin	
mesenger	messenger
mesh, -ed, -ing	
mesige	message
mesmerise, -rised, -rising	
mesmerism	
mess, -ed, -ing	
message	
messenger	
Messiah	
Messianic	
messmate	
Messrs	
mesure	measure
metabolic	
metabolise, -lised, -lising	
metabolism	
metafisicul	metaphysical
metafisics	metaphysics
metafor	metaphor
metaforic	metaphoric
metaforicul	metaphorical
metal, -alled, -alling (element)	
metal	mettle (energy)
metalic	metallic
metallic	
metallurgic	
metallurgical, -ly	
metallurgist	
metallurgy	

metalurgey	metallurgy
metamorfic	metamorphic
metamorfosus	metamorphosis
metamorphic	
metamorphosis, -ses	
metaphor	
metaphoric	
metamorphical, -ly	
metaphrase, -phrased, -phrasing	
metaphysical, -ly	
metaphysics	
metastasise, -sised, -sising	
mete, meted, meting (measure)	
mete	meat (flesh)
mete	meet (contact)
meteor (streak)	
meteor	metier (trade)
meteoric, -ally	
meteorite	
meteorological, -ly	
meteorology	
meter (measure)	
meter	metre (distance)
methadone	
methane	
methed	method
methedrine	
methilate	methylate
metho	
method	
methodical, -ly	
Methodist	
methodology, -gies	
methylate, -lated, -lating	
meticulous, -ly	
meticulus	meticulous
metier (trade)	
metier	meteor (streak)
metiorology	meteorology
metre (distance)	
metre	meter (measure)
metric	
metricate, -cated, -cating	
metrication	
metric system	

Word	Correct spelling
metronome	
metropolis, -lises	
metropolitan	
mettle (energy)	
mettle	metal (element)
metul	mettle (energy)
mew, -ed, -ing	
mews (stables)	
mews	muse (think)
mezanine	mezzanine
mezzanine	
mi	my
mia-mia	
miander	meander
miaow, -ed, -ing	
miasma, -mas, -mata	
miasmatical	
miasmic	
mica	
mice	
microbe	
microbial	
microbic	
microbiological	
microbiologist	
microbiology	
micro-economics	
microfiche	
microfilm	
microfone	microphone
micrometer	
micron	
microphone	
microprocessor	
microprosessor	microprocessor
microscope	
microscopic, -ally	
microwave	
midair	
midday	
middel	middle
middle, -led, -ling	
middleman, -men	
middle-of-the-road	
middlewait	middleweight
middleweight	
middling	
middul	middle
middy, -dies (beer)	
middy	midi (skirt)
midel	middle
midge	
midget	
midi (skirt)	
midi	middy (beer)
midil	middle
midling	middling
midnight	
midnite	midnight
mid-off	
mid-on	
midriff	
midshipman, -men	
midst	
midul	middle
mid wicket	
midwife, -wives	
mien (show)	
mien	mean (intend)
miff	
mige	midge
might (power)	
might	mite (small)
mighty, -tier, -tiest	
migit	midget
migraine	
migrane	migraine
migrant	
migrate, -grated, -grating	
migration	
migratory	
migreat	migrate
mika	mica
mikado, -dos	
miksamotosis	myxomatosis
mikscher	mixture
mikschur	mixture
mikser	mixer
miksture	mixture
mil (millilitre)	
mil	mill (grind)
mild, -ly	
mildew, -ed, -ing	
mildu	mildew

mile	
mileage	
milestone	
mileniem	millennium
milenium	millennium
milet	millet
milibar	millibar
milieu	
mililiter	millilitre
milimeter	millimetre
miliner	milliner
miling	milling
milinry	millinery
milion	million
milionair	millionaire
milipeed	millipede
milisha	militia
militancy	
militansy	militancy
militant, -ly	
militarism	
militarist	
militaristic, -ally	
military	
militia	
milk, -ed, -ing	
milksop	
milky, -kier, -kiest	
Milky Way	
mill, milled, milling (grind)	
millennial, -ly	
millennium, -niums, -nia	
miller	
millet	
millibar	
millligram	
millilitre	
millimetre	
milliner	
millinery	
million	
millionaire	
millipede	
millpond	
millstone	
millwheel	
milyou	milieu

mime, mimed, miming	
mimic, -icked, -icking	
mimicry, -ries	
mimosa	
minaret	
mince, minced, mincing	
mincemeat	
mincer	
mind, minded, minding	
mindful, -ly	
mine, mined, mining	
minefield	
miner (worker)	
miner	minor (less)
miner	myna (bird)
mineral	
mineralogical, -ly	
mineralogist	
mineralogy	
minestrone	
minestroney	minestrone
minestrony	minestrone
minesweeper	
mingel	mingle
mingle, -led, -ling	
mingul	mingle
mingy, -gier, -giest	
mini	
miniature	
minibus	
minicher	miniature
minichur	miniature
minim	
minimal, -ly	
minimise, -mised, -mising	
minimiser	
minimum, -mums, -mia	
minion	
miniscule	minuscule
miniskirt	
minister	
ministerial, -ly	
ministration	
ministrative, -ly	
ministrey	ministry
ministry, -tries	
minit	minute

mink, minks (animal)
  minks — minx (girl)
minnow, -nows
minor (lesser)
  minor — miner (worker)
  minor — myna (bird)
minority, -ties
  minow — minnow
  minse — mince
minstrel
mint, -ed, -ing
minuet
minus
minuscule
minute, -uted, -uting
minx (girl)
  minx — minks (animals)
  minyouet — minuet
  miopia — myopia
  miow — miaow
  miracel — miracle
miracle
  miracul — miracle
miraculous, -ly
  miraculus — miraculous
mirage
mire, mired, miring
  mirer — mirror
  miriad — myriad
mirrnyong
mirror, -ed, -ing
mirth
mirthful, -ly
  mis — miss
  misadvencher — misadventure
  misadvenchur — misadventure
misadventure
  misal — missal
misanthrope
misanthropic, -ally
misanthropist
misanthropy
misapprehension
misappropriate, -ated, -ating
misappropriation
  misapropriate — misappropriate

misbehave, -haved, -having
miscarriage
miscarry, -ried, -rying
  miscariage — miscarriage
  miscarie — miscarry
  miscarige — miscarriage
miscast, -cast, -casting
miscellaneous, -ly
miscellany, -nies
mischance
  mischanse — mischance
mischief
  mischievious — mischievous
mischievious, -ly
  mischif — mischief
  mischivus — mischievous
misconceive, -ceived, -ceiving
misconceiver
  misconcepshun — misconception
misconception
  misconcieve — misconceive
misconduct
  misconsepshun — misconception
misconstrue, -strued, -struing
miscreant
misdeed
misdemeanour
  misdemener — misdemeanour
misdo, -did, -done, -doing
  mise — mice
  miselanius — miscellaneous
  miselany — miscellany
  miself — myself
  miseltoe — mistletoe
miser
miserable, -ly
  miserabul — miserable
misere
miserly
misery, -ries
misfit, -fitted, -fitting
misfortune
misgiving
mishap
  mishapen — misshapen
  mishion — mission
mishmash

misile	missile
misiltoe	mistletoe
misis	misses
misive	missive
misus	missus
mislay, -laid, -laying	
misle	missal (book)
misle	missile (weapon)
mislead, -led, -leading	
misleader	
misleed	mislead
misnoma	misnomer
misnomer	
misogynist	
misogynous	
misogyny	
misojonist	misogynist
misojonous	misogynous
misojony	misogyny
mispell	misspell
misplace, -placed, -placing	
misplacement	
misplase	misplace
misprint, -ed, -ing	
misrabul	miserable
misrepresent, -ed, -ing	
miss, misses	
miss, missed, missing	
missal (book)	
missal	missile (weapon)
misselaney	miscellany
misselanius	miscellaneous
misselany	miscellany
misses (fail)	
misses	missus (wife)
misshape, -shaped, -shaping	
missile (weapon)	
missile	missal (book)
mission	
missionary, -ries	
missive	
misspell, misspelt, misspelling	
missus (wife)	
mist (cloud)	
mist	missed
mistake, -took, -taking	
mistaken	
misteltoe	mistletoe
mister	
misterey	mystery
misterius	mysterious
mistery	mystery
mistic	mystic
mistic	mystique
mistify	mystify
mistletoe	
mistreat, -ed, -ing	
mistress	
mistrial	
mistrust, -ed, -ing	
misty, -tier, -tiest	
misul	missal
misul	missile
misultoe	mistletoe
misunderstand, -stood, -standing	
misuse, -used, -using	
mite (small)	
mite	might (power)
miten	mitten
miter	mitre
mith	myth
mithical	mythical
mithology	mythology
mitie	mighty
mitigate, -gated, -gating	
mitre, -tred, -tring	
mitt	
mitten	
mix, mixed, mixing	
mixamotosis	myxomatosis
mixcher	mixture
mixchur	mixture
mixer	
mixture	
mix-up	
mizzenmast	
mnemonics	
mo	mow
moa (bird)	
moa	mower (lawn)
moan, moaned, moaning	
moaner	

moat
mob, mobbed, mobbing
mobile, -ly
mobiliety mobility
mobilisation
mobilise, -lised, -lising
mobility
moccasin
mock, mocked, mocking
mocker
mockery, -ries
mockingbird
mockry mockery
mock-up
modal (manner)
modal model (example)
moddul modal
moddul model
mode
model, -elled, -elling (example)
modeller
moden modern
moderate, -rated, -rating
moderation
moderator
modern, -ly
modernity, -ties
modest, -ly
modesty, -ties
modicum
modifi modify
modifiable
modifiabul modifiable
modification
modifier
modify, -fied, -fying
modlin maudlin
modul model
modular
modulate, -lated, -lating
modulation
modulator
module
moduler modular
modulur modular
mogo
mogul
mohair
Mohammedan
mohare mohair
moiety, -ties
moischer moisture
moischur moisture
moisen moisten
moisun moisten
moist, -ly
moisten, -ed, -ing
moisture
mokasin moccasin
moke
molar
molases molasses
molasses
molasus molasses
mold mould
mole
molecular, -ly
molecule
molest, -ed, -ing
molestation
molicodle mollycoddle
molicodul mollycoddle
moll
mollify, -fied, -fying
mollusc
mollycoddle, -dled, -dling
moloch
Molotov cocktail
molt malt (liquor)
molt moult (lose)
molten
molusk mollusc
molybdenum
moment
momentarily
momentary
momentous, -ly
momentum, -ta
monakey monarchy
monarch
monarchal, -ly
monarchic, -ally
monarchist

monarchy, -chies	
monastery, -teries	
monastic, -ally	
monasticism	
monastry	monastery
Monday	
mone	moan
monetary, -rily	
money, monies	
moneychanger	
money-grubber	
money-grubbing	
moneylender	
money market	
money order	
monga	monger
mong	
monger	
Mongol	
Mongolian	
Mongolism	
Mongoloid	
mongoose, -gooses	
mongrel	
mongrul	mongrel
moniter	monitor
monitor, -ed, -ing	
monk	
monkey, -keys	
monkey, -keyed, -keying	
monkey-wrench	
monochromatic, -ally	
monochrome	
monochromic	
monocle	
monocled	
monocul	monocle
monogamist	
monogamous	
monogamus	monogamous
monogamy	
monograf	monograph
monogram	
monograph	
monokrome	monochrome
monokside	monoxide
monolith	
monolithic	
monolog	monologue
monologue	
monoplain	monoplane
monoplane	
monopoley	monopoly
monopolisation	
monopolise, -lised, -lising	
monopoly, -lies	
monorail	
monosilabic	monosyllabic
monosilabul	monosyllable
monosyllabic, -ally	
monosyllable	
monotone	
monotonous, -ly	
monotonus	monotonous
monotony	
monoxide	
monsoon	
monsoonal	
monster	
monstera deliciosa	
monstrosity, -ties	
monstrous, -ly	
monstrus	monstrous
montage	
month	
monument	
monumental, -ly	
mooch, -ed, -ing	
mood	
moody, -dier, -diest	
moon	
moonlight	
moonshine	
moonstone	
moony, -nier, -niest	
moor, -ed, -ing (land)	
moor	more (further)
Moor (Muslim)	
moorhen	
moose, moose (animal)	
moose	mouse (rodent)
moose	mousse (food)
moosli	muesli
moot	

moovabul	moveable
moove	move
mop, mopped, mopping	
mope, moped, moping	
moped	
mopoke	
moral, -ly	
moralise, -lised, -lising	
moralist	
moralistic	
moralitey	morality
morality, -ties	
morass	
moratorium, -toria, -toriums	
moray, -rays (eel)	
morays	mores (custom)
morbid, -ly	
morbidity	
mordant, -ly	
mordern	modern
more, most (further)	
more	moor (tie up)
moreover	
mores (custom)	
morfine	morphine
morg	morgue
morgage	mortgage
morganatic, -ally	
morgige	mortgage
morgue	
moribund, -ly	
moribundity	
Mormon	
Mormonism	
morn (morning)	
morn	mourn (sorrow)
mornay	
mornful	mournful
morning (day)	
morning	mourning (sor-
rowing)	
moron	
moronic	
morose, -ly	
morover	moreover
morow	morrow
morphine	

morrow	
morse code	
morsel	
mortafy	mortify
mortal, -ly	
mortality, -ties	
mortar	
mortarboard	
mortgage, -gaged, -gaging	
mortgagee	
mortgagor	
mortice, -ticed, -ticing	
mortifi	mortify
mortification	
mortify, -fied, -fying	
mortiss	mortice
mortuary, -ries	
mos	moss
mosaic	
moselle	
moshun	motion
mosk	mosque
moskito	mosquito
mosque	
mosquito, -toes	
moss	
most, -ly	
mot	
mote (dust)	
mote	moat (ditch)
motel	
moter	motor
motervate	motivate
motet	
moth, moths	
mothballs	
mother	
mother-in-law, mothers-in-law	
motherland	
mother-of-pearl	
motif (figure)	
motif	motive (reason)
motion, -ed, -ing	
motivate, -vated, -vating	
motivation	
motivational	
motive (reason)	

Word	Correct spelling
motive	motif (figure)
motle	mottle
motley, -leys	
motly	motley
moto	motto
motor, -ed, -ing	
motorbike	
motorcycle	
motorcyclist	
motorist	
mottle, -tled, -tling	
motto, -tos	
mould, moulded, moulding	
moulder, -ed, -ing	
mouldy, -dier, -diest	
moult, -ed, -ing (lose)	
moult	malt (liquor)
mound	
mount, mounted, mounting	
mountain	
mountaineer	
mountainous, -ly	
mountenus	mountainous
mountun	mountain
mourn, -ed, -ing (sorrow)	
mourn	morn (morning)
mourner	
mournful, -ly	
mourning (sorrowing)	
mourning	morning (day)
mouse, mice (rodent)	
mouse, moused, mousing	
mouse	moose (animal)
mouse	mousse (food)
moussaka	
mousse (food)	
moustache	
mousy, -sier, -siest	
mouth, mouths	
mouthful, -fuls	
mouthpeace	mouthpiece
mouthpiece	
mouth-to-mouth	
movabel	moveable
movabul	moveable
move, moved, moving	

Word	Correct spelling
moveable, -ly	
movement	
movie	
mow, mowed, mowing	
mower	
mownd	mound
mownt	mount
mowntain	mountain
mowntenus	mountainous
mowntun	mountain
mowse	mouse
mowth	mouth
mozzarella	
Mr., Messrs.	
Mrs.	
Ms.	
much, more, most	
muchooal	mutual
mucilage	
mucilaginous	
muck, mucked, mucking	
muckrake, -raked, -raking	
muck-up	
mucky, -ier, -iest	
mucous (of mucus)	
mucus	
mud, mudded, mudding	
muddie (crab)	
muddie	muddy (dirty)
muddle, -dled, -dling	
muddler	
muddy, -died, -dying (dirty)	
muddy, -dier, -diest (dirty)	
muddy	muddie (crab)
mudel	muddle
mudflat	
mudflow	
mudguard	
mudhopper	
mudlark	
mudle	muddle
mudrunner	
mudskipper	
mudslinger	
muesli	
muezzin	
muff, -ed, -ing	

muffin
muffle, -fled, -fling
muffler
mufful muffle
mufin muffin
mufti, -tis
mug, mugged, mugging
mugga
mugger
muggins
muggy, -gier, -giest
mukus mucous
mukus mucus
mulatto, -tos, -toes
mulberie mulberry
mulberry, -ries
mulch, -ed, -ing
mule
muleteer
mulga
mulgara
mulish, -ly
mull, -ed, -ing
mullet, -lets, -let
mulligatawny
mullion
mullock
mulloway
multaple multiple
multch mulch
multicultural
multifaceted
multifarious, -ly
multifarius multifarious
multifaseted multifaceted
multigrade
multilateral, -ly
multimillionaire
multinashionul multinational
multinational
multipartite
multiple
multiple sclerosis
multipli multiply
multiplication
multiplicative, -ly
multiplicity, -ties
multiplier
multiplisity multiplicity
multiply, -plied, -plying
multipul multiple
multitude
multitudinous, -ly
multitudinus multitudinous
mulyun mullion
mum
mumble, -bled, -bling
mumbo jumbo
mumbul mumble
mumie mummy
mumifi mummify
mummer
mummification
mummify, -fied, -fying
mummy, -mies
mummy, -mied, -mying
mumps
mumy mummy
munch, munched, munching
munchies
mundain mundane
mundane, -ly
Munday Monday
munetry monetary
mungrel mongrel
municipal, -ly
municipality, -ties
munie money
munishun munition
munisipality municipality
munk monk
munky monkey
munth month
muny money
mur myrrh
mural
murder, -ed, -ing
murderer
murderess
murderous, -ly
murk, -ily
murky, -kier, -kiest
murmer murmur
murmur, -ed, -ing

murrain	
murth	mirth
murtle	myrtle
mus	mews (stables)
mus	muse(think)
muscat	
muscatel	
muscle, -cled, -cling (body)	
muscle	mussel (fish)
muscle-bound	
Muscovy duck	
muscular, -ly	
muscularity	
muse, mused, musing (think)	
muse	mews (stables)
musel	muscle (body)
musel	mussel (fish)
museum	
mush, -ed, -ing	
mushroom, -ed, -ing	
mushy, -ier, -iest	
music	
musical, -ly	
musician	
musishun	musician
musk	
muskatel	muscatel
musket	
musketeer	
musketry	
muskrat, -rats	
Muslim, -lims	
muslin	
mussel (fish)	
mussel	muscle (body)
must	
mustache	moustache
mustash	moustache
mustang	
mustard	
muster, -ed, -ing	
musterd	mustard
mustie	musty
mutant, -ly	
mutate, -tated, -tating	
mutation	
mute, muted, muting	
muter	mutter
mutilate, -lated, -lating	
mutilation	
mutilator	
mutinear	mutineer
mutineer	
mutinous, -ly	
mutinus	mutinous
mutiny, -nies	
mutiny, -nied, -nying	
muton	mutton
mutt	
mutter, -ed, -ing	
mutton	
mutton-bird	
mutton-chops	
mutual, -ly	
mutuality	
muu-muu	
muzak	
muzul	muzzle
muzzle, -zled, -zling	
myall	
myna (bird)	
myna	miner (worker)
myna	minor (less)
myopia	
myopic	
myriad	
myrrh	
myrtle	
myself	
mysterious, -ly	
mysterius	mysterious
mystery, -ries	
mystic (symbol)	
mystical, -ly	
mysticism	
mystification	
mystify, -fied, -fying	
mystique (secret)	
mystisism	mysticism
mystry	mystery
myth	
mythical, -ly	
mythology, -gies	
myxomatosis	

Nn

nab, nabbed, nabbing
nabor neighbour
nachur nature
nachurul natural
nack knack
nacker knacker
nacker nacre
nacre (pearl)
nacreous
nadir
nag, nagged, nagging
nagger
nail, nailed, nailing
naive, -ly
naivety
naked, -ly
nakedness
nakid naked
nale nail
namby-pamby, -bies
name, named, naming
namely
namesake
nanie nanny
nankeen kestrel
nanny, -ies
nannygai
nanny-goat
nany nanny
nap, napped, napping
napalm
naparm napalm
nape
napery
naphtha
naphthalene
napie nappy
napkin
nappe (rock)
nappy, -pies (cloth)
napsack knapsack
naptha naphtha
narate narrate
narative narrative
narcissism
narcissistic
narcissus, -cissuses, -cissi
narcosis
narcotic
nark, -ed, -ing
narl gnarl
narow narrow
narrate, -rated, -rating
narration
narrative, -ly
narrator
narrow, -ly
narsissism narcissism
narsissistic narcissistic
narsisus narcissus
nasal, -ly
nasalisation
nasalise, -lised, -lising
nasality
nascence
nascency
nascent, -ly
nasel nasal
nash gnash
nashun nation
nashunal national
nastie nasty
nasty, -tier, -tiest
nat gnat
natal
natch
natel natal
nater natter
nateral natural
naty natty
nation
national, -ly
nationalism
nationalist
nationalistic, -ally

Word	Correct spelling
nationality, -ties	
nation-state	
native	
Nativity	
Natsi	Nazi
natter, -ed, -ing	
natty, -tier, -tiest	
natul	natal
natur	nature
natural, -ly	
naturalisation	
naturalise, -lised, -lising	
naturalism	
naturalist	
naturalistic	
nature	
naturopathy	
naty	natty
naught	
naughty, -tier, -tiest	
nausea	
nauseate, -ated, -ating	
nauseation	
nauseous, -ly	
nautical, -ly	
nautilus, -luses	
naval (ship)	
naval	navel (body)
nave (church)	
nave	knave (rogue)
navel (body)	
navel orange	
navie	navvy
navie	navy
navigabel	navigable
navigable, -bly	
navigate, -gated, -gating	
navigation	
navigator	
navul	naval (ship)
navul	navel (body)
navvy, -vies (worker)	
navy, -vies (warships)	
naw	gnaw
nay (no)	
nay	neigh (horse)
naybour	neighbour

Word	Correct spelling
nayl	nail
Nazi, -zis	
Nazism	
nead	knead
nead	need
neadel	needle
neadil	needle
neadle	needle
neadless	needless
neap	
near, -ed, -ing	
nearby	
nearly	
nearside	
neat, -ly	
nebula, -lae, -las	
nebulous, -ly	
nebulus	nebulous
necesarey	necessary
necesitate	necessitate
necesitey	necessity
necessarily	
necessary, -saries	
necessitate, -tated, -tating	
necessity, -ties	
neck	
neckerchief	
neckliss	necklace
necklace	
necksus	nexus
necktie	
necromancer	
necromancy	
necromanser	necromancer
necromansey	necromancy
necrofilia	necrophilia
necrofiliac	necrophiliac
necrofilism	necrophilism
necrophilia	
necrophiliac	
necrophilism	
necropolis, -lises	
nectar	
nectarine	
nee (name)	
nee	knee (limb)
need, -ed, -ing (necessary)	

need knead (dough)
need kneed (use knee)
needful, -ly
needle, -dled, -dling
needless, -ly
needlework
needul needle
neel kneel
neer near
ne'er-do-well
neet neat
nefarious, -ly
nefarius nefarious
nefew nephew
negate, -gated, -gating
negation
negative, -tived, -tiving
negativity
negatory
neglect, -ed, -ing
neglectful, -ly
negligee
negligence
negligense negligence
negligent, -ly
negligibility
negligible, -bly
negligibul negligible
neglijay negligee
negoshabul negotiable
negoshiate negotiate
negotiability
negotiable, -bly
negotiant
negotiate, -ated, -ating
negotiation
Negro, -groes
Negroid
neice niece
neigh (horse)
neigh nay (no)
neighbor neighbour
neighbour
neighbourhood
neighbouring
neighbourly
neither (nor)
neither nether (below)
nek neck
neklace necklace
neklis necklace
nekrofilia necrophilia
nekropolis necropolis
nell knell
nemesis, -ses
nemisis nemesis
nemonics mnemonics
neofite neophyte
Neolithic
neologise, -gised, -gising
neon
neophyte
nephew
nephrism
nephritic
nephritis
nepotism
Neptune
nerd
nerve, nerved, nerving
nerve centre
nerve-racking
nerveous nervous
nerveous nervous
nervous, -ly
nervy, -vier, -viest
nesessary necessary
nesessitate necessitate
nesessitey necessity
nesessity necessity
nesle nestle
nest, -ed, -ing
nestle, -tled, -tling
nesul nestle
net, netted, netting
netball
netha neither (nor)
netha nether (below)
nether (below)
nether neither (nor)
nettle, -tled, -tling
nettul nettle
network

Word	Correct spelling
neumatic	pneumatic
neural, -ly	
neuralgia	
neuralgic	
neuritic	
neuritis	
neurological, -ly	
neurologist	
neurology	
neurone	
neurosis, -ses	
neurotic, -ally	
neuter	
neutral, -ly	
neutralisation	
neutralise, -lised, -lising	
neutrality	
neutron	
neva	never
never-never	
nevertheless	
new (novel)	
new	gnu (animal)
new	knew
newclear	nuclear
newcleus	nucleus
newcomer	
newfangled	
Newfoundland	
newmatic	pneumatic
newmonia	pneumonia
newral	neural
newrologist	neurologist
newrone	neurone
newrosis	neurosis
newrotic	neurotic
news	
newsagency	
newsagent	
newscast, -cast, -casting	
newscaster	
newsletter	
newsman, -men	
newspaper	
newspeak	
newsprint	
news reader	
newsreel	
newt	
newter	neuter
newtralise	neutralise
newtron	neutron
New Zealander	
next	
next of kin	
nexus, nexus	
ni	nigh
nib	
nibbel	nibble
nibble, -bled, -bling	
nibbler	
nibul	nibble
nice, nicer, nicest	
nicety, -ties	
niche	
nick, -ed, -ing	
nickel, -elled, -elling	
nickerbockers	knickerbockers
nickers	knickers
nickle	nickel
nicknack	knick-knack
nickname, -named, -naming	
nicks	nix
nicotine	
niece	
niether	neither
nifarius	nefarious
nife	knife
niftie	nifty
nifty, -tier, -tiest	
nigel	niggle
nigerd	niggard
niggard	
niggle, -gled, -gling	
nigh	
night, -ly (time)	
night	knight (lord)
nightcap	
nightclub	
nightdress	
nightingale	
nightjar	
nightmare	
nightmarish	

nostrim — nostrum
nostrum
nosy, -sier, -siest
not (denial)
not — knot (tie)
nota bene
notability
notable, -bly
notarial, -ly
notary, -ries
notation
notch, -ed, -ing
note, noted, noting
notefy — notify
nothing
notice, -ticed, -ticing
noticeable, -bly
noticeabul — noticeable
notifiable
notification
notifier
notify, -fied, -fying
notion
notional, -ly
not negotiable
notories — notorious
notoriety, -ties
notorious, -ly
notorius — notorious
notwithstanding
nougar — nougat
nougat
nought
noughts-and-crosses
noun
nourish, -ed, -ing
nourishingly
nourishment
nouns
nouveau riche, nouveaux riches
novel
novelette
novelist
novella, novellas, novelle
novelty, -ties
November
novice

novitiate
now
nowadays
nowhere
nowing — knowing
nowledge — knowledge
noxious, -ly
noxius — noxious
nozzle
nozzul — nozzle
nu — gnu (animal)
nu — knew
nu — new (novel)
nuance
nuanse — nuance
nub
nubile
nuckle — knuckle
nuclear
nuclear bomb
nuclear energy
nuclear family
nuclear fishun — nuclear fission
nuclear fission
nuclear fusion
nuclear power
nuclear reaction
nuclear reactor
nucleus, -clei, -cleuses
nude, -ly
nudge, nudged, nudging
nudism
nudist
nudity
nuge — nudge
nugget
nuisance
nulifi — nullify
null
nulla-nulla
nullification
nullify, -fied, -fying
num — numb
numatic — pneumatic
numb, numbed, numbing
number, -ed, -ing
numberless

Word	Correct spelling
numberplate	
numbness	
numbskull	
numeracy	
numeral	
numerasy	numeracy
numerate, -rated, -rating	
numeration	
numerator	
numerical, -ly	
numericul	numerical
numerological	
numerology	
numerous, -ly	
numerus	numerous
numismatics	
numismatist	
numonia	pneumonia
nun (woman)	
nun	none (no one)
nunnery, -neries	
nupshal	nuptial
nuptial	
nural	neural
nuralgia	neuralgia
nurcher	nurture
nuritis	neuritis
nurologist	neurologist
nurone	neurone
nurosis	neurosis
nurotic	neurotic
nurse, nursed, nursing	
nursery, -eries	
nursrey	nursery
nurture, -tured, -turing	
nurve	nerve
nusance	nuisance
nuse	news
nuspaper	newspaper
nut, nutted, nutting	
nuter	neuter
nutcracker	
nutmeg	
nutral	neutral
nutrient	
nutriment	
nutrishun	nutrition
nutrishus	nutritious
nutrition	
nutritional, -ly	
nutritionist	
nutritious, -ly	
nutron	neutron
nuts	
nutshell	
nutty, -tier, -tiest	
nuty	nutty
nuzul	nuzzle
nuzzle, -zled, -zling	
nylon	
nymf	nymph
nymph	
nymphomania	
nymphomaniac	

opaline
opaque, opaqued, opaquing
opasity opacity
opeate opiate
open, -ed, -ing
openly
open-minded
open-range
open-verdict
opera
operable, -bly
operabul operable
operate, -rated, -rating
operater operator
operatic, -ally
operation
operational, -ly
operative, -ly
operator
operetta
ophthalmic
ophthalmologist
ophthalmology
opiate, -ated, -ating
opine, opined, opining
opinion
opinionated
opinyun opinion
opium
oponent opponent
oportune opportune
oportunitey opportunity
opose oppose
oposishun opposition
oposite opposite
oposition opposition
opossum
oposum opossum
opponency
opponent
opportune, -ly
opportunism
opportunist
opportunity, -ties
oppose, -posed, -posing
opposite
opposition
oppress, -ed, -ing
oppression
oppressive, -ly
oppressor
opprobrious, -ly
opprobrium
oprabul operable
oprate operate
opreshun oppression
opresive oppressive
opress oppress
opshun option
opshunul optional
opt, -ed, -ing
opthalmic ophthalmic
opthalmology ophthalmology
optic
optical, -ly
optician
optics
optimism
optimist
optimistic, -ally
optimum, -ma, -mums
option
optional, -ly
optishun optician
optometrist
optometry
opulence
opulense opulence
opulent, -ly
opus, opuses, opera
or
or awe (dread)
or oar (boat)
or ore (rock)
ora aura
oracle
oracul oracle
oracular, -ly
oral, -ly (spoken)
oral aural (hear)
orangatang orang-outang
orange
orang-outang
orashun oration

orater	orator
oration	
orator	
oratorical, -ly	
oratorio, -rios	
oratory, -ries	
oratrey	oratory
orb	
orbit, -ed, -ing	
orbital	
orcestra	orchestra
orcestral	orchestral
orcestrate	orchestrate
orchard	
orchardist	
orchestra	
orchestral, -ly	
orchestrate, -trated, -trating	
orchestration	
orchid	
orcid	orchid
ordain, -ed, -ing	
ordanal	ordinal
ordane	ordain
ordeal	
ordenrey	ordinary
order, -ed, -ing	
orderly, -lies	
orderliness	
ordinal	
ordinance (law)	
ordinariness	
ordinary, -ries	
ordination	
ordinry	ordinary
orditer	auditor
orditrey	auditory
ordnance (weapons)	
ordnance	ordinance (law)
ordure	
ore (rock)	
ore	oar (boat)
ore	or, (either)
ore	awe (dread)
oregano	
orfan	orphan
orfanage	orphanage
orfanaje	orphanage
orful	awful
orfun	orphan
organ	
organdie, -dies	
organic, -ally	
organisation	
organise, -nised, -nising	
organism	
organist	
organza	
orgasm	
orgenism	organism
orger	auger (tool)
orger	augur (omen)
orgey	orgy
orgiastic	
orgy, -gies	
orical	auricle (ear)
orical	oracle (seer)
oriel	
orient	
oriental	
orientate, -tated, -tating	
orientation	
orienteering	
orifice	
orifise	orifice
origami	
origin	
original, -ly	
originality, -ties	
originate, -nated, -nating	
oringe	orange
oriole	
orjy	orgy
orkestra	orchestra
orkestral	orchestral
orkestrate	orchestrate
orkestration	orchestration
orkid	orchid
ornament	
ornamental, -ly	
ornamentation	
ornate, -ly	
ornimant	ornament
orning	awning

ornithologist
ornithology
orotund
orphan
orphanage
Orphism
orris
orspishus — auspicious
orstruck — awestruck
orsum — awesome
ort — aught
ort — ought
orthedoks — orthodox
orthodontic
orthodontics
orthodontist
orthodox
orthodoxy, -doxies
orthografey — orthography
orthography, -phies
orthopaedic
orthopaedics
orthopaedist
orthopaedy
orthopeadic — orthopaedic
orthority — authority
oscilation — oscillation
oscillate, -lated, -lating (move)
oscillate — osculate (kiss)
oscillation
oscillator
oscilloscope
osculate, -lated, -lating (kiss)
osculate — oscillate (move)
oseanic — oceanic
oselot — ocelot
oshun — ocean
osier
osifi — ossify
osler — ostler
osmosis
ospray — osprey
osprey, -preys
ossifi — ossify
ossification
ossify, -fied, -fying
ossilate — oscillate
ossilation — oscillation
ossiloscope — oscilloscope
osteapath — osteopath
ostensible, -bly
ostensibul — ostensible
ostentation
ostentatious, -ly
osteoarthritis
osteomyelitis
osteopath
osteopathic
osteopathy
ostler
ostracise, -cised, -cising
ostracism
ostrasise — ostracise
ostrasism — osatracism
ostrich
ote — oat
oter — otter
oth — oath
other
otherwise
otherworldly
otic
otiose, -ly
otiosity
otoman — ottoman
otter
ottoman, -mans
ouch
ought (should)
ought — aught (any part)
ouija
oul — owl
ounce
ounse — ounce
our (us)
our — hour
ourly — hourly
ours
ourself, -selves
oust, ousted, ousting
ouster
out, -ed, -ing
outback

outbilding outbuilding
outboard
outbrake outbreak
outbreak
outbuilding
outburst
outcast
outcome
outcri outcry
outcrop, -cropped, -cropping
outcry, -cries
outdate, -dated, -dating
outdo, -done, -doing
outdoor
outdoors
outer
outfall
outfield
outfit, -fitted, -fitting
outflank, -ed, -ing
outfox, -ed, -ing
outgoing
outgrow, -grew, -grown, -growing
outgrowth
outhouse
outhowse outhouse
outlandish, -ly
outlast, -ed, -ing
outlaw
outlawry
outlay, -laid, -laying
outlet
outline, -lined, -lining
outlive, -lived, -living
outlook
outlying
outmode, -moded, -moding
out-of-date
out-of-doors
out-of-pocket
out-of-the-way
outpatient
outpayshent outpatient
outperform, -ed, -ing
outplay, -ed, -ing
outpoint, -ed, -ing
outpooring outpouring
outpost
outpouring
output
outrage, -raged, -raging
outrageous, -ly
outraygus outrageous
outrider
outrigger
outright
outrite outright
outset
outside
outsider
outsize
outskirts
outspoken, -ly
outstanding, -ly
outstretch, -ed, -ing
outstrip, -stripped, -stripping
outward, -ly
outwards
outweigh
outwit, -witted, -witting
ouze ooze
ov of
oval, -ly
ovarey ovary
ovary, -ries
ovate
ovation
oven
ovenproof
ovenware
ovenwear ovenware
over, -ly
overall
overarm
overawe, -awed, -awing
overawl overall
overbalance, -anced, -ancing
overbalanse overbalance
overbare overbear
overbear, -bore, -borne, -bearing
overbid, -bid, -bidding
overboard
overbord overboard
overbridge

overcast, -cast, -casting
overcharge, -charged, -charging
overcoat
overcome, -came, -come, -coming
overdew overdue
overdo, -did, -done, -doing
overdose, -dosed, -dosing
overdraft
overdraw, -drew, -drawn, -drawing
overdress, -ed, -ing
overdrive, -drove, -driven, -driving
overdu overdue
overdue
overestimate, -mated, -mating
overestimation
overflow, -flowed, -flowing
overgrown
overhang, -hung, -hanging
overhaul, -ed, -ing
overhawl overhaul
overhead
overhear, -heard, -hearing
overhearer
overhed overhead
overherd overheard
overhere overhear
overjoid overjoyed
overjoyed
overkill
overland
overlander
overlap, -lapped, -lapping
overlay, -laid, -laying
overleaf
overleef overleaf
overlie, -lay, -lain, -lying (lie over)
overlie overly
overlook
overly (excessively)
overly overlie
overnight
overnite overnight
overore overawe
overought overwrought
overpass
overpower, -ed, -ing
overeach overreach
overeech overreach
overiding overriding
overreach, -ed, -ing
override, -rode, -ridden, -riding
overrool overrule
overrule, -ruled, -ruling
overrun, -ran, -run, -running
overule overrule
overun overrun
overseas (abroad)
oversee, -saw, -seen, -seeing
overseer
overshadow, -ed, -ing
overshoot, -shot, -shooting
oversight
oversite oversight
overstate, -stated, -stating
overstatement
overstay, -ed, -ing
overstep, -stepped, -stepping
overstock, -ed, -ing
oversubscribed
overt, -ly
overtake, -taken, -taking
overtaks overtax
overtax
overthrow, -thrown, -throwing
overtime, -timed, -timing
overtone
overture, -tured, -turing
overturn, -ed, -ing
overview
overwait overweight
overwate overweight
overweight
overwelm overwhelm
overwerk overwork
overwhelm, -ed, -ing
overwork, -worked, -working
overwrought
ovine
ovipares oviparous
oviparis oviparous
oviparous, -ly
oviparus oviparous
ovoid (egg)
ovoid avoid (evade)

ovulate, -lated, -lating	
ovulation	
ovule	
ovum, ova	
owa	hour
owa	our
owe, owed, owing (debt)	
owe	oh (cry)
owl	
own, -ed, -ing	
ownce	ounce
owner	
ownership	
ownly	only
owst	oust
owt	out
ox, oxen	
oxalis	
oxidate, -dated, -dating	
oxidation	
oxide	
oxidisable	
oxidisabul	oxidisable
oxidisation	
oxidise, -dised, -dising	
oxidiser	
oxigenate	oxygenate
oxyacetylene	
oxygen	
oxygenate, -nated, -nating	
oxygenation	
oxygenise, -nised, -nising	
oxymoron, -mora	
oyster	
Oz	
ozone	
ozonize, -ized, -izing	
ozonosphere	

Pp

pace, paced, pacing
pacemaker
pacer
pach   patch
pachwork   patchwork
pacific, -ally
pacification
pacifier
pacifism
pacifist
pacify, -fied, -fying
pack, -ed, -ing
package
packer
packet
packhorse
packije   package
pact
pad, padded, padding
paddle, -dled, -dling
paddler
paddle-steamer
paddock
paddul   paddle
paddy, -dies
paddy, -wagon
pade   paddy
padie   paddy
padlock, -ed, -ing
padre
padrey   padre
pady   paddy
paediatrician
paediatrics
pagan
paganism
page, paged, paging
pageant
pageantry, -ries
pagentry   pageantry
pageboy
pager
pagoda
pail (bucket)
pail   pale (white)
pain (ache)
pain   pane (glass)
painful, -ly
pain-killer
painstaking, -ly
paint, -ed, -ing
painter
pair, -ed, -ing (two)
pair   pare (trim)
pair   pear (fruit)
pakeha
pal, palled, palling (friend)
palace
palase   palace
palatable, -bly
palatal, -ly (taste)
palate (mouth)
palate   palette (board)
palate   pallet (bed)
palate   pellet (ball)
palatial, -ly (palace)
pale, paled, paling (white)
pale, paler, palest
pale   pail (bucket)
palette (board)
palette   pallet (bed)
paliate   palliate
palid   pallid
palindrome
paling
palisade, -saded, -sading
pall, palled, palling (satiate)
pallbearer
pallet (bed)
pallet   palette (paint)
pallet   pellet (ball)
palliate, -ated, -ating
palliation
palliative, -ly
pallid, -ly

Entry	Correct spelling
pall-mall (game)	
pall-mall	pell-mell (haste)
pallor	
palm, -ed, -ing	
palmist	
palmistry	
palmy, -mier, -miest	
palomino, -nos	
palor	pallor
palpable, -bly	
palpabul	palpable
palpitate, -tated, -tating	
palpitation	
palsie	palsy
palsied	
palsy, -sies	
paltrie	paltry
paltriness	
paltry, -trier, -triest	
pamplet	pamphlet
pampas	
pamper, -ed, -ing	
pamphlet	
pamphleteer	
pan, panned, panning	
panacea	
panache	
Panama hat	
panash	panache
pancake, -caked, -caking	
pancreas	
pancreatic	
panda (animal)	
pandemonium	
pander, -ed, -ing (indulge)	
pane (glass)	
pane	pain (ache)
paneful	painful
panegyric, -ally	
panel, -elled, -elling	
panellist	
panestaking	painstaking
pang	
panic, -icked, -icking	
paniced	panicked
panicky	

Entry	Correct spelling
panic-stricken	
panigiric	panegyric
panik	panic
pannier	
pannikin	
panorama	
panoramic, -ally	
pansie	pansy
pansy, -sies	
pant, -ed, -ing	
pantaloon	
pantechnicon	
pantheism	
pantheist	
pantheistic, -ally	
pantheon	
panther	
panthion	pantheon
panties	
pantihose	
pantingly	
pantograf	pantograph
pantograph	
pantomime	
pantomine	pantomime
pantrey	pantry
pantry, -ries	
pants	
panza	panzer
panzer	
pap	
papa	
papacy, -cies	
papal	
papasy	papacy
paper	
paperback	
paperbark	
paperboy	
paperclip	
paper-mache	papier-mâché
paperwait	paperweight
paperweight	
papier-mâché	
papirus	papyrus
papism	
papoose	

papouse papoose
pappa papa
pappoose papoose
papprika paprika
pappyrus papyrus
paprica paprika
paprika
papul papal
papyrus, -ri
parable
parabola
parabul parable
parachute
paracide parricide
paracleet paraclete
paraclete
parade, -raded, -rading
paradice paradise
paradigm
paradime paradigm
paradise
paradoks paradox
paradox
parady parody
parafernalia paraphernalia
paraffin
parafin paraffin
parafrase paraphrase
paragon
paragraf paragraph
paragraph
parakeet
parakete parakeet
paralax parallax
paralel parallel
paralelagram parallelogram
paralise paralyse
paralisis paralysis
paralitic paralytic
parallax
parallel, -leled, -leling or -lelled, -lelling
parallelogram
paralyse, -lysed, -lysing
paralysis
paralytic
paramedical
parameter
paramiter parameter
paramoor paramour
paramount
paramour
paramownt paramount
paranoia
paranoiac
paranoid
parapet
paraphernalia
paraphrase, -phrased, -phrasing
paraplegic
paraplijic paraplegic
parashoot parachute
parashute parachute
parasite
parasitic, -ally
parasitism
parasol
parasoll parasol
paratrooper
parboil, -ed, -ing
parboyle parboil
parcel, -celled, -celling
parch, -ed, -ing
parchment
pardon, -ed, -ing
pardonable
pardonabul pardonable
pardoner
pare (trim)
pare pair (two
pare pear (fruit)
parent
parentage
parental, -ly
parenthesis, -ses
parentige parentage
parfait
parfay parfait
pariah
parie parry
parish, parishes
parishioner
parishoner parishioner
pariside parricide

parisidul parricidal
parity
park, -ed, -ing
parka
parket parquet
parking-meter
Parkinson's disease
parlament parliament
parlance
parlans parlance
parlay parley
parlement parliament
parlementarey parliamentary
parlementry parliamentary
parler parlour
parlermade parlour-maid
parley, -leyed, -leying
parliament
parliamentarian
parliamentary
parlour
parlour-maid
parm palm
parmist palmist
parochial, -ly
parochialism
parody, -dies
parody, -died, -dying
parograf paragraph
parograph paragraph
parokial parochial
paroksism paroxysm
parole, -roled, -roling
paroll parole
parot parrot
paroxysm
parquet, -queted, -queting
parranoia paranoia
parricide
parrot
parry, parried, parrying
parse, parsed, parsing
parsel parcel
parshal partial
parshialitey partiality
parsimonious, -ly
parsimonius parsimonious
parsimony
parsley
parslie parsley
parsly parsley
parsnip
parson
parsonage
parsonige parsonage
parsul parcel
part, -ed, -ing
partake, -took, -taken, -taking
partial, -ly
partiality, -ties
participant
participate, -pated, -pating
participle
participul participle
particle
particul particle
particular, -ly
partie party
partime part-time
partisan
partishun partition
partisipant participant
partisipate participate
partisipul participle
partition, -ed, -ing
partly
partner, -ed, -ing
partridge
partrige partridge
part-time
party, -ties
pars pass
pary parry
pasabul passable
pascal paschal
paschal
pascher pasture
pase pace
pasemaker pacemaker
paserby passer-by
pashonate passionate
pashun passion
pasific pacific
pasify pacify

pasige passage
pasinger passenger
pasive passive
pasivitey passivity
Pasover Passover
paspalum
pasport passport
pass, passed, passing
passable, -bly
passabul passable
passage, -saged, -saging
passbook
passé
passenger
passer-by, passers-by
passige passage
passion
passionate, -ly
passionfruit
passive, -ly
passivity
Passover
passport
password
past
pasta (dough)
pasta pastor (priest)
paste, pasted, pasting
pasteboard
pastel
pasterise pasteurise
pasteurise, -ed, -ing
pastiche
pastie pasty
pastime
pastor (priest)
pastoral, -ly
pastoralist
pastrami
pastry, -tries
pasture, -ed, -ing
pasty, -ties
pasword password
pat, patter, patting
patay pâté
patch, -ed, -ing
patchwork
patchy, patchier, patchiest
pâté
patella, -tellae
paten pattern
patent, -ed, -ing
patent-leather
pater patter
patern pattern
paternal, -ly
paternalism
paternity
path
pathetic, -ally
pathological, -ly
pathology, -gies
pathos
patie patty
patience (calm)
patient, patients (ill)
patient, -ly
patina
patio, patios
patiserey patisserie
patisserie
patois, patois
patriarch
patriarchal, -ly
patriarchy, -archies
patriark patriarch
patrician
patricide
patrimony, -monies
patriot
patriotic, -ally
patriotism
patrishun patrician
patriside patricide
patrol, patrolled, patrolling
patron
patronage
patroness
patronige patronage
patronise, -ed, -ing
patter, -ed, -ing
pattern, -ed, -ing
patty, -ies
paturnal paternal

Word	Correct spelling
paturnitey	paternity
patwa	patois
paucity	
paun	pawn
paunch, paunches	
paunchy	
pauper	
pause, paused, pausing (stop)	
pause	paws (feet)
pave, paved, paving	
pavement	
pavilion	
pavlova	
paw (foot)	
paw	poor (needy)
paw	pore (skin)
paw	pour (flow)
pawcelain	porcelain
pawch	porch
pawk	pork
pawkupine	porcupine
pawl	pall
pawlbarer	pall-bearer
pawlsied	palsied
pawlsy	palsy
pawltrey	paltry
pawn, -ed, -ing	
pawnbroker	
pawnbroking	
pawnch	paunch
pawnografey	pornography
pawpaw	
pawper	pauper
pawpus	porpoise
pawse	pause (stop)
pawselin	porcelain
pawshun	portion
pawsitey	paucity
pay, paid, paying	
payable	
payabul	payable
payload	
payment	
paynt	paint
payola	
payroll	
payshence	patience
payshent	patient
paytent	patent
pea	
peace (calm)	
peace	piece (part)
peaceable, -bly	
peaceabul	peaceable
peaceful, -ly	
peach, peaches	
peacock	
peak, -ed, -ing (top)	
peak	peek (look)
peak	pique (anger)
peal, -ed, -ing (ring)	
peal	peel (skin)
peanut	
peap	peep
pear (fruit)	
pear	pair (two)
pear	pare (trim)
pearage	peerage
pearce	pierce
pearl (gem)	
pearl	purl (knit)
pearly, -lies	
peasant	
peasantry	
peashooter	
peashuter	peashooter
peat	
pebble	
pecadillo, -loes, -los	
pecan	
peck, -ed, -ing	
peckish, -ly	
pecock	peacock
pectin	
pectoral	
peculiar, -ly	
peculiarity, -ties	
pecuniary	
pedagog	pedagogue
pedagogic, -ally	
pedagogue	
pedagogy	
pedal, -alled, -alling (bike)	
pedant	

pedantic, -ally
pedantry, -ries
peddle, -dled, -dling (sell)
  peddle — pedal (bike)
pederast
pederastic, -ally
pederasty
pedestal, -stalled, -stalling
pedestrian
pedicure
pedigree
pedlar
peek, -ed, -ing (look)
  peek — peak (top)
  peek — pique (anger)
peel, -ed, -ing (skin)
  peel — peal (ring)
peep, -ed, -ing
peepshow
peer, -ed, -ing (look)
  peer — pier (wharf)
peerage
peeress
  peerige — peerage
peerless, -ly
peevish
peewee
peewit
peg, pegged, pegging
  peice — piece
pejorative, -ly
  pek — peck
  pekant — piquant
Pekinese
Pekingese
  pekish — peckish
pelargonium
pelican
pellet (ball)
  pellet — palate (mouth)
  pellet — palette (board)
  pellet — pallet (bed)
pell-mell (haste)
  pell-mell (game) — pall-mall
pellucid, -ly
pelmet
pelt, -ed, -ing
  pelusid — pellucid
pelvis, -ves
pen, penned, penning
penal
penalisation
penalise, -lised, -lising
penalty, -ties
penance
  penanse — penance
  penant — pennant
pence
penchant
pencil, -cilled, -cilling
pendant
pendent
pending
pendulous, -ly
pendulum
  pendulus — pendulous
penetrable, -bly
  pentrabul — penetrable
penetrate, -trated, -trating
penetration
penfriend
penguin
  pengwin — penguin
penicillin
  peniless — penniless
peninsula
penis, -nes, -nises
  penisilin — penicillin
  penitenshary — penitentiary
  penitenshul — penitential
penitent, -ly
penitential, -ly
penitentiary, -ries
penknife, -knives
pen-name
pennant
penniless
pennon
penny, pennies, pence
penny-farthing
penny-pinching
penological
penologist

Word	Correct spelling
penology	
pen-pusher	
pense	pence
penshun	pension
penshuner	pensioner
pensil	pencil
pension	
pensionable	
pensionabul	pensionable
pensioner	
pensive, -ly	
pentagon	
pentathalon	pentathlon
pentathlon	
penthouse	
penthowse	penthouse
pent-up	
penultimate, -ly	
penumbra, -brae, -bras	
penurious, -ly	
penury	
penut	peanut
peon	
peony, -nies	
people, -pled, -pling	
pep, pepped, pepping	
peper	pepper
pepermint	peppermint
pepery	peppery
pepper	
peppercorn	
peppermint	
peppery	
pep pill	
pep talk	
peptic	
perambulate, -lated, -lating	
perambulation	
perambulator	
perambulatory	
per annum	
per capita	
perceivable, -bly	
perceive, -ceived, -ceiving	
per cent	
percentage	
percentige	percentage

Word	Correct spelling
percentile	
percepshun	perception
perceptabul	perceptible
perceptible, -bly	
perception	
perceptive, -ly	
perceptual, -ly	
percession	procession
perch, perches	
perch, -ed, -ing	
perchase	purchase
percipience	
percipient	
percolate, -lated, -lating	
percolater	percolator
percolation	
percolator	
percushun	percussion
percussion	
percussionist	
percussive	
perdishun	perdition
perdition	
peregrinate, -nated, -nating	
peremptoriness	
peremptory, -torily	
perennial, -ly	
perfeckshun	perfection
perfect, -ed, -ing	
perfectible	
perfectibul	perfectible
perfection	
perfectionism	
perfectionist	
perfidious, -ly	
perfidius	perfidious
perfidy, -dies	
perforate, -rated, -rating	
perforation	
perforce	
perform, -ed, -ing	
performance	
performanse	performance
perfume, -fumed, -fuming	
perfumery, -ries	
perfunctory, -torily	
perfunctry	perfunctory

pergarey perjury
pergative purgative
pergatry purgatory
perge purge
pergola
perhaps
perhibit prohibit
periferal peripheral
perifery periphery
peril, -rilled, -rilling
perilous, -ly
perilus perilous
perimeter
period
periodic
periodical, -ly
peripatetic
peripheral, -ly
periphery, -ries
periscope
perish, -ed, -ing
perishable
perishabul perishable
perisher
peritonitis
periwinkle
perjure, -jured, -juring
perjurer
perjury, -ries
perk, -ed, -ing
perkushun percussion
perky, -kier, -kiest
perl pearl (gem)
perl purl (knit)
perloin purloin
perloyn purloin
perm, -ed, -ing
permananse permanence
permanence
permanency, -cies
permanent, -ly
permanganate
permeability
permeable
permeate, -ated, -ating
permeation
permiate permeate
permisabul permissible
permishun permission
permissible, -bly
permission
permissive, -ly
permissiveness
permit, -mitted, -mitting
permutation
permute, -muted, -muting
pernicious, -ly
perniciousness
pernickety
pernishus pernicious
perokside peroxide
peroration
peroxide, -ided, -iding
perpechual perpetual
perpechuate perpetuate
perpendicular, -ly
perpendicularity
perpetrate, -trated, -trating
perpetrater perpetrator
perpetration
perpetrator
perpetual, -ly
perpetuate, -ated, -ating
perpetuation
perpetuator
perpetuity, -ties
perport purport
perpose purpose
perquisite (profit)
perquisite (necessary) prerequisite
per say per se
per se
perse purse
persecushun persecution
persecute, -cuted, -cuting
persecution
persecutor
persepshun perception
perseptabul perceptible
perseve persevere
perseverance
persevere, -vered, -vering
Persian

persimmon
persist, -ed, -ing
persistence
person
personable, -bly
personage
personal, -ly (private)
personal — personnel (employees)
personalise, -lised, -lising
personality, -ties
persona non grata
personate, -ated, -ating
personible — personable
personification
personify, -fied, -fying
personnel (employees)
personnel — personal (private)
perspective, -ly
perspeks — perspex
perspektive — perspective
perspex
perspicacious, -ly
perspicacity
perspicuous, -ly
perspicuousness
perspiration
perspire, -spired, -spiring
persuade, -suaded, -suading
persuader
persuashun — persuasion
persuasion
persuasive, -ly
persuit — pursuit
perswade — persuade
perswasion — persuasion
pert, -ly
pertness
pertain, -ed, -ing
pertane — pertain
pertinacious, -ly
pertinacity
pertinent, -ly
perturb, -ed, -ing
perturbable
peruse, -rused, -rusing
pervade, -vaded, -vading
pervasion
pervasive, -ly
perverse, -ly
pervershun — perversion
perversion
perversity, -ties
pervert, -ed, -ing
perverter
pervurse — perverse
pervurshun — perversion
pervurt — pervert
pesabul — peaceable
pesant — peasant
pesary — pessary
pese — peace
pesimism — pessimism
pesimist — pessimist
pessary, -ries
pessimism
pessimist
pest
pester, -ed, -ing
pesticide
pestilence
pestilense — pestilence
pestilent, -ly
pestiside — pesticide
pestle
pesul — pestle
pet, petted, petting
petal
petard
peteet — petite
peter, -ed, -ing
peticoat — petticoat
petie — petty
petishun — petition
petite
petition, -ed, -ing
petrel (bird)
petrel — petrol (fuel)
petrify, -fied, -fying
petrol (fuel)
petrol — petrel (bird)
petroleum
petrul — petrel (bird)

petrul	petrol (fuel)
petticoat	
pettily	
pettiness	
petty, -tier, -tiest	
petulance	
petulant, -ly	
petunia	
pevish	peevish
pew	
pewter	
phalanger	
phalanx, -anxes or -anges	
phalus	phallus
phallic	
phallus, phalluses, phalli	
phantasm	
phantasmagoria	
phantom	
Pharaoh	
pharisaic	
pharisee	
pharmaceutical, -ly	
pharmacist	
pharmacy, -cies	
pharyngitis	
pharynx, pharynges, pharynxes	
phase, phased, phasing	
pheasant	
phenacetin	
phenix	phoenix
phenol	
phenomenal, -ly	
phenomenon, -mena	
phesant	pheasant
phial (vessel)	
philander, -ed, -ing	
philanderer	
philanthropic, -ally	
philanthropist	
philanthropy, -pies	
philarmonic	philharmonic
philatelist	
philately	
philharmonic	
philippines	
philosofer	philosopher
philosofical	philosophical
philosofy	philosophy
philosopher	
philosophical, -ly	
philosophise, -phised, -phising	
philosophy, -phies	
philter	philtre
philtre, -tred, -tring	

For phis- words, look under **phys-**.

phlegm	
phlegmatic, -ally	
phlem	phlegm
phlox	
phobia	
phobic	
phoenix	
phone	
phonetic, -ally	
phonograf	phonograph
phonogram	
phonograph	
phony, phonier, phoniest	
phosfate	phosphate
phosforus	phosphorus
phosphate	
phosphor	
phosphorescent	
phosphorus	
photo, photos	
photocopier	
photocopy, -pies	
photocopy, -copied, -copying	
photoelectric	
photo-finish	
photogenic	
photograf	photograph
photograph, -graph, -graphing	
photographic, -ally	
photography	
photostat, -stated, -stating	
photosynthesis	
phrase, phrased, phrasing	
phraseology	
phrenetic, -ally	
phylactery, -teries	

physic (medicine)
physical, -ly
physician
physicist
physics
physiognomy, -mies
physiological, -ly
physiology
physiotherapist
physiotherapy
physique
pi (Greek letter)
pi — pie (food)
pianist
piano, pianos
pianoforte
piatsa — piazza
piazza
pibald — piebald
picador
picancy — piquancy
picaniny — piccaninny
piccaninny, -nies
piccolo, -los
pich — pitch
picinic — picnic
pick, -ed, -ing
pickaxe, -axed, -axing
picket, -ed, -ing
pickle, -led, -ling
pickpocket
pick-up
picnic, -nicked, -nicking
picnicker
pictorial, -ly
picture, -tured, -turing
picturesque
pidgin (talk)
pidgin — pigeon (bird)
pie (food)
pie — pi (Greek letter)
piebald
piece, pieced, piecing (part)
piece — peace (calm)
piecemeal
piecework
pier (wharf)
pier — peer (look)
pierce, pierced, piercing
pierse — pierce
piety, -ties
pig, pigged, pigging
pigeon (bird)
pigeon — pidgin (talk)
pigeonhole, -holed, -holing
pigeon-toed
pigery — piggery
piggery, -geries
piggyback
pig-headed
pigiback — piggyback
pigin — pidgin (talk)
pigin — pigeon (bird)
pig-iron
piglet
pigment
pigmentation
pigmy, -mies
pigskin
pigstick, -ed, -ing
pigsticker
pigsty, -sties
pigtail
pigtale — pigtail
pijamas — pyjamas
pikau
pike, piked, piking
pikelet
pilchard
pile, piled, piling
pile-up
pilfer, -ed, -ing
pilferage
pilferer
pilferige — pilferage
pilgrim
pilgrimage
pilgrimige — pilgrimage
pilige — pillage
pilion — pillion
pill
pillage, -laged, -laging
pillager

pillar
pillbox, -boxes
pillion
pillory, -ries
pillory, -ried, -rying
pillow, pillows
pilon — pylon
pilory — pillory
pilot, -ed, -ing
pilotage
pilow — pillow
pilyun — pillion
pilsener
pimp, -ed, -ing
pimple
pimply, -plier, -pliest
pimpul — pimple
pin, pinned, pinning
pinacle — pinnacle
pinafore
pinball
pince-nez
pincers
pinch, -ed, -ing
pincher
pincushion
pine, pined, pining
pineapple
pineappul — pineapple
pin-feather
ping, -ed, -ing
ping-pong
pinion, -ed, -ing
pink, -ed, -ing
pinnacle, -cled, -cling
pinpoint, -ed, -ing
pinprick
pinsers — pincers
pinstripe
pint
pintuck, -ed, -ing
pin-up
pinyun — pinion
pionear — pioneer
pioneer, -ed, -ing
pious, -ly
pip, pipped, pipping

pipe, piped, piping
pipedream
pipeline
pipi
pipit
pippin
pipsqueak
piquancy
piquant, -ly
pique, piqued, piquing
piracy
piramid — pyramid
piranha
pirasy — piracy
pirate, -rated, -rating
piratical, -ly
pire — pyre
pirooet — pirouette
pirouette, -etted, -etting
piscatorial
Pisces
pistachio, -chios
pistil (flower)
pistol (gun)
piston
pit, pitted, pitting
pitanse — pittance
pitapat, -patted, -patting
pitch, -ed, -ing
pitch-black
pitchblende
pitcher (baseball)
pitcher — picture (image)
pitchfork, -ed, -ing
pitchi
piteous, -ly
piter-pater — pitter-patter
pitfall
pith
pithead
pithy, -ier, -iest
pitiable, -ly
pitiabul — pitiable
pitiful, -fully
pitiless, -ly
pittance
pittanse — pittance

pitter-patter
pittosporum
pituitary, -taries
pituri
pity, pities
pity, pitied, pitying
  pius   pious
pivot, -ed, -ing
pivotal, -ly
pixie, pixies
pixy, pixies
pizza
pizzicato
placability
placable, -bly
  placabul   placable
placard, -ed, -ing
placate, -cated, -cating
placatory
place, placed, placing (position)
  place   plaice (fish)
placebo, -bos, -boes
placement
placenta, -tas, -tae
placental
placid, -ly
placidity
placket
  plagarism   plagiarism
  plage   plague
plagiarise, -rised, -rising
plagiarism
plagiarist
plague, plagued, plaguing
plaice (fish)
plaid (cloth)
plain, -ly (clear)
  plain   plane (flat)
plain-clothes
plain-spoken
plains wanderer
plaint
plaintiff (sue)
plaintive, -ly (sad)
plait, -ed, -ing (braid)
  plait   plate (dish)
  plaket   placket

plan, planned, planning
plane, planed, planing (flat)
  plane   plain (clear)
planet
planetarium
planetary
plank
plankton
planner
plant, -ed, -ing
plantation
planter
  plantif   plaintiff (sue)
  plantive   plaintive (sad)
plaque
  plase   place (position)
  plase   plaice(fish)
  plasenta   placenta
  plasid   placid
plasma
plaster, -ed, -ing
plasterboard
plasterer
plastic, -ally
  plasticene   plasticine
plasticine
plasticity
  plastisene   plasticine
plate, plated, plating (dish)
  plate   plait (braid)
plateau, -eaus, -eaux
platelet
  plater   platter
platform
  platichude   platitude
platinum
  platipus   platypus
platitude
platitudinous
  plato   plateau
platonic
platoon
platter
platypus, -puses, -pi
plaudit
plausible, -bly
  plausibul   plausible

play, -ed, -ing
playback
playboy
player
playful, -ly
playground
play-off
playrite   playwright
playwright
plaza
plea, pleas (request)
plead, -ed, -ing
pleas   please (satisfy)
pleasant, -ly
pleasantry, -tries
please, pleased, pleasing (satisfy)
pleasurable, -bly
pleasurabul   pleasurable
pleat, -ed, -ing
plebean   plebeian
plebeian
plebiscite
plebisite   plebiscite
plectrum, -tra, -trums
pledge, pledged, pledging
plee   plea
pleed   plead
pleet   pleat
plege   pledge
plenary, -rily
plenipotentiary, -ries
plenitude
plenteous, -ly
plentiful, -ly
plentius   plenteous
plenty
plesant   pleasant
plese   pleas (requests)
plese   please (satisfy)
plesurabul   pleasurable
plesure   pleasure
plethora
pleurisy
pli   ply
pliable, -bly
pliabul   pliable
pliant, -ly

pliers
plight, -ed, -ing
Plimsoll line
plinth
plite   plight
pliwood   plywood
plod, plodded, plodding
plodder
ploi   ploy
plonk, -ed, -ing
ploomage   plumage
plootocrasy   plutocracy
plooviul   pluvial
plop, plopped, plopping
plot, plotted, plotting
plough, -ed, -ing
ploughshare
plover
plow   plough
ploy
pluck, -ed, -ing
plucky, -ily
plug, plugged, plugging
plum (fruit)
plum   plumb (test)
plumage
plumb, -ed, -ing (test)
plumber
plumbline
plume, plumed, pluming
plumige   plumage
plumline   plumbline
plummer   plumber
plummet, -ed, -ing
plump, -ed, -ing
plunder, -ed, -ing
plunge, plunged, plunging
plural
pluralism
plurality, -ties
plurasy   pleurisy
plus
plus-fours
plush
plutocracy, -cies
plutocrat
plutonium

pluvial
ply, plies
ply, plied, plying
plywood
pneumatic, -ally
pneumonia
poach, -ed, -ing
poacher
pock poach
pock
pocket, -ed, -ing
pocket-book
pocket-knife, -knives
pocket-money
pockmark
pod, podded, podding
poddy
podiatrist
podiatry
podium, -dia
poem
poet
poetess
poetic
poetical, -ly
poetry
pogrom
poignancy
poignant, -ly
poinancy poignancy
poinant poignant
poinsettia
point, -ed, -ing
point-blank
pointedly
pointer
pointillism
pointless, -ly
poise, poised, poising
poison, -ed, -ing
poisoner
poisonous, -ly
poke, poked, poking
poker
pokey, pokies (machine)
poky, -kier, -kiest (small)
polar (region)
polar poler (horse)
polarise, -rised, -rising
polarity
polaroid
pole, poled, poling (stick)
pole poll (vote)
polemic
polemical, -ly
polen pollen
poler (horse)
poler polar (region)
polese police
police, -liced, -licing
policeman, -men
policewoman, -women
policy, -cies
poligamus polygamous
poligamy polygamy
poliglot polyglot
poligon polygon
polinate pollinate
Polineshun Polynesian
poliomyelitis
polip polyp
polish, -ed, -ing
polisy policy
politburo
polite, -ly
politic
polithene polythene
political, -ly
politician
politicise, -cised, -cising
politicking
politics
politishun politician
polka, -kaed, -kaing
poll, -ed, -ing (vote)
poll pole (stick)
pollard
pollen
pollinate, -nated, -nating
pollination
pollster
pollutant
pollute, -luted, -luting
pollution

Word	Correct spelling
polo	
polo-neck	
poltegist	poltergeist
poltergeist	
poltise	poultice
poltry	poultry
polushun	pollution
polute	pollute
polyandrous	
polyandry	
polyanthus	
polyester	
polygamist	
polygamous, -ly	
polygamy	
polyglot	
polygon	
Polyneshun	Polynesian
Polynesian	
polyp	
polysaturated	
polythene	
polyunsaturated	
pomander	
pomegranate	
pomel	pommel
Pomeranian	
pommel, -melled, -melling	
pommy, -mies	
pomp	
pompom	
pomposity	
pompous, -ly	
poncho, -chos	
ponder, -ed, -ing	
ponderous, -ly	
ponderus	ponderous
ponie	pony
pontiff	
pontifical, -ly	
pontificate, -cated, -cating	
pontoon	
pony, -nies	
ponytail	
pooch	
poodle	
poodul	poodle

Word	Correct spelling
pool, -ed, -ing	
poop, -ed, -ing	
poor, -ly (needy)	
poor	paw (foot)
poor	pore (skin)
poor	pour (flow)
poorhouse	
pop, popped, popping	
popcorn	
pope	
popery	
popet	poppet
popie	poppy
popish, -ly	
poplar (tree)	
poplin	
popourri	potpourri
poppet	
poppy, -pies	
poppycock	
populace	
popular, -ly (known)	
popularise, -rised, -rising	
popularitey	popularity
popularity	
populase	populace
populate, -lated, -lating	
population	
populer	popular
populous, -ly	
populus	populous
popy	poppy
por	paw (foot)
por	poor (needy)
por	pore (skin)
por	pour (flow)
porcelain	
porcelane	porcelain
porch	
porcupine	
pore (skin)	
pore	paw (foot)
pore	poor (needy)
pore	pour (flow)
porfrey	porphyry
poridge	porridge
porige	porridge

pork	
porkupine	porcupine
pornografy	pornography
pornographer	
pornographic	
pornography	
porosity	
porous	
porphyry, -ries	
porpoise, -poises	
porpus	porpoise
porridge	
porselin	porcelain
porshun	portion
porslin	porcelain
port	
portable	
portal	
portend, -ed, -ing	
portenshus	portentous
portent	
portentous, -ly	
porter	
portfolio, -lios	
porthole	
portico, -coes, -cos	
portion, -ed, -ing	
portly, -lier, -liest	
portmanteau, -teaus, -teaux	
portrait	
portraiture	
portray, -ed, -ing	
portrayal	
portret	portrait
portul	portal
porus	porous
poschur	posture
pose, posed, posing	
poser	
poseshun	possession
posess	possess
posessive	possessive
posey	posy
posh, -ly	
poshun	potion
posibility	possibility
posibul	possible
posishun	position
position	
positive, -ly	
posse	
possess, -ed, -ing	
possession	
possessive, -ly	
possessor	
possible, -bly	
possibility, -ties	
possibul	possible
possum	
post, -ed, -ing	
postage	
postal	
postcard	
postcode	
postdate, -dated, -dating	
poster	
posterier	posterior
posterior, -ly	
posterity	
postern	
postgraduate	
posthaste	
posthumous, -ly	
posthumus	posthumous
postige	postage
post-mortem	
post-office	
postpone, -poned, -poning	
postponement	
postulant	
postulate, -lated, -lating	
postumus	posthumous
posture, -tured, -turing	
posy, -sies	
pot, potted, potting	
potable	
potash	
potasium	potassium
potassium	
potato, -toes	
pot-bellied	
pot-belly, -lies	
potency	
potenshul	potential

Word	Correct spelling
potensy	potency
potent	
potentate	
potential, -ly	
potentiality, -ties	
poter	potter
potery	pottery
pothole	
potion	
potluck	
potpourri, -ris	
pottage	
potter, -ed, -ing	
pottery, -ries	
potty, -ties	
pouch, pouches	
poulterer	
poultice, -ticed, -ticing	
poultise	poultice
poultry	
pounce, pounced, pouncing	
pound, -ed, -ing	
pour, -ed, -ing	
pour	poor (needy)
pour	pore (skin)
pout, -ed, -ing	
poverty	
poverty-stricken	
powch	pouch
powder, -ed, -ing	
powdery	
power, -ed, -ing	
powerful, -ly	
powerhouse	
powerless, -ly	
pownce	pounce
pownd	pound
powt	pout
pow wow, -wowed, -wowing	
pox	
practicable, -bly	
practicabul	practicable
practical, -ly	
practicality	
practice, -ticed, -ticing	
practician	
practise, -tised, -tising	

Word	Correct spelling
practishun	practician
practishuner	practitioner
practitioner	
pragmatic, -ally	
pragmatism	
pragmatist	
prairey	prairie
prairie	
praise, praised, praising	
praiseworthy, -thily	
pram	
prance, pranced, prancing	
prandial, -ly	
prang, -ed, -ing	
prank	
pranse	prance
prarey	prairie
prase	praise
prate, prated, prating	
prattle, -tled, -tling	
pratul	prattle
prawn	
pray, -ed, -ing (beg)	
pray	prey (hunt)
prayer	
prayerbook	
preach, -ed, -ing	
preacher	
preamble	
preambul	preamble
prearrange, -ranged, -ranging	
precarious, -ly	
precaution	
precautionary	
precautionry	precautionary
precawshun	precaution
precede, -ceded, -ceding (before)	
precede (ahead)	proceed
precedence	
precedent (law)	
precedent (head)	president
precept	
preceptor	
prech	preach
precinct	

precious, -ly
precipatation — precipitation
precipice
precipise — precipice
precipitant, -ly
precipitate, -tated, -tating
precipitation
precipitous, -ly
precipitus — precipitous
precis (summary)
precise, -ly (exact)
precishun — precision
precision
preclude, -cluded, -cluding
precocious, -ly
precocity
preconceive, -ceived, -ceiving
preconcieve — preconceive
preconsepshun — preconception
preconception
preconseve — preconceive
precoshus — precocious
precursor
predater — predator
predator
predatory
predecessor
predesessor — predecessor
predestination
predestine, -tined, -tining
predetermination
predetermine, -mined, -mining
predicament
predicate, -cated, -cating
predicative, -ly
predict, -ed, -ing
predictable, -bly
predictabul — predictable
prediction
predictor
predilecshun — predilection
predilection
predispose, -posed, -posing
predisposition
predominance
predominant, -ly
predominate, -ated, -ating

pre-eminence
pre-eminent, -ly
pre-empt, -ed, -ing
pre-emptory
preen, -ed, -ing
prefabricate, -cated, -cating
prefabrication
preface, -faced, -facing
prefatory, -rily
prefect
prefecture
prefer, -ferred, -ferring
preferable, -bly
preference
preferense — preference
preferenshul — preferential
preferential, -ly
preferment
prefice — preface
prefiks — prefix
prefix
pregnancy, -cies
pregnansy — pregnancy
pregnant, -ly
prehensile
prehistoric, -ally
prejudge, -judged, -judging
prejudgment
prejudice, -diced, -dicing
prejudicial, -ly
prejudise — prejudice
prejudishul — prejudicial
prelate
preliminary, -aries
prelude, -luded, -luding
premarital
premature, -ly
premenstrual tension
premier (chief)
premiere (first performance)
premise, -ised, -ising
premises
premium
premonishun — premonition
premonition
premonitory
prenatal

prene preen
preoccupation
preoccupy, -pied, -pying
preparation
preparatory, -rily
preparatry preparatory
prepare, -pared, -paring
preponderance
preponderant, -ly
preposition
preposterous, -ly
prerekwisit prerequisite
prerequisite (necessary)
prerequisite (profit) perquisite
prerogative
pres press
presage, -saged, -saging
prescripshun prescription
prescription
prescriptive, -ly
presede precede
presedence precedence
presedent precedent
presedent president
preseed precede
preseleckshun preselection
preselect, -ed, -ing
preselection
presence
presense presence
present, -ed, -ing
presentable, -bly
presentation
presentiment
presently
presept precept
preservation
preservative
preserve, -served, -serving
presher pressure
presherise pressurise
preshus precious
preside, -sided, -siding
presidency
presidenshul presidential
presidensy presidency
president
presidential
presige presage
presinct precinct
presipice precipice
presipis precipice
presipitate precipitate
presipitus precipitous
presise precise
press, -ed, -ing
press-up
pressure, -sured, -suring
pressurisation
pressurise, -rised, -rising
prest priest
prestege prestige
presthood priesthood
prestige
prestigious, -ly
prestigus prestigious
presto
presume, -sumed, -suming
presumption
presumptuous, -ly
presumshun presumption
presumtuus presumptuous
presuppose, -posed, -posing
presupposition
pretence
pretend, -ed, -ing
pretender
pretense pretence
pretenshun pretension
pretenshus pretentious
pretension
pretentious, -ly
preternatural, -ly
pretext
pretie pretty
prettily
prettiness
pretty, -tier, -tiest
prety pretty
pretzel
prevail, -ed, -ing
prevale prevail
prevalence

prevalense	prevalence
prevalent, -ly	
prevaricate, -cated, -cating	
prevarication	
prevenshun	prevention
prevent, -ed, -ing	
preventable, -bly	
preventabul	preventable
preventative, -ly	
prevention	
preventive, -ly	
preview, -ed, -ing	
previous, -ly	
prey, -ed, -ing (hunt)	
prey	pray (beg)
pri	pry
price, priced, pricing	
priceless, -ly	
prick, -ed, -ing	
prickle, -led, -ling	
prickly, -lier, -liest	
prickul	prickle
pride, prided, priding	
prie	pry
prier	prior
priery	priory
priest	
priesthood	
priestly, -lier, -liest	
prig	
priggish, -ly	
prim, primmer, primmest	
primacy	
prima donna	
prima-facie	
primary, -ries	
primer	
primeval, -ly	
primitive, -ly	
primogenitor	
primogeniture	
primordial, -ly	
primrey	primary
primrose	
primula	
primus	
prince	
princedom	
princely, -lier, -liest	
princess	
principal (head)	
principality, -ties	
principle (law)	
principul	principal (head)
prinse	prince
prinsess	princess
prinsipal	principal
prinsipality	principality
print, -ed, -ing	
printer	
printery, -ries	
print-out	
prion	
prior	
priority, -ties	
priority-paid	
priory, -ries	
prise, prised, prising (move)	
prise	price (cost)
prise	prize(award)
prism	
prismatic, -ally	
prison	
prisoner	
prissy, -ier, -iest	
pristeen	pristine
pristine	
privacy, -cies	
privasy	privacy
privisy	privacy
private, -ly	
privateer	
privation	
privelage	privilege
privet	
privie	privy
privilege, -leged, -leging	
privy, -vies	
prize, prized, prizing (award)	
prizm	prism
probability, -ties	
probable, -ly	
probabul	probable

probate, -bated, -bating
probation
probationer
probe, probed, probing
probible — probable
probity
problem
problematic, -ally
procedural, -ly
procedure
proceed, -ed, -ing
proceshun — procession
process, -ed, -ing
procession
processional, -ly
processor
proclaim, -ed, -ing
proclamation
proclaym — proclaim
procrastinate, -nated, -nating
procrastination
procrastinator
procreate, -ated, -ating
proctor
procurable
procurabul — procurable
procure, -cured, -curing
procurer
prod, prodded, prodding
prodigal, -ly
prodigality, -ties
prodigious, -ly
prodigus — prodigious
prodigy, -gies
prodijus — prodigious
produce, -duced, -ducing
producer
producible
producshun — production
product
production
productive, -ly
productivity
produse — produce
produser — producer
profane, -faned, -faning
profanely
profanity, -ties
profecy (noun) — prophecy
profecy — prophesy (verb)
profer — proffer
profeser — professor
profeshunal — professional
profesor — professor
profess, -ed, -ing
professional, -ly
professionalism
professor
professorial, -ly
profet — profit (gain)
profet — prophet (seer)
proffer, -ed, -ing
proficiency, -cies
proficient, -ly
profile, -filed, -filing
profishency — proficiency
profishent — proficient
profit, -ed, -ing
profitable, -bly
profitabul — profitable
profiteer, -ed, -ing
profitless
profligacy
profligate, -ly
pro-forma
profound, -ly
profownd — profound
profundity, -ties
profuse, -ly
profushun — profusion
profusion
progenitor
progeny, -nies
prognosis, -noses
prognostic
prognosticate, -cated, -cating
prognostication
program, -grammed, -gramming
programmable
programme
programmer
progreshun — progression
progress, -ed, -ing

progression
progressive, -ly
prohibishun prohibition
prohibit, -ed, -ing
prohibition
prohibitive, -ly
projecshun projection
project, -ed, -ing
projectile
projection
projectionist
projector
proksimate proximate
proksy proxy
prolapse, -lapsed, -lapsing
proletarian
proletariat
proliferate, -rated, -rating
prolific, -ally
prolog prologue
prologue
prolong, -ed, -ing
prolongation
prom
promenade, -naded, -nading
prominence
prominense prominence
prominent, -ly
promiscuity, -ties
promiscuous, -ly
promiscuus promiscuous
promise, -mised, -mising
promissory
promontory, -ries
promontry promontory
promoter
promotion
promp prompt
prompt, -ed, -ing
prompter
promulgate, -gated, -gating
promulgation
prone
prong, -ed, -ing
pronoun
pronounce, -nounced, -nouncing
pronouncement
pronown pronoun
pronownse pronounce
pronto
pronunciation
prood prude
proof, -ed, -ing
proofread, -read, -reading
proofreader
proon prune
proove prove
prop, propped, propping
propaganda
propagate, -gated, -gating
propagation
propagator
propane
propel, -pelled, -pelling
propellant (noun)
propellent (adjective)
propeller
propensity, -ties
proper, -ly
property, -ties
prophecy, cies
prophesy, -sied, -sying
prophet
prophetess
prophetical, -ly
prophilactic prophylactic
prophylactic
propishiate propitiate
propishus propitious
propitiate, -ated, -ating
propitious, -ly
proponent
proporshunal proportional
proportion
proportional, -ly
proportionate, -ly
proposal
propose, -posed, -posing
proposer
proposishun proposition
proposition
propound, -ed, -ing
propownd propound
proprietary

proprieter	proprietor
proprietor	
proprietry	proprietary
propriety, -ties	
propulsion	
pro-rata	
prorogue, -rogued, -roguing	
prosaic, -ally	
proscenium, -nia	
proscribe, -scribed, -scribing	
proscription	
prose	
prosecushun	prosecution
prosecute, -cuted, -cuting	
prosecution	
prosecutor	
prosedure	procedure
proseed	proceed
proselite	proselyte
proselyte, -lyted, -lyting	
proselytise, -tised, -tising	
prosess	process
prosicute	prosecute
prosilite	proselyte
prosilitise	proselytise
prosody	
prospect, -ed, -ing	
prospective, -ly	
prospector	
prospectus	
prosper, -ed, -ing	
prosperity, -ties	
prosperous, -ly	
prosperus	prosperous
prostate gland	
prosthesis, -ses	
prostitushen	prostitution
prostitute, -tuted, -tuting	
prostitution	
prostrate, -trated, -trating	
prostration	
protagonist	
protea	
protecshun	protection
protect, -ed, -ing	
protection	
protectionist	
protective, -ly	
protector	
protectorate	
proteen	protein
protégé	
protein	
protest, -ed, -ing	
Protestant	
Protestantism	
protestation	
protocol	
proton	
prototipe	prototype
prototype	
protract, -ed, -ing	
protractor	
protrood	protrude
protrooshun	protrusion
protrude, -ruded, -ruding	
protrusion	
protruberance	
protruberant, -ly	
proud, -ly	
provable	
prove, proved, proven, proving	
provender	
proverb	
proverbial, -ly	
provide, -vided, -viding	
providence	
providense	providence
provident, -ly	
providential, -ly	
provider	
province	
provincial, -ly	
provinshul	provincial
provishun	provision
provision	
provisional, -ly	
proviso	
provocation	
provocative, -ly	
provoke, -voked, -voking	
provost	
prow	
prowd	proud

prowess
prowl, -ed, -ing
proximate, -ly
proximity
proxy, proxies
prozaic prosaic
prude
prudence
prudense prudence
prudent, -ly
prudential, -ly
prudish, -ly
prune, pruned, pruning
prunus
prurience
prurient, -ly
Prushan Prussian
Prussian
pry, pried, prying
psalm
psalmist
psaltery, -teries
pseudo
pseudonym
psyche
psychedelic
psychiatric, -ally
psychiatrist
psychiatry
psychic, -ally
psychoanalyse, -lysed, -lysing
psychoanalysis
psychoanalyst
psychological, -ly
psychologist
psychology, -gies
psychopath
psychopathy
psychosis, -ses
psychosomatic
psychotherapist
pschotherapy
psychotic

> For psyco- words, look under **psycho-** .

psykey psyche
psykic psychic
ptomaine
puberty
pubes
pubescence
pubescent
pubic
publesher publisher
public, -ly
publican
publication
publicise, -cised, -cising
publicity
publish, -ed, -ing
publisher
publisise publicise
publisity publicity
puce
puck
pucka (genuine)
pucker, -ed, -ing (fold)
pudding
puddle, -dled, -dling
puddul puddle
puding pudding
puerile, -ly
puerility, -ties
puff, -ed, -ing
puffin
puffy, -fier, -fiest
pufy puffy
pugilism
pugilist
pugilistic, -ally
pugnacious, -ly
pugnacity
pugnasity pugnacity
pug-nosed
pukka
pulchritude
pulie pulley
pulkritude pulchritude
pull, -ed, -ing
pullet
pulley, -leys
pullover
pulmonary

Word	Correct spelling
pulmonry	pulmonary
pulp, -ed, -ing	
pulpit	
pulpwood	
pulpy, -pier, -piest	
pulsar	
pulsate, -ated, -ating	
pulsation	
pulsator	
pulse, pulsed, pulsing	
pulser	pulsar
pulverise, -rised, -rising	
puma	
pumice	
pumise	pumice
pumkin	pumpkin
pummel, -melled, -melling	
pump, -ed, -ing	
pumpernickel	
pumpkin	
pun, punned, punning	
punative	punitive
punch, -ed, -ing	
punch-drunk	
punch-up	
punctilious, -ly	
puntilius	punctilious
punctual, -ly	
punctuality	
punctuate, -ated, -ating	
punctuation	
puncture, -tured, -turing	
pundit	
pungency	
pungent, -ly	
punie	puny
punish, -ed, -ing	
punishable	
punishment	
punitive, -ly	
pungensy	pungency
punjent	pungent
punk	
punnet	
punt, -ed, -ing	
punter	
puny, -nier, -niest	
pup, pupped, pupping	
pupet	puppet
pupie	puppy
pupil	
puppet	
puppeteer	
puppetry	
puppy, -pies	
pur annum	per annum
puray	puree
purceive	perceive
purchase, -chased, -chasing	
purdah	
pure, purer, purest	
puree, -reed, -reeing	
purgative, -ly	
purgatory	
purgatry	purgatory
purge, purged, purging	
purifie	purify
purify, -fied, -fying	
purile	puerile
puritan	
puritanical, -ly	
puritanism	
puritie	purity
purity	
purje	purge
purjery	perjury
purl, -ed, -ing (knit)	
purl	pearl (gem)
purloin, -ed, -ing	
puroolense	purulence
purple, -pled, -pling	
purport, -ed, -ing	
purpose	
purposeful, -ly	
purpul	purple
purr, -ed, -ing	
purser	
pursuant, -ly	
pursue, -sued, -suing	
pursuit	
pursute	pursuit
purulence	
purulent, -ly	
purvay	purvey

purvey, -ed, -ing
purveyor
pus
  puse puce
push, -ed, -ing
pushbike
push-button
pushover
push-up
pushy
pusillanimous, -ly
pussyfoot
put, put, putting
putative, -ly
  puter pewter
  putie putty
putrefaction
putrefy, -fied, -fying
putrescent
putrid, -ly
  putrify putrefy
putt, -ed, -ing
putter
putty, -ties
putty, puttied, puttying
put-upon
  puty putty
  puzel puzzle
puzzle, -zled, -zling
  pye pi (Greek letter)
  pye pie (food)
pygmy, -mies
pyjamas
pylon
pyramid
pyramidal, -ly
pyre
pyrex
  pyric pyrrhic
pyrotechnics
pyrrhic
pythagoras
python
pyx

Qq

queue	
quack, -ed, -ing	
quackery, -eries	
quad (timber)	
quadrangle	
quadrangul	quadrangle
quadrant	
quadrafonic	quadraphonic
quadraphonic	
quadrasonic	
quadratic	
quadril	quadrille
quadrille	
quadrillion	
quadriplegia	
quadriplegic	
quadruped	
quadrupedal	
quadruple, -pled, -pling	
quadruplet	
quadrupul	quadruple
quaff, quaffed, quaffing	
quagmire	
quail	
quaint, -ly	
quaintness	
quake, quaked, quaking	
Quaker	
Quakerism	
qualification	
qualifi	qualify
qualified	
qualifier	
qualify, -fied, -fying	
qualitative, -ly	
quality, -ties	
qualm	
quandary, -ries	
quandong	
quandry	quandary
quango	
quantifi	quantify
quantifiable	
quantification	
quantify, -fied, -fying	
quantitative, -ly	
quantity, -ties	
quarantine, -tined, -tining	
quarel	quarrel
quarey	quarry
quark	
quarm	qualm
quarrel, -relled, -relling	
quarreller	
quarrelsome, -ly	
quarry, -ries	
quarry, -ried, -rying	
quart, quarts	
quarter	
quarterdeck	
quarterly	
quartermaster	
quartet	
quartile	
quarto, -tos	
quartz (rock)	
quartz	quarts (measures)
quash, -ed, -ing	
quasi	
quatrain	
quattrocento	
quaver, -ed, -ing	
quavery	
quay (wharf)	
que	cue (billiards)
que	queue (line)
queasy, -sier, -siest	
queasiness	
queen, -ly	
queer, -ly	
queerness	
quell, -ed, -ing	
queller	
quench, -ed, -ing	

Word	Correct spelling
quenchable	
quenchless	
querie	query
querulous, -ly	
querulousness	
querulus	querulous
query, -ries	
query, -ried, -rying	
queschun	question
quest, -ed, -ing	
quester	
question, -ed, -ing	
questionable, -bly	
questionair	questionnaire
questioner	
questionnaire	
questyun	question
queue, queued, queuing	
quibble, -bled, -bling	
quibbler	
quibel	quibble
quich	quiche
quiche	
quick, -ly	
quicken	
quickie	
quicklime	
quickness	
quicksand	
quicksilver	
quickstep	
quick-tempered	
quick-witted	
quid, quid, quids	
quid pro quo	
quiescence	
quiescent, -ly	
quiesense	quiescence
quiet, -ly (silent)	
quiet	quite (rather)
quieten, -ed, -ing	
quietness	
quill	
quilt	
quilted	

Word	Correct spelling
quince	
quinella	
quinine	
quinse	quince
quinsy, -sies	
quintesense	quintessence
quintessence	
quintessential	
quintet	
quintette	
quintuple, -pled, -pling	
quintuplet	
quintupul	quintuple
quip, quipped, quipping	
quipster	
quire (paper)	
quire	choir (sing)
quirk	
quish	quiche
quisine	cuisine
quit, quitted or quit, quitting	
quite (rather)	
quite	quiet (silent)
quits	
quitter	
quiver, -ed, -ing	
quivery	
quixotic	
quixotism	
quiz, quizzes	
quiz, quizzed, quizzing	
quizzical, -ly	
quod (prison)	
quod	quad (timber)
quoit	
quokka	
quorum	
quoshent	quotient

For other **quo-** words, look under **qua-** .

Word	Correct spelling
quota	
quotation	
quote, quoted, quoting	
quotient	

Rr

rabbi, -bis
rabbinical
rabbit, -bited, -biting
rabbiter
rabble, -bled, -bling
rabblerouser
rabi — rabbi
rabid, -ly
rabies
rabit — rabbit
rabud — rabid
rabul — rabble
raccoon
race, raced, racing
racecorse — racecourse
racecourse
racegoer
racehorse
racer
racetrack
raceway
racial, -ly
racialism
racialist
racism
racist
rack, -ed, -ing
rack-and-pinion
racket, -ed, -ing
racketeer
rackit — racket
raconter — raconteur
raconteur
racquet
racy, -cier, -ciest
radar
raddle, -led, -ling
rade — raid
radeo — radio
radial, -ly
radialogy — radiology
radial-ply
radian
radiance
radianse — radiance
radiant, -ly
radiate, -ated, -ating
radiater — radiator
radiation
radiator
radical, -ly
radicalism
radicul — radical
radii
radio, -dioed, -dioing
radioactive
radioastronomy
radiografy — radiography
radiogram
radiographer
radiography
radiologist
radiology
radiotelephone
radiotherapy
radish
radiul — radial
radium
radius, radii, radiuses
raffia
raffish, -ly
raffle, -led, -ling
raft
rafter
rag, ragged, ragging
ragamuffin
rage, raged, raging
raglan
ragout, -gouted, -gouting
ragtime
raid, -ed, -ing
rail, -ed, -ing
raillery, -ries
railroad
railway

raiment	
rain, -ed, -ing (water)	
rain	reign (rule)
rain	rein (bridle)
rainbird	
rainbow	
raincoat	
rainfall	
rainforest	
raise, raised, raising (lift)	
raise	rays (beams)
raisin	
raison d'être	
raisun	raisin
raje	rage
rake, raked, raking	
rakish, -ly	
rakket	racket
rale	rail
ralie	rally
rally, -lies	
rally, -lied, -lying	
ram, rammed, ramming	
ramble, -bled, -bling	
rambler	
rambul	ramble
ramification	
ramify, -fied, -fying	
ramp	
rampage, -paged, -paging	
rampageous, -ly	
rampagius	rampageous
rampant, -ly	
rampart	
ramrod	
ramshackle	
ramshackul	ramshackle
ranch	
rancher	
rancid	
rancidity	
rancorous, -ly	
rancour	
rancur	rancour
rancurus	rancorous
random, -ly	
randy	
rane	rain (water)
rane	reign (rule)
rane	rein (bridle)
range, ranged, ranging	
rangefinder	
ranger	
rangul	wrangle
rank, -ed, -ing	
rankle, -kled, -kling	
ransack, -ed, -ing	
ransid	rancid
ransom, -ed, -ing	
ransome	ransom
ransum	ransom
rant, -ed, -ing	
rap, rapped, rapping (strike)	
rap	wrap (cover)
rapacious, -ly	
rapacity	
rapashus	rapacious
rapasity	rapacity
rapcher	rapture
rape, raped, raping	
rapid, -ly	
rapid-fire	
rapier	
rapine	
rapist	
rapport	
rapprochement	
rapsody	rhapsody
rapt (engrossed)	
rapt (cover)	wrapped
rapture	
rapturous, -ly	
rapturus	rapturous
rare, rarer, rarest	
rarefacshun	rarefaction
rarefaction	
rarefy, -fied, -fying	
rarely	
raring	
rarity, -ties	
rasbery	raspberry
rascal	
rascality, -ties	

rascally	
rase, rased, rasing (destroy)	
rase	race (run)
rase	raise (lift)
rash, -ly	
rashal	racial
rashalist	racialist
rasher	
rashio	ratio
rashness	
rashul	racial
rashun	ration
rashunalise	rationalise
rasin	raisin
rasism	racism
rasist	racist
raskul	rascal
rasp, -ed, -ing	
raspberry, -ries	
rat, ratted, ratting	
ratabul	rateable
ratchet	
rate, rated, rating	
rateo	ratio
ratepayer	
rath	wrath
rather	
ratification	
ratify, -fied, -fying	
ratio, -tios	
ration, -ed, -ing	
rational, -ly (reasonable)	
rationale (statement)	
rationalise, -lised, -lising	
rationalism	
rationality, -ties	
rat-race	
rattan	
rattle, -tled, -tling	
rattlesnake	
rattletrap	
ratty, -tier, -tiest	
ratul	rattle
raucous, -ly	
raucus	raucous
ravage, -aged, -aging	
ravager	
rave, raved, raving	
ravel, -elled, -elling	
raven	
ravene	ravine
ravenous, -ly	
ravige	ravage
ravine	
ravioli	
ravish, -ed, -ing	
raw (uncooked)	
raw	roar (noise)
rawcus	raucous
rawhide	
ray	
rayon	
rays (beams)	
rays	raise (lift)
rays	raze (destroy)
raze, razed, razing (destroy)	
razer	razor
razoo	
razor	
reach, -ed, -ing	
reacktion	reaction
react, -ed, -ing	
reaction	
reactionary	
reactive, -ly	
reactor	
read, read, reading (book)	
read	red (colour)
read	reed (plant)
readable, -bly	
readabul	readable
reader	
readership	
readily	
readiness	
ready, readied, readying	
ready, readier, readiest	
ready-made	
reaf	reef
reafforest, -ed, -ing	
reafforestation	
reagent	
reak	reek (smell)
reak	wreak (inflict)

Word	Correct spelling
real, -ly (true)	
real	reel (wind)
realign, -ed, -ing	
realisation	
realise, -lised, -lising	
realism	
realist	
realistic, -ally	
reality, -ties (fact)	
realm	
realter	realtor
realtor	
realty (real estate)	
ream, reamed, reaming	
reap, -ed, -ing	
reaper	
reappear, -ed, -ing	
rear, -ed, -ing	
reargard	rearguard
rearguard	
rearmament	
reason, -ed, -ing	
reasonable, -bly	
reasonabul	reasonable
reassemble, -bled, -bling	
reassembul	reassemble
reassert, -ed, -ing	
reassertion	
reassess, -ed, -ing	
reassessment	
reassurance	
reassure, -sured, -suring	
reath	wreath
rebate, -bated, -bating	
rebel, -belled, -belling	
rebellion	
rebellious, -ly	
rebelyun	rebellion
rebild	rebuild
rebound, -ed, -ing	
rebownd	rebound
rebuff, -ed, -ing	
rebuild, -built, -building	
rebuke, -buked, -buking	
rebut, -butted, -butting	
rebutal	rebuttal
rebuttal	
recalcitrance	
recalcitrant	
recall, -ed, -ing	
recant, -ed, -ing	
recantation	
recapitulate, -lated, -lating	
recapitulation	
recede, -ceded, -ceding	
receipt	
receit	receipt
receive, -ceived, -ceiving	
receiver	
receivership	
recent, -ly	
recepe	recipe
recepshun	reception
recepshunist	receptionist
receptacle	
receptacul	receptacle
reception	
receptionist	
receptive, -ly	
receshun	recession
recess, -ed, -ing	
recessive, -ly	
rech	retch (vomit)
rech	wretch (victim)
recidivism	
recidivist	
reciept	receipt
recieve	receive
recipe	
recipient	
reciprocal, -ly	
reciprocate, -cated, -cating	
reciprocation	
reciprocity	
reciprosity	reciprocity
recital	
recitation	
recite, -cited, -citing	
reck	wreck
reckage	wreckage
reckless, -ly	
reckon, -ed, -ing	
reclaim, -ed, -ing	
reclamation	

reclassify, -fied, -fying
recline, -clined, -clining
recluse
recognisable, -bly
  recognisabul — recognisable
recognise, -nised, -nising
  recognishun — recognition
recognition
recoil, -ed, -ing
  recolecshun — recollection
recollect, -ed, -ing
recollection
recommend, -ed, -ing
recommendation
reconcile, -ciled, -ciling
reconciliation
recondite
recondition, -ed, -ing
reconnaissance
  reconnoiter — reconnoitre
reconnoitre, -tred, -tring
reconsider, -ed, -ing
  reconsile — reconcile
  reconsiliation — reconciliation
reconstruct, -ed, -ing
reconstruction
  recoop — recoup
record, -ed, -ing
recorder
  recorse — recourse
recount, -ed, -ing
recoup, -ed, -ing
recourse
recover, -ed, -ing
recovery, -eries
  recownt — recount
recreant, -ly
recreation
recriminate, -nated, -nating
recrimination
recriminatory
recruit, -ed, -ing
recruitment
  recrute — recruit
rectangle
  rectangul — rectangle
rectangular, -ly
rectification
rectifier
rectify, -fied, -fying
rectilinear, -ly
  rectilinier — rectilinear
rectitude
rector
rectory, -ries
rectum
recumbency
  recumbensy — recumbency
recumbent, -ly
recuperate, -rated, -rating
recuperation
recuperative
recur, -curred, -curring
recurrence
  recurrense — recurrence
recurrent, -ly
recyclable
  recyclabul — recyclable
recycle, -cycled, -cycling
  recycul — recycle
red, redder, reddest (colour)
  red — read (book)
redbreast
  redbrest — redbreast
redden, -ed, -ing
reddish
  reddy — ready
redeem, -ed, -ing
redeemable, -ably
redeemer
  redempshun — redemption
redemption
redemptive
  reden — redden
  redeploi — redeploy
redeploy, -ed, -ing
redeployment
redevelop, -ed, -ing
redevelopment
red-handed
  redie — ready
redistribute, -buted, -buting
redistribution
redolence

redolent, -ly	
redouble, -led, -ling	
redoubtable, -bly	
redound, -ed, -ing	
redoutabul	redoutable
redress, -ed, -ing	
redskin	
reduce, -duced, -ducing	
reducksun	reduction
reduction	
redundancy, -cies	
redundansy	redundancy
reduplicate, -cated, -cating	
redwood	
reed (plant)	
reed	read (book)
reedwarbler	
reedy, reedier, reediest	
reef, -ed, ing	
reefer	
reek, -ed, -ing (smell)	
reek	wreak (inflict)
reel, -ed, -ing (wind)	
reel	real (true)
re-elect, -ed, -ing	
re-election	
re-entry, -tries	
refer, -ferred, -ferring	
referee, -reed, -reeing	
reference	
referense	reference
referendum, -da, -dums	
referent	
referral	
refill, -ed, -ing	
refine, -fined, -fining	
refinement	
refinery, -ries	
refleckshun	reflection
reflect, -ed, -ing	
reflection	
reflector	
refleks	reflex
reflex	
refloat, -ed, -ing	
reform, -ed, -ing	
reformation	
reformatory, -ries	
reformer	
refrackshun	refraction
refraction	
refractive, -ly	
refrain, -ed, -ing	
refrence	reference
refresh, -ed, -ing	
refresher	
refreshment	
refrigerant	
refrigerate, -rated, -rating	
refrigerater	refrigerator
refrigeration	
refrigerator	
refuel, -elled, -elling	
refuge	
refugee	
refulgence	
refulgent, -ly	
refund, -ed, -ing	
refurbish, -ed, -ing	
refusal	
refuse, -fused, -fusing	
refutation	
refute, -futed, -futing	
regain, -ed, -ing	
regal, -ly (royal)	
regale, -galed, -galing (feast)	
regalia	
regane	regain
regard, -ed, -ing	
regardless, -ly	
regatta	
regeme	regime
regency, -cies	
regenerate, -rated, -rating	
regeneration	
regenerative, -ly	
regent	
regime	
regimen	
regiment	
regimental	
regimentation	
region	
regional, -ly	

regionalism
register, -ed, -ing
registrar
registration
registry, -tries
regon   region
regreshun   regression
regress, -ed, -ing
regression
regressive, -ly
regret, -gretted, -gretting
regretabul   regrettable
regretful, -ly
regrettable, -bly
regualation   regulation
reguard   regard
regular, -ly
regularity
regulate, -lated, -lating
regulation
regulator
regulatory
reguler   regular
regurgitate, -tated, -tating
rehabilitate, -tated, -tating
rehabilitation
rehash, -ed, -ing
rehearsal
rehearse, -hearsed, -hearsing
reherse   rehearse
reign, -ed, -ing (king)
reign   rain (water)
reign   rein (bridle)
reimburse, -bursed, -bursing
reimbursement
rein, -ed, -ing (bridle)
rein   rain (water)
rein   reign (rule)
reincarnation
reindeer, -deer
reinforce, -forced, -forcing
reinforcement
reinstate, -stated, -stating
reiterate, -rated, -rating
reiteration
reiterative, -ly
rejeckshun   rejection

reject, -ed, -ing
rejection
rejeme   regime
rejister   register
rejoice, -joiced, -joicing
rejoin, -ed, -ing
rejoinder
rejoise   rejoice
rejoovenate   rejuvenate
rejuvenate, -nated, -nating
rejuvenation
rekord   record

For rekw- words, look under **requ-** .

relaks   relax
relapse, -lapsed, -lapsing
relate, -lated, -lating
relation
relative, -ly
relativity
relax, -ed, -ing
relaxation
relay, -ed, -ing
release, -leased, -leasing
relegate, -gated, -gating
relegation
releif   relief
relent, -ed, -ing
relentless, -ly
relese   release
relevance
relevancy
relevanse   relevance
relevant, -ly
releve   relieve
reli   rely
reliable, -bly
reliability
reliabul   reliable
reliance
reliant
relic
relief
relieve, -lieved, -lieving
religion
religious, -ly

religun religion
religus religious
relinkwish relinquish
relinquish, -ed, -ing
relish, -ed, -ing
relm realm
reluctance
reluctanse reluctance
reluctant, -ly
rely, relied, relying
remain, -ed, -ing
remainder
remains
remand, -ed, -ing
remark, -ed, -ing
remarkable, -bly
remedial, -ly
remedy, -dies
remedy, -died, -dying
remember, -ed, -ing
remembrance
remembranse remembrance
remind, -ed, -ing
reminder
reminisce, -nisced, -niscing
reminiscence
reminiscent, -ly
reminisense reminiscence
reminisent reminiscent
reminiss reminisce
remishun remission
remiss, -ly
remission
remit, -mitted, -mitting
remittance
remnant
remonstrate, -trated, -trating
remonstrative
remooval removal
remoove remove
remorse
remorseful, -ly
remote, remoter, remotest
remotely
removable
removalist
remove, -moved, -moving

remunerate, -rated, -rating
remuneration
remunerative, -ly
ren wren
Renaissance
renal
rench wrench
rend, rent, rending
render, -ed, -ing
rendezvous, -voused, -vousing
rendition
renegade
renege, reneged, reneging
renew, -ed, -ing
renounce, -nounced, -nouncing
renovate, -vated, -vating
renovater renovator
renovation
renovator
renown
renowned
rent, -ed, -ing
rental
rentul rental
renue renew
renunciation
reorganisation
reorganise, -nised, -nising
repair, -ed, -ing
repairer
reparable, -bly
reparation
repartee
repast
repatriate, -ated, -ating
repatriation
repay, -paid, -paying
repeal, -ed, -ing
repeat, -ed, -ing
repeatedly
repeater
repel, -pelled, -pelling
repellant repellent
repellent, -ly
repent, -ed, -ing
repentance
repentanse repentance

repentant, -ly
repercushun repercussion
repertoire
repertory, -ries
repetishus repetitious
repetition
repetitious, -ly
repetry repertory
repitition repetition
replace, -placed, -placing
replacement
replay, -played, -playing
replenish, -ed, -ing
replenishment
replete
replica
reply, -plies
reply, -plied, -plying
report, -ed, -ing
reportable
reporter
repose, -posed, -posing
repository, -tories
repositry repository
reposseshun repossession
repossess, -ed, -ing
repossession
reprehenshun reprehension
reprehensible, -bly
reprehension
represent, -ed, -ing
representation
representational
representative, -ly
represhun repression
repress, -ed, -ing
repressabul repressible
repressible
repression
repressive, -ly
reprieve, -prieved, -prieving
reprimand, -ed, -ing
reprint, -ed, -ing
reprisal
reprisul reprisal
reproach, -ed, -ing
reproachable, -bly

reprobate, -bated, -bating
reprobation
reproch reproach
reproduce, -duced, -ducing
reproducshun reproduction
reproduction
reproof, -ed, -ing
reprove, -proved, -proving
reproval
reptile
reptilian
republic
republican
republicanism
repudiate, -ated, -ating
repudiation
repugnance
repugnanse repugnance
repugnant, -ly
repulse, -pulsed, -pulsing
repulsion
repulsive, -ly
reputable, -bly
reputabul reputable
reputation
repute, -puted, -puting
request, -ed, -ing
requiem
requierment requirement
require, -quired, -quiring
requirement
requisishun requisition
requisite
requisition
rerite rewrite
reritten rewritten
rerote rewrote
rescind, -ed, -ing
rescue, -cued, -cuing
rescuer
research, -ed, -ing
researcher
reseat receipt
resede recede
reseipt receipt
resemble, -bled, -bling
resembul resemble

Word	Correct
resent, -ed, -ing (hurt)	
resent	recent (new)
resentful, -ly	
resentment	
resepshun	reception
reseptacul	receptacle
reseptive	receptive
reserch	research
reservation	
reserve, -served, -serving	
reservoir	
resess	recess
resesshun	recession
resession	recession
reset, -set, -setting	
reseve	receive
resevoir	reservoir
reside, -sided, -siding	
residence	
residenshul	residential
resident	
residential	
residivision	recidivism
residual, -ly	
residuary	
residue	
resign, -ed, -ing	
resignation	
resilience	
resilient, -ly	
resin	
resind	rescind
resinous	
resinus	resinous
resipe	recipe
resipient	recipient
resiprocul	reciprocal
resiprosity	reciprocity
resist, -ed, -ing	
resistance	
resitation	recitation
resistor	
resite	recite
resolute, -ly	
resolution	
resolve, -solved, -solving	
resonance	

Word	Correct
resonant, -ly	
resonate, -nated, -nating	
resorce	resource
resort, -ed, -ing	
resound, -ed, -ing	
resource	
resourceful, -ly	
respect, -ed, -ing	
respectability, -ties	
respectable, -bly	
respectabul	respectable
respectful, -ly	
respective, -ly	
respiration	
respirator	
respiratory	
respiratry	respiratory
respite	
resplendent, -ly	
responce	response
respond, -ed, -ing	
respondent	
response	
responsibility, -ties	
responsible, -bly	
responsive, -ly	
rest, -ed, -ing (sleep)	
rest	wrest (grab)
restaration	restoration
restaurant	
resterant	restaurant
restful, -ly	
restitushion	restitution
restitution	
restive, -ly	
restle	wrestle
restler	wrestler
restless, -ly	
restoration	
restorative	
restore, -stored, -storing	
restrain, -ed, -ing	
restraint	
restricshun	restriction
restrict, -ed, -ing	
restriction	
restrictive, -ly	

restructure, -tured, -turing
result, -ed, -ing
resultant
resumay résumé (review)
résumé (review)
resume, -sumed, -suming (take up)
resumption
resurgence
resurgent
resurrect, -ed, -ing
resurrection
resuscitate, -tated, -tating
resuscitation
resuscitator
resusitation resuscitation
retail, -ed, -ing
retain, -ed, -ing
retainer
retaliate, -ated, -ating
retaliation
retard, -ed, -ing
retardation
retch, -ed, -ing (vomit)
retch wretch (victim)
retention
retentive, -ly
reticence
reticent, -ly
retina, -nas, -nae
retinew retinue
retinue
retire, -tired, -tiring
retirement
retisent reticent
retoric rhetoric
retoricul rhetorical
retort, -ed, -ing
retrace, -traced, -tracing
retract, -ed, -ing
retractable
retrase retrace
retread, -treaded, -treading
retreat, -ed, -ing
retred retread
retreive retrieve
retrench, -ed, -ing
retrenchment
retribushun retribution
retribution
retrieve, -trieved, -trieving
retrievable
retrieval
retriever
retroactive, -ly
retrograde, -graded, -grading
retrogreshun retrogression
retrogress, -ed, -ing
retrogression
retrogressive, -ly
retro-rocket
retrospect
retrospective, -ly
return, -ed, -ing
reunion
reunite, -nited, -niting
rev, revved, revving
revalie reveille
revaluation
revalue, -ued, -uing
revalueation revaluation
reveal, -ed, -ing
reveille (bugle call)
revel, -elled, -elling
revelation
reveller (festivity)
revelry, -ries
revenew revenue
revenge, -venged, -venging
revenue
reverberate, -rated, -rating
reverberation
reverberatory
revere, -vered, -vering (respect)
reverence
reverend
reverense reverence
reverent, -ly
reverie (daydream)
reversal
reverse, -versed, -versing
reversion
revert, -ed, -ing
revertabul revertible
revertible

review, -ed, -ing (survey)
review revue (theatre)
revile, -viled, -viling
revise, -vised, -vising
revishun revision
revision
revival
revivalism
revive, -vived, -viving
revocation
revoke, -voked, -voking
revolt, -ed, -ing
revolushun revolution
revolution
revolutionary, -ries
revolutionise, -nised, -nising
revolutionry revolutionary
revolve, -volved, -volving
revolver
revue (theatre)
revue review (survey)
revulshun revulsion
revulsion
reward, -ed, -ing
rhapsodical, -ly
rhapsodise, -dised, -dising
rhapsody, -dies
rhesus
rhetoric
rhetorical, -ly
rheumatic
rheumatism
rheumatoid arthritis
rhinestone
rhino, -nos
rhinoceros, -roses, -ros
rhododendron
rhombus, -buses, -bi
rhubarb
rhyme, rhymed, rhyming (verse)
rhythm
rhythmical, -ly
rib, ribbed, ribbing
ribald
ribaldry
ribbon
rice
rich, -ly
riches
Richter scale
rick, -ed, -ing
rickets
rickety
rickshaw
ricochet, -ed, -ing
ricshore rickshaw
rid, rid or ridded, ridding
ridance riddance
riddance
riddle, -dled, -dling
ride, rode, ridden, riding
rider
ridge, ridged, ridging
ridicule, -culed, -culing
ridiculous, -ly
ridiculus ridiculous
ridul riddle
rie rye (grain)
rie wry (askew)
Riesling
rife
riffraff
rifle, -fled, -fling
rift
riful rifle
rig, rigged, rigging
right, -ed, -ing (correct)
right rite (ceremony)
right write (inscribe)
righteous, -ly
rightful, -ly
right-handed
right-winger
rigid, -ly
rigidity
rigmarole
rigor mortis
rigorous, -ly
rigorus rigorous
rigour
rig-out
rigul wriggle
rile, riled, riling
rim, rimmed, rimming (edge)

rime, rimed, riming (frost)
rime — rhyme (verse)
rind
ring, ringed, ringing (surround)
ring, rang, rung, ringing (bell)
ring — wring (squeeze)
ringbark, -ed, -ing
ringer
ringer — wringer
ring-in
ringleader
ringlet
ringtail possum
ringworm
rink
rinse, rinsed, rinsing
riot, -ed, -ing
riotous, -ly
riotus — riotous
rip, ripped, ripping
ripcord
ripe, riper, ripest
ripen, -ed, -ing
rip-off
ripper
ripple, -pled, -pling
rippul — ripple

> If the word is not under **ri-** look under **re-**.

rip-roaring
rip-tide
rise, rose, risen, rising
risk, -ed, -ing
riskay — risqué
riskily
risky, -kier, -kiest
risqué
rissole
rist — wrist
rit — writ
rite (ceremony)
rite — right (correct)
rite — write (inscribe)
riter — writer
rithe — writhe
ritten — written
ritual,-ly
rival, -valled, -valling
rivalry, -ries
river
rivergum
rivet, -ed, -ing
rivulet
ro — roe (fish)
ro — row (boat
roach, -ches
road (street)
road — rode (did ride)
roadblock
roadworthiness
roadworthy
roar, -ed, -ing (noise)
roar — raw (uncooked)
roast, -ed, -ing
rob, robbed, robbing
robber
robbery, -ries
robe, robed, robing
robery — robbery
robin
robot
robust, -ly
rock, -ed, -ing
rocker
rockery, -ries
rocket, -ed, -ing
rocketry
rock'n'roll
rock-wallaby
rococo
rod
rodayo — rodeo
rode (did ride)
rode — road (street)
rodent
rodeo, -deos
rodio — rodeo
roe (fish)
roe — row (boat)
roge — rogue
rogish — roguish
rogue, rogued, roguing
roguery, -gueries

roguish,-ly	
role (character)	
roll, -ed, -ing (turn)	
roll bar	
rollcall	
roller	
roller-skate, -skated, -skating	
rolling-pin	
rollick, -ed, -ing	
rollmop	
roll-up	
roly-poly	
Roman Catholic	
romance, -manced, -mancing	
romantic, -ly	
romanticise, -cised, -cising	
romanticism	
romanticist	
Romany, -nies (gipsy)	
rombus	rhombus
rome	roam
romp, -ed, -ing	
rondo, -dos	
roneo, -ed, -ing	
rong	wrong
roo (kangaroo)	
roo	rue (regret)
roodiment	rudiment
roof, roofs	
roofless	
roof-rack	
rooful	rueful
rooge	rouge
rooin	ruin
rooinous	ruinous
rook, -ed, -ing	
rookery, -ries	
rookie	
rool	rule
roolet	roulette
room, -ed, -ing	
roomatism	rheumatism
roomer	rumour
roomy, -mier, -miest	
roon	ruin
roopee	rupee
roorul	rural

roose	ruse
roost, -ed, -ing	
rooster	
root, -ed, -ing (plant)	
root	route (way)
ropable	
rope, roped, roping	
ropeable	
ropeway	
ropey	
ropy, ropier, ropiest	
ror	roar (noise)
ror	raw (uncooked)
rort	
rosary, -ries	
rosay	rosé (wine)
rose, rosed, rosing (flower)	
rosé (wine)	
rosella	
rosemary	
rosery	rosary
roset	rosette
rosette	
rosewood	
rosie	rosy
rosily	
rost	roast
roster	
rostrum, -trums, -tra	
rosy, rosier, rosiest	
rot, rotted, rotting	
rotary	
rotate, -tated, -tating	
rotation	
rote (routine)	
rote	wrote (did write)
roten	rotten
roter	rotor
rotisserie	
rotor	
rotten, -ly	
rotund, -ly	
rotundity	
roudy	rowdy
rouge, rouged, rouging	
rough, -ly	

roughage
roughen, -ed, -ing
roughshod
rought — wrought
roulet — roulette
roulette, -letted, -letting
round, -ed, -ing
roundabout
rounders
roundly
round-up
rouse, roused, rousing
rouseabout
rout, routed, routing (defeat)
route (way)
route — root (plant)
routeen — routine
routine
rove, roved, roving
rover
row, -ed, -ing (boat)
row — roe (fish)
rowdie — rowdy
rowdily
rowdy, -dier, -diest
rowel, -elled, -elling
rowlock
rownd — round
rowse — rouse
rowt — rout
royal, -ly
royalist
royalty, -ties
rub, rubbed, rubbing
rubber
rubbish
rubbishy
rubble
rubella
ruber — rubber
rubicund
rubie — ruby
rubish — rubbish
rubric
rubul — rubble
ruby, -bies
ruck, -ed, -ing
rucksack
ruckshun — ruction
ruction
rudder
ruddy, -dier, -diest
rude, ruder, rudest (rough)
rude — rued (regret)
rudely
rudeness
ruder — rudder
rudimentary
rudiments
rudy — ruddy
rue, rued, ruing (regret)
rued — rude (rough)
rueful, -ly (pity)
ruf — rough (coarse)
ruffen — roughen
ruffian
ruffle, -fled, -fling (annoy)
rufful — ruffle
rufian — ruffian
rufige — roughage
rufle — ruffle
ruful — rueful
rug, rugged, rugging
rugby
ruin, -ed, -ing (destroy)
ruin — rune (letter)
ruination
ruinous, -ly
ruinus — ruinous
rule, ruled, ruling
ruler
rum
rumatism — rheumatism
rumba
rumble, -bled, -bling
rumbul — rumble
rumen, -mina
rumer — rumour
rumige — rummage
ruminant
ruminate, -nated, -nating
rummage, -maged, -maging
rumour, -ed, -ing
rump

Word	Correct
rumple, -pled, -pling	
rumpul	rumple
rumpus	
run, ran, run, running	
runabout	
rune (letter)	
rune	ruin (destroy)
rung (did ring)	
rung (squeezed)	wrung
run-in	
runner	
runner-up	
runny	
run-off	
run-of-the-mill	
run-on	
runt	
runway	
rupcher	rupture
rupee	
rupture, -tured, -turing	
rural, -ly	
ruse	
rush, -ed, -ing	
Rushun	Russian
rusit	russet
rusk	
russet	
Russian roulette	
rust, -ed, -ing	
rustic, -ally	
rusticity, -ties	
rustle, -tled, -tling	
rustproof	
rusty, -tier, -tiest	
rut, rutted, rutting	
ruthless, -ly	
rye (grain)	
rye	wry (askew)
rye-grass	
ryme	rhyme
rythm	rhythm

Ss

Sabath	Sabbath
Sabbath	
sabbatical	
sabbaticul	sabbatical
sabel	sable
saber	sabre
Sabin vaccine	
sable	
sabot	
sabotage, -taged, -taging	
saboteur	
sabre, -bred, -bring	
sabre-toothed	
sac (bag)	
sac	sack (hessian)
sacarin	saccharin
saccharin	
sacerdotal, -ly	
sachay	sachet
sachel	satchel
sachet	
sack, -ed, -ing	
sackarin	saccharin
sackcloth	
sacrament	
sacramental, -ly	
sacred, -ly	
sacredness	
sacrement	sacrament
sacrifice, -ficed, -ficing	
sacrificial, -ly	
sacrifise	sacrifice
sacrifishul	sacrificial
sacriledge	sacrilege
sacrilege	
sacrilegious, -ly	
sacrilige	sacrilege
sacriligus	sacrilegious
sacrosanct	
sad, sadder, saddest	
sadden, -ed, -ing	
saddle, saddled, saddling	
saddleback	
saddler	
saddlery, -ries	
sadern	sadden
sadler	saddler
sadlery	saddlery
sadism	
sadist	
sadistic, -ally	
sadul	saddle
safari, -ris	
safe, safer, safest	
safegard	safeguard
safeguard	
safekeeping	
safely	
safety, -ties	
saffire	sapphire
saffron	
safire	sapphire
safron	saffron
saftie	safety
sag, sagged, sagging	
saga	
sagacious, -ly	
sagacity, -ties	
sagasity	sagacity
sagayshus	sagacious
sage, sager, sagest	
Sagittarius	
sago	
said	
sail (boat)	
sail	sale (sold)
sailsman	salesman
sailboard	
sailcloth	
sailor	
sailplane, -planed, -planing	
saint, -ly	
sainted	
sainthood	
saintliness	

sake
  sakred — sacred
  sakson — Saxon
  saksophone — saxophone
salaam
salacious, -ly
salad
salamander
salami
  salamy — salami
salaried
salary, -ries (wage)
  salary — celery (food)
  salasious — salacious
sale (sold)
  sale — sail (boat)
saleability
saleable, -ly
  saleabul — saleable
  salene — saline
salesgirl
saleslady, -dies
salesman, -men
salesmanship
salesroom
saleswoman, -women
saleyard
  salie — sally
salience
  saliense — salience
salient, -ly
saline
salinity
saliva
salivary
salivate, -vated, -vating
salivation
sallow
sallowish
sally, -lies
sally, -lied, -lying
  salm — psalm

> For all other sall- words, look under sal-.

salmon
salmonella
salon
  saloobrius — salubrious
saloon
  saloot — salute
  salow — sallow
salt, -ed, -ing
saltbush
saltcellar
  saltery — psaltery
  saltseller — saltcellar
salubrious, -ly
  salubrius — salubrious
  salud — salad
salutary
salutation
salute, -luted, -luting
salvage, -vaged, -vaging (save)
  salvage — selvedge (edge)
salvager
salve, salved, salving
salver
  salvidge — salvage (save)
  salvidge — selvedge (edge)
salvo, -vos, -voes
sal volatile
  samantic — semantic
samba
same
  samon — salmon
samovar
Samoyed
sampan
sample, -pled, -pling
sampler
  sampul — sample
samurai
  samuri — samurai
  sanatarium — sanitarium
sanatorium, -toriums, -toria
  sancshun — sanction
sanctification
sanctify, -fied, -fying
sanctimonious, -ly
  sanctimonius — sanctimonious
sanction, -ed, -ing
sanctity, -ties
sanctuary, -ries

sanctum, -tums
sand, -ed, -ing
sandal
sandalwood
sandbag, -bagged, -bagging
sandbank
sandblast, -ed, -ing
sandfly, -flies
sandpaper, -ed, -ing
sandpiper
sandshoe
sandsoap
sandstone
sandul sandal
sandwhich sandwich
sandwich, -wiches
sandwitch sandwich
sane, saner, sanest (not mad)
sane seine (net)
sanely
saneness
sang
sangfroid
sanguinary
sanguine, -ly
sangwin sanguine
sanitarium, -tariums, -taria
sanitary
sanitation
sanitorium sanatorium
sanity
sank

For all other sank- words, look under sanct- .

sanskrit
Santa Claus
Santa Klaus Santa Claus
sap, sapped, sapping
saper sapper
sapience
sapiency
sapient, -ly
sapling
sapper
sapphire
sappling sapling

sapwood
sarcasm
sarcastic, -ally
sarcofagus sarcophagus
sarcophagus, -gi, -guses
sardeen sardine
sardine, -dines
sardonic, -ally
sargent sergeant
sari
sarong
sarsaparilla
sartorial, -ly
sary sari
saserdotal sacerdotal
sash
sashay (trip)
sashay sachet (bag)
sashiate satiate
sassafras
Sassenach
Satan (devil)
Satanic, -ally
Satanism
Satanist
satay
satchel
sate, sated, sating
sateen (cotton)
satellite
Saten Satan (devil)
saten sateen (cotton)
saten satin (silk)
Saterday Saturday
satiabel satiable
satiable, -ly
satiate, -ated, -ating
satiation
satin (silk)
satinwood
satire (sarcasm)
satire satyr (a god)
satiric
satirical, -ly
satirist
satisfacshun satisfaction
satisfaction

satisfactorily	
satisfactory	
satisfactry	satisfactory
satisfiabul	satisfiable
satisfy, -fied, -fying	
saturate, -rated, -rating	
saturation	
Saturday	
Saturn (planet)	
saturn	sauterne (wine)
saturnine, -ly	
satyr (a god)	
satyr	satire (sarcasm)
sauce (liquid)	
sauce	source (origin)
saucepan	
saucer	
saucerer	sorcerer
saucery	sorcery
saucily	
sauciness	
saucy, -cier, -ciest	
sauerkraut	
sauna	
saunter, -ed, -ing	
saurian	
sausage	
sausy	saucy
sauté, -téed, -téeing	
sauterne (wine)	
sauturn	sauterne
savage, savaged, savaging	
savagely	
savagery, -ries	
savana	savanna
savanna	
savant	
save, saved, saving	
saveloy	
saver (keeper)	
saver	savour (taste)
savier	saviour
savige	savage
savigery	savagery
savigry	savagery
saving	
saviour	
savoir-faire	
savory, -vories (herb)	
savour, -ed, -ing (taste)	
savour	saver (keeper)
savoury, -vouries (tasty)	
savoy	
savvy	
saw, sawed, sawing (cut)	
saw	soar (rise)
saw	sore (hurt)
sawcer	saucer
sawcey	saucy
sawdid	sordid
sawdust	
sawmill	
sawna	sauna
sawnter	saunter
sawpit	
saws	sauce (liquid)
saws	source (origin)
sawser	saucer
sawsey	saucy
saxhorn	
saxofone	saxophone
saxofonist	saxophonist
Saxon	
saxophone	
saxophonist	
say, said, saying	
sayance	seance
say-so	
scab, scabbed, scabbing	
scabbard	
scabees	scabies
scabies	
scaffold	
scaffolding	
scalar	
scald, -ed, -ing (burn)	
scald	scold (chide)
scale, scaled, scaling	
scaliwag	scallywag
scallop, -ed, -ing	
scallywag	
scalp, -ed, -ing	
scalpel	
scalper	

scalpul scalpel
scamp
scamper, -ed, -ing
scan, scanned, scanning
scandal
scandalise, -lised, -lising
scandalmonger
scanner
scanshun scansion
scansion
scant
scantness
scanty, scantier, scantiest
scapegoat
scapula, -lae
scar, scarred, scarring
scarab
scarce, scarcer, scarcest
scarcely
scarceness
scarcity, -ties
scare, scared, scaring
scarecrow
scaremonger
scarf, scarfs, scarves
scarify, -fied, -fying
scarlet
scarp
scarper
scarsity scarcity
scary, scarier, scariest
scate skate
scathing, -ly
scatter, -ed, -ing
scatterbrain
scatty, -tier, -tiest
scavenge, -venged, -venging
scavenger
sceme scheme
scenario, -narios
scene (view)
scene seen (to see)
scenery, -neries
scenic, -ally
scent (perfume)
scent cent (coin)
scent sent (to send)

scepter sceptre
sceptic
sceptical, -ly
scepticism
sceptre
scerge scourge
scermish skirmish
schedule, -uled, -uling
schematic, -ally
scheme, schemed, scheming
schemer
schism
schismatic
schizofrenia schizophrenia
schizoid
schizophrenia
schizophrenic
schnapper
schnapps
scholar
scholarly
scholarship
scholastic, -ally
scholasticism
school, -ed, -ing
schoolboy
schoolgirl
schooner
sciatic
sciatica
science
scientific, -ally
scientist
scimitar
scintillate, -lated, -lating
sciolism
scion
scissors
scitsofrenia schizophrenia
sclerosis, -ses
scoff, -ed, -ing
scolar scholar
scolarship scholarship
scolastic scholastic
scold, -ed, -ing (chide)
scold scald (burn)
scollop

scone
scool school
scoop, -ed, -ing
scooter
scope
scorch, -ed, -ing
score, scored, scoring
scorer
scorn, -ed, -ing
scornful, -ly
Scorpio
scorpion
scorpiun scorpion
Scotch
scotch, -ed, -ing
scot-free
Scotsman, -men
Scotswoman, -women
Scottish
scoundrel
scoundrul scoundrel
scour, -ed, -ing (scratch)
scour scow (barge)
scourge, scourged, scourging
scout, -ed, -ing
scow (barge)
scow scour (scratch)
scowl, -ed, -ing
scowndrel scoundrel
scowt scout
scrabble, -bled, -bling
scrabbul scrabble
scrag, scragged, scragging
scraggly, -glier, -gliest
scraggy, -gier, -giest
scram, scrammed, scramming
scramble, -bled, -bling
scrambul scramble
scrap, scrapped, scrapping
scrapbook
scrape, scraped, scraping
scraper
scrappily
scrappy, -pier, -piest
scrapy scrappy
scratch, -ed, -ing
scrawl, -ed, -ing
scrawny, -nier, -niest
scream, -ed, -ing
screamer
scree
screech, -ed, -ing
screed
screen, -ed, -ing
screenplay
screw, -ed, -ing
screwball
screwdriver
screwtinise scrutinise
screwy, screwier, screwiest
scribal (writer)
scribble, -bled, -bling (write)
scribbler
scribbul scribble
scribe, scribed, scribing
scrim
scrimage scrimmage
scrimmage, -maged, -maging
scrimp, -ed, -ing
scrip (receipt)
scripcher scripture
script (handwriting)
scriptural, -ly
Scripture
scrofula
scrofulous, -ly
scroll
scroo screw
scrotem scrotum
scrotum
scrounge, scrounged, scrounging
scrounger
scrownge scrounge
scrub, scrubbed, scrubbing
scrubber
scrubby, -bier, -biest
scruff
scruffy, scruffier, scruffiest
scrum, scrummed, scrumming
scrumage scrummage
scrummage
scrumpshus scrumptious
scrumptious, -ly
scrumptiousness

scrumshus	scrumptious
scrunch, -ed, -ing	
scruple, -pled, -pling	
scrupul	scruple
scrupulosity	
scrupulous, -ly	
scrupulousness	
scrutinise, -nised, -nising	
scrutiny, -nies	
scuba	
scud, scudded, scudding	
scuff, -ed, -ing	
scuffle, -fled, -fling	
scuful	scuffle
scul	scull (row)
scul	skull (head)
sculery	scullery
scull, -ed, -ing (row)	
scull	skull (head)
scullery, -leries	
scullion	
scullyon	scullion
sculpcher	sculpture
sculpt, -ed, -ing	
sculpter	sculptor
sculptor	
sculptress	
sculptural, -ly	
sculpture, -tured, -turing	
scum, scummed, scumming	
scummy, -mier, -miest	
scungie	scungy
scungy	
scurf	
scurge	scourge
scurie	scurry
scurilus	scurrilous
scurrilous, -ly	
scurrulus	scurrilous
scurry, -ries	
scurry, -ried, -rying	
scurvey	scurvy
scurvily	
scurvy, -vier, -viest	
scury	scurry
scuttel	scuttle
scuttle, -tled, -tling	

scuttlebutt	
scuttul	scuttle
scythe, scythed, scything	
sea (ocean)	
see	see (look)
sea-anemone	
seaboard	
seabord	seaboard
seafarer	
seafaring	
seafood	
seagoing	
seagull	
seahorse	
seal, -ed, -ing	
sealant	
sealer	
sea-level	
sealing (close)	
sealing	ceiling (roof)
seam, -ed, -ing (join)	
seam	seem (appear)
seaman, -men (sailors)	
seamanship	
seamen	semen (seed)
seamstress	
seamy, -mier, -miest	
sean	scene (view)
sean	seen (to see)
seance	
seanse	seance
seaplane	
sear, -ed, -ing (burn)	
sear	seer (prophet)
search, -ed, -ing	
searcher	
searchlight	
search-warrant	
sea-scout	
sea-shell	
seashore	
seasickness	
seaside	
season, -ed, -ing	
seasonable, -bly	
seasonabul	seasonable
seasonal, -ly	

Word	Correct spelling
seat, -ed, -ing	
seawards	
seaweed	
seaworthiness	
seaworthy	
sebaceous	
sebashus	sebaceous
secaters	secateurs
secateurs	
secede, -ceded, -ceding	
secesshun	secession
secession	
secetary	secretary
seclude, -cluded, -cluding	
seclushun	seclusion
seclusion	
second, -ed, -ing	
secondary, -arily	
secondary boycott	
second-class	
second-degree	
second-hand	
secondly	
second-rate	
secondry	secondary
seconds	
secratery	secretary
secrecy, -cies	
secreshun	secretion
secresy	secrecy
secret, -ly	
secretarial	
secretariat	
secretariul	secretarial
secretary, -ries	
secrete, -creted, -creting	
secretion	
secretive, -ly	
secretry	secretary
secshun	section
sect	
sectar	sector
sectarian	
sectarianism	
section	
sectional, -ly	
secter	sector
sector	
secular, -ly	
secularism	
secularist	
securable	
securabul	securable
secure, -cured, -curing	
security, -ties	
sed	said
sedament	sediment
sedan	
sedate, -dated, -dating	
sedation	
sedative	
sedentary	
sedentery	sedentary
seder	cedar
sedge	
sediment	
sedimentary	
sedimentation	
sedimentery	sedimentary
sedishun	sedition
sedishus	seditious
sedition	
seditious, -ly	
seditive	sedative
seduce, -duced, -ducing	
seducer	
seducshun	seduction
seduction	
seductive, -ly	
seductiveness	
sedulous	
sedulus	sedulous
see, saw, seen, seeing (look)	
see	sea (ocean)
seed, seeded, seeding (plant)	
seed	cede (yield)
seediness	
seedling	
seedy, seedier, seediest	
seefarer	seafarer
seefood	seafood
seege	siege
seegull	seagull
seek, sought, seeking	

Wrong	Right
seel	seal
seelant	sealant
seeler	sealer
see-level	sea-level
seeling	ceiling (roof)
seeling	sealing (close)
seem, -ed, -ing (appear)	
seem	seam (join)
seeman	seaman (sailor)
seemly, -lier, -liest	
seemstress	seamstress
seemy	seamy
seen (to see)	
seen	scene (view)
seenery	scenery
seenic	scenic
seenile	senile
seep, -ed, -ing	
seepage	
seepige	seepage
seequel	sequel
seer (prophet)	
seer	sear (burn)
searsucker	seersucker
seersucker	
seesaw	
seese	cease
seesfire	ceasefire
seeshore	seashore
seesun	season
sect	seat
seethe, seethed, seething	
seeweed	seaweed
seeze	seize
seezure	seizure
sege	sedge
segment	
segmentation	
segregate, -gated, -gating	
segregation	
segregationist	
seige	siege
seine (net)	
seine	sane (not mad)
seismagraf	seismograph
seismic	
seismograph	
seismologist	
seismology	
seize, seized, seizing	
seizure	
sekaters	secateurs
sekond	second
sekrete	secrete
seks	sex
sekshun	section
sekstant	sextant
seksual	sexual
seksy	sexy
sekt	sect
sektor	sector
sekular	secular
sekure	secure
sekwel	sequel
sekwense	sequence
sekwin	sequin
Selcius	Celsius
seldom, -ly	
selebrate	celebrate
selebrity	celebrity
seleckshun	selection
select, -ed, -ing	
selecter	selector
selection	
selective, -ly	
selectivity	
selector	
seler	cellar (room)
seler	seller (goods)
selerity	celerity
selery	celery (food)
selery	salary (wage)
selestial	celestial
self, selves	
self-addressed	
self-aggrandisement	
self-assurance	
self-centred	
self-confessed	
self-confidence	
self-confident	
self-conscious, -ly	
self-contained	
self-defence	

self-denial	
self-destruct	
self-determination	
self-employed	
self-evident, -ly	
self-fertilisation	
self-government	
self-image	
self-imidge	**self-image**
self-important, -ly	
self-interest	
selfish, -ly	
selfishness	
selfless, -ly	
self-made	
self-opinionated	
self-pollination	
self-possessed	
self-raising flour	
self-respect	
self-righteous, -ly	
self-rule	
self-sacrifice	
self-service	
self-sown	
self-starter	
self-sufficient	
self-willed	
selibacy	**celibacy**
selibat	**celibate**
selibrate	**celebrate**
sell, sold, selling (goods)	
sell	**cell (prison)**
seller (goods)	
seller	**cellar (room)**
sellofane	**cellophane**
sellophane	**cellophane**
sell-out	
sellullar	**cellular**
selluloid	**celluloid**
sellulose	**cellulose**
sellvage	**salvage (save)**
sellvedge	**selvedge (edge)**
Selsius	**Celsius**
selular	**cellular**
seluloid	**celluloid**
selulose	**cellulose**
selvage (edge)	
selvedge (edge)	
selvedge	**salvage (save)**
semafor	**semaphore**
semantic	
semaphore, -phored, -phoring	
semblance	
semblanse	**semblance**
semen (seed)	
semen	**seamen (sailors)**
semester	
semibreve	
semicercul	**semicircle**
semicircle	
semicircular	
semicolon	
semiconductor	
semidetached	
seminal, -ly	
seminar	
seminary, -aries	
seminery	**seminary**
semiprecious	
semipreshus	**semiprecious**
semiquaver	
Semite	
semitery	**cemetery**
Semitic	
semitone	
semitrailer	
semolina	
sena	**senna**
senario	**scenario**
senat	**senate**
senate	
senater	**senator**
senator	
senatorial	
senatoriul	**senatorial**
send, sent, sending	
sender	
senile	
senilitey	**senility**
senility	
senior	
seniority, -ties	

senna
senotaf	cenotaph
sensability	sensibility
sensabul	sensible

sensation
sensational, -ly
sensationalise, -ised, -ising
sensationalism
sensationalist

sensatise	sensitise

sense, sensed, sensing
senser	censer (incense)
senser	censor (books)
senser	sensor (device)
senshual	sensual
senshur	censure (blame)

sensible, -bly
sensibility, -ties
sensibul	sensible

sensitise, -tised, -tising
sensitivity, -ties
sensor (device)
sensor	censer (incense)
sensor	censor (books)
sensorey	sensory
sensorious	censorious

sensory, -orily
sensual, -ly
sensualist
sensualitey	sensuality

sensuality, -ties
sensuous, -ly
sensus	census

sent (to send)
sent	cent (money)
sent	scent (perfume)
sentenary	centenary

sentence, -tenced, -tencing
sentenchus	sententious
sentennial	centennial

sententious, -ly
senter	centre

sentience
sentient, -ly
sentigrade	Centigrade
sentigram	centigram

sentiment
sentimental, -ly
sentimentalism
sentimentalist
sentimentality, -ties
sentimeter	centimetre

sentinel, -nelled, -nelling
sentipede	centipede
sentor	centaur
sentral	central
sentralise	centralise
sentrey	sentry
sentrifugal	centrifugal
sentifuge	centrifuge
sentripetal	centripetal

sentry, -tries
sentupul	centuple
senturion	centurion
sentury	century
senyor	senior
senyority	seniority

sepal
separable, -bly
separabul	separable

separate, -rated, -rating
separately
separation
separationist
separator
seperabul	separable
seperate	separate
seperation	separation
sephalitis	cephalitis

sepia
sepoy
sepsis
September
septennial, -ly
septer	sceptre

septet
septic
septicaemia
septisemia	septicaemia

septuagenarian
sepulchral, -ly
sepulchre
sepulchrul	sepulchral
sepulker	sepulchre

sequel	
sequence	
sequense	sequence
sequenshul	sequential
sequential, -ly	
sequester, -ed, -ing	
sequestration	
sequin	
ser	sir
seraf	seraph
serafic	seraphic
seramic	ceramic
seranade	serenade
serch	search
seremony	ceremony
seraph, -aphs, -aphim	
seraphic, -ally	
serch	search
sere (dry)	
sere	sear (burn)
serebrul	cerebral
sereen	serene
serees	series
serenade, -naded, -nading	
serendipity	
serene, -ly	
serenitey	serenity
serenity, -ties	
seres	series
sereze	cerise
serf (slave)	
serf	surf (sea)
serfdom	
serge (cloth)	
serge	surge (rush)
sergeant	
serial, -ly (part)	
serial	cereal (grain)
serialisation	
serialise, -lised, -lising	
seribelum	cerebellum
seribrul	cerebral
seribrum	cerebrum
series	
serif	
serimonial	ceremonial
serimonius	ceremonious
serimony	ceremony
serious, -ly	
seriousness	
serius	serious
serjent	sergeant
serloin	sirloin
serly	surly
serman	sermon
sermise	surmise
sermon	
sermount	surmount
sername	surname
serpent	
serpentine	
serplice	surplice (gown)
serplus	surplus (extra)
serprise	surprise
serrate, -rated, -rating	
serration	
serry, -ried, -rying	
sertain	certain
sertainty	certainty
sertax	surtax
sertifiabul	certifiable
sertificate	certificate
sertify	certify
sertitude	certitude
serum, sera, serums	
servant	
servay	survey
servaylanse	surveillance
serve, served, serving	
server	
servery, serveries	
servical	cervical
service, -viced, -vicing	
serviceability	
serviceable, -bly	
serviceabul	serviceable
serviceman, -men	
servicewoman, -women	
serviet	serviette
serviette	
serviks	cervix
servile, -ly	
servility	
servitude	

Word	Correct spelling
servival	survival
servive	survive
serviver	survivor
servix	cervix
sesame	
sesayshun	cessation
sese	cease
seseed	secede
seseshun	secession
seshun	cession (yield)
seshun	session (period)
sesless	ceaseless
seson	season
sesonabul	seasonable
sesonal	seasonal
sespit	cesspit
sesquicentenary, -ries	
sesseshun	secession
session (period)	
session	cession (yield)
set, set, setting	
setback	
setee	settee
seter	setter
setul	settle
settee	
setter	
settle, -tled, -tling	
settlement	
settler	
settul	settle
set-up	
seudo	pseudo
seudonim	pseudonym
sevear	severe
seven	
seventeen	
seventeenth	
seventh	
Seventh-Day Adventist	
seventieth	
seventy, -ties	
sever, -ed, -ing	
several, -ly	
severance	
severanse	severance
severe, -verer, -verest	
severely	
severitey	severity
severity, -ties	
sew, sewed, sewn, sewing (stitch)	
sew	sow (plant)
sewage	
sewer (drain)	
sewer (stitcher)	
sewer	sower (planter)
sewerage	
sewerige	sewerage
sewige	sewage
sex, -ed, -ing	
sexiness	
sexist	
sextant	
sextet	
sexton	
sexual, -ly	
sexualitey	sexuality
sexuality	
sexy, sexier, sexiest	
sezarian	caesarian
sfere	sphere
sfericul	sperical
sferoid	spheroid
sfincter	sphincter
sfinx	sphinx
sha	shah
shabbily	
shabbiness	
shabby, -bier, -biest	
shaby	shabby
shack	
shackle, -led, -ling	
shackul	shackle
shaddow	shadow
shade, shaded, shading	
shadow, -ed, -ing	
shadowy	
shady, -dier, -diest	
shaft	
shag, shagged, shagging	
shagginess	
shaggy, -gier, -giest	
shagrin	chagrin
shagy	shaggy

shah	
shak	shack
shake, shook, shaken, shaking	
shakedown	
shaker	
Shakespearian	
shake-up	
shakey	shaky
shakily	
shakiness	
shaky, shakier, shakiest	
shal	shall
shalay	chalet
shale	
shalet	chalet
shall (will)	
shall	shell (cover)
shallot	
shallow, -ly	
shallowness	
sham, shammed, shaming	
shamble, -bled, -bling	
shambles	
shambul	shamble
shame, shamed, shaming	
shamefaced, -ly	
shameful, -ly	
shameless, -ly	
shampane	champagne
shampoo, -ed, -ing	
shamrock	
shamy	chamois
shandeleer	chandelier
shandie	shandy
shandy, -dies	
shanghai, -haied, -haiing	
shank	
shan't (shall not)	
shant	shan't
shantung	
shanty, -ties	
shape, shaped, shaping	
shapeliness	
shapely, -lier, -liest	
shaperon	chaperone
sharade	charade
shard	
share, shared, sharing	
sharebroker	
sharefarmer	
shareholder	
shark	
sharkskin	
sharp, -ly	
sharpen, -ed, -ing	
sharpener	
sharper	
sharpness	
sharpshooter	
sharpwitted	
shasee	chassis
shashlik	
shater	shatter
shatow	chateau
shatter, -ed, -ing	
shave, shaved, shaven, shaving	
shaver	
shawl	
sheaf, sheaves	
shear, sheared, shorn, shearing (cut)	
shear	sheer (thin)
shearer	
shearwater	
sheath, sheaths	
sheathe, sheathed, sheathing	
sheave, sheaved, sheaving	
shed, shed, shedding	
shedule	schedule
sheef	sheaf
sheek	chic (smart)
sheek	sheik (ruler)
sheen	
sheep, sheep	
sheep-dip	
sheepdog	
sheepish, -ly	
sheepishness	
sheep-run	
sheepskin	
sheer, -ed, -ing (swerve)	
sheer (thin)	
sheer	shear (cut)
sheet, -ed, -ing	
shef	chef

sheik (ruler)
sheik shake (move)
sheila
sheild shield
shekel
shel shell
shelac shellac
shelf, shelves
shelfish shellfish
shell, -ed, -ing (cover)
she'll (she will)
shell she'll
shellac, -lacked, -lacking
shellfish, -fishes, -fish
shell-shocked
shelly, -lier, -liest
shelter, -ed, -ing
shelve, shelved, shelving
shemozzle
shenanigan
she-oak
sheperd shepherd
shepherd, -ed, -ing
shepherdess
sherbet
sherbut sherbet
sherie sherry
sherif (Muslim leader)
sheriff (law man)
sherry, -ries
shery sherry
sheth sheath
sheves sheaves
shevron chevron
shibboleth
shic chic (smart)
shic sheik (ruler)
shicanery chicanery
shickered
shied
shield, -ed, -ing
shiffon chiffon
shift, -ed, -ing
shiftiness
shiftless, -ly
shifty, -tier, -tiest
shilling shilling

shillelagh
shilling
shimmer, -ed, -ing
shimmery
shimmy, -mies
shimmy, -mied, -mying
shin, shinned, shinning
shindig
shine, shone, shined, shining
shiner
shingel shingle
shingle, -gled, -gling
shingles
shinguls shingles
shiny, shinier, shiniest
ship, shipped, shipping
shipment
shipreck shipwreck
shipright shipwright
shipshape
shipwreck, -ed, -ing
shipwright
shiralee
shirk, -ed, -ing
shirker
shirr, -ed, -ing
shirt
shirty
shish-kebab
shivalrey chivalry
shivalrus chivalrous
shiver, -ed, -ing
shivery
shnaps schnapps
shoal, -ed, -ing
shock, -ed, -ing
shocker
shod
shoddily
shoddiness
shoddy, -dier, -diest
shodie shoddy
shody shoddy
shoe, shoes
shoe, shod, shoeing (footwear)
shoe shoo (scare)
shoehorn

shoelace
shoemaker
shoeshine
shoestring
shofer   chauffeur
shogun
sholder   shoulder
shole   shoal
shoo, -ed, -ing (scare)
shoo   shoe (footwear)
shood   should
shook
shoot, shot, shooting (gun)
shoot   chute (channel)
shooter
shoot-out
shop, shopped, shopping
shopkeeper
shop-lift, -ed, -ing
shop-lifter
shop-soiled
shop-steward
shore, shored, shoring (sea)
shore   sure (certain)
shorely   surely
shorety   surety
shorn
short, -ly
shortage
shortbread
shortbred   shortbread
shortcake
short-change, -changed, -changing
short-circuit, -ed, -ing
shortcoming
shorten, -ed, -ing
shortfall
shorthand
shortidge   shortage
shorts
short-sighted
short-sited   short-sighted
short-wave
shot
shotgun
shot-put
shot-putter

should
shoulder, -ed, -ing
shoulder-blade
shout, -ed, -ing
shove, -ed, -ing
shovel, -ed, -ing
shoveler (bird)
shoveller (bird), (person)
shovinism   chauvinism
shovinist   chauvinist
show, showed, shown, showing
showboat
showdown
shower
showery
showily
showjumper
showjumping
showman, -men
showmanship
show-off
showt   shout
showy, showier, showiest
shrank
shrapnel
shred, shredded, shredding
shredder
shreek   shriek
shrew
shrewd, -ly
shrewish, -ly
shriek, -ed, -ing
shrift
shrike
shrill
shrimp
shrine
shrink, shrank, shrunk, shrinking
shrinkage
shrinkige   shrinkage
shrivel, -elled, -elling
shroo   shrew
shrood   shrewd
shroud
shrowd   shroud
shrub
shrubbery

shrug, shrugged, shrugging
shrunk
shudder, -ed, -ing
  shuffel shuffle
shuffle, -fled, -fling
shun, shunned, shunning
shunt, -ed, -ing
shunter
  shurbet sherbert
  shurk shirk
  shurt shirt
shush, -ed, -ing
shut, shut, shutting
shutdown
shut-eye
shut-out
  shuttel shuttle
shutter
shuttle, -tled, -tling
shuttlecock
  shuttul shuttle
  shuttulcock shuttlecock
  shutul shuttle
  shuve shove
  shuvel shovel
shy, shied, shying
shy, shyer, shyest
shyly
shyness
shyster
  sianide cyanide
  siatic sciatic
  sibernetics cybernetics
sibilant, -ly
sibling
  sicamore sycamore
  sicedelic psychedelic
  siciatry psychiatry
  sicick psychic
sick
sicken, -ed, -ing
sickie
sickle
sickliness
sickly, -lier, -liest
  sickul sickle
  siclamate cyclamate
  siclamen cyclamen
  sicle cycle
  siclic cyclic
  siclist cyclist
  siclone cyclone
  siclotron cyclotron
  sicoanalise psychoanalyse
  sicological psychological
  sicology psychology
  sicopant sycophant
  sicopath psychopath
  sicosis psychosis
  sicosomatic psychosomatic
  sicotherapist psychotherapist
  sicotic psychotic
  sicul cycle
side, sided, siding
sideboard
  sidebord sideboard
sidelight
sideline
  sidelite sidelight
  sider cider
sideshow
sidestep, -stepped, -stepping
sidetrack, -ed, -ing
sideways
  sidel sidle
sidle, -dled, -dling
  sie sigh
siege, sieged, sieging
sienna
  sience science
  siense science
  sientific scientific
  sientist scientist
sierra
siesta
sieve, sieved, sieving
  sieze seize
  sifer cypher
  sifilis syphilis
  sifon syphon
sift, -ed, -ing
  sigar cigar
  sigaret cigarette
sigh, -ed, -ing

sight, -ed, -ing (view)	
sight	cite (quote)
sight	site (place)
sightless, -ly	
sightly, -lier, -liest	
sightseeing	
sightseer	
sigma	
sign, -ed, -ing (mark)	
sign	sine (maths)
signal, -ed, -ing	
signatory, -ries	
signatry	signatory
signature	
signefy	signify
signet (ring)	
signet	cygnet (swan)
significance	
significanse	significance
significant, -ly	
signification	
signifie	signify
signify, -fied, -fying	
signpost	
signul	signal
sign-writer	
sikedelic	psychedelic
sikey	psyche
Sikh	
sikiatrist	psychiatrist
sikiatry	psychiatry
sikick	psychic
siksty	sixty
silabul	syllable
silabus	syllabus
silage	
silence, silenced, silencing	
silencer	
silense	silence
silent, -ly	
silestial	celestial
silf	sylph
silhouette, -etted, -etting	
silica	
silicon (element)	
silicone (synthetic)	
silicosis	

silie	silly
silige	silage
silinder	cylinder
silindricul	cylindrical
silk	
silken	
silkiness	
silk-screen	
silkworm	
silky, -kier, -kiest	
silky oak	
sill	
sillabul	syllable
silliness	
silly, -lier, -liest	
silo, -los	
silogism	syllogism
silt, -ed, -ing	
siluet	silhouette
silver, -ed, -ing	
silverfish, -fish, -fishes	
silverside	
silversmith	
silvery	
sily	silly
simbiosis	symbiosis
simbiotic	symbiotic
simbol	cymbal (music)
simbol	symbol (sign)
simbolicul	symbolical
simbolise	symbolise
simbolism	symbolism
siment	cement
simer	simmer
simetry	symmetry
simfoney	symphony
simian	
similar, -ly	
similarity, -ties	
simile	
similer	similar
simmer, -ed, -ing	
simmetry	symmetry
simpathetic	sympathetic
simpathise	sympathise
simpathy	sympathy
simpel	simple

simper, -ed, -ing
simple, -pler, -plest
simple interest
simpleton
simplicity, -ties
simplification
simplify, -fied, -fying
simplisity simplicity
simplistic, -ally
simply
simposium symposium
simptom symptom
simptomatic symptomatic
simpul simple
simpulton simpleton
simulate, -lated, -lating
simulation
simulator
simultaneous, -ly
simultaynius simultaneous
sin, sinned, sinning
sinagog synagogue
sinamon cinnamon
since
sincere, -cerer, -cerest
sincerely
sincerity, -ties
sinchromesh synchromesh
sincronise synchronise
sine (maths)
sine sign (mark)
sine camera cine camera
sinecure
sinema cinema
sinematograf cinematograph
sinepost signpost
sinew
sinewy
sinful, -ly
sing, sang, sung, singing
singe, singed, singeing
singel single
singer
single, -gled, -gling
single-handed
single-minded
singlet
singsong
singular, -ly
singularity, -ties
singuler singular
sinic cynic
sinical cynical
sinema cinema
sinimatograf cinematograph
sinisism cynicism
sinister, -ly
sink, sank, sunk or sunken, sinking
sinker
sinkhole
sinod synod
sinonim synonym
sinonimus synonymous
sinopsis synopsis
sinoptic synoptic
sinoshure cynosure
sinse since
sinsere sincere
sinserity sincerity
sintax syntax
sinthesis synthesis
sinthesise synthesise
sinthetic synthetic
sinue sinew
sinuous, -ly
sinus, -nuses
sinusitis
sinuus sinuous
sip, sipped, sipping
sipet sippet
sipher cipher
siphon, -ed, -ing
sippet
sipress cypress
sir
sirca circa
sircharge surcharge
sire, sired, siring
siren
siringe syringe
sirloin
sirosis cirrhosis
sirup syrup
sirus cirrus

sisal	
sise	size
sism	schism
sismic	seismic
sismograf	seismograph
sismologist	seismologist
sissers	scissors
sissy	
sist	cyst
sistem	system
sistematic	systematic
sistematise	systematise
sister	
sister-in-law, sisters-in-law	
sisterly	
sistern	cistern
sit, sat, sitting	
sitadel	citadel
sitar	
sitation	citation
site, sited, siting (place)	
site	cite (state)
site	sight (view)
sitely	sightly
siteseeing	sightseeing
siteseer	sightseer
sitey	city
sithe	scythe
sitie	city
sit-in	
sitizen	citizen
sitric	citric
sitrus	citrus
sitter	
situate, -ated, -ating	
situation	
sive	sieve
sivere	severe
sivic	civic
sivilian	civilian
sivilisation	civilisation
sivilise	civilise
sivilitey	civility
six	
six-shooter	
sixteen	
sixteenth	

sixth, -ly	
sixtieth	
sixty, -ties	
size, sized, sizing	
sizeable, -bly	
sizeabul	sizeable
sizemic	seismic
sizers	scissors
sizul	sizzle
sizzle, -zled, -zling	
sizzler	
sizzul	sizzle
skane	skein
skate, skated, skating	
skateboard	
skater	
skedule	schedule
skee	ski
skeem	scheme
skein	
skeletal	
skeleton	
skeletul	skeletal
skematic	schematic
skeme	scheme
skeptic	sceptic
skepticism	scepticism
skepticul	sceptical
skerick	skerrick
skermish	skirmish
skerrick	
skert	skirt
sketch, -ed, -ing	
sketcher	
sketchily	
sketchiness	
sketchy, sketchier, sketchiest	
skew, -ed, -ing	
skewer	
ski, skis, ski	
ski, skied, skiing	
skid, skidded, skidding	
skiff	
skil	skill
skilet	skillet
skilful, -ly	
skilfulness	

skilite	skylight
skill	
skilled	
skillet	
skillion	
skillyun	skillion
skim, skimmed, skimming	
skimp, -ed, -ing	
skimpily	
skimpiness	
skimpy, skimpier, skimpiest	
skin, skinned, skinning	
skin-deep	
skindiver	
skindiving	
skiney	skinny
skinflint	
skinhead	
skink	
skinny, -nier, -niest	
skip, skipped, skipping	
skiper	skipper
ski-pole	
skipper	
skirmish	
skirt, -ed, -ing	
skiscraper	skyscraper
skit (making fun)	
skite, skited, skiting (boast)	
skitsofrenia	schizophrenia
skittel	skittle
skittish, -ly	
skittle, skittled, skittling	
skivvy	
skol, skolled, skolling	
skua	
skue	skew
skulk, -ed, -ing	
skull (head)	
skull	scull (row)
skullcap	
skunk	

For all skw- words, look under **squ-** .

sky, skied or skyed, skying	
skydiver	
skylark	
skylight	
skyline	
skylite	skylight
skyrocket	
skyscraper	
slab	
slack, -ly	
slacken, -ed, -ing	
slacks	
slag, slagged, slagging	
slain	
slake, slaked, slaking	
slaken	slacken
slalom	
slam, slammed, slamming	
slander, -ed, -ing	
slanderer	
slanderous, -ly	
slane	slain
slang	
slangy	
slant, -ed, -ing	
slap, slapped, slapping	
slapdash	
slapstick	
slash, -ed, -ing	
slasher	
slat	
slate, slated, slating	
slater	
slatern	slattern
slather, -ed, -ing	
slattern, -ly	
slaughter, -ed, -ing	
slaughterhouse	
Slav	
slave, slaved, slaving	
slaver	
slavish, -ly	
slavishness	
Slavonic	
slawter	slaughter
slay, slew, slain, slaying (kill)	
slay	sleigh (sledge)
sleazy, -zier, -ziest	
sled, sledded, sledding	

sledge	
sledge-hammer	
sleek, -ly	
sleekness	
sleep, slept, sleeping	
sleeper	
sleepily	
sleepiness	
sleepless, -ly	
sleep-out	
sleepy, sleepier, sleepiest	
sleet	
sleeve	
sleeved	
slege	sledge
sleigh (sledge)	
sleight (skill)	
sleight	slight (small)
slender, -ly	
slept	
sleuth	
slew	
sli	sly
slice, sliced, slicing	
slick, -ly	
slide, slid, sliding	
slight, -ly (small)	
slight	sleight (skill)
slim, slimmed, slimming	
slim, slimmer, slimmest	
slime	
slimily	
sliminess	
slimy, slimier, slimiest	
sling, slung, slinging	
slink, slunk, slinking	
slinky, slinkier, slinkiest	
slip, slipped, slipping	
sliper	slipper
slipknot	
slipnot	slipknot
slipper	
slippery, -perier, -periest	
sliprale	sliprail
sliprail	
slipshod	
slip-stitch	

slipstream	
slipway	
slise	slice
slit, slit, slitting	
slite	slight
slither, -ed, -ing	
sliver	
slo	sloe (fruit)
slo	slow (not fast)
slob	
slobber, -ed, -ing	
slobbery	
sloe (fruit)	
sloe	slow (not fast)
slog, slogged, slogging	
slogan	
sloop	
sloose	sluice
slooth	sleuth
slop, slopped, slopping	
slope, sloped, sloping	
slopily	sloppily
sloppiness	
sloppily	
sloppy, -pier, -piest	
slopy	sloppy
slosh, -ed, -ing	
slot, slotted, slotting	
sloth	
slothful, -ly	
slouch, -ed, -ing	
slough (skin)	
sloven, -ly	
slovenliness	
slow, -ed, -ing (not fast)	
slow	sloe (fruit)
slow	slough (skin)
slowch	slouch
slowcoach	
slow-motion	
sludge	
sludgy, sludgier, sludgiest	
slue	slew
sluff	slough
sluggard	
sluggardly	
sluggish, -ly	

sluice, sluiced, sluicing
slum, slummed, slumming
slumber, -ed, -ing
slump, -ed, -ing
slung
slunk
slur, slurred, slurring
slurie slurry
slurp, -ed, -ing
slurry
slush
slushy, -shier, -shiest
slut
sluttish, -ly
sly, slyer, slyest or slier, sliest
slyly
slyness
smack, -ed, -ing
small
smallgoods
smallpox
small-time
smarmy
smart, -ed, -ing
smart, smarter, smartest
smart alec
smarten, -ed, -ing
smartly
smash, -ed, -ing
smasher
smattering
smear, -ed, -ing
smeer smear
smell, smelled or smelt, smelling
smelly, smellier, smelliest
smelter
smidgin
smile, smiled, smiling
smirch, -ed, -ing
smirk, -ed, -ing
smite, smote, smiting
smith
smithereens
smithey smithy
smithy, smithies
smitten
smock, -ed, -ing

smog
smoggy, smoggier, smoggiest
smogy smoggy
smoke, smoked, smoking
smoke-bush
smoker
smokescreen
smokestack
smoko
smoky, smokier, smokiest
smolder smoulder
smooch, -ed, -ing
smoodge, smoodged, smoodging
smooth, -ed, -ing
smoothly
smoothness
smorgasbord
smother, -ed, -ing
smoulder, -ed, -ing
smudge, smudged, smudging
smug, smugger, smuggest
smuge smudge
smuggle, smuggled, smuggling
smuggler
smuggul smuggle
smugle smuggle
smugly
smurch smirch
smurk smirk
smut
smuttily
smuttiness
smutty, smuttier, smuttiest
smuty smutty
snack
snaffle, -fled, -fling
snafful snaffle
snag, snagged, snagging
snagger
snail
snake, snaked, snaking
snakebite
snaky, snakier, snakiest
snale snail
snap, snapped, snapping
snapdragon
snaper snapper

snapper
snappily
snappiness
snappy, -pier, -piest
snapshot
snapy   snappy
snare, snared, snaring
snarl, -ed, -ing
snatch, -ed, -ing
sneak, -ed, -ing
sneaker
sneek   sneak
sneeker   sneaker
sneer, -ed, -ing
sneeze, sneezed, sneezing
snib, snibbed, snibbing
snick, -ed, -ing
snicker, -ed, -ing
snide
snif   sniff
snifel   sniffle
sniff, -ed, -ing
sniffle, -fled, -fling
sniffful   sniffle
sniger   snigger
snigger, -ed, -ing
snip, snipped, snipping (cut)
snipe, sniped, sniping (shoot)
sniper
snipet   snippet
snippet
snitch, -ed, -ing
snivel, -elled, -elling
sniveller
snivul   snivel
snob
snobbery
snobbish, -ly
snood
snook
snooker, -ed, -ing
snoop, -ed, -ing
snoopy
snooze, snoozed, snoozing
snore, snored, snoring
snorkel
snorkle   snorkel
snorkul   snorkel
snort, -ed, -ing
snout
snow, -ed, -ing
snowball
snowey   snowy
snowflake
snow job
snowline
snowman, -men
snowplough
snowshoe, -shoed, -shoeing
snowt   snout
snowy, snowier, snowiest
snub, snubbed, snubbing
snuff, -ed, -ing
snuffle, -fled, -fling
snug, snugger, snuggest
snuggle, -gled, -gling
so (in this way)
so   sew (stitch)
so   sow (pig, plant)
soak, -ed, -ing
so-and-so
soap, -ed, -ing
soapbox
soapie
soap opera
soappy   soapy
soapstone
soapy, soapier, soapiest
soar, -ed, -ing (fly)
soar   sore (hurt)
sob, sobbed, sobbing
sober, -ed, -ing
sobriety
sobrikay   sobriquet
sobriquet
so-called
soccer
sociability
sociable, -bly
sociabul   sociable
social, -ly
socialisation
socialise, -lised, -lising
socialism

socialist	
socialistic, -ally	
socialite	
society, -ties	
socioeconomic, -ally	
sociologist	
sociology	
sociul	social
sock, -ed, -ing	
socker	soccer
socket	
sockit	socket
sockeye	
sod	
soda	
soda-water	
sodden	
soden	sodden
sodium	
sodomite	
sodomy	
sofa	
sofar	sofa
sofen	soften
sofism	sophism
sofist	sophist
sofisticate	sophisticate
sofistication	sophistication
sofistry	sophistry
soft, -ly	
softball	
soften, -ed, -ing	
soft-pedal, -alled, -alling	
soft-soap	
software	
softwear	software
soggily	
sogginess	
soggy, -gier, -giest	
sogie	soggy
sogy	soggy
soia	soya
soil, -ed, -ing	
soiray	soiree
soiree	
soiya	soya
sojern	sojourn
sojourn, -ed, -ing	
soke	soak
solace, -aced, -acing	
solar	
solareum	solarium
solarium, -laria	
solass	solace
solatude	solitude
sold	
solder, -ed, -ing	
soldier, -ed, -ing	
soldierly	
sole (shoe)	
sole	soul (spirit)
solecism	
soled	solid
soleful	soulful
solem	solemn
solemn, -ly	
solemnisation	
solemnise, -nised, -nising	
solemnitey	solemnity
solemnity, -ties	
solenoid	
soler	solar
solesism	solecism
solfa, -faed, -faing	
solger	soldier
solicit, -ed, -ing	
solicitation	
soliciter	solicitor
solicitor	
solicitous, -ly	
solicitude	
solicitus	solicitous
solid, -ly	
solidarity, -ties	
solidifi	solidify
solidification	
solidify, -fied, -fying	
solid-state	
solilokwy	soliloquy
soliloquy, -quies	
solisit	solicit
solisitor	solicitor
solisitus	solicitous
solitaire	

solitary, -taries
solitude
  soljer — soldier

> For soll- words,
> look under sol-.

solo, -los
soloist
solstice
  solstiss — solstice
solubility, -ties
soluble, -bly
  solubul — soluble
  solushun — solution
solution
solvable
solve, solved, solving
solvency
  solvensy — solvency
solvent
  somber — sombre
  sombraro — sombrero
sombre, -ly
sombrero
some (few)
  some — sum (total)
somebody, -bodies
somehow
someone
  somersalt — somersault
somersault
something
sometime
somewhat
somewhere
somnambulism
somnolence
  somnolense — somnolence
son (boy)
  son — sun (star)
sonar
sonata
  soner — sonar
song
songster
songstress
sonic
sonic boom
  sonick — sonic
son-in-law, sons-in-law
sonnet
sonny, -nies
sonorous, -ly
  sonorus — sonorous
  soo — sue
  soocher — suture
  soocrose — sucrose
  sooet — suet
  sooflay — souffle
sook
sooky
soon
  soop — soup
soot (chimney)
  soot — suit (clothes)
sooth (truth)
soothe, soothed, soothing (calm)
soothsayer
  soovenir — souvenir
sop, sopped, sopping
  sope — soap
sophism
sophist
sophisticate, -cated, -cating
sophistication
sophistry, -ries
soporific
sopping
soppy, -pier, -piest
soprano, -pranos, -prani
sorbet
  sorce — sauce (liquid)
  sorce — source (origin)
sorcerer
sorceress
sorcery, -ceries
  sord — sword
sordid, -ly
  sordust — sawdust
sore, sorer, sorest (hurt)
  sore — saw (cut)
  sore — soar (rise)
  sorel — sorrel
  sorey — sorry

sorghum	
sorgum	sorghum
sorie	sorry
sorna	sauna
sornter	saunter
sorority, -ties	
sorow	sorrow
sorrel	
sorrow	
sorrowful, -ly	
sorry, -rier, -riest	
sort (type)	
sort	sought (looked)
sortee	sortie
sortie, -tied, -tieing	
soshable	sociable
soshal	social
soshalise	socialise
sosietey	society
sosige	sausage
so-so	
sot	
soto vochay	sotto voce
sotto voce	
soufflé	
sough (rustling sound)	
sough	sow (pig)
sought (looked)	
soul (spirit)	
soul	sole (shoe)
sound, -ed, -ing	
soundbox	
sounding-board	
soundproof	
soundtrack	
soundwave	
soup	
sour, -ed, -ing	
source (origin)	
source	sauce (liquid)
souse, soused, sousing	
south	
south-east	
south-easter	
south-eastern	
southerly	
southern	
Southern Cross	
southward, -ly	
south-west	
south-wester	
south-western	
souvenir	
sovereign	
sovereignty, -ties	
soverin	sovereign
soviet	
sovrenty	sovereignty
sow, sowed, sowing (pig, plant)	
sow	sew (stitch)
sown (planted)	
sown	sewn (stitched)
sownd	sound
sowr	sour
sowth	south
soy	
soya	
spa	
space, spaced, spacing	
spaceship	
spacious, -ly	
spade, spaded, spading	
spadework	
spagetti	spaghetti
spaghetti	
span, spanned, spanning	
spaner	spanner
spangle, -gled, -gling	
spangul	spangle
Spaniard	
spaniel	
spank, -ed, -ing	
spanner	
Spanyard	Spaniard
spanyel	spaniel
spar, sparred, sparring (fight)	
spare, spared, sparing (extra)	
spark, -ed, -ing	
sparkle, -kled, -kling	
sparkler	
sparkul	sparkle
sparow	sparrow
sparrow	
sparrowhawk	

sparse, sparser, sparsest
sparsity
Spartan
spase — space
spashus — spacious
spasm
spasmodic, -ally
spastic, -ally
spat (did spit)
spatal — spatial
spate (sudden)
spatial, -ly
spatter, -ed, -ing
spatula
spawn, -ed, -ing
spay, -ed, -ing
speak, spoke, spoken, speaking
speakeasy, -easies
speaker
spear, -ed, -ing
spearmint
spec (gamble)
spec — speck (spot)
special, -ly
specialisation
specialise, -lised, -lising
specialist
speciality, -ties
specialty, -ties
species, -cies
specific, -ly
specification
specify, -fied, -fying
specimen
specious, -ly
speck, -ed, -ing (spot)
speck — spec (gamble)
speckle, -kled, -kling
spectacle
spectacul — spectacle
spectacular, -ly
spectator
specter — spectre
spectre
spectroscope
spectrum, -tra
speculate, -lated, -lating
speculation
speculator
speech
speed, sped, speeding
speedometer
speedway
speek — speak
speer — spear
spekul — speckle
spel — spell
spell, spelt or spelled, spelling
spellbound
spencer
spend, spent, spending
spendthrift
sperm
spern — spurn
spert — spurt
speshal — special
speshalist — specialist
speshus — specious
spesify — specify
spesimen — specimen
spew, -ed, -ing
sphere
spherical, -ly
spheroid
sphinx
spi — spy
spice, spiced, spicing
spick-and-span
spicy, spicier, spiciest
spider
spidery
spiel, -ed, -ing
spigot
spike, spiked, spiking
spill, spilt or spilled, spilling
spillage
spillige — spillage
spin, spun, spinning
spina bifida
spinach
spinaker — spinnaker
spinal
spindle, -dled, -dling
spin-dry, -dried, -drying

spine
spinifex
spinige — spinach
spinnaker
spinner
spin-off
spinster
spiny, spinier, spiniest
spiral, -ralled, -ralling
spire
spirel — spiral
spirichual — spiritual
spirichualist — spiritualist
spirit, -ed, -ing
spiritual, -ly
spiritualism
spiritualist
spirituality, -ties
spise — spice
spisy — spicy
spit, spat, spitting
spite, spited, spiting
spiteful, -ly
spitfire
spittle
spittoon
spittul — spittle
spiv
splash, -ed, -ing
splashdown
splatter, -ed, -ing
splay, -ed, -ing
spleen
splender — splendour
splendid, -ly
splendour
splice, spliced, splicing
splicer
splint
splinter, -ed, -ing
splise — splice
split, split, splitting
split-level
splurge, splurged, splurging
splutter, -ed, -ing
spoil, spoilt, spoiling
spoilage
spoilsport
spoke
spoken
spokesperson
sponge, sponged, sponging
sponger
spongy, -gier, -giest
sponser — sponsor
sponsor, -ed, -ing
sponsorship
spontaneity, -ties
spontaneous, -ly
sponteneity — spontaneity
spoof, -ed, -ing
spook, -ed, -ing
spool
spoon, -ed, -ing
spoonbill
spoonerism
spoon-feed, -fed, -feeding
spoor (trail)
spoor — spore (germ)
sporadic, -ally
spore, spored, sporing (germ)
spore — spoor (trail)
sporran
sport, -ed, -ing
sportive, -ly
sportsman, -men
sportswoman, -women
spot, spotted, spotting
spotlight, -ed, -ing
spotlite — spotlight
spouse
spout, -ed, -ing
spowse — spouse
spowt — spout
sprain, -ed, -ing
sprane — sprain
sprang
sprat
sprawl, -ed, -ing
spray, -ed, -ing
spread, spread, spreading
spread-eagle, -gled, -gling
spred — spread
spree

sprie	spry
sprightly, -lier, -liest
spring, sprang, sprung, springing
springboard
springbok, -boks
spring-clean, -ed, -ing
spring-loaded
springy, -gier, -giest
sprinkle, -kled, -kling
sprinkler
sprinkul	sprinkle
sprint, -ed, -ing
sprit (pole)
sprite, -ly (elf)
sprocket
sproose	spruce
sprout, -ed, -ing
sprowt	sprout
spruce, spruced, sprucing
spruce, sprucer, sprucest
sprung
spry, spryer, spryest
spud, spudded, spudding
spume, spumed, spuming
spun
spunge	sponge
spunk
spunky, spunkier, spunkiest
spur, spurred, spurring
spurious, -ly
spurius	spurious
spurm	sperm
spurn, -ed, -ing
spurt, -ed, -ing
sputnik
sputter, -ed, -ing
sputum, sputa
spy, spies
spy, spied, spying
squabble, -bled, -bling
squabul	squabble
squad
squadron
squalid, -ly
squall, -ed, -ing
squalor
squander, -ed, -ing
square, squared, squaring
squarely
square-rigged
squash, -ed, -ing
squat, squatted, squatting
squatter
squattocracy
squaw
squawk, -ed, -ing
squeak, -ed, -ing
squeal, -ed, -ing
squeamish, -ly
squeeze, squeezed, squeezing
squelch, -ed, -ing
squib, squibbed, squibbing
squid, squids, squid
squiggle, -gled, -gling
squiggly
squiggul	squiggle
squint, -ed, -ing
squire, squired, squiring
squirm, -ed, -ing
squirrel
squirt, -ed, -ing
squiz, -ed, -ing
squod	squad
squodron	squadron
squolid	squalid
squonder	squander
squosh	squash
squot	squat
stab, stabbed, stabbing
stabilisation
stabilise, -lised, -lising
stabiliser
stability, -ties
stable, -bled, -bling
stabul	stable
staccato
stack, -ed, -ing
stadium, -dia, -diums
staf	staff
staff, -ed, -ing
stag
stage, staged, staging
stagecoach
stager	stagger

stagflation
stagger, -ed, -ing
staghorn
stagnant, -ly
stagnate, -nated, -nating
stagnation
staid, -ly (calm)
staid (stopped) — stayed
staidium — stadium
stain, -ed, -ing
stainless, -ly
stair (step)
stair — stare (look at)
staircase
stairwell
stake, staked, staking (post)
stake — steak (meat)
stalactite
stalagmite
stale, staled, staling
stale, staler, stalest
stalemate, -mated, -mating
stalion — stallion
stalk, -ed, -ing (hunt)
stalk — stork (bird)
stall, -ed, -ing
stallion
stalwart, -ly
stalwert — stalwart
stamen
stamena — stamina
stamer — stammer
stamina
stammer, -ed, -ing
stamp, -ed, -ing
stampede, -peded, -peding
stance
stanchion
stanchun — stanchion
stand, stood, standing
standard
standardise, -dised, -dising
stand-by
standerd — standard
stand-in
stand-offish, -ly

standstill
stane — stain
stank
stanse — stance
stanza
staple, -pled, -pling
stapler
stapul — staple
star, starred, starring
starboard
starbord — starboard
starch, -ed, -ing
star-crossed
stardom
stare, stared, staring (look at)
stare — stair (step)
starfish, -fishes, -fish
stargaze, -gazed, -gazing
stargazer
stark, -ly
starkers
starling
start, -ed, -ing
startch — starch
starter
startle, -tled, -tling
starvation
starve, starved, starving
stash, -ed, -ing
stashun — station
stashunry — stationary
stashunry — stationery
state, stated, stating
stateliness
stately, -lier, -liest
statement
stateroom
statesman, -men
stateswoman, -women
static, -ally
station, -ed, -ing
stationary (still)
stationer (sells paper)
stationery (paper)
statistical, -ly
statistician
statistics

statistishun	statistician
stattic	static
statuary, -aries (statues)	
statue	
statuesk	statuesque
statuesque, -ly	
stature	
status	
status quo	
statute	
statutory (law)	
statutry	statutory
staunch, -ed, -ing	
stave, staved, staving	
stawk	stalk
stay, stayed, staying	
stead	
steadfast, -ly	
steadily	
steady, steadied, steadying	
steady, steadier, steadiest	
steak (meat)	
steak	stake (post)
steal, stole, stolen, stealing (rob)	
steal	steel (metal)
stealth	
stealthily	
stealthy, -thier, -thiest	
steam, -ed, -ing	
steam-engine	
steamer	
steamroller	
sted	stead
stedfast	steadfast
stedy	steady
steed	
steel, -ed, -ing (metal)	
steel	steal (rob)
steely	
steep, -ed, -ing	
steeple	
steeplechase	
steepul	steeple
steer, -ed, -ing	
steerage	
steerige	steerage
steersman, -men	
stelth	stealth
stem, stemmed, stemming	
stench	
stencil, -cilled, -cilling	
stenografer	stenographer
stenografy	stenography
stenographer	
stenography	
stensil	stencil
step, stepped, stepping, (pace)	
stepladder	
steppe (plain)	
stereo, stereos	
stereogram	
stereophonic	
stereotype, -typed, -typing	
sterile, -ly	
sterilisation	
sterilise, -lised, -lising	
steriliser	
sterio	stereo
steriofonic	stereophonic
steriotype	stereotype
sterling	
stern, -ly	
sternum	
stethoscope	
stetson	
stevedore, -dored, -doring	
stew, -ed, -ing	
steward	
stewardess	
sti	sty
stich	stitch
stick, stuck, sticking	
sticker	
stickler	
stick-up	
sticky, stickier, stickiest	
stickybeak	
stif	stiff
stifen	stiffen
stiff	
stiffen, -ed, -ing	
stiffener	
stifle, -fled, -fling	
stiful	stifle

stigma, -mas, -mata	
stigmatise, -tised, -tising	
stikler	stickler
stil	still
stile (steps)	
stile	style (type)
stiletto, -tos	
stilish	stylish
stilist	stylist
still, -ed, -ing	
stillbirth	
stillborn	
still-life	
stilt	
stilted, -ly	
stilton	
stilus	stylus
stimie	stymie
stimulant	
stimulate, -lated, -lating	
stimulation	
stimulator	
stimulus, -li, -luses	
sting, stung, stinging	
stingray	
stingy, -gier, -giest	
stink, stank, stunk, stinking	
stinker	
stinkhorn	
stinkpot	
stint, -ed, -ing	
stipend	
stipendiary, -ries	
stipple, -pled, -pling	
stipul	stipple
stipulate, -lated, -lating	
stipulation	
stir, stirred, stirring	
stirling	sterling
stirrup	
stirup	stirrup
stitch, -ed, -ing	
stoat	
stock, -ed, -ing	
stockade, -aded, -ading	
stockbroker	
stock-car	
stocking	
stockman, -men	
stockpile, -piled, -piling	
stocktaking	
stockwhip	
stocky, -kier, -kiest	
stodgily	
stodgy, -gier, -giest	
stogy	stodgy
stoical, -ly	
stoicism	
stoisism	stoicism
stoke, stoked, stoking	
stoker	
stole	
stolen	
stolid, -ly	
stoma, stomata	
stomach	
stomach-ache	
stomick	stomach
stone, stoned, stoning	
stonefish	
stonemason	
stoneware	
stony, stonier, stoniest	
stood	
stooge, stooged, stooging	
stool	
stoop, stooped, stooping	
stop, stopped, stopping	
stopcock	
stope, stoped, stoping	
stopgap	
stoppage	
stopper	
stopwatch	
store, stored, storing	
storey (floor)	
storey	story (tale)
storie	storey (floor)
storie	story (tale)
storige	storage
stork (bird)	
stork	stalk (hunt)
storm, -ed, -ing	
stormily	

stormy, -mier, -miest
story, -ries (tale)
  story storey (floor)
stout, -ly
stove, stoved, stoving
stow, -ed, -ing
stowaway
  stowt stout
straddle, -dled, -dling
  straf strafe
strafe, strafed, strafing
straggle, -gled, -gling
straggler
straight (line)
  straight strait (passage)
straightaway
straighten, -ed, -ing
straightforward, -ly
strain, -ed, -ing
strainer
strait (passage)
  strait straight (line)
straiten
straitjacket
straitlaced
strand
  strane strain
strange, stranger, strangest
strangle, -gled, -gling
strangler
stranglehold
  strangul strangle
strangulate, -lated, -lating
strangulation
strap, strapped, strapping
strapper
strasbourg
strata
stratagem
strata title
  strate straight (line)
  strate strait (passage)
  strategie strategy
strategic, -ally
strategist
strategy, -gies
stratification
stratify, -fied, -fying
  stratigem stratagem
  stratosfere stratosphere
stratosphere
stratum, strata
straw
  strawberie strawberry
strawberry, -ries
stray, -ed, -ing
streak, -ed, -ing
streaky, streakier, streakiest
stream, -ed, -ing
streamer
streamline, -lined, -lining
  streek streak
  streem stream
street
strength
strengthen, -ed, -ing
strenuous, -ly
  strenuus strenuous
streptomycin
stress, -ed, -ing
stretch, -ed, -ing
stretcher
strew, strewed, strewn, strewing
striate, -ated, -ating
striation
  strick strict
stricken
strict, -ly
stricture
stride, strode, striding
stridence
strident, -ly
strife
strike, struck, stricken, striking
strikebound
strikebreaker
  striknun strychnine
strine
string, strung, stringing
stringency
  stringensy stringency
stringent, -ly
stringer
stringy, -gier, -giest

strip, stripped, stripping
stripe, striped, striping
stripling
stripper
striptease
strive, strove, striven, striving
strobe
stroboscope
strode
stroke, stroked, stroking
stroll, -ed, -ing
stroller
strong, -ly
stronghold
stroo — strew
strop, stropped, stropping
stroppie — stroppy
stroppy, stroppier, stroppiest
strove
struck
struckcher — structure
structure, -tured, -turing
strudel
struggle, -gled, -gling
struggler
strugul — struggle
strum, strummed, strumming
strummer
strumpet
strung
strut, strutted, strutting
strychnine
stu — stew
stuard — steward
stub, stubbed, stubbing
stubble
stubbly
stubborn, -ly
stuben — stubborn
stucco, -coes, -cos
stuck-up
stud, studded, studding
student
studie — study
studied
studio, -dios
studious, -ly
studius — studious
study, studies
study, studied, studying
stuf — stuff
stuff, -ed, -ing
stuffily
stuffy, -fier, -fiest
stufy — stuffy
stuko — stucco
stultifie — stultify
stultify, -fied, -fying
stumble, -bled, -bling
stumbul — stumble
stump, -ed, -ing
stump-jump plough
stun, stunned, stunning
stunner
stunt, -ed, -ing
stuntman, -men
stupefie — stupefy
stupefy, -fied, -fying
stupendous, -ly
stupendus — stupendous
stupid, -ly
stupidity, -ties
stupify — stupefy
stupor
sturdie — sturdy
sturdily
sturdy, -dier, -diest
sturgeon
sturgun — sturgeon
sturling — sterling
sturn — stern
stuter — stutter
stutter, -ed, -ing
stutterer
stuward — steward
St Vitus dance
sty, sties
style (type)
style — stile (steps)
stylish, -ly
stylist
stylistic, -ally
stymie, -mied, -mieing
styptic

suage	sewage
suave, -ly	
suavity, -ties	
sub, subbed, subbing	
subaltern	
subcomitee	subcommittee
subcommittee	
subconscious, -ly	
subconshus	subconscious
subcontinent	
subcontract, -ed, -ing	
subcontractor	
subculture	
subcutaneous, -ly	
subdivide, -vided, -viding	
subdivishun	subdivision
subdivision	
subdue, -dued, -duing	
subeditor	
suberb	suburb
suberban	suburban
subgigate	subjugate
subgroup	
subheading	
subjecshun	subjection
subject, -ed, -ing	
subjection	
subjective, -ly	
subjectivity	
sub judice	
subjugate, -gated, -gating	
subjugation	
subjunctive	
sublimate, -mated, -mating	
sublimation	
sublime, -limed, -liming	
subliminal, -ly	
sublimity, -ties	
sublimminal	subliminal
submarine	
submerge, -merged, -merging	
submishun	submission
submission	
submissive, -ly	
submit, -mitted, -mitting	
submurge	submerge
subnormal, -ly	
subordinate, -nated, -nating	
subordination	
suborn, -ed, -ing	
subpena	subpoena
subpoena, -naed, -naing	
subscribe, -ribed, -ribing	
subscriber	
subscription	
subsection	
subsekwent	subsequent
subsequent, -ly	
subservience	
subservient, -ly	
subset	
subside, -sided, -siding	
subsidence	
subsidie	subsidy
subsidise, -dised, -dising	
subsidy, -dies	
subsist, -ed, -ing	
subsistence	
subsistense	subsistence
subsistent, -ly	
subsoil	
substance	
substandard	
substanshul	substantial
substantial, -ly	
substantiate, -ated, -ating	
substation	
substitute, -tuted, -tuting	
subtefuge	subterfuge
subterfuge	
subterranean	
subtitle, -tled, -tling	
subtitul	subtitle
subtle, -tly	
subtlety, -ties	
subtracshun	subtraction
subtraction	
subtropical	
suburb	
suburban	
suburbia	
subversion	
subversive	
subvert, -ed, -ing	

subway
succeed, -ed, -ing
success
successful, -ly
succession
successive, -ly
successor
succinct, -ly
succour, -ed, -ing (aid)
succulent, -ly
succumb, -ed, -ing
such
suchure — suture
suck, -ed, -ing
sucker (dupe)
suckshun — suction
suckulent — succulent
suckum — succumb
sucrose
sucsede — succeed
sucseshun — succession
sucses — success
sucseser — successor
sucsesful — successful
sucsint — succinct
suction
sudden, -ly
suds
sue, sued, suing
suede
suer — sewer
suet (meat)
sufer — suffer
suffer, -ed, -ing
sufferance
sufferanse — sufferance
suffice, -ficed, -ficing
sufficiency
sufficient, -ly
suffiks — suffix
suffishensy — sufficiency
suffix
suffocate, -cated, -cating
suffocation
suffrage
suffragette
suffuse, -fused, -fusing

suffusion
sufocashun — suffocation
sufocate — suffocate
sufrajet — suffragette
sufrance — sufferance
sufrige — suffrage
sufuse — suffuse
sugar
sugary
sugeschun — suggestion
sugest — suggest
suggest, -ed, -ing
suggestive, -ly
suicidal
suicide, -cided, -ciding
suiside — suicide
suit, -ed, -ing (clothes)
suit — suet (meat)
suitability
suitable, -bly
suitcase
suite (rooms)
suiter — suitor
suitor
sulk, -ed, -ing
sulky, sulkier, sulkiest
sullage
sullen, -ly
sully, -lied, -lying
sulphur
sulphuric
sultan
sultana
sultrie — sultry
sultriness
sultry, -trier, -triest
sum, summed, summing (total)
sum — some (few)
sumbody — somebody
sumhow — somehow
summarine — submarine
summarise, -rised, -rising
summary, -ries (short)
summary (warm) — summery
summation
summer

summerhouse
summerise | summarise
summery (warm)
summery (short) | summary
summit
summon, -ed, -ing (call)
summons, -monses (court)
sumo
sums
sump
sumptuous, -ly
sun, sunned, sunning (star)
sun | son (boy)
sun inlaw | son-in-law
sunbake, -baked, -baking
sunburn, -ed, -ing
sundae (ice-cream)
Sunday (day)
sundeck
sunder, -ed, -ing
sundial
sundown
sundowner
sundries
sundry, -rily
sunfish, -fishes, -fish
sunflower
sung
sunglasses
sunk
sunken
sunlamp
sunny, -nier, -niest
sunshine
sunspot
sunstroke
suntan, -tanned, -tanning
sup, supped, supping
super
superannuate, -ated, -ating
superannuation
superb, -ly
supercharge, -charged, -charging
supercilious, -ly
superficial, -ly
superfishul | superficial
superfluity, -ties
superfluous, -ly
superfosfate | superphosphate
superhuman, -ly
superimpose, -posed, -posing
superintendent
superior, -ly
superiority
superlative, -ly
superman, -men
supermarket
supernatural, -ly
supernumerary, -aries
superphosphate
superpower
supersaturate, -rated, -rating
supersede, -seded, -seding
supersonic
superstructure
supervise, -vised, -vising
supervishun | supervision
supervision
supervisor
supervisory
supervisry | supervisory
supine, -ly
suple | supple
suplement | supplement
suport | support
suposition | supposition
supper
supplant, -ed, -ing
supple, -pler, -plest
supplement
supplementation
supplementary
suppliant, -ly
supplier
supply, -plied, -plying
support, -ed, -ing
supporter
supposable, -bly
supposabul | supposable
suppose, -posed, -posing
supposition
suppository, -ries
suppress, -ed, -ing

suppression
suppressive
suppurate, -rated, -rating
suppuration
supremacy
supremasy   supremacy
supreme, -ly
supres   suppress
supreshun   suppression
suprintend   superintend
supul   supple
sur   sir
surcharge, -charged, -charging
surcingle

For other surc- words, look under circ- .

sure, -ly (certain)
sure   shore (sea)
sureptishus   surreptitious
surety, -ties
surf, -ed, -ing (sea)
surf   serf (slave)
surface, -faced, -facing
surfboard
surfeet   surfeit
surfeit, -ed, -ing
surfer
surfie
surfis   surface
surge, surged, surging
surgen   surgeon
surgeon
surgery, -geries
surgical, -ly
surly, -lier, -liest
surly   surely
surmise, -mised, -mising
surmount, -ed, -ing
surname
surogat   surrogate
surpass, -ed, -ing
surplice (garment)
surplis   surplice
surplus (extra)
surprise, -prised, -prising
surrealism
surrealist
surrender, -ed, -ing
surreptishus   surreptitious
surreptitious, -ly
surrogate
surround, -ed, -ing
surtaks   surtax
surtax
surveillance
survey, -veys
surveyor
survival
survive, -vived, -viving
survivor
susceptibility
susceptible, -bly
suspect, -ed, -ing
suspend, -ed, -ing
suspender
suspense
suspicion
suspicious, -ly
suspishun   suspicion
sustain, -ed, -ing
sustayn   sustain
sustenance
sustenanse   sustenance
sut   soot
sutable   suitable
suter   suitor
suthen   southern
sutlety   subtlety
sutul   subtle
suture, -tured, -turing
swab, swabbed, swabbing
swaddle, -dled, -dling
swade   suede
swag
swagger, swaggered, swaggering
swagman, -men
swain
swallow, -ed, -ing
swam
swamp, -ed, -ing
swampy, -pier, -piest
swan
swank, -ed, -ing

swap, swapped, swapping
sware swear
swarm, -ed, -ing
swarthy, -thier, -thiest
swashbuckler
swastika
swat, swatted, swatting
swathe, swathed, swathing
sway, -ed, -ing
swear, swore, sworn, swearing
sweat, -ed, -ing
sweater
sweatshop
swede
sweep, swept, sweeping
sweeper
sweepstake
sweet, -ly (taste)
sweet suite (rooms)
sweetbread
sweeten, -ed, -ing
sweetener
sweethart sweetheart
sweetheart
swell, swelled, swollen, swelling
swelter, -ed, -ing
swerve, swerved, swerving
swet sweat
sweter sweater
swich switch
swift, -ly
swill, -ed, -ing
swim, swam, swum, swimming
swimmer
swimsuit
swindle, -dled, -dling
swindul swindle
swine
swing, swung, swinging
swipe, swiped, swiping
swirl, -ed, -ing
swish, -ed, -ing
switch, -ed, -ing
switchboard
swivel, -elled, -elling
swob swab
swollen
swollow swallow
swomp swamp
swoon, -ed, -ing
swoop, -ed, -ing
sword
swordfish
sworm swarm
sworn
swot, swotted, swotting
swum
swurl swirl
swurve swerve
syanide cyanide
sybarite
sybaritic, -ally
sycamore
sycedelic psychedelic
syche psyche
syciatrist psychiatrist
syciatry psychiatry
sycick psychic
syclone cyclone
sycoanalise psychoanalyse
sycoanalisis psychoanalysis
sycofant sycophant
sycological psychological
sycologist psychologist
sycology psychology
sycophant
sycophantic, -ally
sycosis psychosis
sycotherapist psychotherapist
sycotherapy psychotherapy
sycotic psychotic
Sydney
Sydneysider
syfilis syphilis
sygnet cygnet
sylable syllable
sylf sylph
sylinder cylinder
syllabic, -ally
syllable
syllabus, -buses, -bi
syllogise, -gised, -gising
syllogism
syllogistic, -ally

sylph
sylvan
sylvun sylvan
symbiosis
symbiotic, -ally
symbol (sign)
symbol cymbal (music)
symbolic, -ally
symbolise, -lised, -lising
symbolism
symbolist
symfony symphony
symmetrical, -ly
symmetry, -tries
sympathetic, -ally
sympathey sympathy
sympathise, -ised, -ising
sympathiser
symphonic
symphony, -nies
symposium, -siums, -sia
symptom
symptomatic
synagog synagogue
synagogue
synanym synonym
synchromesh
synchronisation
synchronise, -nised, -nising
synchronous, -ly
synchronus synchronous
syncopate, -pated, -pating
syncopation
syndical
syndicalism
syndicate, -cated, -cating
syndication
syndrome
synic cynic
synical cynical
synod
synodal
synonimus synonymous
synonym
synonymous, -ly
synopsis, -ses
synoptic, -ally
syntactical, -ly
syntaks syntax
syntax
synthesis, -ses
synthesise, -ised, -ising
synthesiser
synthetic, -ally
sypher cipher
syphilis
syphilitic
syphon, -ed, -ing
syringe, -ringed, -ringing
syrup
syrupy
system
systematic
systematical, -ly
systematisation
systematise, -tised, -tising
systemic, -ally
systole
sythe scythe
Szechuan
Szechwan

Tt

tab, tabbed, tabbing
tabacco — tobacco
tabard
tabasco
tabasko — tabasco
tabby, -bies
tabel — table
tabie — tabby
table, -bled, -bling
tableau, -leaux, -leaus
tablespoon
tablespoonful, -fuls
tablet
tablit — tablet
tablo — tableau
tabloid
tabloyd — tabloid
taboo, -boos
taboo, -booed, -booing
tabul — table
tabular
tabulate, -lated, -lating
tabulation
taby — tabby
tachometer
tacit, -ly
taciturn
tack, -ed, -ing
tackie — tacky
tackle, -led, -ling
tackler
tackometer — tachometer
tackul — tackle
tacky, -kier, -kiest
taco
tact
tactic
tactical, -ly
tactician
tactics
tactile
tactyle — tactile
tadpole
taffeta
tafita — taffeta
tag, tagged, tagging
tail (end)
tail — tale (story)
tailgate
tailor, -ed, -ing
tailor-made
taint, -ed, -ing
taipan
take, took, taken, taking
takeover
taks — tax
taksation — taxation
taksi — taxi
talc
talcum powder
tale (story)
tale — tail (end)
talent
talented
talie — tally
talisman, -mans
talk, -ed, -ing
talk — talc
talkative, -ly
talkback
tall
tallboy
tallow
tallowwood
tally, -lies (score)
tally, -lied, -lying (score)
tally — telly (T.V.)
Talmud
talon
talor — tailor
talow — tallow
tamale
tamarind
tamborine — tambourine
tambourine

tame, tamed, taming
tame, tamer, tamest
tameable
tam-o'-shanter
tamper, -ed, -ing
tampon
tan, tanned, tanning
tanbark
tandem
tang
tangenshul — tangential
tangent
tangential, -ly
tangerine
tangible, -bly
tangibul — tangible
tangle, -gled, -gling
tango, -gos
tango, -goed, -going
tangul — tangle
tanjent — tangent
tank
tankard
tanker
tannin
tantalise, -lised, -lising
tantamount
tantamownt — tantamount
tantrum
tap, tapped, tapping
tap-dancing
tape, taped, taping
taper, -ed, -ing
tape-recorder
tapestry, -tries
tapeworm
tapioca
tapistry — tapestry
tappet
taproot
tar, tarred, tarring
tarantella (dance)
tarantula (spider)
tardie — tardy
tardily
tardy, -dier, -diest
tare (weight)
tare — tear (rip)
target
targit — target
tarie — tarry
tarif — tariff
tariff
tarmac
tarnation
tarnish, -ed, -ing
tarot
tarow — tarot
tarpaulin
tarpollun — tarpaulin
tarragon
tarrif — tariff
tarry, ries
tarry, -ried, -rying
tartan
tartar
tartare sauce
tarter — tartar
tartily
tarty
tasit — tacit
tasiturn — taciturn
task
taskmaster
tassel, tasselled, tasselling
tassul — tassel
taste, tasted, tasting
tastebud
tasteful, -ly
tasty, -tier, -tiest
tatoo — tattoo
tattle, -led, -ling
tattoo, -toos
tattoo, -tooed, -tooing
tattul — tattle
tatty
taudry — tawdry
taught (teach)
taught — taut (tight)
taught — tort (law)
taunt, -ed, -ing
Taurus
taut, -ly (tight)
taut — taught (teach)

taut	tort (law)
tautological, -ly	
tautology, -gies	
taven	tavern
tavern	
tawdrily	
tawdry, -drier, -driest	
tawny, -nier, -niest	
tax, taxed, taxing	
taxable	
taxabul	taxable
taxation	
tax-deductible	
taxi, taxis	
taxi, taxied, taxiing	
taxicab	
taxidermy	
taxie	taxi
taxonomy, -mies	
tea (drink)	
tea	tee (golf)
teach, taught, teaching	
teachable, -ably	
teachabul	teachable
teacher	
tea-chest	
teacup	
teal	
team, -ed, -ing (group)	
team	teem (rain)
teamster	
teapot	
tear (crying)	
tear, tore, torn, tearing (rip)	
tear	tare (weight)
tear	tier (row)
tearful, -ly	
tearjerker	
tease, teased, teasing	
teaspoon	
teat	
teath	teeth (noun)
teathe	teethe
tea-tree	
tech	teach
techer	teacher
technical, -ly	
technicality, -ties	
technician	
technicolour	
technique	
technocracy	
technological, -ly	
technologist	
technology	
tecneek	technique
tecnical	technical
tecnicality	technicality
tecnishun	technician
tecnocrasy	technocracy
tecnology	technology
tedious, -ly	
tee, teed, teeing (golf)	
tee	tea (drink)
teech	teach
teek	teak
teel	teal
teem, -ed, -ing (rain)	
teem	team (group)
teenager	
teese	tease
tee-shirt	
teet	teat
teeter, -ed, -ing	
teeth (noun)	
teethe, teethed, teething	
teetotal, -ly	
teetotaller	
teflon	
tekneek	technique
teknical	technical
teknicality	technicality
teknicolor	technicolour
teknishun	technician
teknocrasy	technocracy
teknology	technology
tekst	text
tekstile	textile
teksture	texture
telecast, -ed, -ing	
telecommunication	
telefone	telephone
telefonist	telephonist
telefoto	telephoto

telegraf	telegraph
telegram	
telegraphic	
telegraphist	
telegraphy	
teleks	telex
telepathic	
telepathist	
telepathy	
telephone, -phoned, -phoning	
telephonic, -ally	
telephonist	
telephoto lens	
teleprinter	
telescope, -coped, -coping	
televise, -vised, -vising	
televishun	television
television	
telex	
telifone	telephone
telifonist	telephonist
teligram	telegram
teliphoto	telephoto
teliscope	telescope
telivise	televise
telivishun	television
tell, told, telling	
teller	
telltale	
telly, tellies (T.V.)	
temerity	
temper, -ed, -ing	
tempera	
temperament	
temperamental, -ly	
temperance	
temperanse	temperance
temperate, -ly	
Temperate Zone	
temperature	
tempest	
tempestuous, -ly	
tempestuus	tempestuous
template	
temple	
templut	template
tempo, -pos	
temporal, -ly	
temporarily	
temporary	
temporise, -rised, -rising	
tempory	temporary
temprament	temperament
tempratcher	temperature
tempremental	temperamental
tempt, -ed, -ing	
temptation	
tempter	
temtation	temptation
tenable, -bly	
tenabul	tenable
tenacious, -ly	
tenancy	
tenansy	tenancy
tenant	
tend, -ed, -ing	
tendency, -cies	
tendenshus	tendentious
tendentious, -ly	
tender, -ed, -ing	
tenderfoot, -foots, -feet	
tenderly	
tendon	
tendril	
tenement	
tenet	
teniment	tenement
tenis	tennis
tennis	
tenon	
tenor	
tenpin bowling	
tense, tensed, tensing	
tense, tenser, tensest	
tenshun	tension
tension	
tent	
tentacle	
tentative, -ly	
tenterhook	
tenth	
tenuous, -ly	
tenure	
tenuus	tenuous

tenyer tenure
tepee
tepid, -ly
teracota terracotta
terain terrain
terarium terrarium
terazo terrazzo
terban turban
terbid turbid
terbine turbine
terbo turbo
terbulent turbulent
terf turf
tergid turgid
teribul terrible
terier terrier
terific terrific
terifie terrify
teritry territory
terjid turgid
terkey turkey
terkwoise turquoise
term
termagant
terminable, -ly
terminabul terminable
terminal, -ally
terminate, -nated, -nating
termination
terminology, -gies
terminus, -ni, -nuses
termite
termoil turmoil
tern (bird)
tern turn (move)
ternip turnip
teror terror
terorist terrorist
terpentine turpentine
terpitude turpitude
terrace, -raced, -racing
terracotta
terrain
terrarium, -rariums, -raria
terrazzo
terrestrial, -ly
terrible, -bly

terribul terrible
terrier
terrific, -ally
terrify, -fied, -fying
terrine
territorial, -ly
territory, -ries
terror
terrorise, -rised, -rising
terrorism
terrorist
terse, terser, tersest
tersely
tertiary, -ries
tertle turtle
terylene
teselate tessellate
teselation tessellation
tespoon teaspoon
tessellate, -ated, -ating
tessellation
test, -ed, -ing
testament
testicle
testicul testicle
testifie testify
testify, -fied, -fying
testimonial
testimony, -nies
testis, testes
test-tube
testy, -tier, -tiest
tetanus
tete-a-tete
tether, -ed, -ing
tetragon
tetrahedron, -drons, -dra
texchur texture
text
textbook
textile
textual, -ly
texture, -tured, -turing
thach thatch
thalidomide
than
thank, -ed, -ing

Word	Correct spelling
thankful, -ly	
thankless, -ly	
thanksgiving	
that, those	
that's (that is)	
thats	that's
thatch, -ed, -ing	
thaw, -ed, -ing	
thay	they
theater	theatre
theatre	
theatrical, -ly	
theft	
their (possessive)	
their	there (at that place)
theirs (possessive)	
theirs	there's (there is)
theism	
theist	
theistic, -ally	
theif	thief
theives	thieves
theiving	thieving
thematic, -ally	
theme	
themselves	
then	
thence	
thense	thence
theocracy, -cies	
theocrasy	theocracy
theocrat	
theodolite	
theological, -ly	
theologian	
theology, -gies	
theolojun	theologian
theorem	
theoretic	
theoretical, -ly	
theorise, -rised, -rising	
theorist	
theorm	theorem
theory, -ries	
theosofie	theosophy
theosophical, -ly	
theosophist	
theosophy	
therapeutic, -ally	
therapey	therapy
therapist	
therapy, -pies	
therd	third
there (at that place)	
there	their (possessive)
there	they're (they are)
thereabouts	
thereby	
therefore	
therem	theorem
therein	
thereof	
thereon	
there's (there is)	
theres	theirs (possessive)
theres	there's (there is)
theretic	theoretic
thereticul	theoretical
therey	theory
thereupon	
therewith	
therise	theorise
therist	theorist
therm	
thermal, -ly	
thermodynamic, -ally	
thermometer	
thermometrical, -ly	
thermonuclear	
thermoplastic	
thermos	
thermostat	
thermostatic, -ally	
Thersday	Thursday
therst	thirst
thersty	thirsty
therteen	thirteen
therty	thirty

thesaurus, -sauri	
these	
thesis, -ses	
thesorus	thesaurus
Thespian	
they'd (they had)	
theyd	they'd
they'll (they will)	
theyll	they'll
they're (they are)	
theyre	they're
they've (they have)	
theyve	they've
thi	thigh
thick, -ly	
thicken, -ed, -ing	
thickener	
thicket	
thickhead	
thickness	
thickset	
thickskinned	
thief, thieves	
thieve, thieved, thieving	
thievish, -ly	
thigh	
thimble	
thimbul	thimble
thime	thyme
thin, thinned, thinning	
thin, thinner, thinnest	
thine	
thiner	thinner
thing	
thingamajig	
think, thought, thinking	
think-tank	
thinly	
thinner	
thinness	
third, -ly	
third-degree	
thirm	therm
thiroid	thyroid
thirst, -ed, -ing	
thirstily	
thirsty, -tier, -tiest	
thirteen	
thirteenth	
thirtie	thirty
thirtieth	
thirty, -ties	
this, these	
thisis	thesis
thisle	thistle
thisorus	thesaurus
thistle	
thistledown	
thisul	thistle
thitha	thither
thither	
tho	though
thong	
thor	thaw
thoraks	thorax
thorax, thoraces, thoraxes	
thorn	
thorny, -nier, -niest	
thorough, -ly (absolute)	
thorough	through (pass)
thoroughbred	
thoroughfare	
thort	thought
those	
thou (you)	
though (but)	
thought (did think)	
thoughtful, -ly	
thoughtless, -ly	
thousand	
thousandth	
thowsand	thousand
thrall	
thrash, -ed, -ing	
thread, -ed, -ing	
threat	
threaten, -ed, -ing	
thred	thread
three	
three-dimensional	
threepence	
three-quarter	
threesome	
thresh, -ed, -ing	

threshold	
thret	threat
threw (did throw)	
threw	through (between)
threwout	throughout
thrice	
thrift	
thrifty, -tier, -tiest	
thrill, -ed, -ing	
thriller	
thrips, thrips	
thrise	thrice
thrive, throve, thrived, thriving	
thro' (through)	
throat	
throb, throbbed, throbbing	
throe (spasm)	
throe	throw (toss)
thrombosis, -oses	
throne (chair)	
throne	thrown (tossed)
throng, -ed, -ing	
throo	threw (tossed)
throo	through (between)
throte	throat
throttle, -tled, -tling	
throttul	throttle
through (pass)	
through	thorough (absolute)
through	threw (tossed)
throughout	
throve	
throw, threw, thrown, throwing (toss)	
throw	throe (spasm)
throwaway society	
thrown (tossed)	
thrown	throne (chair)
thrum, thrummed, thrumming	
thrush	
thrust, thrust, thrusting	
thud, thudded, thudding	
thug	
thuggery	
thuggish, -ly	
thum	thumb
thumb, -ed, -ing	
thump, -ed, -ing	
thunder, -ed, -ing	
thunderbolt	
thunderclap	
thunderous, -ly	
thunderstruck	
thundery	
thundrus	thunderous
thurer	thorough
thurerbred	thoroughbred
thurerfare	thoroughfare

For thurm- words, look under **therm-** .

Thursday	
thurst	thirst
thurteen	thirteen
thurty	thirty
thus	
thwart, -ed, -ing	
thwort	thwart
thyme (plant)	
thyroid	
tiara	
tibia, tibiae, tibias	
tic (twitch)	
tick, -ed, -ing (sound)	
ticker	
ticket	
tickle, -led, -ling	
ticklish	
tickul	tickle
ticoon	tycoon
tic-tac	
tidal	
tiddler	
tiddlywinks	
tide, tided, tiding (ocean)	
tide	tied (bound)
tidie	tidy
tidily	
tidings	
tidul	tidal
tidy, tidied, tidying	
tidy, tidier, tidiest	

tie, tied, tying
tier, (row)
  tier tear (crying)
  tier tire (weary)
  tier tyre (wheel)
  tif tiff
tiff
tiffin
  tifoid typhoid
  tifoon typhoon
  tifus typhus
tiger
  tigeress tigress
tight, -ly
tighten, -ed, -ing
tightrope
tights
tigress
tiki
tile, tiled, tiling
till, -ed, -ing
tiller
tilt, -ed, -ing
timber, -ed, -ing (wood)
timbre (sound)
timbrel
  timbrul timbrel
time, timed, timing (clock)
  time thyme (plant)
timekeeper
timeless, -ly
timely, -lier, -liest
timepiece
timetable
timid, -ly
timidity
timorous, -ly
  timorus timorous
timpano, -ni
tin, tinned, tinning
  tinchur tincture
tincture, -tured, -turing
tinder
tinderbox
tine
tinea
tinge, tinged, tingeing
tingle, tingled, tingling
  tingul tingle
  tinie tiny
tinker, -ed, -ing
tinkle, -led, -ling
  tinkture tincture
  tinkul tinkle
tinny, -nier, -niest
tin-pot
tinsel, -selled, -selling
tinselly
  tinsul tinsel
tint, -ed, -ing
tintack
tiny, tinier, tiniest
tip, tipped, tipping
  tipe type
  tipewriter typewriter
  tipical typical
  tipify typify
  tipist typist
  tipografy typography
tipple, -led, -ling
tipsily
tipsy, -sier, -siest
tiptoe, -toed, -toeing
tiptop
  tipul tipple
tirade
  tiranical tyrannical
  tiranise tyrannise
  tirant tyrant
  tiranus tyrannous
  tirany tyranny
tire, tired, tiring (weary)
  tire tier (row)
  tire tyre (wheel)
tiresome
  tiresum tiresome
'tis (it is)
  tis 'tis (it is)
  tis tizz (anxiety)
  tishoo tissue
tissue, -sued, -suing
tit
titan
titanic

titavation titivation
titbit
tite tight
titen tighten
tites tights
tithe, tithed, tithing
titian
titillate, -lated, -lating
titillation
titivate, -vated, -vating
titivation
title, -tled, -tling (name)
titrate, -trated, -trating
titter, -ed, -ing
tittillate titillate
tittle (dot)
tittle-tattle, -tled, -tling
titul title
titular
tizz (anxiety)
to (towards)
to too (also)
to two (number)
toad
toadfish
toadstool
toady, toadies
toady, toadied, toadying
toast, -ed, -ing
toaster
toastmaster
toastmistress
tobacco
tobacconist
tobaco tobacco
tobogan toboggan
toboggan
tobogganist
tocsic toxic
tocsin (alarm)
tocsin toxin (poison)
today
toddle, -dled, -dling
toddler
toddy, -dies
tode toad
todler toddler
todstool toadstool
todul toddle
tody toddy
toe, toed, toeing (foot)
toe tow (pull)
toey
tofee toffee
toff
toffee (sweet)
toffy (rich)
tog, togged, togging
together
togetherness
toggle, -gled, -gling
toggul toggle
toheroa
toi toy
toil, -ed, -ing
toilet
toiletrain toilet-train
toiletry, -tries
toilet-train
token
toksic toxic
toksin tocsin (alarm)
toksin toxin (poison)
tol toll
told
tole toll
tolerable, -bly
tolerance
toleranse tolerance
tolerant, -ly
tolerate, -rated, -rating
tolerense tolerance
toll, -ed, -ing
tolrabul tolerable
tomahawk
tomahork tomahawk
tomarto tomato
tomato, -toes
tomb
tomboy
tombstone
tome
tomfoolery
tomorow tomorrow

Word	Correct spelling
tomorrer	tomorrow
tomorrow	
ton	
tonal, -ly	
tongs	
tongue, tongued, tonguing	
tongue-tied	
tongue-twister	
tonic	
tonight	
tonite	tonight
tonnage	
tonne	
tonnige	tonnage
tonsher	tonsure
tonsil	
tonsillectomy, -mies	
tonsillitis	
tonsure, -sured, -suring	
too (also)	
too	to (towards)
too	two (number)
took	
tool, -ed, -ing	
toom	tomb
toomstone	tombstone
toon	tune
toor	tour
toot, -ed, -ing	
tooth, teeth	
toothache	
toothake	toothache
toothbrush, -brushes	
toothcomb	
toothless	
toothpaste	
toothy, -thier, -thiest	
tootle, -tled, -tling	
tootul	tootle
top, topped, topping	
topas	topaz
topaz	
topic	
topical, -ly	
topknot	
topless, -ly	
topmast	

Word	Correct spelling
topografer	topographer
topografy	topography
topper	
topple, -pled, -pling	
toppul	topple
topsail	
topside	
topsoil	
topsy-turvy	
tor (hill)	
tor	tore (ripped)
tor	tour (trip)
torch	
torcher	torture
torchlight	
torchlite	torchlight
tore (ripped)	
tore	tour (trip)
toreador	
torent	torrent
torid	torrid
torism	tourism
torment, -ed, -ing	
tormenter	tormentor
tormentor	
torn	
tornado, -does, -dos	
tornament	tournament
torney	tawny
tornt	taunt
torpedo, -does	
torpedo, -doed, -doing	
torper	torpor
torpid, -ly	
torpidity	
torpor	
torque	
torrenshul	torrential
torrent	
torrential, -ly	
torrid, -ly	
torshun	torsion
torsion, -ally	
torso, -sos	
tort (law)	
tort	taught (teach)
tort	taut (tight)

Word	Correct spelling
tortilla	
tortoise	
tortoiseshell	
tortology	tautology
tortuous, -ly	
torture, -tured, -turing	
torturer	
tortus	tortoise
tortuus	tortuous
toss, tossed, tossing	
toss-up	
tost	toast
tot, totted, totting	
total, -talled, -talling	
totalisator	
totalitarianism	
totality, -ties	
totally	
tote, toted, toting	
totem	
toter	totter
totter, -ed, -ing	
tottery	
totul	total
touch, -ed, -ing (feel)	
touchdown	
touché (good point)	
touchily	
touchline	
touchstone	
touch-type, -typed, -typing	
touchy, -chier, -chiest	
tough, -ly	
toughen, -ed, -ing	
toupee	
tour, -ed, -ing (trip)	
tour	tor (hill)
tour	tore (ripped)
tourer	
tourism	
tourist	
tournament	
tournikay	tourniquet
tourniquet	
tousle, -sled, -sling	
tout, -ed, -ing	
tow, -ed, -ing (pull)	
tow	toe (foot)
toward	
towards	
towel, -elled, -elling	
tower, -ed, -ing	
towl	towel
town	
town-planner	
township	
towring	towering
towsl	tousle
towt	tout
toxic, -ally	
toxicity	
toxin (poison)	
toxin	tocsin (alarm)
toy, -ed, -ing	
toyl	toil
toylet	toilet
trace, traced, tracing	
tracer	
tracery, -ries	
trachea, tracheae	
trachoma	
track, -ed, -ing	
trackshun	traction
tracksuit	
tract	
tractable, -bly	
tracter	tractor
traction	
tractor	
trade, traded, trading	
trade-in	
trademark	
trader	
tradesman, -men	
tradeswoman, -women	
tradishun	tradition
tradition	
traditional, -ly	
traduce, -duced, -ducing	
traducer	
traduse	traduce
traffic, -ficked, -ficking	
trafficable	
trafficator	

trafficker
trafic traffic
tragedian
tragedienne
tragedy, -dies
tragic
tragical, -ly
tragicomedy, -dies
trail, -ed, -ing
trailblazer
trailer
train, -ed, -ing
trainee
trainer
traipse, traipsed, traipsing
trait
traiter traitor
traitor
traitorous, -ly
traitrous traitorous
trajectory, -ries
trajectry trajectory
trajedy tragedy
trakia trachea
trakshun traction
tram, trammed, tramming
tramcar
tramline
trammel, -melled, -melling
tramp, -ed, -ing
trample, -pled, -pling
trampoline, -lined, -lining
trampul trample
tramul trammel
trance, tranced, trancing
trane train
trankwil tranquil
trankwility tranquillity
tranquil, -ly
tranquilliser
tranquillity
transact, -ed, -ing
transaction
transactor
transceiver
transcend, -ed, -ing
transcendent
transcendental, -ally
transcribe, -scribed, -scribing
transducer
transe trance
transend transcend
transept
transfer, -ferred, -ferring
transferal
transference
transfigure, -ured, -uring
transfiks transfix
transfix, -ed, -ing
transform, -ed, -ing
transformation
transformer
transfuse, -fused, -fusing
transfusion
transgress, -ed, -ing
transgression
transgressor
transient, -ly
transishun transition
transister transistor
transistor
transit, -sited, -siting
transition
transitional, -ly
transitory
translate, -lated, -lating
translation
translator
translucent, -ly
transmigrate, -grated, -grating
transmigration
transmigratory
transmishun transmission
transmission
transmit, -mitted, -mitting
transmitter
transom
transparency, -cies
transparensy transparency
transparent, -ly
transperant transparent
transpire, -spired, -spiring
transplant, -ed, -ing
transplantation

transport, -ed, -ing
transporter
transportation
transpose, -posed, -posing
transsexual
transversal, -ly
transverse, -versed, -versing
transvestism
transvestite
trap, trapped, trapping
trapdoor
trapeze
trapezium, -zuims, -zia
trapper
trappings
trapse — traipse
trase — trace
trash
trashy, trashier, trashiest
trate — trait
trater — traitor
traterus — traitorous
trauma, -mata, -mas
traumatic
travail, -ed, -ing (labour)
travale — travail
travel, -elled, -elling (tour)
traveller
travelog — travelogue
travelogue
traverse, -versed, -versing
travesty, -ties
travesty, -tied, -tying
trawl, -ed, -ing
trawler
trawma — trauma
trawmatic — traumatic
treacherous, -ly
treachery, -eries
treacle
tread, trod, trodden, treading
treadle, -dled, -dling
treadmill
treason
treasonable, -bly
treasonous, -ly
treasonus — treasonous

treasure, -ured, -uring
treasurer
treasure-trove
treasury, -uries
treat, -ed, -ing
treatable
treatise
treatiss — treatise
treatment
treaty, -ties
treble, -bled, -bling
trebul — treble
trecherus — treacherous
trechery — treachery
tred — tread
tree
treecul — treacle
treet — treat
treetis — treatise
treetment — treatment
treety — treaty
trefoil
trek, trekked, trekking
trekker
trellis
tremble, -bled, -bling
trembly, -blier, -bliest
trembul — tremble
tremendous, -ly
tremendus — tremendous
tremer — tremor
tremolo, -los
tremor
tremulous, -ly
tremulus — tremulous
trench, -ed, -ing
trenchant, -ly
trend
trendiness
trendy, -dier, -diest
treo — trio
trepidation
treshure — treasure
treshury — treasury
treson — treason
trespass, -ed, -ing
trespasser

tress
tressul — trestle
trestle
trevally
tri — try
triad
trial
triangel — triangle
triangle
triangul — triangle
triangular, -ly
tribal, -ly
tribalism
tribe
tribul — tribal
tribulation
tribunal
tribune
tributary, -ries
tribute
tributry — tributary
trice, triced, tricing
triceps
trick, -ed, -ing
trickery, -eries
trickle, -led, -ling
trickster
tricky, -kier, -kiest
tricolour
tricycle
trident
tried
triel — trial
triennial, -ly
triennium, -enniums, -ennia
trifecta
trifle, trifled, trifling
trifler
triful — trifle
trigger, -ed, -ing
trigonometrical, -ly
trigonometry
trilby, -bies
trillion
trilogy, -gies
trim, trimmed, trimming
trim, trimmer, trimmest

trimaran
trimester
trimmer
trinity, -ties
trinket
trio, trios
trip, tripped, tripping
tripartite
tripe
triple, -pled, -pling
triplet
triplicate, -cated, -cating
tripod
tripple — triple
triptick — triptych
triptych
tripul — triple
trise — trice
trisicul — tricycle
trite, triter, tritest
tritely
triumf — triumph
triumph
triumphal
triumphant, -ly
trivia
trivial, -ly
triviality, -ties
trod
trodden
troff — trough
trofy — trophy
troglodyte
troika
trolie — trolley
troll, -ed, -ing
trolley, -leys
trollop
trolop — trollop
troly — trolley
trombone
trombonist
troo — true
trooant — truant
trooly — truly
troop, -ed, -ing (soldier)
troop — troupe (band)

trooper
  troos — truce
  trooth — truth
  troothful — truthful
trophy, -phies
tropic
tropical, -ly
  trorma — trauma
  trormatic — traumatic
trot, trotted, trotting
troth
trotter
troubadour
trouble, -bled, -bling
troublemaker
troublesome, -ly
troubleshooter
trough
trounce, trounced, trouncing
troupe (band)
trousers
trousseau, -seaux, -seaus
trout
trowel, -elled, -elling
  trownce — trounce
  trowsers — trousers
  trowt — trout
truancy
  truansy — truancy
truant
  trubul — trouble
truce
truck, -ed, -ing
truckie
truculence
  truculense — truculence
truculent, -ly
trudge, trudged, trudging
true, truer, truest
true-blue
  truf — trough
truffle
  truful — truffle
  truge — trudge
truism
  trulie — truly
trump, -ed, -ing
trumpery, -ries
trumpet
trumpeter
truncate, -cated, -cating
truncheon
  trunchon — truncheon
trundle, -dled, -dling
  trundul — trundle
trunk
  truseau — trousseau
truss, -ed, -ing
trust, -ed, -ing
trustee
trustful, -ly
  trustwerthy — trustworthy
trustworthy
trusty, trustier, trustiest
truth
truthful, -ly
try, tries
try, tried, trying
  tryce — trice
  trycycle — tricycle
  trype — tripe
tryst
  tryte — trite
  tryumph — triumph
tsar
T-shirt
tuan
tub, tubbed, tubbing
tuba, -bas, -bae (instrument)
tubby, -bier, -biest
tube, tubed, tubing
tuber (plant)
tuberculosis
tuberculous
tubular
  tuch — touch
  tuchy — touchy
tuck, -ed, -ing
tucker
Tuesday
  tuf — tough
  tuffen — toughen
tuffet
tuft, -ed, -ing

Word	Correct spelling
tug, tugged, tugging	
tugboat	
tuishun	tuition
tuition	
tuk	tuck
tuksedo	tuxedo
tulip	
tulle	
tumble, -bled, -bling	
tumbler	
tumbleweed	
tumbul	tumble
tumer	tumour
tumescent	
tumour	
tumult	
tumultuous, -ly	
tumultuus	tumultuous
tuna (fish)	
tundra	
tune, tuned, tuning	
tuneful, -ly	
tuner (radio)	
tung	tongue
tungsten	
tunic	
tunige	tonnage
tunnel, -nelled, -nelling	
tunnul	tunnel
turban	
turbid, -ly	
turbine	
turbojet	
turboprop	
turbot, -bots, -bot	
turbulence	
turbulense	turbulence
turbulent, -ly	
tureen	
turet	turret
turf, turfs, turves	
turgid, -ly	
turgidity	
turjid	turgid
turkey, -keys	
Turkish	
turkwoise	turquoise
turm	term
turmeric	
turminabul	terminable
turminal	terminal
turminate	terminate
turminus	terminus
turmite	termite
turmoil	
turn, -ed, -ing (rotate)	
turn	tern (bird)
turncoat	
turnikay	tourniquet
turniket	tourniquet
turnip	
turnout	
turnover	
turnstile	
turntable	
turpentine	
turpitude	
turquoise	
turret	
turse	terse
turshury	tertiary
turtle	
turtledove	
turtleneck	
turtul	turtle
Tusday	Tuesday
tusk, -ed, -ing	
tussle, -sled, -sling	
tussock	
tusul	tussle
tutelage	
tutelige	tutelage
tuter	tutor
tutor	
tutorial	
tutoriul	tutorial
tutu	
tuxedo, -dos	
twaddle, -dled, -dling	
twain	
twang	
twangy	
tweak, -ed, -ing	
tweed	

tweek	tweak
tweet	
tweeter	
tweezers	
twelfth	
twelth	twelfth
twelve	
twentieth	
twenty, -ties	
twice	
twich	twitch
twiddle, -dled, -dling	
twidul	twiddle
twig, twigged, twigging	
twiggy	
twilight	
twilite	twilight
twill (fabric)	
'twill (it will)	
twill	'twill (it will)
twin, twinned, twinning	
twine, twined, twining	
twinge, twinged, twinging	
twinkle, -kled, -kling	
twinkul	twinkle
twin-set	
twirl, -ed, -ing	
twist, -ed, -ing	
twitch, -ed, -ing	
twitcher	
twitchy	
twitter, -ed, -ing	
two (number)	
two	to (towards)
two	too (also)
two-dimensional	
two-faced	
twopence	
twostep	
two-time, -timed, -timing	
two-tooth	
'twould (it would)	
twould	'twould
two-up	
twurl	twirl
tycoon	
tyfoid	typhoid
tyfoon	typhoon
tyfus	typhus
tympanic	
tympanum, -nums, -na	
type, typed, typing	
typecast, -cast, -casting	
typeface	
typescript	
typeset, -set, -setting	
typesetter	
typewriter	
typhoid	
typhoon	
typhus	
typical, -ly	
typify, -fied, -fying	
typist	
typographical, -ally	
typography	
tyranical	tyrannical
tyrannical, -ly	
tyrannise, -nised, -nising	
tyranny, -nies	
tyrant	
tyrany	tyranny
tyre (wheel)	
tyre	tire (weary)
tyro, -ros	
tzar	

Uu

ubikwity	ubiquity
ubiquitous, -ly	
ubiquity	
U-boat	
ubote	U-boat
uda	udder
udder	
ufologist	
ug	ugh
ug boot	
ugh	
uglee	ugly
ugliness	
ugly, -lier, -liest	
ugly duckling	
ukelele	
ukulele	
ulcer	
ulcerate, -rated, -rating	
ulceration	
ulcerous, -ly	
ullage, ullaged, ullaging	
ulsa	ulcer
ulserate	ulcerate
ulserayshun	ulceration
ulserus	ulcerous
ultamatum	ultimatum
ulteeria	ulterior
ultemo	ultimo
ulterior, -ly	
ultimate, -ly	
ultimatum, -tums, -ta	
ultimit	ultimate
ultimo	
ultra	
ultramareen	ultramarine
ultramarine	
ultrasound	
ultraviolet	
ululate, -lated, -lating	
umber	
umberella	umbrella
umbilical cord	
umbilicus, -bilici	
umbra, -brae	
umbrage	
umbrageous, -ly	
umbrella	
umbridge	umbrage
umpire, -pired, -piring	
umpyre	umpire
umpteen	
umpteenth	
unable	
unabul	unable
unaccompanied	
unaccountable, -bly	
unaccustomed	
unacustumed	unaccustomed
unakumpneed	unaccompanied
unanimity	
unanimous, -ly	
unanimus	unanimous
unapproachable, -bly	
unaprochibul	unapproachable
unassuming, -ly	
unattached	
unattended	
unatural	unnatural
unavailing, -ly	
unavaleing	unavailing
unaware	
unawares	
unawear	unaware
unbalance, -anced, -ancing	
unbecoming, -ly	
unbecuming	unbecoming
unbeknown	
unbeknownst	
unbeleif	unbelief
unbeleiver	unbeliever
unbeleiving	unbelieving
unbelief	
unbeliever	
unbelieving, -ly	

unbend, -bent or -bended, -bending	
unbenown	unbeknown
unblinking, -ly	
unblushing, -ly	
unborn	
unbosom, -ed, -ing	
unbounded, -ly	
unbownded	unbounded
unbrideld	unbridled
unbridled	
unburden, -ed, -ing	
uncalled-for	
uncanny, -nily	
unceremonious, -ly	
uncertain, -ly	
uncharitable, -ly	
uncharted	
uncircumcised	
uncle	
unclean, -ly	
uncomfortable, -ly	
unconfortibul	uncomfortable
uncommon, -ly	
uncommunicative, -ly	
uncomon	uncommon
uncompromising, -ly	
unconcerned, -ly	
uncondishunal	unconditional
unconditional, -ly	
unconnected, -ly	
unconscionable, -bly	
unconscious, -ly	
unconshunibul	unconscionable
unconshus	unconscious
unconstitutional, -ly	
unconventional, -ly	
uncooth	uncouth
uncouth, -ly	
uncover, -ed, -ing	
unction	
unctuous, -ly	
uncumftibul	uncomfortable
uncut	
uncuver	uncover
undaunted	
undecided	
undefined	
undemonstrative, -ly	
undeniable, -bly	
undeniabul	undeniable
under	
under-age	
underarm	
undercarriage	
undercarridge	undercarriage
underclose	underclothes
underclothes	
undercoat	
undercote	undercoat
undercover	
undercurent	undercurrent
undercurrent	
undercut, -cut, -cutting	
undercuver	undercover
underdeveloped	
underdeveloping	
underdevelopment	
underdevelopt	underdeveloped
underdog	
underdone	
underdun	underdone
underestamate	underestimate
underestimate, -mated, -mating	
underexpose, -exposed, -exposing	
underexposhur	underexposure
underexposure	
underexpows	underexpose
underfoot	
undergo, -went, -gone, -going	
undergraduate	
undergrajuate	undergraduate
undergroth	undergrowth
underground	
undergrowth	
underhand	
underite	underwrite
underlay, -laid, -laying	
underlie, -lay, -lain, -lying	
underlieing	underlying
underline, -lined, -lining	
underling	
underly	underlie
underlying	
undermine, -mined, -mining	

underneath	
underneeth	underneath
undernourish, -ed, -ing	
undernurish	undernourish
underpants	
underpass	
underpin, -pinned, -pinning	
underplay, -played, -playing	
underprivileged	
underproof	
underprufe	underproof
underscaw	underscore
underscore, -scored, -scoring	
undersecretary, -taries	
undersell, -sold, -selling	
undershot	
undersign	
undersine	undersign
understand, -stood, -standing	
understanding	
understait	understate
understate, -stated, -stating	
understatement	
understayt	understate
understood	
understudy, -studied, -studying	
undertaik	undertake
undertaiker	undertaker
undertake, -took, -taken, -taking	
undertaker	
under-the-counter	
undertoan	undertone
undertoe	undertow
undertone	
undertow	
underware	underwear
underwear	
underworld	
underwrite, -written, -writing	
undesirable, -bly	
undesiribul	undesirable
undeveloped	
undevelupt	undeveloped
undew	undue
undewlate	undulate
undewly	unduly
undo, -did, -done, -doing	
undoo	undo
undoubted, -ly	
undowted	undoubted
undress, -dressed, -dressing	
undue	
undulate, -lated, -lating	
undulation	
undulatory	
unduly	
undur	under
undying	
undyou	undue
unearned	
unearned income	
unearth, -ed, -ing	
unearthly	
uneasily	
uneasiness	
uneasy, -easier, -easiest	
unecessary	unnecessary
uneducated	
uneekwell	unequal
uneesy	uneasy
uneeven	uneven
unekwivacal	unequivocal
unemployed	
unemployment	
unequal, -ly	
uneque	unique
unequivocal, -ly	
unerring, -ly	
unesesary	unnecessary
uneven, -ly	
unevenness	
unfailing, -ly	
unfair, -ly	
unfaling	unfailing
unfare	unfair
unfamiliar, -ly	
unfamiliarity	
unfeeling, -ly	
unfemilyer	unfamiliar
unfinished	
unfit, -fitted, -fitting	
unflagging, -ly	
unflapibul	unflappable
unflappable, -bly	

unfold, -ed, -ing
unforchinate unfortunate
unforeseen
unforgettable
unformed
unforsean unforeseen
unfortunate, -ly
unfounded, -ly
unfowld unfold
unfownded unfounded
unfrock, -ed, -ing
unfurl, -ed, -ing
ungainliness
ungainly
unganely ungainly
ungarded unguarded
ungodliness
ungodly
ungracious, -ly
ungrashus ungracious
unguarded, -ly
unguent
ungulate
unhappily
unhappiness
unhappy, -pier, -piest
unhealthily
unhealthiness
unhealthy, -thier, -thiest
unheard-of
unhelthy unhealthy
unherdoff unheard-of
unhinge, -hinged, -hinging
unhinj unhinge
unholey unholy
unholy, -lier, -liest
unholesum unwholesome
uni
unicameral
unicellular
uniceluler unicellular
unicorn
unidirechunal unidirectional
unifacation unification
unification
uniform, -ly
uniformity, -ties

unify, -fied, -fying
unike unique
unilateral, -ly
unilatrel unilateral
unimaginable, -ably
unimaginabul unimaginable
unimpeachable, -ably
unimpeechibul unimpeachable
unimployed unemployed
unimprooved unimproved
unimproved
uninhibited
uninspired
uninspiring
union
union card
unionisation
unionise, -nised, -nising
unionist
unionistic
Union Jack
unique, -ly
uniqueness
unirve unnerve
unisex
unisexual, -ly
unisexuality
unison
unit
Unitarian
Unitarianism
unitary
unite, united, uniting
unit trust
unity, -ties
universal, -ly
universal suffrage
universe
university, -ties
unkempt
unkemt unkempt
unkind, -ly
unkined unkind
unkle uncle
unknit, -knitted, -knitting
unknown
unlawful, -ly

unlearned, -ly	
unlearnt	
unleash, -ed, -ing	
unleavened	
unleesh	unleash
unlerned	unlearned
unlernt	unlearnt
unles	unless
unless	
unlettered	
unlike	
unlikelihood	
unlikely	
unlikelyhood	unlikelihood
unlimited	
unlisted	
unload, -ed, -ing	
unlode	unload
unlooked-for	
unluckily	
unluckiness	
unlucky	
unluckyly	unluckily
unmake, -made, -making	
unmanageable, -bly	
unmanagebul	unmanageable
unmanliness	
unmanly	
unmannerliness	
unmannerly	
unmenchunabul	unmentionable
unmentionable, -bly	
unmistakable, -bly	
unmistakabul	unmistakable
unmitigated, -ly	
unmooved	unmoved
unmoved	
unnatural, -ly	
unnecessary, -rily	
unnerve, -nerved, -nerving	
unnesesarily	unnecessarily
unnesesary	unnecessary
unobtrusif	unobtrusive
unobtrusive, -ly	
unofficial, -ly	
unofishel	unofficial
unorganised	

unorgenized	unorganised
unpalatable, -bly	
unpalatabul	unpalatable
unparaleled	unparalleled
unparalleled	
unparraleled	unparalleled
unpicked	
unplaced	
unplaised	unplaced
unpolished	
unpopular, -ly	
unpopularity	
unpopuler	unpopular
unprecedented, -ly	
unpresidented	unprecedented
unprincipled	
unprinsipled	unprincipled
unprintable	
unprintibul	unprintable
unprofeshunel	unprofessional
unprofessional, -ly	
unproffessinal	unprofessional
unkwalified	unqualified
unqualified	
unquestionable, -bly	
unquestionibul	unquestionable
unravel, -elled, -elling	
unravell	unravel
unreal, -ly	
unrealistic, -ally	
unreckonized	unrecognised
unredeamed	unredeemed
unredeemed	
unreel	unreal
unreelistic	unrealistic
unreesenibul	unreasonable
unrekwited	unrequited
unrelaited	unrelated
unrelated	
unrelenting, -ly	
unreleived	unrelieved
unrelieved	
unremiting	unremitting
unrepeatable, -bly	
unrepeetibul	unrepeatable
unrequited, -ly	
unrest	

unrivalled	
unriveled	unrivalled
unrooly	unruly
unruffled	
unrufled	unruffled
unruly	
unsafe, -ly	
unsaif	unsafe
unsaterated	unsaturated
unsaturated	
unsavery	unsavoury
unsavoury	
unscathed	
unschooled	
unscrew, -ed, -ing	
unscrupulous	
unskru	unscrew
unskuled	unschooled
unseasonable, -bly	
unseat, -seated, -seating	
unseesenibul	unseasonable
unseet	unseat
unsecured	
unsecurred	unsecured
unseemliness	
unseemly	
unseemlynes	unseemliness
unseen	
unselfish, -ly	
unsellfish	unselfish
unserviceable	
unservisabul	unserviceable
unsetled	unsettled
unsettled	
unshakable, -bly	
unshakeable, -bly	
unshakibul	unshakeable
unshore	unsure
unsightly	
unsitely	unsightly
unskild	unskilled
unskilled	
unsociability	
unsociable, -bly	
unsolicited	
unsolisited	unsolicited
unsoshabul	unsociable

unsound, -ly	
unsownd	unsound
unspeakable, -bly	
unspeekabul	unspeakable
unspoilt	
unspoylt	unspoilt
unstable, -bly	
unstabul	unstable
unsteady, -dily	
unstedie	unsteady
unstructured	
unstruxured	unstructured
unstudied	
unstudyed	unstudied
unsubstanshul	unsubstantial
unsubstantial, -ly	
unsung	
unsure	
unswerving, -ly	
unswurving	unswerving
untangel	untangle
untangle, -gled, -gling	
untapped	
untenable, -bly	
unthinkable, -bly	
unthinkabul	unthinkable
unthinking, -ly	
untidie	untidy
untidiness	
untidy, -died, -dying	
untidy, -dier, -diest	
untie, -tied, -tying	
until	
untill	until
untimely	
unto	
untoo	unto
untold	
untouchable	
untouchabul	untouchable
untooward	untoward
untoward, -ly	
untroo	untrue
untrooth	untruth
untrue	
untruth	
unturned	

unushual unusual
unusual, -ly
unutterable, -bly
unutterabul unutterable
unvale unveil
unveil, -ed, -ing
unvoiced
unvoised unvoiced
unwarented unwarranted
unwarranted
unweeldy unwieldy
unwelcome, -ly
unwellcum unwelcome
unwholesome, -ly
unwieldiness
unwieldy
unwiling unwilling
unwilling, -ly
unwillingness
unwind, -wound, -winding
unwined unwind
unwitting, -ly
unworldliness
unworldly
unworthily
unworthiness
unworthy
unwritten
up, upped, upping
up-and-coming
up-beat
upbrade upbraid
upbraid, -ed, -ing
upbringing
up-country
updait update
update, -dated, -dating
upeld upheld
uper upper
up-end, -ended, -ending
upgrade, -graded, -grading
upgraid upgrade
upheaval
upheevul upheaval
upheld
uphill
uphold, -held, -holding
upholster, -ed, -ing
upholsterer
upholstery, -ries
upill uphill
upkeep
uplift
up-market
upold uphold
upolster upholster
upon
upper
upper case
upper chamber
uppercut
upper hand
upper house
uppermost
upright
uprising
uprite upright
uproar
uproarious, -ly
uproot, -ed, -ing
uprore uproar
upset, -set, -setting
upshot
upside down
upstage, -staged, -staging
upstairs
upstaje upstage
upstanding
upsurge, -surged, -surging
upsurje upsurge
upswing, -swung, -swinging
uptaik uptake
uptake
up-tempo
uptight
uptite uptight
up-to-date
up-too-date up-to-date
upturn, -ed, -ing
upward, -ly
upwards
upwood upward
uranic
uranium

Uranus
urban (town)
urbane, -ly (civilised)
urbanity, -ties
urchin
urea
urear urea
ureter
urethra, -thrae, -thras
urethral
urge, urged, urging
urgency
urgent, -ly
urinal
urinary
urinate, -nated, -nating
urination
urine
urinel urinal
urinous
urj urge
urjensy urgency
urjent urgent
urn (jug)
urn earn (gain)
urogenital
urojenital urogenital
urology
urolojy urology
ursine
usability
usable
usableness
usabul usable
usage
usaje usage
use, used, using
useable
useabul useable
used
useful, -ly
usefulness
useless, -ly
uselessness
usher
usherette
usual, -ly
ushuel usual
ushuelly usually
usurp, usurped, usurping
usurpation
usurper
usury, -ries
utalisation utilisation
ute
utensil
utensle utensil
uterine
uterus, uteri
utilisation
utilise, -lised, -lising
utilitarian
utilitarianism
utility, -ties
utmost
utopia
utopian
utopianism
utta utter
utter, uttered, uttering
utterly
uttermost
U-turn
uttur utter
uturus uterus
uvula, -las, -lae
uxorious, -ly
uxoriousness

Vv

vacancy, -cies
vacansy — vacancy
vacant, -ly
vacate, -cated, -cating
vacation
vaccinate, -nated, -nating
vaccination
vaccine
vaccuum — vacuum
vacency — vacancy
vacillate, -lated, -lating
vacseen — vaccine
vacsinate — vaccinate
vacsination — vaccination
vacsine — vaccine
vacuity, -ties
vacuous, -ly
vacuum
vacuum-packed
vacuum-sealed
vacuus — vacuous
vagabond
vagary, -ries
vagarious
vagarius — vagarious
vage — vague
vagina, -nas, -nae
vaginal
vagrancy, -cies
vagransy — vagrancy
vagrant, -ly
vague, vaguer, vaguest
vaguely
vail — vale (valley)
vail — veil (cover)
vain, -ly (proud)
vain — vane (blade)
vain — vein (blood)
vainglorious, -ly
vainglorius — vainglorious
vainglory
vajina — vagina
valadation — validation
valantine — valentine
valay — valet
vale (valley)
vale — veil (cover)
valedicshun — valediction
valediction
valedictory
valedictry — valedictory
valentine
valer — valour
valerus — valorous
valese — valise
valet, -leted, -leting
valiant, -ly
valid, -ly
validate, -dated, -dating
validation
validity, -ties
valise
valley, -leys
valor — valour
valorous, -ly
valorus — valorous
valour
valuable, -bly
valuation
value, -ued, -uing
valuer
valve, valved, valving
valvular
valy — valley
valyu — value
valyubul — valuable
valyuless — valueless
vamoose, -moosed, -moosing
vamp, -ed, -ing
vampire
van
vandal
vandalism
vandul — vandal
vane (blade)

vane	vain (proud)
vane	vein (blood)
vaneer	veneer
vangard	vanguard
vanglorius	vainglorious
vanguard	
vanilla	
vanish, -ed, -ing	
vanity, -ties	
vankwish	vanquish
vanquish, -ed, -ing	
vantage	
vapid, -ly	
vaporise, -rised, -rising	
vaporiser	
vaporous, -ly	
vapour	
variability	
variable, -bly	
variabul	variable
variance	
varianse	variance
variant	
variation	
varicolored	varicoloured
varicoloured	
varicose	
varied	
variegate, -gated, -gating	
varietal, -ly	
variety, -ties	
various, -ly	
varius	various
varnish, -ed, -ing	
vary, varied, varying	
vascular, -ly	
vase	
vasectomy, -mies	
vaseline	
vasillate	vacillate
vast, -ly	
vat, vatted, vatting	
Vatican	
vaudavil	vaudeville
vaudeville	
vault, -ed, -ing	
vaunt, -ed, -ing	
veal	
vector	
veel	veal
veemense	vehemence
veement	vehement
veer, -ed, -ing	
vegatation	vegetation
vegetable	
vegetabul	vegetable
vegetarian	
vegetarianism	
vegetate, -tated, -tating	
vegetation	
vegetative, -ly	
vegetabul	vegetable
vehemence	
vehement, -ly	
vehicle	
vehicular	
veicular	vehicular
veil, -ed, -ing (cover)	
veil	vale (valley)
vein (blood)	
vein	vain (proud)
vein	vane (blade)
veks	vex
veksashus	vexatious
vektor	vector
Velcro	
veldt	
vellum	
velocipede	
velocity, -ties	
velodrome	
veloor	velour
velour	
velum	vellum
velt	veldt
velvet	
velveteen	
velvety	
venal, -ly	
venality, -ties	
vend, -ed, -ing	
vender	vendor
vendetta	
vendor	

Entry / misspelling	Correct spelling
veneer	
venerability	
venerable, -bly	
venerabul	venerable
venerate, -rated, -rating	
veneration	
venereal	
venerial	venereal
venetian blind	
venew	venue
vengeance	
vengeful, -ly	
vengense	vengeance
venial, -ly	
venison	
venom	
venomous, -ly	
venomus	venomous
venous (of veins)	
venous	Venus (planet)
vent, -ed, -ing	
ventalation	ventilation
ventilate, -lated, -lating	
ventilation	
ventilator	
ventral, -ly	
ventricle	
ventricul	ventricle
ventrilokwism	ventriloquism
ventriloquism	
ventriloquist	
venture, -tured, -turing	
venturer	
venturesome, -ly	
venturous, -ly	
venturus	venturous
venue	
Venus (planet)	
venus	venous (of veins)
veracious, -ly (honest)	
veracious (greedy)	voracious
veracity, -ties	
veranda	
verashus	veracious
verasity	veracity

Entry / misspelling	Correct spelling
verb	
verbal, -balled, -balling	
verbalise, -lised, -lising	
verbally	
verbatim	
verbel	verbal
verbena	
verbiage	
verbige	verbiage
verbose, -ly	
verbosity	
verdant, -ly	
verdict	
verdure	
verdurous	
verge, verged, verging	
verger	
vergin	virgin
verie	vary
verifiable, -bly	
verification	
verifie	verify
verify, -fied, -fying	
verily	
verisimilitude	
veritable, -bly	
vermicelli	
vermilion	
vermin	
verminous, -ly	
vermouth	
vernacular, -ly	
vernal, -ly	
vernier	
versatile, -ly	
versatility	
verse, verses (poem)	
verses	versus (against)
versification	
versify, -fied, -fying	
version	
versus (against)	
versus	verses (poems)
vertebra, -brae	
vertebrate	
verteks	vertex
vertex, -tices	

vertical, -ly	
vertiginous, -ly	
vertiginus	vertiginous
vertigo, -goes	
verve	
very, -rier, -riest	
vesa	visa
vespers	
vessel	
vest, -ed, -ing	
vestal	
vestibul	vestibule
vestibule	
vestige	
vestigial, -ly	
vestment	
vestrie	vestry
vestry, -tries	
vestul	vestal
vesture, -tured, -turing	
vet, vetted, vetting	
vetenary	veterinary
vetenry	veterinary
veteran	
veterinary, -ries	
veto, -toes	
veto, -toed, -toing	
vex, -ed, -ing	
vexation	
vexatious, -ly	
veza	visa
vi	vie
via	
viability	
viable, -bly	
viabul	viable
viaduct	
vial (tube)	
vial	vile (bad)
vialate	violate
vialin	violin
viand	
viaticum, -ca, -cums	
vibes	
vibrant, -ly	
vibrate, -brated, -brating	
vibration	

vibrater	vibrator
vibrator	
viburnum	
vicar	
vicarage	
vicarige	vicarage
vicarious, -ly	
vicarius	vicarious
vice	
vice-chairman, -men	
vice-chancellor	
vice-president	
vicer	vicar
viceregal, -ly	
viceroi	viceroy
viceroy	
vice versa	
vicinity, -ties	
vicious, -ly (evil)	
vicious	viscous (thick)
vicissitude	
vicount	viscount
victer	victor
victim	
victimisation	
victimise, -mised, -mising	
victor	
Victorian	
victorious, -ly	
victorius	victorious
victory, -ries	
victual, -ualled, -ualling	
victualler	
video	
videophone	
videotape, -taped, -taping	
vidio	video
vie, vied, vying	
vieing	vying
Vietnamese, -ese	
view, -ed, -ing	
viewer	
viewfinder	
viewpoint	
viger	vigour
vigil	
vigilance	

vigilanse	vigilance
vigilant, -ly (watchful)	
vigilante (law enforcer)	
vigneron	
vignette, -gnetted, -gnetting	
vigoro	
vigorous, -ly	
vigorus	vigorous
vigour	
viksen	vixen
vilafication	vilification
vilain	villain
vile, viler, vilest (bad)	
vile	vial (tube)
vilely	
vilification	
vilifie	vilify
vilifier	
vilify, -fied, -fying	
vilige	village
villa	
village	
villager	
villain	
villainous, -ly	
villainy, -nies	
villanus	villainous
vim	
vinaigrette	
vindicate, -cated, -cating	
vindication	
vindictive, -ly	
vine	
vinegar	
vinegary	
vineyard	
vinigar	vinegar
vino	
vintage, -taged, -taging	
vintige	vintage
vinul	vinyl
vinyl	
viola	
violate, -lated, -lating	
violation	
violator	
violence	
violense	violence
violent, -ly	
violet	
violin	
viper	
viperous, -ly	
viperus	viperous
virago, -goes, -gos	
viral	
virgin	
virginal, -ly	
virginity	
Virgo	
virile	
virility, -ties	
virtual, -ly	
virtue	
virtuoso	
virtuous, -ly	
virtuus	virtuous
virulence	
virulense	virulence
virulent, -ly	
virus, viruses	
visa, -saed, -saing	
visage	
vis-a-vis	
viscera	
viscosity	
viscount	
viscountess	
viscous, -ly, (thick)	
viscous	vicious (evil)
viscuus	viscous (thick)
vise	vice
vise-chairman	vice-chairman
vise-president	vice-president
visera	viscera
viseregal	viceregal
viseversa	vice versa
vishiate	vitiate
vishun	vision
vishunry	visionary
vishus	vicious (evil)
visibility, -ties	
visible, -bly	
visibul	visible

visinity	vicinity
vision	
visionary, -ries	
visionry	visionary
visissitude	vicissitude
visit, -ed, -ing	
visitant	
visitation	
visiter	visitor
visitor	
viskosity	viscosity
vista	
visual, -ly	
visualise, -lised, -lising	
visuul	visual
visuulise	visualise
vital, -ly	
vitality, -ties	
vitamin	
vitel	vital
vitiate, -ated, -ating	
viticulture	
vitreous, -ly	
vitrification	
vitrifie	vitrify
vitrify, -fied, -fying	
vitriol	
vitriolic	
vituperate, -rated, -rating	
viul	vial (tube)
viul	vile (bad)
vivacious, -ly	
vivasious	vivacious
viva voce	
vivid, -ly	
vivisecshun	vivisection
vivisect, -ed, -ing	
vivisection	
vivisectionist	
vixen	
vocabulary, -ries	
vocal, -ly	
vocalisation	
vocalise, -lised, -lising	
vocalist	
vocation	
vocational, -ly	
vociferous, -ly	
vociferus	vociferous
vodka	
voge	vogue
vogue	
voice, voiced, voicing	
void, -ed, -ing	
voiige	voyage
voile	
voise	voice
volatile	
volatility	
volcanic, -ally	
volcano, -noes, -nos	
voley	volley
volishun	volition
volition	
volley, -leys	
volley, -ed, -ing	
volleyball	
volt	
voltage	
voltaic	
voltmeter	
voluble, -bly	
volubul	voluble
volume	
volumetric, -ally	
voluminous, -ly	
voluminus	voluminous
voluntarily	
voluntary, -taries	
volunteer, -ed, -ing	
voluptuous, -ly	
voluptuus	voluptuous
vomit, -ed, -ing	
voodoo, -doos	
voodoo, -dooed, -dooing	
voodooism	
voracious, -ly (greedy)	
voracious	veracious (honest)
voracity	
vorasious	voracious
vortex, -texes, -tices	
vortical, -ly	
vosiferus	vociferous

votary, -ries
vote, voted, voting
voter
votive, -ly
vouch, -ed, -ing
voucher
vouchsafe, -safed, -safing
vow, -ed, -ing
vowch — vouch
vowcher — voucher
vowel
vowul — vowel
voyage, -aged, -aging
voyager
voyd — void
voyeur
voyeurism
voyse — voice
vue — view
vulcanise, -nised, -nising
vulcanism
vulcanite
vulcher — vulture
vulgar, -ly
vulgarism
vulgarity, -ties
vulnerability
vulnerable, -bly
vulnerabul — vulnerable
vulpine
vulture
vulva, -vae, -vas
vurb — verb
vurchoo — virtue
vurchual — virtual
vurchuus — virtuous
vurgin — virgin
vurtue — virtue
vurtuous — virtuous
vye — vie

Ww

wack — whack
wad, wadded, wadding
waddle, -dled, -dling
waddy, -dies (club)
waddy — wadi (channel)
wade, waded, wading
wader
wadi, -dies (channel)
wadi — waddy (club)
wadle — waddle
wadul — waddle
wafe — waif
wafer
wafery
waffle, -fled, -fling
waful — waffle
wag, wagged, wagging
wage, waged, waging
wager
waggish, -ly
waggle, -gled, -gling
waggly
wagon
wagtail
wagul — waggle
wahine
waif
wail, wailed, wailing (cry)
wail — wale (welt)
wail — whale (mammal)
wainscot, -scotted, -scotting
wainwright
waipiro
waist (body)
waist — waste (squander)
waistband
waistcoat
waistline
wait (stay)
wait — weight (amount)
waiter
waitey — weighty
waitress
waive, waived, waiving (forgo)
waive — wave (ocean)
waiver (law)
waiver — waver (sway)
wake, woke, woken, waking
wakeful, -ly
waken, -ened, -ening
waks — wax
walabey — wallaby
wale, waled, waling (welt)
wale — wail (cry)
wale — whale (mammal)
walk, -ed, -ing
walkabout
walkathon
walker
walkie-talkie
walkout
walkover
wall
wallaby, -bies
wallaroo
wallet
walleyed
wallflower
wallop, -ed, -ing
wallow, -ed, -ing
wallpaper
wall-to-wall
walnut
walop — wallop
walow — wallow
walrus, -ruses
walts — waltz
waltz, -ed, -ing
wampum
wan, wanner, wannest (pale)
wan — won (win)

wand	
wanda (ghost)	
wander, -ed, -ing (walk)	
wander	wonder (think)
wanderer	
wanderlust	
wane, waned, waning	
wangle, -gled, -gling	
wangler	
wangul	wangle
want, -ed, -ing	
wanton, -ly (lewd)	
wanton (dough)	won ton
war, warred, warring	
warant	warrant
warantee	warranty
waratah	
warble, -bled, -bling	
warbler	
war cry	
ward	
warden	
wardress	
wardrobe	
ware (goods)	
ware	wear (cover)
ware	where (place)
warehouse	
warehowse	warehouse
warey	wary
warf	wharf
warfare	
warhead	
warily	
wariness	
warior	warrior
warlike	
warlock	
warm, -ed, -ing	
warm-blooded	
warmonger	
warmongering	
warmth	
warn, -ed, -ing (signal)	
warn	worn (tired)
warp, -ed, -ing	

warrant, -ed, -ing	
warrant officer	
warrantor	
warranty, -ties	
warren	
warrigal	
warrior	
wart (lump)	
wart	wort (plant)
wart-hog	
warves	wharves
wary, warier, wariest	
was	
wash, -ed, -ing	
washboard	
washer	
washing soda	
wash-out	
wasn't (was not)	
wasnt	wasn't
wasp	
waspish, -ly	
wassail	
wassailer	
wastage	
waste, wasted, wasting (squander)	
waste	waist (body)
wasteful, -ly	
wasteland	
wastrel	
wat	watt (power)
wat	what (question)
watch, -ed, -ing	
watchdog	
watchful, -ly	
watchman, -men	
watchword	
wate	wait (stay)
wate	weight (measure)
water, -ed, -ing	
waterbed	
water-buffalo	
water-closet	
watercolour	
watercolourist	
water-column	

watercourse
watercress
waterfall
waterfowl
waterfront
waterfrontage
watergate
waterhole
watering-can
watering hole
waterlily
waterlog, -logged, -logging
waterloo
watermark
watermelon
water-pistol
water-polo
waterproof
water-rat
water-repellent
watershed
water-ski, -ski'd or skied, -skiing
watertable
watertight
  watertite — watertight
water-tower
water-vapour
waterway
waterwheel
waterworks
watery
  watige — wattage
watt (power)
  watt — what (question)
wattage
wattle, -tled, -tling
wattlebird
wave, waved, waving (ocean)
  wave — waive (forgo)
waveband
wavefront
wavelength
waver, wavered, wavering (sway)
  waver — waiver (law)
wavily
waviness
wavy, -vier, -viest

wax, waxed or waxen, waxing
waxen
  waxflour — waxflower
waxflower
waxplant
waxwork
way (method)
  way — weigh (amount)
  way — whey (liquid)
waybill
wayfarer
waylay, -laid, -laying
way-out
wayward, -ly
  waywerd — wayward
we (us)
  we — wee (little)
weak, -ly (feeble)
  weak — week (time)
weaken, -ed, -ing
weakling
weakly, -lier, -liest (feebly)
  weakly — weekly (time)
weal (hurt)
  weal — wheel (disc)
wealth, -ily
wealth tax
wealthy, -thier, -thiest
wean, -ed, -ing
weaner
weapon
wear, wore, worn, wearing (cover)
  wear — ware (goods)
  wear — where (place)
  wearey — weary
wearisome, -ly
weary, -rier, -riest
weary, -ried, -rying
weasel
  weat — wheat
weather, -ed, -ing (rain)
  weather — wether (geld)
  weather — whether (if)
weatherboard
weathercock
weathervane
weave, wove or weaved, weaving

weave — we've (we have)
web, webbed, webbing
webfoot, -feet
webfooted
wed, wedded or wed, wedding (join)
we'd
wed — we'd (we had)
Wedensday — Wednesday
wedge, wedged, wedging
wedge-tailed eagle
wedgie
wedlock
Wednesday
wee, weer, weest (small)
weed, weeded, weeding
weediness
weedul — wheedle
weedy, -dier, -diest
week (time)
week — weak (feeble)
weekday
weeken — weaken
weekend
weekender
weekling — weakling
weekly, -lies (time)
weekly — weakly (feebly)
weel — weal (hurt)
weel — wheel (disc)
weelbarow — wheelbarrow
weeld — wield
ween — wean
weep, wept, weeping
weeping willow
weet — wheat
weevil
weeze — wheeze
weft
wege — wedge
weigh, -ed, -ing
weight, -ily
weightiness
weightlessness
weighty, -tier, -tiest
weild — wield
weir (dam)
weird, -ly
weja — ouija
welch, -ed, -ing
welcher
welcome, -comed, -coming
weld, -ed, -ing
welder
welfare
welfare state
well, better, best
we'll (we will)
well-appointed
well-balanced
well-being
well-born
well-bred
well-connected
well-disposed
well-grounded
well-heeled
well-informed
well-known
well-meaning
well-off
well-preserved
well-read
well-rounded
well-to-do
welsh, -ed, -ing
welt
welter
welth — wealth
wen (swelling)
wen — when (at what time)
wench
wend, wended, wending
wenever — whenever
Wensday — Wednesday
went
wepon — weapon
wept
wer — weir (dam)
werd — weird
were (was)
were — where (place)
we're (we are)
were — we're (we are)

Word	Correct spelling
wereabouts	whereabouts
wereas	whereas
werefore	wherefore
weren't (were not)	
werent	weren't
weresoever	wheresoever
wereupon	whereupon
werever	wherever
werewithal	wherewithal
werewolf, -wolves	
werey	weary
werisum	wearisome
werk	work

For other werk- words, look under **work-**.

Word	Correct spelling
werld	world

For other werl- words, look under **worl-**.

Word	Correct spelling
werm	worm

For other wer- words, look under **wor-**.

Word	Correct spelling
Wesleyan	
west	
West End	
westerly, -lies	
western	
westerner	
Westernise, -nised, -nising	
westernmost	
Westminster system	
westward	
westwardly	
westwards	
wet, wetted, wetting (soak)	
wet, wetter, wettest	
wet	whet (sharpen)
wether, -ed, -ing (geld)	
wether	weather (rain)
wether	whether (if)
wetherboard	weatherboard
wethercock	weathercock
wethervane	weathervane
wetsuit	
wettex	
we've (we have)	
weve	weave (cloth)
weve	we've (we have)
weevel	weevil
whack, whacked, whacking	
whacko	
whale, whales (mammal)	
whale, whaled, whaling	
whaleboat	
whalebone	
whaler	
whaler shark	
wham, whammed, whamming	
wharf, wharves, wharfs	
wharfey	wharfie
wharfie	
what (question)	
what	watt (energy)
whata	
what-d'ye-call-it	
whatever	
whatnot	
whatsoever	
wheat	
wheat germ	
wheatmeal	
whedul	wheedle
wheedle, -dled, -dling	
wheel (disc)	
wheel	weal (hurt)
wheelbarrow	
wheelchair	
wheeler-dealer	
wheet	wheat
wheeze, wheezed, wheezing	
wheezy, -zier, -ziest	
whelk	
whelp	
when	
whenever	
where (place)	
where	ware (goods)
where	wear (cover)
whereabouts	
whereas	
wherefore	
wheresoever	

whereupon
wherever
wherewithal
 wherl whirl (spin)
 wherl whorl (circle)
wherry, -ries
whet, whetted, whetting (sharpen)
 whet wet (soak)
whether (if)
 whether weather (rain)
 whether wether (geld)
whew
whey (liquid)
 whey way (method)
 whey weigh (measure)
which (what)
 which witch (magic)
whichever
whiff
whiffle, -fled, -fling
while, whiled, whiling (time)
 while wile (trick)
whilst
whim
whimper, -ed, -ing
whimsey, -sies
whimsical, -ally
whimsicality, -ties
whimsy, -sies
whine, whined, whining (complain)
 whine wine (grape juice)
whinge, whinged, whingeing
whinny, -nies
whinny, -nied, -nying
whip, whipped, whipping
whipbird
whipcord
whiplash
whippersnapper
whippet
whipping boy
whip-round
whirl (spin)
 whirl whorl (circle)
whirligig
whirlpool
whirlwind
whirr, whirred, whirring
whisk, whisked, whisking
whisker
whiskey, -keys (U.S., Irish)
whisky, -kies (Scotch, Canadian)
whisper, -ed, -ing
whist
whistle, -tled, -tling
whistler
 whisul whistle
whit (jot)
 whit wit (humour)
white, whiter, whitest
whitebait, -bait
whitecap
white-collar
white-elephant
white ensign
white-eye
whitefish, -fishes, -fish
white flag
white lie
white light
white pointer
white slave
whitewash
whither (where)
 whither wither (shrivel)
whiting
whitlow
whittle, -tled, -tling
 whitul whittle
whiz, whizzed, whizzing
who
whoa (stop)
 whoa woe (sorrow)
who'd (who would)
 whod who'd
whodunit
whoever
whole (all)
 whole hole (opening)
wholegrain
wholehearted
wholemeal

whole number
wholesale, -saled, -saling
wholesome, -ly
who'll (who will)
  wholl — who'll
wholly (entirely)
  wholly — holy (good)
whom
  whom — womb (uterus)
whoop (cry)
  whoop — hoop (ring)
whoopee
whooping cough
whoops
whoops-a-daisy
whoosh
whop, whopped, whopping
whopper
whore, whored, whoring
  whore — who're
who're (who are)
whorl (circle)
  whorl — whirl (spin)
whorled
who's (who has)
  whos — who's
whose (possessive)
whosoever
  whur — whirr
  whurl — whirl (spin)
  whurl — whorl (circle)
who've (who have)
  whove — who've
why, whys
  wich — which (question)
  wich — witch (magic)
wick
wicked, -ly
wickedness
wicker
wickerwork
wicket
wicket-keeper
wide, wider, widest
wide-angle
widely
widen, -ed, -ing
widespread
widgie
widow, -ed, -ing
widower
width
wield
  wierd — weird
wife, wives
wig, wigged, wigging
wiggle, -gled, -gling
wiggly
  wiggul — wiggle
wigwam
wilco
wild, -ly
wildcat, -catted, -catting
wildcat strike
wilderness
wildfire
wild flower
wildfowl
wild-goose chase
wildlife
Wild West
wile (trick)
  wile — while (time)
wilful, -ly
wiliness
will, willed, willing
willingness
will-o'-the-wisp
willow
willowy
willpower
willy-nilly
  wilst — whilst
wilt, wilted, wilting
wily, -lier, -liest
  wim — whim
  wimen — women

For other **wi-** words, look under **whi-**.

wimple, -pled, -pling
win, won, winning
wince, winced, wincing

winch, winched, winching
wind, -ed, -ing (air)
wind, wound, winding (turn)
windbag
windbreak
windcheater
winder
windfall
wind gauge
windjammer
windlass
windmill
window
window-dressing
window-shop, -shopped, -shopping
windpipe
windrow
windscreen
windsock
windsurf, -ed, -ing
windsurfer
wind-tunnel
windvane
windward
windy, windier, windiest
wine, wined, wining (grape juice)
wine — whine (complain)
wing, winged, winging
winger
wingspan
wingspread
wink, -ed, -ing
winkle, -kled, -kling
winnings
winnow, -ed, -ing
winnower
winsome, -ly
winsomeness
winter
wintery
wintry
wip — whip

For other wip- words, look under **whip-**.

wipe, wiped, wiping
wipe-out
wiper
wire, wired, wiring
wireless
wirrah
wirl — whirl (spin)
wirl — whorl (circle)
wirr — whirr
wiry, wirier, wiriest
wisdom
wisdom tooth, -teeth
wise, wiser, wisest
wisecrack
wisecracker
wish, wished, wishing
wishbone
wishful, -ly
wishy-washy
wisk — whisk

For other wis- words, look under **whis-**.

wisp, wisped, wisping
wisteria
wistful, -ly
wistfulness
wit (humour)
wit — whit (jot)

For other wit- words, look under **whit-**.

witch (magic)
witch — which (question)
witchcraft
witchdoctor
witchetty grub
witch-hunt
witch-hunting
with
withdraw, -drew, -drawn, -drawing
withdrawal
withdrawal sympton
withdrawn
withdroo — withdrew
wither, -ed, -ing (shrivel)
wither — whither (where)

withers
withhold, -held, -holding
withholder
within
  withold — withhold
without
withstand, -stood, -standing
witness, -ed, -ing
witticism
  wittisism — witticism
witty, -tier, -tiest
wives
  wiz — whiz
wizard
wizened
  wo — whoa (stop)
  wo — woe (sorrow)
wobbegong
wobble, -bled, -bling
wobble board
  woble — wobble
  wobul — wobble
  wod — wad
  wodle — waddle
  wodul — waddle
woe (sorrow)
  woe — whoa (stop)
woebegone
woeful, -ly
  woft — waft
  woful — woeful
  wolet — wallet
wok
wolf, wolves
wolfish, -ly
wolfhound
wolfram
wolf spider
wolf-whistle, -led, -ling
  wolop — wallop
  wolow — wallow
wolves
  wom — womb
woman, women
womanise, -nised, -nising
womaniser
womanish, -ly
womanly
womb
wombat
women
women's lib
women's liberation
womera
won (win)
  won — one (number)
wonder, -ed, -ing (think)
  wonder — wander (walk)
wonderful, -ly
wonderland
wonderment
wondrous, -ly
  wondrus — wondrous
wonky, wonkier, wonkiest
wont (accustomed)
  wont — want (need)
  wont — won't (will not)
won't (will not)
won ton (dough)
  wonton — wanton (lewd)
woo, wooed, wooing
wood (timber)
  wood — would (will)
woodblock
woodcarving
woodchip
woodchuck
woodcut
wooden, -ly
woodenness
woodwind
woodwork
woody, woodier, woodiest
wooer
woof, -ed, -ing
woofer
wool
wool classer
wool classing
woolclip
  woolen — woollen
  woolf — wolf
wool-gatherer
wool-gathering

woolgrower	
wool-growing	
woollen	
woollies	
woolly, -lier, -liest	
woolshed	
wool-stapler	
wool-stapling	
woom	womb
wooman	woman
woomera	
woond	wound
woozily	
wooziness	
woozy	
wop	whop (hit)
wor	war
worble	warble
worbul	warble
word, worded, wording	
worden	warden
wordily	
wordiness	
wordless, -ly	
word processor	
wordrobe	wardrobe
wordy, -dier, -diest	
wore	
worf	wharf
worfair	warfare
work, worked, working	
workable	
workaday	
workaholic	
workbench	
workbox	
worker	
work force	
workhorse	
workhouse	
working capital	
working class, -classes	
working model	
working party, -parties	
workman, -men	
work-out	
works committee	
workshop	
work-to-rule	
worl	whirl (spin)
worl	whorl (circle)
world (earth)	
world	whirled (spun)
world-class	
worldliness	
worldly, -lier, -liest	
worm, wormed, worming	
worm	warm (heat)
wormhole	
wormwood	
wormy, wormier, wormiest	
worn (tired)	
worn	warn (signal)
worn-out	
worp	warp
worrier	
worrisome	
worry, -ries	
worry, -ried, -rying	
worse	
worsen, -ed, -ing	
worship, -shipped, -shipping	
worshipper	
worst	
worsted	
wort (plant)	
wort	wart (lump)
worth	
worthily	
worthiness	
worthless, -ly	
worthwhile	
worthy, -thier, -thiest	
wos	was

For other **wo-** words, look under **wa-**.

would (will)	
would	wood (timber)
would-be	
wouldn't (would not)	
wouldnt	wouldn't
wound, wounded, wounding (injure)	
wove	

woven
wowser
wrack (seaweed)
wraith
wrangle, -gled, -gling
wrangler
wrangul — wrangle
wrap, wrapped or wrapt, wrapping
wrapper
wrath
wrathful, -ly
wreak, -ed, -ing
wreath, wreaths (flowers)
wreathe, -thed, -thing (encircle)
wreck, -ed, -ing
wreckage
wrecker
wrek — wreck
wren
wrench, -ed, -ing
wrest, wrested, wresting
wrestle, -tled, -tling
wrestler
wretch
wretched, -ly
wri — wry
wrick, wricked, wricking
wriggle, -gled, -gling
wriggler
wriggly
wrigul — wriggle
wright (worker)
wring, wrung, wringing
wringer
wrinkle, -kled, -kling
wrinkly
wrinkul — wrinkle
wrist
wristpin
wristwatch
writ
write, wrote, written, writing
write — right (true)
write — rite (ceremony)
write — wright (worker)
write-off, written-off, writing-off
writer
writhe, writhed, writhing
written
wrong
wrongdoing
wroth
wrought
wrought iron
wrung
wry, wrier, wriest
wun — one (number)
wun — won (win)
wunce — once
wunder — wonder
wunse — once
wur — whirr
wurl — whirl (spin)
wurl — whorl (circle)
wurley
wurlitzer
wurrung
wurrup
wye, wyes

Xx

X-axis
X chromosome

X cromosome	X chromosome
xenofobia	xenophobia

xenophobe
xenophobia
xenophobic

xerograf	xerograph
xerografic	xerographic
xerografy	xerography

xerograph
xerographic
xerography

xeroks	xerox

xerox
Xmas
X-ray
X-ray tube
xylocarp

xylofone	xylophone
xylograf	xylograph
xylografer	xylographer
xylografic	xylographic
xylografy	xylography

xylograph
xylographer
xylographic
xylography
xyloid
xylophagous
xylophone
xylophonic
xylophonist

Yy

y	why
yabber	
yabbie	yabby
yabby, yabbies	
yacht	
yachting	
yack	yak
yahoo	
yahweh	
yak, yakked, yakking	
yakka	
yam	
yandie	yandy
yandy	
Yang	
yank, yanked, yanking (pull)	
Yank (American)	
yap, yapped, yapping	
yard	
yardarm	
yardstick	
yarmelke	
yarmulke	
yarn, -ed, -ing	
yarran	
yaw, -ed, -ing	
yaw	yore (long ago)
yaw	your
yaw	you're (you are)
yawl	
yawn, -ed, -ing	
yaws (disease)	
yaws	yours
Y-axis	
yay	yea
Y chromosome	
Y cromosome	Y chromosome
ye	
yea	
yeah	
yeald	yield
year	
yearbook	
yearling	
yearly, -lies	
yearn, -ed, -ing	
yeast	
yeasty, yeastier, yeastiest	
yeeld	yield
yeer	year
yeest	yeast
yell, -ed, -ing	
yellow	
yellowcake	
yellowish	
yellow pages	
yellow peril	
yelosih	yellowish
yelow	yellow
yelp, -ed, -ing	
yen, yenned, yenning	
yeoman, -men	
yern	yearn
yes, yeses	
yes-man, -men	
yesterday	
yesteryear	
yet	
yeti	
yety	yeti
yew (tree)	
yew	ewe (sheep)
yew	you (person)
yewse	use
yewshual	usual
yewshuul	usual
yewsual	usual
yewsuul	usual

For other ye- words, look under **u-**.

Yiddish	
yield, yielded, yielding	
Yin	
yippee	

yob
yodel, -delled, -delling
yodeller
  yodle — yodel
  yodul — yodel
yoga
  yogert — yoghourt
  yogert — yoghurt
  yogert — yogurt
yoghourt
yoghurt
yogurt
yogi, -gis
yogism
yoicks
yoke, yoked, yoking (frame)
  yoke — yolk (egg)
yokel
  yokle — yokel
  yokul — yokel
yolk (egg)
  yoman — yeoman
Yom Kippur
yonder
yoo-hoo
yore (long ago)
  yore — yaw (move)
  yore — your
  yore — you're (you are)
  yors — yours
yorker
Yorkshire pudding
  yot — yacht
you (person)
  you — ewe (sheep)
  you — yew (tree)
you'd (you would)
  youd — you'd
you'll (you will)
  youll — you'll
young
youngster

your (possessive)
  your — yaw (move)
  your — yore (long ago)
  your — you're (you are)
you're (you are)
  youre — you're
yours
yourself, -selves
youth, youths
youthful, -ly
you've (you have)
  youve — you've
  yowey — yowie
yowie
yowl, yowled, yowling
yoyo, -yos
yuan
  yuckey — yucky, yukky
  yuckie — yucky, yukky
yucky, yuckier, yuckiest
yuk
yukky, yukkier, yukkiest
yule (Christmas)
  yule — you'll (you will)
yummy, yummier, yummiest
  yung — young
  yungster — youngster
  yurn — yearn
  yuse — use
  yuseful — useful
  yusual — usual
  yusuul — usual
  yutensle — utensil
  yutensul — utensil
  yuterine — uterine
  yuteris — uterus
  yuterus — uterus
  yuth — youth
  yutilise — utilise
  yutopia — utopia

For other yu- words, look under **u-**.

Zz

zabaglione
zany, -nier, -niest
zap, zapped, zapping
zar tsar
zeal
zealot
zealotry
zealous, -ly
zebra
zebra crossing
zebu
zeel zeal
zefer zephyr
zelot zealot
zelous zealous
Zen
zenith
zenithal
zenofobia xenophobia
zenophobia xenophobia
zepher zephyr
zephyr
zeplen zeppelin
zeppelin
zercon zircon
zero, -ros
zero, -roed, -roing
zeroks xerox
zero population growth
zerox xerox
zest
zestful, -ly
zigote zygote
zigzag, -zagged, -zagging
zilch
zillion
zilofone xylophone
zilophone xylophone
zinc
zing
zink zinc
zinnia
Zion
Zionism
Zionist
Zionistic
zip, zipped, zipping
zip-fastener
zipper
zippy, -pier, -piest
zircon
zirconium
zither
zodiac
zodiacal
zombie, -bies
zombiism
zomby zombie
zone, zoned, zoning
zonk, zonked, zonking
zoo
zoochiney zucchini
zoochini zucchini
zoologey zoology
zoological, -ly
zoologist
zoology, -gies
zoom, zoomed, zooming
zot, zotted, zotting
zucchini, zucchini, zucchinis
Zulu, -lus, -lu
Zuni, -nis, -ni
zwieback
zygote